Speak Spanish Now
for
Law Offices

Speak Spanish Now
for
Law Offices

A Customized Learning Approach for Legal Professionals

Brian K. Jones

CAROLINA ACADEMIC PRESS

Durham, North Carolina

Library of Congress Cataloging-in-Publication Data

Jones, Brian K. (Brian Keith), 1971-
Speak Spanish now for law offices : a customized learning approach for legal professionals / Brian K. Jones.
    p. cm.
Includes bibliographical references.
ISBN 978-1-59460-863-6 (alk. paper)
1. Law--United States--Terminology. 2. Spanish language--Conversation and phrase books (for lawyers)
3. Spanish language--Conversation and phrase books--English. I. Title.
KF156.J66 2011
468.2'42102434--dc23
                    2011037174

CAROLINA ACADEMIC PRESS
700 Kent Street
Durham, North Carolina
Tel: (919) 489-7486
Fax: (919) 493-5668
www.cap-press.com

Printed in the United States of America.

Contents

Preface: A Customized Learning Approach to Language

The purpose of this text is to assist those in the legal profession with effective, immediate communication with Spanish-speaking persons. Therefore, this book's approach is to teach straightforward, oral communication that requires the learner to verbally produce while minimally relying on listening skills. It is primarily intended as one-way communication and does not require the learning of grammar or the development of written communiqué. However, certain anticipated responses have been included for you. Upon successfully learning the phrases from the text, the learner will be able to manage situations they commonly encounter on a daily basis, give instructions and make requests, ascertain personal information and interact with Spanish-speaking persons in a culturally appropriate manner.

Using This Text

This text has been designed to promote communication in Spanish for legal professionals, with its principal focus on the functions of paralegals/legal assistants. However, other legal professionals such as attorneys and legal secretaries, just to name a few, will find this text practical. Since not all sections of the text may be specific to your job duties, the text allows you to pick and choose what you will learn and concentrate on those areas that are most beneficial to you and your respective job duties. The pages have been perforated so you can easily remove sections you will not use in order to customize the book or make the most used pages more portable.

In learning the words and phrases in this text, you will be concentrating on oral communication. You will only write in Spanish if you wish prepare note cards to be used during an activity unless it is a requirement of your curriculum. Grammatical explanations are not necessary for any of the information you will be learning. Your instructor will lead you through a variety of oral exercises that will help you internalize these phrases and their meanings. The accompanying CD will enable you to listen to the phrases and practice their pronunciation. Your instructor may also choose to provide you with strategies that will make the CD more beneficial to you as a study aid. The CD may be used in class but is also highly recommended as an independent study aid.

The chapters have been broken down into sections and designated titles to help you manage the selection of the material you will choose to learn and/or utilize in the preparation of scripts (meaning, preparing ahead of time a guide or *script* of the discourse to be used when speaking with a Spanish-speaker in order to facilitate communication). However, make sure to peruse the text in its entirety for miscellaneous phrases you may find beneficial in your interactions with Spanish-speaking persons. Feel free to integrate phrases from multiple sections and/or chapters in order to customize the information you will need to convey to and/or obtain from the other person. It is highly suggested that you reference *Chapter 1—Getting Started* and *Chapter 2—Collecting Basic Personal Information in Person and by Phone* frequently, as these two chapters contain phrases you will mostly likely use on a regular basis when preparing scripts to be used with Spanish speakers. Throughout all chapters, the phrases and expressions follow a logical order for their delivery. However, there is no prescribed sequence you must follow when preparing scripts. How you decide to utilize and combine the phrases and expressions will be based solely on your own practical needs.

Immediately before each set of phrases, you will find a section titled **BEFORE YOU BEGIN**. These sections present pertinent information that will enable the learner to better understand the cultural differences between the Hispanic and Anglo cultures and thus manage a situation more effectively. Current statistics and important relevant information that focus on the Hispanic population have been included.

After the presentation of the last phrase in each chapter, you will find a **NOTES** section has been included which provides additional information about vocabulary used in the phrases for that chapter as well as guidelines for how to correctly manipulate certain phrases when addressing males, females, individuals and groups, etc.

Each chapter then concludes with written and oral activities that correspond to the material in order to provide comprehensive practice of the phrases and expressions you are studying. These activities may be utilized in variety of ways—homework assignments, in-class pair and/or group work (in addition to the activities provided in the instructor's activities manual), review, etc. Answers are not provided for the written and oral activities as these are based directly on the phrases and vocabulary found in the respective chapter. Consult the appropriate chapter(s) when correcting your work. Remember that some activities may encompass multiple chapters.

Pronunciation

The purpose of the **pronunciation patterns** found directly above each Spanish phrase is to immediately generate proper or nearly proper pronunciation. By following these easy guidelines, communication becomes instantaneous. The words and sounds used in the **pronunciation patterns** are based on those used in English, so you will say what you see. Practice exercises to aid you in interpreting the **pronunciation patterns** and to prepare you for making those sounds correctly follow these brief explanations. Be sure to follow them in the designated order.

Instructions for Reading the **Pronunciation** Patterns

1. The separation of words has been indicated by one or more spaces.

   ex. **boo^ay**-nohs **dee**-ahs. (two-word phrase)
        Buenos días.

2. The separation of syllables has been indicated by a *hyphen*.

   ex. **boo^ay**-nohs **dee**-ahs. (each word has two syllables)
        Buenos días.

3. Syllables written in *bolded letters* are emphasized when spoken.

   ex. **boo^ay**-nohs **dee**-ahs. (emphasis on **boo^ay** and **dee**)
        Buenos días.

4. Syllables written in *letters not bolded* are not emphasized.

   ex. **boo^ay**-nohs **dee**-ahs. (no emphasis on -nohs and -ahs)
        Buenos días.

5. The *upward pointing arrow*, or the (^) sign, indicates a combination of sounds to be pronounced as one (1) syllable (one sound).

   ex. **boo^ay**-nohs **dee**-ahs. (**boo^ay** is one sound)
        Buenos días.

6. The *double r* you will see indicates a rolled or trilled "r" sound.

   ex. rray-goo-**lahr**. (rr of rray is rolled/trilled)
        Regular.

The double r, or "rr" in Spanish, is represented by "rr" in the pronunciation key. Do the best you can to imitate the sound but do not get frustrated, as long as you are making the effort you will be understood. Keep practicing and it will come with time. Likewise, anyone who has any prior knowledge of Spanish pronunciation may know that the *Spanish v* is often pronounced as a *soft English b*, although some dialects of spoken Spanish do pronounce the *Spanish v* the same as the *English v*. However, for the sake of consistency and simplicity, the *Spanish v* has been represented as the *letter b* in the pronunciation patterns throughout the text and may be pronounced as such. Additionally, the *Spanish t*, often sounds like the combination *th* or a soft letter *d* in spoken Spanish. Since our purpose here is to promote comprehensible communication without creating frustrating guidelines for exact pronunciation, the letter *t* is simply represented as the letter itself in the pronunciation guide and may be pronounced as such.

Introduction Exercise

With a partner or as a group, randomly select phrases from the text, analyze them and identify each of the above elements from the **pronunciation patterns** explanations. Do not practice pronunciation yet. Just become familiar with how to interpret the **pronunciation patterns**. <u>You must practice the following pronunciation exercises thoroughly before attempting to read the pronunciation patterns for the phrases in this text!</u>

Getting Started

Just like any other muscle in your body that is not accustomed to certain motions and movements, the tongue and mouth are no different. These exercises will help you warm up these muscles and form the correct positions with your mouth and tongue to produce relatively authentic Spanish pronunciation from the very beginning.

Pronunciation Exercise 1

This oral exercise is to help you become used to the basic sounds you will use and see throughout this text, all of which are based on the five basic vowel sounds of the Spanish alphabet—A, E, I, O, U. Though they are the same five vowels found in English, their sounds are rather different. In order to facilitate their production, in practicing this exercise, say exactly what you see as you would in English. Start by saying the words and sounds, going column by column (in sequence according to numbers). Do this as a class, then small groups, next in pairs, and finally individually. Remember, the sounds **bolded** in the first column should be applied to the combinations you will practice in each column that follows. These bolded sounds are the actual sounds of the corresponding Spanish vowel.

Spanish Vowel	#1	#2	#3	#4	#5	#6	#7	#8	#9
A	h**ah**	**ah**	bah	kah	lah	mah	sah	tah	yah
E	d**ay**	**ay**	bay	kay	lay	may	say	tay	yay
I	s**ee**	**ee**	bee	kee	lee	mee	see	tee	yee
O	**oh**	**oh**	boh	koh	loh	moh	soh	toh	yoh
U	f**oo**d	**oo**	boo	koo	loo	moo	soo	too	yoo

Pronunciation Exercise 2

The second practice exercise builds upon the previous one by introducing you to sound combinations you will use and see throughout the text. Practice these in the same manner as the first set. Remember to make letters linked with the upward pointing arrow (^) one syllable (one sound).

#1	#2	#3	#4	#5	#6
tah	boo^ay	tree	ahr	nahs	tahr
chah	tay	kree	ayr	nays	tayr
grah	poo^ay	moo^ee	eer	nees	teer
blah	tray	ghee*	ohr	nohs	tohr
trah	goo^ay	flee	oor	noos	toor

* this *g* is like the letter *g* in the word *get* followed by the *ee* sound.

Pronunciation Exercise 3

Starting with column 1, make sure to emphasize the bolded letters according to the pronunciation key. Once again, remember to make letters linked with the upward pointing arrow (^) one syllable (one sound).

#1	#2	#3	#4
gah-nahs	ah-**sayr**	**tee**^ay-nay	nah-see-**mee**^ayn-toh
dohn-day	ays-pahn-**yohl**	**kee**^ay-rayn	sah-rahm-**pee**^ohn
pah-gahn	rrays-pee-**rahr**	kee-**see**^ay-rah	dee^ah-**bay**-tays
ahn-yoh	door-**meer**	ees-**toh**-ree^ah	ee-payr-tayn-**see**^ohn
koo^ahn-toh	rray-say-**tahr**	**see**^ayn-toh	see-**ghee***^ayn-tay

* this *g* is like the letter *g* in the word *get* followed by the *ee* sound.

Pronunciation Exercise 4

Look through the text paying attention only to the pronunciation key and practice random examples as a class, then in pairs.

Speak Spanish Now
for
Law Offices

Chapter 1

Getting Started

Before You Begin

The Hispanic culture is a very respectful one full of customs and traditions. Regardless of a person's socioeconomic rank, the expectation of mutual respect still exists. Spanish-speakers lean toward formality, even in their treatment of one another. Using phrases and expressions that are characteristic of familiar relationships—such as using the first name of a person instead of the appropriate title and last name for a person you have just met—may be considered rude or interpreted as poor manners. The words and phrases you learn throughout this text, unless otherwise noted, exemplify the etiquette practiced by Hispanics. All of them are appropriate for the environment in which you will use them and the interactions you will have with Spanish-speakers. Remember that being courteous is the key to establishing trust with Hispanics.

I. Greetings, Courtesy Expressions and Goodbyes

*sah-**loo**-dohs, ayks-pray-**see^oh**-nays day kohr-tay-**see**-ah ee days-pay-**dee**-dahs*
Saludos, expresiones de cortesía y despedidas

English	Pronunciation & Spanish
1. Hello.	*oh-lah.* Hola.
2. Good morning.	*boo^ay-nohs **dee**-ahs.* Buenos días.[1]
3. Good afternoon.	*boo^ay-nahs **tahr**-days.* Buenas tardes.[1]
4. Good evening. / Good night.	*boo^ay-nahs **noh**-chays.* Buenas noches.[1]
5. With whom is your appointment today?	*kohn kee^ayn ays soo **see**-tah oh^ee?* ¿Con quién es su cita hoy?
6. Print your name here, please.	*ahs-**kree**-bah soo **nohm**-bray ayn **lay**-trahs day **mohl**-day ah-**kee**, pohr fah-**bohr**.* Escriba su nombre en letras de molde aquí, por favor.[2]
Sign here, please.	*feer-may ah-**kee**, pohr fah-**bohr**.* Firme aquí, por favor.

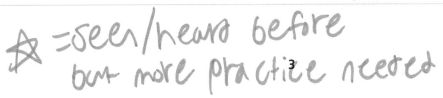

☆ =seen/heard before
but more practice needed

3

7. You may have a seat and someone will be with you shortly.

*poo^ay-day(n) sayn-**tahr**-say ee **ahl**-ghee^ayn lay(s) ah-tayn-day-**rah** **prohn**-toh.*
Puede(n) sentarse y alguien le(s) atenderá pronto.[3]

---

8. Sir / Mr.

*sayn-**yohr**.*
Señor.

---

9. Ma'am / Mrs.

*sayn-**yoh**-rah.*
Señora.[4]

---

10. Miss / Ms.

*sayn-yoh-**ree**-tah.*
Señorita.[4]

---

11. Welcome to [insert establishment name here].

*bee^ayn-bay-**nee**-doh/dah a [insert establishment name here].*
Bienvenido/a a [insert establishment name here].[5]

---

12. How are you (today)?

*koh-moh ays-**tah** (oh^ee)?*
¿Cómo está (hoy)?

---

13. (Very) well/fine. (And you?)

*(moo^ee) bee^ayn. (ee oos-**tayd**?)*
(Muy) bien. (¿Y Ud.?)[6]

---

14. Okay.

*rray-goo-**lahr**.*
Regular.

---

15. So, so.

*ah-**see**, ah-**see**.*
Así, así.

---

16. Not (very) well.

(moo^ee) mahl.
(Muy) mal.[7]

---

17. More or less.

*mahs oh **may**-nohs.*
Más o menos.

---

18. I'm sorry.

*loh **see^ayn**-toh.*
Lo siento.

---

19. Until later.

***ahs**-tah **loo^ay**-goh.*
Hasta luego.

---

20. Goodbye.

*ah-**dee^ohs**.*
Adiós.

---

21. Thank you (very much).

*(**moo**-chahs) **grah**-see^ahs.*
(Muchas) gracias.

---

22. Please.

*pohr fah-**bohr**.*
Por favor.

---

23. You're welcome.

*day **nah**-dah.*
De nada.

---

24. Excuse me.
[stating excuse me **before** an action]

*kohn payr-**mee**-soh.*
Con permiso.

25. Excuse me. [to get someone's attention]	*dees-**kool**-pay.* Disculpe.
26. Pardon. [stating excuse me **after** an action]	*payr-**dohn**.* Perdón.
27. Okay / Fine.	*ays-**tah** bee^ayn.* Está bien.[8]
28. Have a nice day.	*kay **pah**-say oon boo^ayn **dee**-ah.* Qué pase un buen día.
29. At your service.	*ah soos **ohr**-day-nays.* A sus órdenes.[9]
30. A pleasure (to see you).	*moo-choh **goos**-toh (**bayr**-loh/lah).* Mucho gusto (verlo/la).[10]
31. Yes.	*see.* Sí.
32. No.	*noh.* No.
33. Of course.	*koh-moh noh. / pohr soo-**poo^ays**-toh.* Cómo no. / Por supuesto.
34. No problem.	*noh ah^ee proh-**blay**-mah.* No hay problema.
35. I don't know.	*noh say.* No sé.
36. I'm not sure.	*noh ays-**toh^ee** say-**goo**-roh/rah.* No estoy seguro/a.[5]

II. Useful Expressions for Communication Management

*ayks-pray-**see^oh**-nays **oo**-tee-lays **pah**-rah ayl mah-**nay**-hoh day koh-moo-nee-kah-**see^ohn***
Expresiones útiles para el manejo de comunicación

English	Pronunciation & Spanish
1. I'm ...	*soh^ee ...* Soy ... [11]
He / She is ...	*ays ...* Es ... [11]
Mr. ___.	*ayl sayn-**yohr** ___.* el señor ___.
Mrs. ___.	*lah sayn-**yoh**-rah ___.* la señora ___.
Ms. ___.	*lah sayn-yoh-**ree**-tah ___.* la señorita ___.
2. I'm ...	*soh^ee ...* Soy ... [11]
He / She is ...	*ays ...* Es ... [11]
an attorney.	*ah-boh-**gah**-doh/dah.* abogado/a. [12]
a defense attorney.	*ah-boh-**gah**-doh/dah day-fayn-**sohr**(-ah)* abogado/a defensor/a. [12]
a district attorney.	*fees-**kahl**.* fiscal.
a public defendor.	*ah-boh-**gah**-doh/dah day oh-**fee**-see^oh.* abogado/a de oficio. [12]
a paralegal / a legal assistant.	*ah-sees-**tayn**-tay lay-**gahl**.* asistente legal.
a legal secretary.	*say-kray-**tah**-ree^oh/ah hoo-dee-**see^ahl**.* secretario/a judicial. [12]
a law clerk.	*pah-**sahn**-tay.* pasante.
a victim witness assistant.	*ah-sees-**tayn**-tay day **beek**-tee-mahs ee tays-**tee**-gohs.* asistente de víctimas y testigos.
3. I'm going to assist you.	*boh^ee ah ah-tayn-**dayr**-lay(s).* Voy a atenderle(s). [13]
4. He / She is going to assist you.	*bah ah ah-tayn-**dayr**-lay(s).* Va a atenderle(s). [13]

5. Do you speak (a little) English?

*ah-blah (oon **poh**-koh day) een-**glays**?*
¿Habla (un poco de) inglés?

6. Does someone here speak English?

*ahl-ghee^ayn ah-**kee** ah-blah een-**glays**?*
¿Alguien aquí habla inglés?

7. Yes.

see.
Sí.

8. No.

noh.
No.

9. A little.

*oon **poh**-koh.*
Un poco.

10. I don't speak Spanish.

*noh **ah**-bloh ays-pahn-**yohl**.*
No hablo español.

11. I speak very little Spanish.

*ah-bloh moo^ee **poh**-koh ays-pahn-**yohl**.*
Hablo muy poco español.

12. Excuse me.
[to get someone's attention][14]

*dees-**kool**-pay(n).*
Disculpe(n).

13. Wait (right) here.

*ays-**pay**-ray(n) ah-**kee** (**mees**-moh).*
Espere(n) aquí (mismo).[14]

14. Follow me, please.

*see-gah(n)-may, pohr fah-**bohr**.*
Síga(n)me, por favor.[14]

15. Have a seat.

*see^ayn-tay(n)-say, pohr fah-**bohr**.*
Siénte(n)se, por favor.[14]

16. I'll be right back.

*yah **boo^ayl**-boh.*
Ya vuelvo.

17. Just a moment, please.

*oon moh-**mayn**-toh, pohr fah-**bohr**.*
Un momento, por favor.

18. I don't understand. Please repeat it (slower).

*noh kohm-**prayn**-doh. pohr fah-**bohr**, rray-**pee**-tah-loh (mahs days-**pah**-see^oh).*
No comprendo. Por favor, repítalo (más despacio).

19. Thank you for your patience.

*lay(s) ah-grah-**days**-koh lah pah-**see^ayn**-see^ah.*
Le(s) agradezco la paciencia.[13]

20. ... will be in soon.

*... **bee^ay**-nay **prohn**-toh.*
... viene pronto.

Someone

ahl-ghee^ayn
Alguien

The attorney

*ayl/lah ah-boh-**gah**-doh/dah*
El/La abogado/a[12]

The paralegal / The legal assistant

*ayl/lah ah-sees-**tayn**-tay lay-**gahl***
El/La asistente legal[12]

The defense attorney	*ayl/lah ah-boh-**gah**-doh/dah day-fayn-**sohr**(-ah)* El/La abogado/a defensor/a[12]
The district attorney	*ayl/lah fees-**kahl*** El/La fiscal[12]
The public defendor	*ayl/lah ah-boh-**gah**-doh/dah day oh-**fee**-see^oh* El/La abogado/a de oficio[12]
The paralegal / The legal assistant	*ayl/lah ah-sees-**tayn**-tay lay-**gahl*** El/La asistente legal[12]
The legal secretary	*ayl/lah say-kray-**tah**-ree^oh/ah hoo-dee-**see^ahl*** El/La secretario/a judicial[12]
The law clerk	*ayl/lah pah-**sahn**-tay* El/La pasante[12]
The victim witness assistant	*ayl/lah ah-sees-**tayn**-tay day **beek**-tee-mahs ee tays-**tee**-gohs* El/La asistente de víctimas y testigos
21. Would you like something to drink?	*kee-**see^ay**-rah(n) **ahl**-goh day bay-**bayr**?* ¿Quisiera(n) algo de beber?[14]
22. Would you like a soft drink or water?	*kee-**see^ay**-rah(n) oon ray-**frays**-koh oh **ah**-goo^ah?* ¿Quisiera(n) un refresco o agua?[14]

Notes

[1] For simplicity's sake, use *Buenos días* from early morning (generally sun-up) to noon, *Buenas tardes* from noon to sun-down and *Buenas noches* from sun-down to early morning. *Buenas noches* may be used as a greeting or a goodbye after sundown as well.

[2] If the client is unable to print or sign his/her name, or you want to make sure there is no error in understanding what is heard or written, reference *Chapter 2—Collecting Basic Personal Information in Person and by Phone*, for phrases that will assist you in requesting a form of identification if dealing with the individual in person.

[3] If speaking to one person use *puede*; if two or more individuals, use *pueden*. Also, use *le* when addressing one person and *les* when addressing two or more.

[4] Though a woman may not appear young, if she is not married or you are unsure of her marital status, she is still a *Señorita*. Also, *señorita* is often abbreviated as *Srta.*, *señora* as *Sra.* and *señor* as *Sr.*

[5] Use *bienvenido* if speaking to a male; use *bienvenida* when addressing a female. If speaking to a group you may say *bienvenidos* (*bee^ayn-bay-nee-dohs*). If you do insert the name of the establishment, do not worry about translating it into Spanish. In the majority of cases, proper names remain in the source language.

[6] The word *usted* is commonly abbreviated as *Ud.* Whenever you see this abbreviation, make sure to say the entire word.

[7] This phrase is a question of wellbeing and not one of a diagnostic nature; the literal translation of *muy mal* is *very badly*.

[8] This is very common for expressing agreement and comprehension. Another possible translation would be the English word *alright*.

[9] Also expressed by the phrase *Para servirle* (*pah-rah sayr-**beer**-lay*) or *Estoy a su servicio* (*ays-**toh**^ee ah soo sayr-**bee**-see^oh*).

[10] If speaking to a *male*, use *verlo*; if speaking to a *female*, use *verla*.

[11] The form *soy* is used when introducing or speaking in first person—this is *I* in English. The form *es* is used when introducing or speaking of someone else, in this case *he* or *she*. Notice that when introducing someone or even oneself, Spanish uses *el* + *title* + *name* for a *male* or *la* + *title* + *name* for a *female*: for example *Soy el señor Smith / Soy la señora Myers*. You would also hear this in the response to the question—¿*Con quién es su cita hoy?* To explain further, let us assume we are talking about two attorneys—*Attorney Johnson* who happens to be a *male* attorney and *Attorney Thomas* who happens to be a *female*. Taking this into account, the responses would be: *Con el abogado Johnson / Con la abogada Thomas*. Note in the first example *el* is used because *Johnson* is a *male*, whereas in the second example, *la* is used since *Thomas* is a *female*.

[12] If given as an option, use the *-o ending* if you or the person you are referencing is *male* and use the *-a ending* if you or the person you are referencing is *female*. Note that not all titles have a *male* and *female* ending since many are used for both sexes. No-

tice that *defensor* is used for a *male* and that *defensora* is used for a *female* when using the title *defense attorney.* Also, when given the option of including *el* or *la* with a title, remember to use *el* for a *male* and use *la* for a *female.*

[13] Use *le* when addressing one person. Use *les* when addressing two or more. Also, since this phrase may be used for *he* or *she*, you may want to incorporate a simple hand gesture towards the person of whom you are speaking to clarify meaning.

[14] The addition of *-n* to these requests will create the plural form used to address two or more people. Also note, when making a request, such as *Siéntense,* you may want to use *por favor* to soften it. Observe that it would sound odd to follow every request with *por favor* if you were giving a series of them. For example: *Síganme por favor y esperen aquí (Follow me please, and wait here).* Notice how only one *por favor* is all that would be necessary.

Practical Activities

A) Meet and Greet

Instructions: Based on the following information, orally compose mini-conversations in which you *meet and greet* the persons indicated in an appropriate manner. Remember to speak ONLY in Spanish.

You say/ask ...	The person says/responds/asks ...
mini-conversation I	
1. Good morning. (to an unmarried female)	Hello.
2. How are you doing?	Not very well.
3. I'm sorry.	Thank you.
4. Until later.	Goodbye.
mini-conversation II	
1. Good afternoon. (to a married male)	Good afternoon.
2. How are you doing?	Very well, thank you. And you?
3. So-so.	It's nice to see you.
4. Thank you.	Have a nice day.
mini-conversation III	
1. Good evening. (to a married female)	Hello. How are you today?
2. Very well. And you?	Fine.
3. At your service.	Thank you very much.
mini-conversation IV	
1. Good morning. I'm Mr./Ms. Smith.	A pleasure. I'm Mr. Martinez.
2. With whom is your appointment today?	Attorney Daniels.
3. Yes, of course. Print your name for me here, please, and sign here.	Okay.
4. Thank you. You may have a seat and someone will be with you shortly.	Thank you sir/miss.

Follow-up: Form pairs and take turns being both characters in the four mini-conversations above. Try to do this without looking back in the chapter as best you can.

B) Appropriate Responses

Instructions: Based on each scenario described below, select the Spanish phrase(s) from this section that would be most appropriate and explain why. Keep in mind, in some instances, there may be multiple correct responses.

1. You need to get someone's attention.

2. You need to leave a conversation to answer the phone.

3. Someone says he/she does not feel well today.

4. You welcome an elderly male who has just come up to the reception desk.

5. Someone asks how you are doing today.

6. You are saying goodbye to a married female in the evening.

C) Introductions

Instructions: From the information provided in numbers 11 and 12 from the NOTES in this chapter, create your own personal introduction below. Include your personal title—*señor, señorita* or *señora*—as well as the professional title descriptive of your position. Make sure to use the correct form depending upon your gender. If your professional title is not listed, just use the appropriate personal title. Then, incorporate the singular form of the phrase from this chapter *I'm going to assist you* and introduce yourself to your two nearest neighbors. Try to do this as much as possible without looking at the Spanish text.

example: (*Mr. Smith, a defense attorney,* introduces himself to classmate.)
"*Soy el señor Smith. Soy abogado defensor. Voy a atenderle.*"

"*Soy* ___el Señor Bronder. Soy abogado defensor. Voy a atenderle___."

After you have made your initial introductions, try introducing your two nearest neighbors to one another using the information he or she just used in his/her own personal introduction.

example: (One classmate introduces *Mr. Smith, a defense attorney,* to yet another classmate.)
"*Es el señor Smith. Es abogado defensor. Va a atenderle.*"

"*Es* ___el Señor ~~Sm~~ burke. Es abogado defensr. va a atenderle___."

Follow-up: What change would be necessary in any of the introductions above as well as the ones you have created if you were introducing yourself or introducing another person to two or more people?

___me = el → yo   multiple people = el → ustedes/ellos___

D) Phrase Fragments

Instructions: Complete each phrase fragment given by either saying the entire phrase aloud or writing the missing information. First, try to do this WITHOUT looking back at the text. After you have attempted to complete them all, compare with nearby classmates. Only consult the text after you and your classmates are unable to successfully complete all phrases by working together. In some cases there may be more than one form that completes the phrase or expression. Lastly, have a classmate say each completed phrase aloud while you provide the English meaning.

1. ¿Con quién ___es su cita hoy___?

2. ¿Quisiera algo ___de beber___?

3. Voy a _____

4. _____ la paciencia.

5. Qué pase _____

6. _____ aquí mismo.

7. Pueden sentarse y _____

8. Hablo muy _____

E) Situations

Instructions: For each situation given, select the appropriate phrases/expressions from this chapter that would best convey the information indicated. Do not forget that hand gestures, such as motioning toward a sign-in sheet when requesting that a client sign in for an appointment or using a hand gesture in the direction you wish someone to follow you, may come in very useful when relying on limited language skills.

1. *A Hispanic couple has just entered your office and begin speaking Spanish. You ask if either of them speak English to which they respond "no." You inform them your Spanish is limited but you introduce yourself and ask them to wait a moment. You thank them for their patience and tell them you will be right back.*

2. *It is one o'clock when a Hispanic female enters your office and greets you. You respond appropriately and inquire as to with whom she has an appointment. She responds and then you ask her to please sign in. You then ask here to take a seat and let her know that Mrs. Jenkins, the legal assistant, will be with her shortly. In the meantime, you offer her something to drink.*

3. *You are ready to call a male client back to meet with his attorney. First, you get his attention and you ask him to follow you back. On the way, you ask how he doing to which he responds, not so well. You tell him you are sorry to hear it. You get to the room where he will meet with the attorney, request that he have a seat and then ask if he would like some water or a soft drink. Finally, let him know that Mr. Ramsey, the attorney, will be in shortly.*

4. *You tell a client you speak very little Spanish. The client responds but you are unable to catch what she says the first time so you let her know and politely ask her to repeat it. You understand she has an appointment, so you show her the sign-in sheet and request that she print her name then sign beside of it. You thank her and ask that she have a seat and someone will be with her shortly.*

F) Cyber-Investigation

Utilize the internet to locate TWO articles that address the cultural norms of the Hispanic community as they relate to their treatment of one another as well as foreigners. You may wish to start your inquiry with a broad topic such as HISPANICS AND CULTURAL NORMS and begin to limit it from there once you are able to glance over your results. Remember, you may also want to restrict your search even more by employing your search engine's advanced search settings.

Once you have located and read the two articles, create a brief summary that highlights pertinent information to share with your class. Do not forget to cite your sources from which you borrowed the information should others wish to read either or both of the articles in their entirety.

Chapter 2

Collecting Basic Information in Person and by Phone

Before You Begin

Hispanics will have varying degrees of language skills, both in Spanish and English. Depending upon their level of education, they may be literate, semi-literate or illiterate in their native language. Also, Spanish may not be their first language either, but rather an indigenous Latin-American language. Likewise, depending upon the length of time they have spent in the United States, their knowledge of the English language and culture will vary greatly. Since a deep sense of pride is innate to the Hispanic culture, it may be difficult to immediately recognize the true abilities of the person with whom you are dealing. However, assess the situation as your interaction progresses with care and respect so as to be sure to avoid causing any shame or embarrassment.

Also of importance, when gathering personal information, is knowledge of the Hispanic surname system. Unlike many Anglo-Americans who have a first, middle and last name, the majority of Hispanics have a first name (or more) followed by two surnames. These surnames consist first of the father's surname followed by the mother's maiden name or surname. It is important to understand how to distinguish these components of a Hispanic name for the purpose of alphabetizing documents, billing, etc. Hispanic names are ordered according to the father's surname unless the person has an expressed preference or a legal change has been made to modify the name.

For example:

If *Sara Montero* and *Pedro García* have a child named *Miguel*, the child's complete name would be *Miguel García Montero*.

His last name is technically *García* and would appear as such on documents. Likewise, he would be alphabetized under the letter *G* for *García*.

I. Personal Data

dah-tohs payr-soh-*nah*-lays
Datos personales

English	Pronunciation & Spanish
1. (Hello), I am ___.	(**oh**-lah) soh^ee ___. (Hola) soy ___.[1]
2. Are you calling on behalf of yourself or someone else?	yah-mah day **pahr**-tay day see **mees**-moh/mah oh day **pahr**-tay day oh-trah payr-**soh**-nah? ¿Llama de parte de sí mismo/a o de parte de otra persona?[2]

15

3. I'm calling on behalf of ...

*yah-moh day **pahr**-tay day ...*
Llamo de parte de ...

myself.

*mee **mees**-moh/mah.*
mí mismo/a.²

another person.

*day **oh**-trah payr-**soh**-nah.*
otra persona.

4. Is the person male or female?

*ays lah **oh**-trah payr-**soh**-nah **ohm**-bray oh moo-**hayr**?*
¿Es la otra persona hombre o mujer?

5. I need to ask you some questions.

*lay nay-say-**see**-toh ah-**sayr** oo-nahs pray-**goon**-tahs.*
Le necesito hacer unas preguntas.

6. I need to ask you some questions about him / her.

*lay nay-say-**see**-toh ah-**sayr** oo-nahs pray-**goon**-tahs **soh**-bray ayl / **ay**-yah.*
Le necesito hacer unas preguntas sobre él / ella.

7. And him ...

ee ayl ...
Y él ...³

And her ...

*ee **ay**-yah ...*
Y ella ...³

And you ...

*ee oos-**tayd** ...*
Y Ud....³

And (proper name) ...

ee (proper name) ...
Y (proper name) ...³

8. What is your ...

koo^ahl ays soo ...
¿Cuál es su ...⁴

full name?

*nohm-bray kohm-**play**-toh?*
nombre completo?

paternal last name/father's last name?

*ah-pay-**yee**-doh pah-**tayr**-no?*
apellido paterno?

maternal last name/mother's maiden name?

*ah-pay-**yee**-doh mah-**tayr**-no?*
apellido materno?

9. My name is ...

*may **yah**-moh ...*
Me llamo ...

His / Her name is ...

*say **yah**-mah ...*
Se llama ...

10. My name is ...

*mee **nohm**-bray ays ...*
Mi nombre es ...

His / Her name is ...

*soo **nohm**-bray ays ...*
Su nombre es ...

11. How do you spell that?
*koh-moh say ays-**kree**-bay **ay**-soh?*
¿Cómo se escribe eso?[4]

12. Do you speak (any) English?
*ah-blah (oon **poh**-koh day) een-**glays**?*
¿Habla (un poco de) inglés?

13. Do you understand (any) English?
*kohm-**prayn**-day (oon **poh**-koh day) een-**glays**?*
¿Comprende (un poco de) inglés?

14. I speak (a little) Spanish.
*ah-bloh (oon **poh**-koh day) ays-pahn-**yohl**.*
Hablo (un poco de) español.

15. I understand (a little) Spanish.
*kohm-**prayn**-doh (oon **poh**-koh day) ays-pahn-**yohl**.*
Comprendo (un poco de) español.

16. Can you read and write?
*sah-bay lay-**ayr** ee ays-kree-**beer**?*
¿Sabe leer y escribir?[4]

17. I'm sorry, I don't understand (very well).
*loh **see^ayn**-toh, noh kohm-**prayn**-doh (moo^ee bee^ayn).*
Lo siento, no comprendo (muy bien).

18. Please write the information for me here.
*pohr fah-**bohr**, ays-**kree**-bah-may lah een-fohr-mah-**see^ohn** ah-**kee**.*
Por favor, escríbame la información aquí.[4]

19. Do you have a nickname?
*tee^ay-nay ahl-**goon** ah-**poh**-doh?*
¿Tiene algún apodo?

   What is the nickname?
*koo-ahl ays ayl ah-**poh**-doh?*
¿Cuál es el apodo?[4]

20. How old are you?
*koo^ahn-tohs **ahn**-yohs **tee^ay**-nay?*
¿Cuántos años tiene?[5]

21. I am ... years old.
*tayn-goh ... **ahn**-yohs*
Tengo ... años.[5]

   He/she is ... years old.
*tee^ay-nay ... **ahn**-yohs*
Tiene ... años.[5]

22. What is your date of birth?
*koo^ahl ays soo **fay**-chah day nah-see-**mee^ayn**-toh?*
¿Cuál es su fecha de nacimiento?[4,5]

23. Where were you born?
*dohn-day nah-**see^oh**?*
¿Dónde nació?[4]

   What is the name of the ...
*koh-moh say **yah**-mah ...*
¿Cómo se llama ...

   town?
*ayl **poo^ay**-bloh?*
el pueblo?

   city?
*lah see^oo-**dahd**?*
la ciudad?

   state?
*ayl ays-**tah**-doh?*
el estado?

24. What is your marital status?

*koo^ahl ays soo ays-**tah**-doh see-**beel**?*
¿Cuál es su estado civil?

Married.

*kah-**sah**-doh/dah.*
Casado/a.[6]

Divorced.

*dee-bohr-**see^ah**-doh/dah.*
Divorciado/a.[6]

Separated.

*say-pah-**rah**-doh/dah.*
Separado/a.[6]

Single.

*sohl-**tay**-roh/rah.*
Soltero/a.[6]

Widowed.

***bee^oo**-doh/dah.*
Viudo/a.[6]

25. What is your current address?

*koo^ahl ays soo dee-rayk-**see^ohn** ahk-**too^ahl**?*
¿Cuál es su dirección actual?[4, 5]

26. What was your previous address?

*koo^ahl foo^ay soo dee-rayk-**see^ohn** ahn-tay-**ree^ohr**?*
¿Cuál fue su dirección anterior?[4, 5]

27. What is your current telephone number?

*koo^ahl ays soo **noo**-may-roh day tay-**lay**-foh-noh ahk-**too^ahl**?*
¿Cuál es su número de teléfono actual?[5]

28. What is the best number to reach you?

*koo^ahl ays ayl may-**hohr noo**-may-roh day tay-**lay**-foh-noh **pah**-ray kohn-tahk-**tahr**-loh/lah?*
¿Cuál es el mejor número de teléfono para contactarlo/la?[5, 7]

29. What is your nationality?

*koo^ahl ays soo nah-see^oh-nah-lee-**dahd**?*
¿Cuál es su nacionalidad?[8]

30. Are you here legally?

*ays-**tah** ah-**kee** lay-gahl-**mayn**-tay?*
¿Está aquí legalmente?[9]

31. Are you …

ays …
¿Es …

a legal resident?

*rray-see-**dayn**-tay lay-**gahl**?*
residente legal?[9]

a U.S. citizen?

*see^oo-dah-**dah**-noh/nah ays-tah-doh-oo-nee-**dayn**-say?*
ciudadano/a estadounidense?[6, 9]

32. Do you have proof of your immigration status?

***tee^ay**-nay **proo^ay**-bah day soo kohn-dee-**see^ohn** mee-grah-**toh**-ree^ah?*
¿Tiene prueba de su condición migratoria?[9]

33. Do you have (photo) identification?

***tee^ay**-nay ee-dayn-tee-fee-kah-**see^ohn** (kohn **foh**-toh)?*
¿Tiene identificación (con foto)?

34. Do you have …

***tee^ay**-nay …*
¿Tiene …

a driver's license?

lee-sayn-see^ah pah-rah kohn-doo-seer?
licencia para conducir?[10]

an immigration number?

noo-may-roh day een-mee-grah-see^ohn?
número de inmigración?[5, 9]

a social security card?

tahr-hay-tah day say-goo-roh soh-see^ahl?
tarjeta de seguro social?

a visa?

bee-sah (bee-sah-doh)?
visa (visado)?[11]

a passport?

pah-sah-pohr-tay?
pasaporte?

35. Are you currently employed?

trah-bah-hah ahk-too^ahl-mayn-tay?
¿Trabaja actualmente?

Where do you work?

dohn-day trah-bah-hah?
¿Dónde trabaja?[4]

How do you spell that?

koh-moh say ays-kree-bay ay-soh?
¿Cómo se escribe eso?[4]

What is the address of your current employer?

koo^ahl ays lah dee-rayk-see^ohn day soo aym-play-ah-dohr ahk-too^ahl?
¿Cuál es la dirección de su empleador actual?[4, 5]

36. What is your profession?

koo^ahl ays soo proh-fay-see^ohn?
¿Cuál es su profesión?

How do you spell that?

koh-moh say ays-kree-bay ay-soh?
¿Cómo se escribe eso?[4]

II. Managing Phone Calls

*ahd-mee-nees-trah-**see^ohn** day yah-**mah**-dahs tay-lay-**foh**-nee-kahs*
Administración de llamadas telefónicas

English	Pronunciation & Spanish
1. Thank you for calling [insert establishment name].	***grah**-see^ahs pohr yah-**mahr** ah [insert establishment name].* Gracias por llamar a [insert establishment name].
For whom are you calling?	***pah**-rah kee^ayn **yah**-mah?* ¿Para quién llama?
2. Are you seeking legal advice?	***boos**-kah kohn-**say**-hoh lay-**gahl**?* ¿Busca consejo legal?
3. Please listen carefully to the following options. Respond with "yes" when you hear the option that best describes your inquiry. Are you seeking legal advice regarding a(n) ... case or matter?	*pohr fah-**bohr**, ays-**koo**-chay kohn koo^ee-**dah**-doh lahs see-**ghee^ayn**-tays oph-**see^oh**-nays. rrays-**pohn**-dah kohn <see> koo^ahn-doh **oh^ee**-gah lah oph-**see^ohn** kay may-**hohr** days-**kree**-bay ayl proh-**poh**-see-toh day soo yah-**mah**-dah. ays-**tah** boos-**kahn**-doh kohn-**say**-hoh lay-**gahl** rray-fay-**rayn**-tay ah oon **kah**-soh oh ah-**soon**-toh ...* Por favor, escuche con cuidado las siguientes opciones. Responda con <sí> cuando oiga la opción que mejor describe el propósito de su llamada. ¿Está buscando consejo legal referente a un caso o asunto ...[12]
criminal	*pay-**nahl**?* penal?
immigration	*mee-grah-**toh**-ree^oh?* migratorio?
personal injury	*rray-lah-see^oh-**nah**-doh kohn lohs **dahn**-yohs payr-soh-**nah**-lays?* relacionado con los daños personales?
employment	*rray-lah-see^oh-**nah**-doh kohn ayl aym-**play**-oh?* relacionado con el empleo?
family law	*rray-lah-see^oh-**nah**-doh kohn ayl day-**ray**-choh fah-mee-**lee^ahr**?* relacionado con el derecho familiar?
real estate	*rray-lah-see^oh-**nah**-doh kohn lohs **bee^ay**-nays rrah-**ee**-says?* relacionado con los bienes raíces?
occupancy of a dwelling?	*rray-lah-see^oh-**nah**-doh kohn lah oh-koo-pah-**see^ohn** day **oo**-nah bee-**bee^ayn**-dah?* relacionado con la ocupación de una vivienda?
financial or bankruptcy	*fee-nahn-**see^ay**-roh oh rray-lah-see^oh-**nah**-doh kohn lah bahn-kah-**rroh**-tah?* financiero o relacionado con la bancarrota?
litigation	*rray-lah-see^oh-**nah**-doh kohn ayl lee-**tee**-hee^oh?* relacionado con el litigio?

4. He/She is not available at the moment.
*noh ays-**tah** dees-poh-**nee**-blay ayn **ays**-tay moh-**mayn**-toh.*
No está disponible en este momento.

5. I'm going to transfer the call to ...
*boh^ee ah pah-**sahr** lah yah-**mah**-dah con ...*
Voy a pasar la llamada con ...

someone who speaks Spanish.
*ahl-ghee^ayn kay **ah**-blah ays-pahn-**yohl**.*
alguien que habla español.

someone else.
*oh-trah payr-**soh**-nah.*
otra persona.

6. Please hold.
*pohr fah-**bohr**, noh **koo^ayl**-gay.*
Por favor, no cuelgue.

7. If no one answers, leave a message.
*see **nah**-dee^ay kohn-**tays**-tah, **day**-hay oon mayn-**sah**-hay.*
Si nadie contesta, deje un mensaje.

8. Speak clearly and slowly.
*ah-blay **klah**-rah ee layn-tah-**mayn**-tay.*
Hable clara y lentamente.

9. Leave your name, telephone number and a brief message.
*day-hay soo **nohm**-bray, **noo**-may-roh day tay-**lay**-foh-noh ee oon **bray**-bay mayn-**sah**-hay.*
Deje su nombre, número de teléfono y un breve mensaje.

10. I'm going to send your call to voicemail.
*boh^ee ah pah-**sahr** lah yah-**mah**-dah ahl boo-**sohn** day bohs.*
Voy a pasar la llamada al buzón de voz.

11. How do you spell ...
*koh-moh say ays-**kree**-bay ...*
¿Cómo se escribe ...

your first name?
*soo pree-**mayr nohm**-bray?*
su primer nombre?[4]

your last name?
*soo ah-pay-**yee**-doh?*
su apellido?[4]

12. Slower, please.
*mahs days-**pah**-see^oh, pohr fah-**bohr**.*
Más despacio, por favor.

13. Repeat it, please.
*rray-**pee**-tah-loh, pohr fah-**bohr**.*
Repítalo, por favor.

14. You have the wrong number.
*say ah ay-kee-boh-**kah**-doh day **noo**-may-roh.*
Se ha equivocado de número.

15. You need to call this number, ___.
*nay-say-**see**-tah yah-**mahr** ah **ays**-tay **noo**-may-roh, ___.*
Necesita llamar a este número, ___.[5]

16. Dial this extension: ___.
*mahr-kay **ays**-tay **noo**-may-roh day ayks-tayn-**see^ohn**: ___.*
Marque este número de extensión: ___.[5]

17. Please call back ...
*pohr fah-**bohr**, **yah**-may ...*
Por favor, llame ...

later.
*mahs **tahr**-day.*
más tarde.

	*mahn-**yah**-nah.*
tomorrow.	mañana.
	*ays-tah **tahr**-day.*
this afternoon.	esta tarde.
	*ays-tah **noh**-chay.*
this evening.	esta noche.
	*mahn-**yah**-nah pohr lah mahn-**yah**-nah.*
tomorrow morning.	mañana por la mañana.
	*mahn-**yah**-nah pohr lah **tahr**-day.*
tomorrow afternoon.	mañana por la tarde.
	*mahn-**yah**-nah pohr lah **noh**-chay.*
tomorrow evening.	mañana por la noche.

	*grah-see^ahs ee kay **pah**-say oon boo^ayn **dee**-ah.*
18. Thank you and have a nice day.	Gracias y qué pase un buen día.

	*see^**ayn**-toh noh poh-**dayr** ah^ee-yoo-**dahr**.*
19. I'm sorry I cannot help.	Siento no poder ayudar.

	*lay dah-**ray** ays-tah een-fohr-mah-**see^ohn** ah **oo**-noh day **noo^ays**-trohs ah-boh-**gah**-dohs.*
20. I will pass this information along to one of our attorneys.	Le daré esta información a uno de nuestros abogados.

	*rray-see-bee-**rah** **oo**-nah yah-**mah**-dah tay-lay-**foh**-nee-kah tahn **prohn**-toh **koh**-moh poh-**see**-blay.*
21. You will hear from someone as soon as possible.	Recibirá una llamada telefónica tan pronto como posible.

	*noh ay-hayr-**say**-mohs …*
22. We don't practice …	No ejercemos …
	*ays-tah **klah**-say day day-**ray**-choh.*
that type of law.	esta clase de derecho.
	*day-**ray**-choh ayn **ay**-sah see^oo-**dahd**.*
in that city.	derecho en esa ciudad.
	*day-**ray**-choh ayn **ay**-sah rray-**hee^ohn**.*
in that region.	derecho en esa región.

	*boy ah **dahr**-lay ayl **noo**-may-roh day tay-**lay**-foh-noh day oon sayr-**bee**-see^oh day rray-fay-**rayn**-see^ah day ah-boh-**gah**-dohs kay **poo^ay**-day ah-tayn-**dayr**-lay ayn ays-pahn-**yohl**. ays poh-**see**-blay kay lay **poo^ay**-dahn ah^ee-yoo-**dahr** mahs.*
23. I'm going to give you the phone number of a lawyer referral service that can assist you in Spanish. They may be able to help you further.	Voy a darle el número de teléfono de un servicio de referencia de abogados que puede atenderle en español. Es posible que le puedan ayudar más.[5]

Notes

[1] Identify yourself appropriately using information from *Chapter 1 — II. Useful Expressions for Communication Management.* If answering the phone, understand there are many regional ways to do so in Spanish, however a simple *Hello (Hola)* will suffice here. It may also be used should you need to place a caller on hold and come back to him/her and verify he/she is still on the line. Lastly, remember the phrases provided in this section are meant to assist with assessments performed in person and over the phone. Therefore, you will select the phrases you will use based on the situation in which you find yourself. Adjust the dialogue accordingly.

[2] If addressing a *male* use the -o ending; if addressing a *female* use the -a ending.

[3] ***Extremely important information:*** You will use these short phrases to navigate between *you, he/him* or *she/her* with ANY of the statements where *you* is translated into English. Notice that most of the Spanish phrases and questions can be used to indicate not only *you,* but also *he/him* or *she/her* as well without having to change any words in the phrase. In such a case, you will first insert either *Y Ud. . . . , Y él . . .* or *Y ella . . .* plus the phrase or question you wish to compose. For example, you realize you are speaking to a caller about a *male.* To ask the male's name you say: "*Y él, ¿Cuál es su nombre completo?*" *(And him, what is his name?).* This clears up any ambiguity about whom you are referencing. In the case of using a proper name, you still must take into consideration whether the person is male or female, then continue with the remainder of the phrase making any necessary adjustments for male or female endings. See note 2 above and notes 6 and 7 below.

[4] If you are face-to-face with an individual and he/she is capable of reading and writing, take advantage of the situation by allowing him or her to write the information for you. Otherwise, if conducting a phone interview or the client is unable to perform this task, ask that he/she spell words that are difficult to understand. Also, consult *Chapter 12 — The Basics — I. The Spanish Alphabet.*

[5] Once again, you may elect to have the client write out this information if possible. Reference *Chapter 12 — The Basics — II. Numbers* for assistance with age, dates, etc. Also, see *Chapter 13 — Telling Time the Easy Way — Days of the Week and Month of the Year.*

[6] Use the *-o (-oh)* ending for a *male* and the *-a (-ah)* ending for a *female.*

[7] Use *lo* if speaking to or about a *male.* Use *la* when speaking to or about a *female.*

[8] See the *Appendix* for a listing of nationalities with their pronunciation in Spanish.

[9] Make sure you are legally aloud to ask these questions. They are only permitted to be asked by certain government agencies, business personnel and legal professionals.

[10] The verb *manejar (mah-nay-**hahr**)* which means *to manage; to drive* is often interchangeable with *conducir.* Therefore, you may also hear *licencia de manejar* for *driver's license.*

[11] Either of these two terms are commonly used for this immigration document.

[12] After you have discovered in what area of law the caller or potential client has interest, select the appropriate section from the table of contents and continue with the expressions and questions you find relevant for the collection of information from that specific chapter or section.

Practical Activities

A) ¿Ud., él o ella? (You, him or her?)

Part I — Instructions: Review the explanation given in number 3 of the **NOTES** for this chapter. Then, taking your queue from the persons indicated in parenthesis, formulate the question in Spanish following the example provided.

For example:

What is your full name? (her) / (him)

Explanation: You have the question from the text "What is your full name? and you see the word "her" in the first set of parenthesis. To formulate this question so that the concept of "her" is conveyed rather than "you," say: "*Y ella, ¿cuál es su nombre completo?*" *(And her, what is her name?).* This clears up any ambiguity about whom is being referenced. Repeat the process with "him" found in the second set of parenthesis: "*Y él, ¿cuál es su nombre completo?*" *(And him, what is his name?).*

Take turns doing this in pairs, groups or as a class and make sure to pay close attention to any differences that occur depending upon whether a *male* or *female* is being addressed. And do not forget to use *Y Ud.,* when referencing *you* should it be necessary.

1. Do you have a nickname? (you) / (him)   *Tienes un apodo?*
2. How old are you? (her) / (you)   *Cuantos años tienes?*
3. What is your marital status? (her) / (him)
4. What is your profession? (you) / (her)   *Cual es tu/su estado civil?*
5. What is your nationality? (him) / (her)   *Cual es el mejor numero de telefono para contactarlo/la?*
6. What is the best number to reach you? (you) / (her)
7. What is the current address of your employer? (him) / (her)
8. Are you seeking legal advice regarding an employment case or matter? (her) / (you)

Part II — Instructions: Using eight of the sixteen questions you formulated in *Part I* above, determine what their possible responses might be. Feel free to write these down or say them aloud to a partner. Take into account, that some questions will have multiple if not infinite possibilities, in which case you should strive to exhaust your answers when possible and/or provide sample responses. This will greatly assist you in preparing yourself to listen for anticipated responses to common questions.

B) Matching Questions and Answers

Instructions: For phone calls, it will be somewhat important to be able to understand simple Spanish words and phrases said by callers. To help you prepare for this, match the Spanish questions below with the Spanish answer. After you have finished, compare your answers with those of a classmate. Finally, have your instructor review the correct responses with you and practice saying each question and answer aloud in Spanish, then translate them into English.

1. _a_ ¿Para quién llama?   a. Tengo 37 años.
2. _c_ ¿Habla un poco de inglés?   b. México.
3. _b_ ¿Cuál es su nombre completo?   c. 2297 Creed St., Raleigh, NC, 49237.

4. f ¿Cómo se escribe eso?   d. No, lo siento. Sólo español.

5. a ¿Cuántos años tiene?   e. Mexicano.

6. i ¿Cuál es su estado civil?   f. Álvaro, A-L-V-A-R-O. Torres, T-O-R-R-E-S.

7. c ¿Cuál es su dirección actual?   g. Para el abogado Johnston.

8. b ¿Dónde nació?   h. Álvaro Torres.

9. j ¿Cuál es su número de teléfono?   i. Soltero.

10. e ¿Cuál es su nacionalidad?   j. 910-555-2874.

Follow-up: Using the questions from this exercise, invent your own answers in Spanish. Then, form groups of three to four people and take turns reading JUST the answers aloud. The other group members will try to match the corresponding question to the answer they hear.

C) Obtaining Personal Information

Part I—Instructions: First, write the numbers one through ten in a column on a piece of paper. Then, choose 10 different items from those listed here and write them in a logical order beside each number:

full name	nickname	past address
father's last name	place of birth	proof of immigration status
here legally	date of birth	employment
marital status	current address	speak any English
phone number	passport	mother's maiden name
U.S. citizen	driver's license	immigration number
read or write	nationality	social security card
age	identification	best phone number for communication
understand any English		

Part II—Instructions: Write your name on the paper and trade with a partner. Have your partner look for the questions in *Section I—Personal Data* of this chapter that would be used to obtain the information from *Part I* above. Remember to take into consideration the gender of the person you will interview for certain questions (hint—reference the name on the paper). You may prepare a script for your interview, but regardless, you will want to practice saying your questions aloud before you conduct the interview. After both of you are comfortable with saying the phrases in Spanish and providing short anticipated responses, take turns interviewing one another using the questions and answers you have both prepared. Do not forget to use the lead-in phrases from the beginning of this section to let the person you will interview know who you are. Reference *Chapter 12* for help with letters and numbers when answering questions.

Follow-up: Present one of your interviews to the class and have various classmates "interpret" into English what is being said as the interview progresses.

D) Phone Calls

One of the most difficult situations you will encounter is speaking a foreign language over the phone. Since the person is not visible, you cannot rely on body language or facial expressions to assist you in oral comprehension. For this reason, it is extremely important to become comfortable with communication strategies that will allow you to successfully manage phone calls with Spanish-speakers.

Part I — Instructions: Read the "phone calls" below, then prepare a script for what you will say in order to successfully manage each one. In preparing your script, you may choose to mark the appropriate phrases/expressions in the text itself or write them on a separate sheet of paper. Review your scripts several times to make sure you have included all of the requisite information.

1. *You answer the phone and realize that a gentleman is speaking Spanish. Introduce yourself, ask the caller to please slow down then state that you speak very little Spanish. Proceed by asking the caller if he speaks and understands any English. Unfortunately, his response is "no." Request that the caller hold while you transfer the call to someone who speaks Spanish. Tell him that if no one answers, to please leave a message. Remind the caller to speak clearly and slowly.*

2. *Upon answering the phone, you immediately hear a young lady speaking Spanish. Introduce yourself and ask if she is seeking legal advice. She answers "yes," which prompts you to find out what it is regarding by providing her with options. You find out she would like to speak to someone regarding a personal injury issue. After noting this, you ask her for her name and phone number. For verification of your comprehension, you request she spell her name. Then, inform her you will pass the information along to one of the attorneys and that someone will contact her.*

3. *You answer the phone by introducing yourself. A voice on the other end asks if you speak Spanish. You respond that you do a little and ask the caller if she is calling for herself or on behalf of someone else. You then ask the caller if she is seeking legal advice to which the caller responds "no." You then inquire as to if there is someone with whom she would like to speak to which she responds "Attorney Greene." Tell her you will transfer the call and to please hold. Inform her that if no one answers, to leave a message.*

4. *A Spanish-speaking caller is inquiring about legal advice regarding family law. Inform the caller that the firm does not practice this type of law but to hold on just a moment and you will be right back. When you return, tell the caller you have a phone number to a referral service that she can call and that she may find more assistance there. Provide the caller with a ten digit number (area code plus seven digit phone number). Ask that she repeat it back to you so you are sure she has the correct number written down. After confirmation of the correct information, tell her goodbye and to have a good day.*

5. *A transferred call rings to your phone. You answer and hear a male state "I was holding" (Estaba esperando/ ays-**tah**-bah asy-pay-**rahn**-doh). You ask for whom he was calling to which he responds "Attorney Davis." Inform him that the attorney is unavailable and that he will need to call back tomorrow afternoon. Then provide him with the correct number and extension he will need. Finally conclude the call by thanking the client and wishing him a nice day.*

Part II — Instructions: Form pairs with a classmate. Place two chairs back to back, then both of you take a sit. Practice each of the five "phone calls" in this manner. This simulation allows you to hear the speaker well but not see him/her. Just as on a phone call, you must rely on your script and communication strategies to help you successfully tend to the caller's needs. Do not forget to incorporate phrases and expressions from the previous chapter as well as this one that will help you complete your tasks.

E) Cyber-Investigation

Using the internet, research literacy rates across the Spanish-speaking countries of Latin America. Then, search for information that provides a demographic breakdown of the origins of Hispanics who have recently arrived to the U.S. — both legally and illegally. Where do the majority of these immigrants originate? What is the average level of education of these individuals? Do you notice any trends that may have some basis on the correlation of literacy rates and immigration? If so, what are they? How would the literacy rate of Hispanic immigrants possibly impact American society, business, etc.? Can you suggest some strategies that might address the challenges brought on by the information you have discovered? Summarize and share your findings below.

Chapter 3

Overview of the American Judicial System[1]

Before You Begin

Since it is unlikely the majority of your Hispanic clients will be familiar with the American judicial system and how it functions, you may wish to share the information from this chapter with them. Notice that there only a few phrases provided before the general overview—which is presented in both English and Spanish—begins. Therefore, no pronunciation key is provided for the content of this chapter. You are not expected to read this information to the client but rather to allow the client to review it or ask a family member or friend to read it aloud to him/her in the case your client is unable to perform this task.

I. Explanation of Information

ayks-plee-kah-see^ohn dah een-fohr-mah-see^ohn
Explicación de información

English	Pronunciation & Spanish
1. Are you able to read in Spanish or English?	*sah-bay lay-ayr ayn ays-pahn-yohl oh ayn een-glays?* ¿Sabe leer en español o en inglés?
Is there someone who can read this information to you?	*ah^ee ahl-ghee-^ayn kay lay poo^ay-dah lay-ayr ays-tah een-fohr-mah-see^ohn?* ¿Hay alguien que le pueda leer esta información?
Please take this with you and ask someone to review it with you.	*pohr fah-bohr, yay-bay-say ays-toh ee pee-dah-lay ah ahl-ghee^ayn kay say loh lay-ah.* Por favor, llévese esto y pídale a alguien que se lo lea.
2. This literature will provide you with a general overview of the American Judicial System.	*ays-tah een-fohr-mah-see^ohn lay dah-rah oon ray-soo-mayn hay-nay-rahl dayl sees-tay-mah hoo-dee-see^ahl ays-tah-doh-oo-nee-dayn-say.* Esta información le dará un resumen general del sistema judicial estadounidense.

*ays eem-pohr-**tahn**-tay kay **tayn**-gah ahl-**goon** koh-noh-see-**mee^ayn**-toh day lohs proh-**say**-sohs een-boh-loo-**krah**-dohs ah^**oon**-kah noh lay ah-**plee**-kayn ah soo **kah**-soh **toh**-dohs lohs proh-**say**-sohs mayn-see^oh-**nah**-dohs ayn **ays**-tah een-fohr-mah-**see^ohn**.*

3. It is important that you be familiar with the processes involved, even if not all of the processes mentioned in this information may apply to your case.

Es importante que tenga algún conocimiento de los procesos involucrados aunque no le apliquen a su caso todos los procesos mencionados en esta información.

II. The American Judicial System[2]

El sistema judicial estadounidense

Our judicial system is known as an *adversarial system* of justice. This means that litigants, or the parties in a case, have the opportunity to present evidence and arguments at trial to an impartial judge or jury, who will then decide the outcome of the case.

Se conoce nuestro sistema judicial como un sistema adversario de justicia. Esto quiere decir que los litigantes, o sean las partes involucradas en un caso, tienen la oportunidad de presentarle pruebas y argumentos durante un juicio a un juez o a un jurado imparcial.

In civil cases, the plaintiff is the person or entity that initiates the case by filing a complaint against one or more defendants. Normally, plaintiffs seek compensation from the defendants for injuries they sustained, which is allegedly caused by some wrongdoing on the part of the defendants. The defendant, on the other hand, is the person or entity who is sued.

En los casos civiles, el demandante es la persona que inicia el caso presentando una denuncia en contra de uno o más demandados. Normalmente, el demandante espera recibir indemnización de los demandados por daños que se han sufrido, los cuales se alegan ocasionados debido a algún malhecho de parte de los demandados. Por otro lado, el demandado es la persona o la entidad contra la cual se ha presentado la denuncia.

In criminal cases, the state initiates the case, usually by issuing a citation through a police officer or by the filing of an indictment or information charging a person with a crime. The person that is charged with a crime is referred to as a defendant.

En los casos penales, normalmente el estado inicia el caso emitiendo una citación mediante un oficial de policía o presentando una acusación formal o información que imputa a una persona de un delito. La persona imputada de un delito se llama el acusado.

If convicted of that crime, the person may be punished by being fined, incarcerated or in rare cases, such as certain murder cases, by execution. Defendants may also be given probation or may be ordered to pay restitution to the victims of their crimes by the court.

Si se juzga a una persona culpable de un delito, puede que los castigos conlleven una multa, el encarcelamiento o en instancias extraordinarias, tales como ciertos casos de homicidio, la pena de muerte. Los tribunales pueden concederles la libertad vigilada a los acusados u obligarlos a pagarles indemnización a las víctimas de sus delitos.

In civil matters, defendants are not incarcerated, unless they have committed some form of criminal contempt, e.g., usually by disobeying a court order.

En casos civiles, no se encarcela a los demandados, a no ser que hayan cometido alguna clase de desacato penal, ej. normalmente desobedeciendo una orden judicial.

In civil cases, each party usually pays for its own legal representation. In addition, each party normally bears their own costs, e.g., filing fees, etc. associated with the case. However, in some instances, the parties may seek to be reimbursed for their fees and costs. This is especially true where a contract between the parties may award fees and costs to the prevailing (winning) party.

En los casos civiles, cada parte suele pagar su propia representación legal. Además, cada parte suele encargarse de sus propios gastos, ej. los pagos de derecho de trámite, etc. asociados con el caso. No obstante, es posible que las partes puedan pedir reembolso de sus pagos y gastos, lo cual es sumamente común cuando un contrato entre las partes pueda obligar a la parte perdedora a compensar a la parte ganadora reembolsándoles los pagos y los gastos que se han acumulado.

If a plaintiff is financially unable to afford the filing fee, the plaintiff may petition the court to waive the fee. In criminal cases, if the defendant is determined to be indigent, the court will appoint an attorney to represent the defendant in the case. In the United States, all defendants have a constitutional right to counsel regardless of their ability to pay for an attorney. This guarantee does not apply in civil cases.

Si un demandante no puede costear el pago de derecho de trámite, el demandante puede peticionar al tribunal que se perdone este pago. En los casos penales, si se determina que el acusado es indigente, el tribunal le asignará un abogado de oficio para representarlo en el caso. En los Estados Unidos, todo acusado goza del derecho constitucional a la representación legal a pesar de su capacidad de pagar a un abogado. Esta garantía no se aplica en los casos civiles.

III. Court Systems

Los sistemas judiciales

The U.S. court system is comprised basically of two distinct systems: a federal court system and individual state court systems.

Básicamente, los sistemas judiciales de los Estados Unidos se ven categorizados en dos sistemas distintos: un sistema judicial federal y otro sistema judicial estatal individual.

At both levels, there are generally three levels of courts—the first being trial courts who have jurisdiction over the case from the time it is filed until it is decided by the judge or jury; appellate courts who then hear cases that are appealed from the trial courts or other agencies; and supreme courts, who generally hear appeals from the appellate courts.

En ambos sistemas, generalmente hay tres niveles de tribunales—el primero es el sistema de tribunales de primera instancia que tienen jurisdicción sobre el caso desde el momento en que se le presenta hasta que un juez o un jurado lo determine; los tribunales de apelación son los que ven los casos apelados de los tribunales de primera instancia u otras agencias; y los tribunales supremos son los que generalmente ven apelaciones de los tribunales de apelación.

Generally, most legal disputes are resolved in state courts, particularly at the trial level. Some states may have two types of trial courts—the first, being a court of general jurisdiction and the second, being a court of special jurisdiction. Though special jurisdiction courts may be known by other names, for example, small claims, they may still try some cases, including traffic-related cases, lesser civil and criminal cases as well as juvenile cases.

En general, se resuelve la mayoría de los conflictos jurídicos en los tribunales estatales, en particular a través de la celebración de un juicio. Puede que algunos estados tengan dos tipos de tribunales de juicio—el primero siendo un tribunal de jurisdicción general y el segundo siendo un tribunal de jurisdicción especial. Aunque puede que se conozcan los tribunales de jurisdicción especial por otros nombres, por ejemplo, los tribunales de reclamos menores, todavía ven algunos casos, los cuales incluyen casos relacionados a las infracciones de tránsito, casos civiles y penales menores así como casos de menores de edad.

Courts of general jurisdiction most often hear cases involving any matter, civil or criminal, that originates in state court. States all use different names for their courts, including District Court, Circuit Court, Superior Court and even Supreme Court, to name a few. Parties should always consult with an attorney to determine the proper court in which to file or defend an action.

Los tribunales de jurisdicción general suelen ver casos que se tratan de cualquier asunto, sea civil o penal, que tienen su inicio en los tribunales estatales. Todo estado tiene nombre diferente para sus tribunales, incluyendo el tribunal del distrito, el tribunal de circuito, el tribunal superior e incluso el tribunal supremo, para nombrar algunos. Los litigantes deben consultar a un abogado para determinar en cuál de los tribunales deben presentar una denuncia o defender un caso.

At the federal level, the U.S. trial courts are known as District Courts. Each District Court has jurisdiction over cases that originate within a specific region of the state or district. Some states may have only one U.S. District Court, such as Minnesota, while others, such as California, will have several.

Se conocen los tribunales de primera instancia estadounidenses como los tribunales de distrito. Cada tribunal de distrito tiene jurisdicción sobre los casos que tienen su inicio dentro de una región específica del estado o distrito. Puede que algunos estados tengan sólo un tribunal de distrito de los Estados Unidos, tal como Minnesota, mientras que otros, tal como California, tendrá varios.

After a case has been tried or a final judgment or order issued by the court, a party who disagrees with the ruling or judgment, may have the right to appeal that decision to the appellate courts within that state or federal circuit. In most states, there is an intermediate layer of appellate courts and a supreme court. Cases that are appealed from trial courts first are heard in Courts of Appeal. From there, if a party disagrees with that court's ruling, the party may have the right to appeal to the supreme court for that state.

Después de que el tribunal ha juzgado un caso, dictado un fallo o expedido una orden, puede que una parte que está en desacuerdo con el fallo o la decisión tenga el derecho de apelar tal decisión a los tribunales de apelación de aquel estado o circuito federal. En la mayoría de los estados, hay un nivel intermedio de los tribunales de apelación y un tribunal supremo. Los tribunales de apelación ven los casos que se apelan de los tribunales de primera instancia. De allí, si una parte queda en desacuerdo con el fallo de ese tribunal, es posible que esta parte tenga el derecho de apelárselo al tribunal supremo de aquel estado.

In the federal system, the same structure exists, except that the appellate courts for a particular circuit may hear cases from multiple states. In the U.S., there are 13 circuits, each having their own Circuit Court of Appeals. From there, cases are appealed to the U.S. Supreme Court, which is based in Washington, DC.

Esta misma estructura existe en el sistema federal salvo que los tribunales de apelación para un circuito particular puedan ver casos de varios estados. Hay 13 circuitos en los E.E.U.U. y cada uno tiene su propio tribunal del circuito de apelaciones. De allí, se apelan los casos al Tribunal Supremo de los Estados Unidos, el cual está ubicado en Washington, DC.

Unlike trial courts, appellate courts usually decide cases based almost entirely on written briefs presented by the litigants. They may also require oral argument before the judges or justices as to the issues being appealed, but these are unlike the trials that have occurred below. Instead, the appellate court may review the trial court records for mistakes or prejudicial errors that occurred and, if a re-trial is necessary, send or *remand* the case back to the trial court for a decision based upon the reasoning contained in the appellate court's opinion. The appellate court may also *affirm* the lower court's decision, *reverse* the decision or *affirm or reverse in part* that decision.

A diferencia de los tribunales de primera instancia, en general los tribunales de apelación determinan casos casi exclusivamente basado en los escritos presentados por los litigantes. Además, es posible que puedan requerir un alegato oral ante los jueces o magistrados relacionado a los asuntos en apelación. Sin embargo, estos juicios son distintos que se celebran en los tribunales inferiores. En contraste, el tribunal de apelación revisa los archivos del tribunal de juicio por errores o equivocaciones perjudiciales que sucedieron y le devuelve o le remite el caso al tribunal de primera instancia para una decisión basada en el razonamiento contenido en la opinión del tribunal de apelación si es menester un nuevo juicio. El tribunal de apelación también puede confirmar la decisión del tribunal inferior, revocar la decisión o confirmar o revocar en parte aquella decisión.

Administrative Courts

Los tribunales administrativos

In addition to trial courts, there are also certain administrative courts in which decisions dealing with administrative law are made. They are often called upon to make decisions when an individual has been denied benefits offered by administrative or public agencies. In such a situation, the individual is looking to have the denial of benefits overturned.

Además de los tribunales de primera instancia, también hay ciertos tribunales administrativos en los cuales se toman decisiones que tratan con la ley administrativa. Muchas veces se les pide que tomen decisiones cuando un individuo ha sido denegado beneficios ofrecidos por una agencia administrativa o pública. En tal situación, el individuo espera que se anule la denegación de beneficios.

IV. The American Common Law System

El sistema *Common Law*

Unlike many countries whose law derives from Roman law and are civil law countries, the United States legal system is very similar to the English system, which is a common law system. In that system, our laws are derived not only from statutes but from precedent—meaning, that as cases are decided, their rulings may be applicable to other cases. Our judges rely upon prior cases to then decide what a particular outcome in another case should be.

A diferencia de muchos países cuyas leyes provienen de la ley romana y se clasifican como países de ley civil, el sistema legal de los Estados Unidos es muy parecido al sistema inglés, el cual es un sistema *Common Law*. En nuestro sistema, se derivan nuestras leyes no sólo de los estatutos sino también de los precedentes—esto significa que es posible que sus fallos les sean aplicables a otros casos. Nuestros jueces se basan en los casos anteriores para decidir cuál debería ser un resultado particular para otro caso.

V. The Litigation Process—From Complaint to Verdict

El proceso de litigación—de la denuncia al veredicto

Generally speaking, the litigation process follows certain guidelines. The basic structure of the litigation process is as follows:

En general, el proceso de litigación sigue ciertas pautas. La estructura básica del proceso de litigación es así:

A complaint is filed, thus launching the process. In the complaint, the plaintiff outlines the alleged wrongdoing perpetrated by the defendant and alleges the damages the plaintiff is requesting in the case.

Se presenta una denuncia que sirve para lanzar el proceso. En la denuncia, el demandante esboza el presunto malhecho perpetrado por el demandado y asevera los daños que el demandante está pidiendo en el caso.

Next, the defendant files a response, or answer, admitting to or denying the allegations contained in the complaint. This response must normally be filed within a specific time period after complaint is served. If you are served with a complaint and summons, you should read the summons carefully and consult legal counsel as to the due dates of any responsive document or answer. Failure to file an answer may subject a party to what is called a default judgment, which allows the plaintiff in a lawsuit to begin enforcing the judgment.

Luego, el demandado presenta una respuesta, o contestación, confesando o negando los alegatos contenidos en la denuncia. Normalmente, se debe presentar esta contestación dentro de un plazo de tiempo especificado después de haber entregado la denuncia. Si se le entrega una denuncia o citación, debe leerla atentamente y consultar a un abogado respecto a las fechas límites de cualquier documento o contestación que se necesitará presentar. Puede que una parte se vea sometida a un fallo por incomparecencia al no presentar una contestación, lo cual le permite al demandante de un juicio a empezar a ejecutar el fallo.

Once the pleadings are filed, then the "discovery" phase follows. During this time, each party has the right to find out what information the opposing party may possess regarding the lawsuit. Discovery allows a party to request information in the possession of another party, to request the production of certain documents, to schedule depositions of potential witnesses, among other things.

Una vez presentados los alegatos escritos, sigue la etapa de "exhibición de pruebas". Durante esta etapa, cada parte tiene el derecho de enterarse de la información que posee la parte contraria referente a la demanda. La exhibición de pruebas le permite a una parte pedir acceso a la información en la posesión de la otra parte, pedir la producción de ciertos documentos, programar deposiciones de posibles testigos, entre otras cosas.

During and after discovery, the parties will normally file any motions that are relevant to the issues in the case. These include motions to compel certain discovery, motions that seek to protect certain privileged or confidential information, motions for summary judgment, and evidentiary motions seeking admission or exclusion of certain evidence, among others.

Durante y después de la etapa de exhibición de pruebas, normalmente las partes presentarán cualesquier peticiones que son pertinentes a los asuntos en el caso. Estas incluyen peticiones para obligar la divulgación de ciertas pruebas, peticiones que procuran proteger cierta información privilegiada y confidencial, peticiones para juicio sumario y peticiones probatorias pidiendo la aceptación o la exclusión de ciertas pruebas, entre otras.

Then, once discovery is completed, the trial phase begins. In most cases, a trial may be either a jury trial or a bench trial. In both civil and criminal cases, there is a constitutional right to a jury trial. However, certain procedures should be followed to preserve that right without waiving it. Parties involved in litigation should consult with their attorneys in this regard.

Una vez concluida la etapa de exhibición de pruebas, comienza la etapa de juicio. En muchos casos, un juicio puede ser un juicio ante un jurado o ante un juez. Tanto en los casos civiles como en los penales, hay un derecho constitucional a un juicio ante jurado. Sin embargo, se deben seguir ciertos procedimientos para conservar ese derecho sin renunciarlo. Las partes involucradas en la litigación deben consultar a sus abogados al respecto.

In a jury trial, a panel of sworn, impartial individuals from the community are called upon to render a decision based upon what is heard and presented to them during the trial. The ultimate goal of the jury in a civil case is to determine which party is right in the litigation as well as to decide what compensation will be made to the winning party. In the criminal case, the goal is to decide whether the defendant is guilty of the crime charged.

En un juicio ante jurado, se agrupa un panel de individuos de la comunidad que son imparciales y que han prestado juramento para llegar a una decisión basada en lo que se oye y lo que se presenta durante el juicio. La meta principal de un jurado en un caso civil es determinar cuál de las partes tiene derecho en la litigación así como decidir qué será la indemnización destinada a la parte ganadora. En el caso penal, la meta principal es determinar si el acusado es culpable del delito imputado.

A bench trial essentially follows the same protocol but rather than allowing the decision to be made by a jury, the decision is made by a judge. However, in both jury and bench trials, the judge will oversee the proceedings and make rulings regarding the evidence and other procedural matters.

Básicamente, un juicio ante un juez sigue el mismo protocolo pero en vez de permitir que un jurado tome una decisión, el juez la toma. Sin embargo, en ambas clases de juicio, el juez supervisa las actuaciones y dicta fallos en lo concerniente a las pruebas y otros asuntos procesales.

A verdict is delivered after the jurors or the judge have had the opportunity to deliberate the facts and information presented during the trial process. In a jury deliberation, members of the jury will gather in a deliberation room to discuss and vote upon the legal proceedings. Each state varies with respect to the number of jurors in agreement that is needed to reach a decision. In some cases, a simple majority prevails, while in others, the decision must be unanimous. Also, each state varies in the number of jurors that are required to serve on a panel.

Se entrega un veredicto después de que los jurados han tenido la oportunidad de deliberar los hechos y la información presentados durante el juicio. Durante una deliberación del jurado, los miembros del jurado se reunirán en la sala de deliberaciones para conferenciar y votar sobre las actuaciones legales. El número de jurados acordados que se necesita para llegar a una decisión varía por estado. En algunos casos, una sencilla mayoría prevalece, mientras que en otros, la decisión ha de ser unánime. Además, el número de personas requerido para componer el panel de jurados varía por estado.

VI. Rules of Court

Las normas del tribunal

At all times, from the beginning of a lawsuit through the filing and hearing of appeals, there are numerous guidelines in place to ensure that all parties are treated fairly. They range from specifics regarding filing a claim, to courtroom etiquette and behavior, to the presentation of evidence. In state and local courts, these guidelines may be determined by committees of judges and court personnel appointed by the state supreme court. At the federal court level, the Chief Justice of the United States appoints committees composed of judges, lawyers and professors to determine these guidelines which then must receive approval by the Judicial Conference of the United States at which time they become law unless Congress modifies them or votes to reject them. Because the rules that apply to such actions can be numerous and because more than one set of rules may apply to any one action, it is best to consult with an experienced attorney regarding applicability of the appropriate rules. Presently, a number of states make such rules available on their court websites.

En todo momento, desde el inicio de una demanda hasta por su presentación y el proceso de apelación, hay varias pautas establecidas para cerciorar que se trata imparcialmente a todas partes involucradas. Estas normas varían desde la presentación de una demanda, las normas de conducta y el protocolo de la sala de audiencias hasta la presentación de pruebas. En los tribunales estatales y locales, puede que estas pautas sean determinadas por comités de jueces y personal judicial designados por el tribunal supremo estatal. Al nivel judicial federal, el Presidente del Tribunal Supremo de los Estados Unidos designa a comités compuestos por jueces, abogados y profesores para determinar estas pautas que luego deben ser aprobadas por la Conferencia Judicial de los Estados Unidos momento en que se convierten en ley a menos que el Congreso los modifique o vote para rechazarlos. Como las reglas que se aplican a tales acciones pueden ser numerosas y como más de una serie de reglas se le puede aplicar a cualquier acción singular, es mejor consultar a un abogado con experiencia respecto a la aplicabilidad de las reglas apropiadas. Actualmente, varios estados disponen de sus pautas en su sitio web del tribunal estatal.

VII. Alternative Dispute Resolutions

Métodos alternativos de solución de disputas

Mediation and Arbitration

Mediación y Arbitraje

Two alternative dispute resolution processes are mediation and arbitration. Mediation is used as a means of resolving a dispute between two or more litigants. In this process, an impartial third party, called a mediator, rather than a judge will preside over the process and help the parties to arrive at a resolution to their dispute. The mediation process is confidential and private. Although mediation may not be obligatory, any decisions made during this process are legally binding. Arbitration, on the other hand, is very similar to the litigation process, allowing the presentation of discovery and testimony of witnesses which take place in an informal trial setting. An arbitrator or panel of arbitrators, also impartial third parties, rather than a judge or jury, will decide the case. Their decision is usually final and is rarely able to be appealed.

Dos métodos alternativos de solución de disputas son la mediación y el arbitraje. Se utiliza la mediación como un medio de resolver una disputa entre dos o más litigantes. En este proceso, un tercero imparcial, conocido como un mediador, en vez de un juez, presidirá el proceso y ayudará a las partes involucradas a alcanzar una solución a la disputa. El proceso de mediación es confidencial y privado. Aunque la mediación no sea obligatoria, cualesquier decisiones tomadas durante este proceso son obligatorias legalmente. El arbitaje, por otro lado, es muy parecido al proceso de litigación, permitiendo la presentación de la divulgación de pruebas y el testimonio de los testigos, lo cual se llevará a cabo en un entorno jurídico e informal para la celebración de juicios. Un árbitro o panel de árbitros, que también son terceros imparciales, en vez de un juez o un jurado, decidirán el caso. Normalmente, su decisión es final y rara vez se puede apelar.

VIII. Governmental and Regulatory Agencies

Agencias gubernamentales y regulatorias

In addition, certain governmental and regulatory agencies also have quasi-judicial roles, including the following:

Además, ciertas agencias gubernamentales y regulatorias hacen papeles cuasi-juidiciales, incluyendo lo siguiente:

U.S. Equal Opportunity Employment Commission (EEOC)

Comisión de igualdad de oportunidades de empleo (EEOC por sus siglas en inglés)

This federal agency is responsible for enforcing laws that make it illegal to discriminate against an applicant for a job or an employee due to ones race, color, religion, sex, national origin, age (40 or older), disability or genetic information as well as retaliation for having reported an employer or potential employer for such discrimination. Any person that feels he/she has been discriminated against may file a claim directly with this organization without any cost to that person. The EEOC will take if upon itself to investigate the allegations on behalf of the complainant.

Esta agencia federal es responsable del hacer cumplir con las leyes que ilegitiman la discriminación contra un solicitante de un trabajo o un empleado debido a su raza, color, religión, género, origin nacional, edad (de 40 años o más), discapacidad o información genética así como represalias por haber denunciado a un empleador o un empleador potencial por tal discriminación. Cualquier persona que siente que ha sido el blanco de discriminación puede hacer una denuncia directamente con esta organización sin costo alguno a esa persona. Esta agencia (EEOC por sus siglas en inglés) se responsabilizará de investigar los alegatos en nombre del denunciante.

U.S. Social Security Administration
Administración de Seguro Social de los Estados Unidos

This federal agency deals with a multitude of issues. However, in the legal arena, its primary function is the approval or denial of disability benefits for individuals unable to work due to some health related issue. To initiate this process, the individual starts by contacting the local SSA office to request a disability application packet. Upon completion and submission of the packet, it is sent to DDS (Disability Determination Section) to see if the person meets the criteria for the pay out of disability benefits.

Esta agencia federal trata con una multitud de asuntos. Sin embargo, en la arena legal, su función principal es la aprobación o la denegación de beneficios para discapacitados, los cuales son aquellos individuos que no pueden trabajar debido a algún asunto relacionado a la salud. Para lanzar este proceso, el individuo se comunica con la oficina local de la Administración de Seguro Social (SSA por sus siglas en inglés) para pedirle un paquete de solicitud de beneficios de discapacidad. Al completar y remitir el paquete, se le manda a la Oficina de Determinación de Discapacidades (DDS por sus siglas en inglés) para decidir si la persona cumple con los criterios establecidos para el desembolso de beneficios por discapacidades.

If a claim is approved, the applicant will receive a letter of confirmation of benefits. In the case it is denied, a letter of denial will be sent to the applicant, who has a limited time period to request reconsideration. Once again, if approval is granted during reconsideration, the applicant will be notified by letter. Likewise, should the claim be denied, the applicant has a limited time period to appeal this decision to an administrative law judge. The judge will then set a hearing for the appeal. The judge will either approve or deny the appeal, though this does not constitute a definitive decision.

Si se aprueba la denuncia, el solicitante recibirá una carta en la que se confirma el otorgamiento de beneficios. En el caso de que el solicitante sea denegado, se le envía una carta de denegación al mismo, el cual tendrá un plazo limitado para pedir una reevaluación. Otra vez, si se concede la aprobación durante la reevaluación, se le informará al solicitante por correo. Asimismo, si se niega la denuncia, el solicitante tiene un plazo limitado para apelar esta decisión a un juez de la ley administrativa. Entonces, el juez o aprobará o denegará la apelación, aunque esto no constituye una decisión definitiva.

A judge's denial of an appeal can then be appealed to the Appeals Council. The claimant does not appear before the Appeals Council, whose decision is based only on documents and appeals documents that are contained in claimant's file. It may take longer than one year for a decision to be issued. However, while awaiting this decision, the claimant may file a new claim with the local SSA and begin the process again although no hearing will be scheduled with an administrative law judge until the Appeal Council has rendered a final decision. Once this occurs, if the decision is once again unfavorable, the new appeal may proceed through the process as previously described.

Se puede apelar la denegación de una apelación hecha por un juez a un Consejo de Apelaciones. El demandante no tiene que comparecer ante el Consejo de Apelaciones, cuya decisión se fundamenta sólo en documentos y los de apelación que se hallan en el expediente del demandante. Puede tardarse más de un año para que se expida una decisión. No obstante, mientras se espera esta decisión, el demandante puede presentar otra denuncia con la oficina local de la Administración de Seguro Social (SSA por sus siglas en inglés) y empezar el proceso de nuevo aunque no se programará ninguna audiencia con un juez de ley administrativa hasta que el Consejo de Apelaciones haya tomado una decisión final. Una vez que esto ocurre, si otra la decisión resulta desfavorable, la nueva apelación puede pasar por el proceso ya descrito anteriormente.

Industrial Commission
Comisión de Bienestar Industrial

An Industrial Commission is a state entity and therefore its independent duties will vary from state to state. However, among its many functions, one of primary importance is its duty to determine if employees who are injured on the job and their dependents qualify for worker's compensation benefits. The commission acts as both judge and jury in reaching such decisions. It should be understood that the interpretation and application of worker's compensation acts which result in either the awarding or denial of such benefits are always subject to judicial review.

Una Comisión de Bienestar Industrial es una entidad estatal y por eso, sus deberes independientes varían de estado a estado. Sin embargo, entre sus múltiples deberes, uno de importancia principal es el de determinar si empleados lastimados en el trabajo y personas a su cargo cumplen con los requisitos para poder recibir los beneficios de indemnización laboral. La comisión hace el papel de juez y jurado en tomar tales decisiones. Se debe entender que la interpretación y la aplicación de los actos de indemnización laboral, los cuales resultarán en el otorgamiento o la denegación de tales beneficios, siempre están sujetos a la revisión judicial.

IX. Settlements
Acuerdos

A settlement, an agreement or arrangement that has been reached by the litigants, may take place at any point during the litigation, mediation or arbitration process. If this occurs, a settlement agreement will be executed and the case will be dismissed. Otherwise, the litigation process or the alternative dispute resolution method will continue until a ruling is made or a decision is reached.

Un acuerdo, un convenio o arreglo que los litigantes han alcanzado, puede tomar lugar en cualquier momento durante el proceso de litigación, mediación o arbitraje. Si esto ocurre, se formalizará un acuerdo de conciliación y se sobreseerá el caso. Si no, el proceso de litigación o el método alternativo de solución de disputas seguirá hasta que se haya dictado un fallo o se haya tomado una decisión.

Notes

[1] This chapter has been provided for informative purposes only. Therefore, you will notice only an extremely beneficial **Cyber-Investigation** has been included. It is HIGHLY recommended that you complete it for valuable cultural information.

[2] You will notice there is NO pronunciation guide to follow. You may elect to show this chapter of the text to Spanish speaking clients and ask them to read it. This will provide them with a concise yet brief overview of the American Judicial System.

Practical Activities

A) Cyber-Investigation

As stated in BEFORE YOU BEGIN from this chapter, it is extremely probable that your potential Hispanic clients will be unfamiliar with the U.S. judicial system, its hierarchy and functions. One of the biggest problems that many of these people encounter, especially recent arrivals, is being the target of scams when seeking legal advice and assistance. Ironically, some of those doing the scamming tend to be fellow Hispanics with lofty promises of quick and easy resolutions to many legal woes, namely illegal immigration issues. With this said, use the internet to search for the following terms and write the meanings beside of each one in the space provided.

1. Search for the *Spanish* meaning of *notario.**
   [* You will be able to find an English translation of the meaning online.]

   notario or **notario público**—(noh-**tah**-ree^oh **poo**-blee-koh)

   _____.

2. Search for the *English* meaning of *notary*.

   notary or **notary public**—

   _____.

3. What are the differences in the duties and legal authority of a *notary* in the *U.S.* versus one in *México*?

U.S.	*México*

4. Research examples in which a person calling him/herself a *notario público* or *notario* here in the U.S. has taken advantage of this title and has defrauded Hispanics with legal issues.

   _____

   _____

   _____

   _____

   _____

   _____

5. Search for the Spanish term *fedatario público*. Write its meaning below.

   fedatario público—(fay-dah-**tah**-ree^oh **poo**-blee-koh)

   _____.

6. According to what you have learned in this **Cyber-Investigation**, circle the letter in front of the term(s) that CORRECTLY correlates to the English meaning of *notary* or *notary public*.

   a) notario or *notario publico*   *b) fedatario público*

Chapter 4

Criminal Law

Before You Begin

One of the biggest problems Hispanics face when dealing with the U.S. judicial system is their lack of understanding. It should be noted that many of these people come from countries where the legal system has broken down and/or has failed to fulfill its role as an effective administrator of the law and its enforcement. Therefore, not only is it difficult to explain to them the intricacies of U.S. legal system and expect them to comprehend it, but it may also be equally challenging for them to place their trust in such a system. For example, the option to accept a plea rather than proceed with a trial may appear to a Hispanic as a confession of guilt when he/she alleges to be innocent. Therefore, convincing the individual to opt for the plea that is being offered rather than to move forward with a trial may not be an easy task, even though the later may carry a more severe punishment.

I. General Questions

*pray-**goon**-tahs hay-nay-**rah**-lays*
Preguntas generales

English	Pronunciation & Spanish
1. What is your name?	*koh-moh say yah-mah?* ¿Cómo se llama?[1]
2. What is the best phone number to use in case we are disconnected?	*koo^ahl ays ayl may-hohr noo-may-roh day tay-lay-foh-noh pah-rah oo-sahr see nohs days-koh-nayk-tah-mohs?* ¿Cuál es el mejor número de teléfono para usar si nos desconectamos?[2]
3. What is your complete mailing address?	*koo^ahl ays lah dee-rayk-see^ohn kohm-play-tah dayl loo-gahr dohn-day rray-see-bay soo koh-rray-oh?* ¿Cuál es la dirección postal completa del lugar donde recibe su correo?[1, 2]
4. What is your date of birth?	*koo^ahl ays soo fay-chah day nah-see-mee^ayn-toh?* ¿Cuál es su fecha de nacimiento?[2]
5. Do you have family?	*tee^ay-nay fah-mee-lee^ah?* ¿Tiene familia?
6. Are you married?	*ays-tah kah-sah-doh/dah?* ¿Está casado/a?[3]
7. What is your spouse's name?	*koh-moh say yay-mah soo kohn-yoo-hay?* ¿Cómo se llama su cónyuge?[1]

41

8. Can your spouse be reached by phone?	*oo-noh say **poo^ay**-day koh-moo-nee-**kahr** kohn soo **kohn**-yoo-hay pohr tay-**lay**-foh-noh?* ¿Uno se puede comunicar con su cónyuge por teléfono?
What is your spouse's telephone number?	*koo^ahl ays ayl **noo**-may-roh day tay-**lay**-foh-noh day soo **kohn**-yoo-hay?* ¿Cuál es el número de teléfono de su cónyuge?[1, 2]
9. Do you have the same address as your spouse?	*tee^**ay**-nay lah **mees**-mah dee-rayk-**see^ohn** kay soo **kohn**-yoo-hay?* ¿Tiene la misma dirección que su cónyuge?
What is your spouse's address?	*koo^ahl ays lah dee-rayk-**see^ohn** day soo **kohn**-yoo-hay?* ¿Cuál es la dirección de su cónyuge?[1, 2]
10. Do you have any children?	*tee^**ay**-nay ee-hohs?* ¿Tiene hijos?
How many?	***koo^ahn**-tohs?* ¿Cuántos?[2]
What is the age of each one?	*koo^ahl ays lah ay-**dahd** day **kah**-dah oo-noh?* ¿Cuál es la edad de cada uno?[2]
11. Who is the person in your family with whom we should speak regarding your bond if you are arrested?	*kee^ayn ays lah payr-**soh**-nah ayn soo fah-**mee**-lee^ah kohn kee^ayn nohs day-**bay**-mohs koh-moo-nee-**kahr** rray-fay-**rayn**-tay ah soo kah^oo-**see^ohn** see say lay ah-**rrays**-tah?* ¿Quién es la persona en su familia con quien nos debemos comunicar referente a su caución si se le arresta?[1]
12. Do you have a job?	*tee^**ay**-nay trah-**bah**-hoh?* ¿Tiene trabajo?
Where?	***dohn**-day?* ¿Dónde?[1]
What do you do?	*ah kay say day-**dee**-kah?* ¿A qué se dedica?[1]
13. Can you spell that for me (slowly)?	*may loh **poo^ay**-day day-lay-tray-**ahr** (layn-tah-**mayn**-tay)?* ¿Me lo puede deletrear (lentamente)?[1]

II. Current Charges and Prior Convictions

*eem-poo-tah-**see^oh**-nays ahk-**too^ah**-lays ee kohn-**day**-nahs ahn-tay-**ree^oh**-rays*
Imputaciones actuales y condenas anteriores

English	Pronunciation & Spanish
1. Have you been (recently) charged with a crime?	*say lay ah ah-koo-**sah**-doh day oon day-**lee**-toh (rray-see^ayn-tay-**mayn**-tay?)* ¿Se le ha acusado de un delito (recientemente)?
When were you charged?	***koo^ayn**-doh say lay ah-koo-**soh**?* ¿Cuándo se le acusó?[4]

Was this a misdemeanor or a felony?

*foo^ay oon day-**lee**-toh may-**nohr** oh mah-**yohr**?*
¿Fue un delito menor o mayor?

2. Do you have a copy of …

*tee^**ay**-nay **koh**-pee^ah day …*
¿Tiene copia de …

the citation?

*lah see-tah-**see^ohn**?*
la citación?

the warrant?

*lah **ohr**-dayn hoo-dee-**see^ahl**?*
la orden judicial?

the indictment?

*lah ah-koo-sah-**see^ohn** fohr-**mahl**?*
la acusación formal?

any document that lists the charges against you?

*ahl-**goon** doh-koo-**mayn**-toh kay ay-noo-**may**-rah lohs **kahr**-gohs ayn soo **kohn**-trah?*
algún documento que enumera los cargos en su contra?

3. Can you fax that to me?

*may lah **poo^ay**-day mahn-**dahr** pohr fahks?*
¿Me la puede mandar por fax?

4. Can you give me the case or file number associated with that?

*may **poo^ay**-day dahr ayl **noo**-may-roh day **kah**-soh oh day ayks-pay-**dee^ayn**-tay ah-soh-**see^ah**-doh kohn **ay**-sah?*
¿Me puede dar el número de caso o de expediente asociado con esa?[2]

5. When is your court date?

*koo^**ahn**-doh ays soo **fay**-chah day pray-sayn-tah-**see^ohn** ahl tree-bo-**nahl**?*
¿Cuándo es su fecha de presentación al tribunal?[4]

In what county (courthouse)?

*ayn (ayl tree-boo-**nahl** day) kay kohn-**dah**-doh?*
¿En (el tribunal de) qué condado?[1]

6. Do you see information on … regarding where you need to go on that date?

*say ah een-dee-**kah**-doh … **dohn**-day **day**-bay pray-sayn-**tahr**-say ayn ah-**kay**-yah **fay**-chah?*
¿Se ha indicado … dónde debe presentarse en aquella fecha?

the citation

*lah see-tah-**see^ohn***
la citación

the warrant

*lah **ohr**-dayn hoo-dee-**see^ahl***
la orden judicial

the indictment

*lah ah-koo-sah-**see^ohn** fohr-**mahl***
la acusación formal

the document that lists the charges against you

*ayl doh-koo-**mayn**-toh kay ay-noo-**may**-rah lohs **kahr**-gohs ayn soo **kohn**-trah*
en el documento que enumera los cargos en su contra

7. Has anyone from the police spoken to you about the case?

*lay ah ah-**blah**-doh **ahl**-ghee^ayn day lah koh-mee-sah-**ree**-ah day poh-lee-**see**-ah **soh**-bray ayl **kah**-soh?*
¿Le ha hablado alguien de la comisaría de policía sobre el caso?

8. Has anyone threatened to swear out a warrant against you?

*ah ah-may-nah-**sah**-doh **ahl**-ghee^ayn kohn ay-may-**teer oo**-nah **ohr**-dayn day ah-**rray**-stoh ayn soo **kohn**-trah?*

¿Ha amenazado alguien con emitir una orden de arresto en su contra?

9. Do you understand that you have a constitutional right to speak with an attorney and to refuse to answer any questions from law enforcement until you have spoken with an attorney?

*kohm-**prayn**-day kay **tee^ay**-nay oon day-**ray**-choh kohns-tee-too-see^oh-**nahl** day ah-**blahr** kohn oon ah-boh-**gah**-doh ee nay-**gahr**-say ah kohn-tays-**tahr** koo^ah-lays-**kee^ayr** pray-**goon**-tahs **ay**-chahs pohr oon oh-fee-**see^ahl** day lahs **foo^ayr**-sahs dayl **ohr**-dayn **poo**-blee-koh **ahs**-tah kay **ah^ee**-yah ah-**blah**-doh kohn oon ah-boh-**gah**-doh?*

¿Comprende que tiene un derecho constitucional de hablar con un abogado y negarse a contestar cualesquier preguntas hechas por un oficial de las fuerzas del orden público hasta que haya hablado con un abogado?

10. If you are arrested, please be sure not to waive this right by answering questions.

*see say lay ah-**rrays**-tah, fah-**bohr** day ah-say-goo-**rahr**-say day noh rray-noon-**see^ahr** ays-tay day-**ray**-choh kohn-tays-**tahn**-doh pray-**goon**-tahs.*

Si se le arresta, favor de asegurarse de no renunciar este derecho contestando preguntas.

The officer will read your rights to you, which include the rights to remain silent and to have an attorney.

*ayl poh-lee-**see^ah** lay lay-ay-**rah** soos day-**ray**-chohs, lohs **koo^ah**-lays kohn-**yay**-bahn lohs day-**ray**-chohs day goo^ahr-**dahr** see-**layn**-see^oh ee tay-**nayr** ah oon ah-boh-**gah**-doh.*

El policía le leerá sus derechos, los cuales conllevan los derechos de guardar silencio y tener a un abogado.

11. Do you have any idea of when you might be arrested?

sah-bay **koo^ahn**-doh **pee^ayn**-sahn ah-rrays-**tahr**-loh/lah?

¿Sabe cuándo piensan arrestarlo/la?[5]

When?

koo^ahn-doh?

¿Cuándo?[2, 4]

Approximately how long do you have before you are arrested?

*koo^ahn-toh **tee^aym**-poh lay **kay**-dah mahs oh **may**-nohs **ahn**-tays day kay say lay ah-**rrays**-tay?*

¿Cuánto tiempo le queda más o menos antes de que se le arreste?[2, 4]

I have a day.

*may **kay**-dah oon **dee**-ah.*

Me queda un día.[6]

I have (#) days.

*may **kay**-dahn (#) **dee**-ahs.*

Me quedan (#) días.[6]

I don't know.

noh say.

No sé.[6]

I'm not sure.

*noh ays-**toh^ee** say-**goo**-roh/rah.*

No estoy seguro/a.[6, 7]

12. Regarding the incident, were there any witnesses?

*rrays-**payk**-toh ahl een-see-**dayn**-tay, ah-**bee**-ah tays-**tee**-gohs?*

Respecto al incidente, ¿había testigos?

Do you know their names and addresses?	*sah-bay soos **nohm**-brays ee dee-rayk-**see**^oh-nays?* ¿Sabe sus nombres y direcciones?
I need you to make a list of their names and addresses to give me.	*nay-say-**see**-toh kay **ah**-gah **oo**-nah **lees**-tah day soos **nohm**-brays ee dee-rayk-**see**^oh-nahs **pah**-rah ayn-tray-**gahr**-may.* Necesito que haga una lista de sus nombres y direcciones para entregarme.
Do you know if the police have spoken with them yet?	*sah-bay see lah poh-lee-**see**-ah lays ah ah-**blah**-doh yah?* ¿Sabe si la policía les ha hablado ya?

13. Have you ever been convicted of any felony?	*say lay ah kohn-day-**nah**-doh day oon day-**lee**-toh mah-**yohr** ahl-**goo**-nah bays?* ¿Se le ha condenado de un delito mayor alguna vez?
When?	*koo^**ayn**-doh?* ¿Cuándo?[4]
Where?	*dohn-day?* ¿Dónde?[1]

14. Have you ever been convicted of a misdemeanor?	*say lay ah kohn-day-**nah**-doh day oon day-**lee**-toh may-**nohr** ahl-**goo**-nah bays?* ¿Se le ha condenado de un delito menor alguna vez?
When?	*koo^**ayn**-doh?* ¿Cuándo?[4]
Where?	*dohn-day?* ¿Dónde?[1]

15. Have you ever been convicted of any traffic offense?	*say lay ah kohn-day-**nah**-doh day **oo**-nah een-frahk-**see**^ohn day **trahn**-see-toh ahl-**goo**-nah bays?* ¿Se le ha condenado de una infracción de tránsito alguna vez?
When?	*koo^**ayn**-doh?* ¿Cuándo?[4]
Where?	*dohn-day?* ¿Dónde?[1]

16. Do you have anyone that we should contact and inform of your ...	*ah^ee **ahl**-ghee^ayn kohn kee^ayn day-**bay**-mohs koh-moo-nee-**kahr**-nohs ay een-fohr-**mahr**-lay day ...* ¿Hay alguien con quien debemos comunicarnos e informarle de ...
charges?	*lohs **kahr**-gohs ayn soo **kohn**-trah?* los cargos en su contra?
situation?	*soo see-too^ah-**see**^ohn?* su situación?

case?	*soo **kah**-soh?* su caso?
What is that person's name and phone number?	***koo^ah**-lays sohn ayl **nohm**-bray ee ayl **noo**-may-roh day tay-**lay**-foh-noh day **ay**-sah payr-**soh**-nah?* ¿Cuáles son el nombre y el número de teléfono de esa persona?[2]

III. Bond

*lah **fee^ahn**-sah / kah^oo-**see^ohn***
La fianza / caucíon

English	Pronunciation & Spanish
1. Have you been bonded out of jail?	*say ah day-poh-see-**tah**-doh **oo**-nah **fee^ahn**-sah **pah**-rah kay say lay lee-**bay**-ray?* ¿Se ha depositado una fianza para que se le libere?
Where are you incarcerated?	***dohn**-day ays-**tah** en-kahr-say-**lah**-doh/dah?* ¿Dónde está encarcelado/a?[1, 3]
What is the address of the location where you are incarcerated?	*koo^ahl ays lah dee-rayk-**see^ohn** day lah loh-kah-lee-dad **dohn**-day ays-**tah** en-kahr-say-**lah**-doh/dah?* ¿Cuál es la dirección de la localidad donde está encarcelado/a?[3]
If you do not know, ask someone.	*see noh lah **sah**-bay, pray-**goon**-tay-lay ah **ahl**-ghee^ayn.* Si no la sabe, pregúntele a alguien.
2. Are you at the [insert county name] county jail?	*ays-**tah** ayn lah **kahr**-sayl dayl kohn-**dah**-doh day [insert county name]?* ¿Está en la cárcel del condado de [insert county name]?
3. Do you know the amount of the bond?	***sah**-bay ayl **mohn**-toh day soo **fee^ahn**-sah?* ¿Sabe el monto de su fianza?
How much is it?	***koo^ahn**-toh ays?* ¿Cuánto es?[2]
Is that secured or unsecured?	*ays lah **fee^ahn**-sah ah-say-goo-**rah**-dah oh noh ah-say-goo-**rah**-dah?* ¿Es la fianza asegurada o no asegurada?

IV. Immigration Status

*kohn-dee-**see^ohn** mee-grah-**toh**-ree^ah*
Condición migratoria

English	Pronunciation & Spanish
1. Which of the following describes your immigration status?	*koo^ahl day lohs see-**ghee^ayn**-tays days-**kree**-bay soo kohn-dee-**see^ohn** mee-grah-**toh**-ree^ah?* ¿Cuál de los siguientes describe su condición migratoria?

United States citizen	*see^oo-dah-**dah**-noh/nah day lohs ays-**tah**-dohs oo-**nee**-dohs* ciudadano/a de los Estados Unidos[3]
legal permanent resident	*rray-see-**dayn**-tay payr-mah-**nayn**-tay lay-**gahl*** residente permanente legal
asylee or refugee	*ah-see-**lah**-doh/dah oh rray-foo-**hee^ah**-doh/dah* asilado/a o refugiado/a[3]
temporary resident alien	*rray-see-**dayhn**-tay taym-poh-**rah**-ree^oh* residente temporario/a[3]
non-resident	*noh rray-see-**dayn**-tay* no residente
temporary protected status	***bah**-hoh proh-tayk-**see^ohn** taym-poh-**rah**-ree^ah* bajo protección temporaria
out of status	*seen kohn-dee-**see^ohn** mee-grah-**toh**-ree^ah **bah**-lee-dah* sin condición migratoria válida
illegal alien	*ayks-trahn-**hay**-roh/rah ee-lay-**gahl*** extranjero/a ilegal[3]
undocumented alien	*ayks-trahn-**hay**-roh/rah een-doh-koo-mayn-**tah**-doh/dah* extranjero/a indocumentado/a[3]
2. Do you have papers that show your residency or immigration status?	***tee^ay**-nay pah-**pay**-lays **pah**-rah proh-**bahr** soo rray-see-**dayn**-see^ah oh soo kohn-dee-**see^ohn** mee-grah-**toh**-ree^ah?* ¿Tiene papeles para probar su residencia o condición migratoria?
Do you have copies of those at home in case we need to provide them as proof of your status?	***tee^ay**-nay **koh**-pee^ahs day **ay**-yohs ayn **kah**-sah ayn **kah**-soh day kay lohs nay-say-see-**tay**-mohs **pah**-rah kohm-proh-**bahr** soo rray-see-**dayn**-see^ah oh soo kohn-dee-**see^ohn** mee-grah-**toh**-ree^ah?* ¿Tiene copias de ellos en casa en caso de que los necesitemos para comprobar su residencia o condición migratoria?
3. Have you spoken with any other attorneys about these issues?	*say ah koh-moo-nee-**kah**-doh kohn **oh**-troh ah-boh-**gah**-doh rray-fay-**rayn**-tay ah **ays**-tohs ah-**soon**-tohs?* ¿Se ha comunicado con otro abogado referente a estos asuntos?
What is full name of the attorney?	*koo^ahl ays ayl **nohm**-bray kohm-**play**-toh dayl ah-boh-**gah**-doh?* ¿Cuál es el nombre completo del abogado?[1]
4. Please understand that until you receive correspondence from us regarding this issue that details the conditions of our agreement to represent you in this matter, we are not your legal representative on this or any other issue.	*fah-**bohr** day ayn-tayn-**dayr** kay **ahs**-tah kay say rray-**see**-bah kohn-feer-mah-**see^ohn** may-**dee^ahn**-tay koh-rrays-pohn-**dayn**-see^ah day noh-**soh**-trohs kohn rrays-**payk**-toh ah **ays**-tay ah-**soon**-toh ayn lah koo^ahl say day-**tah**-yahn lohs **play**-sohs day **noo^ays**-troh ah-**koo^ayr**-doh **pah**-rah rray-pray-sayn-**tahr**-loh/lah, noh **soh**-mohs soo rray-pray-sayn-**tahn**-tay lay-**gahl** ayn **ays**-tay nee en neen-**goon oh**-troh ah-**soon**-toh.* Favor de entender que hasta que se reciba confirmación mediante correspondencia de nosotros con respecto a este asunto en la cual se detallan las condiciones de nuestro acuerdo para representarlo/la, no somos su representante legal en este ni en ningún otro asunto.[5]

Notes

[1] Reference *Chapter 12 — The Basics — I. The Alphabet* for aiding in comprehension.

[2] Reference *Chapter 12 — The Basics — II. Numbers* for aiding in comprehension.

[3] Use the *-o* ending with a male and the *-a* ending with a female.

[4] Reference *Chapter 13 — Telling Time the Easy Way — II. Days of the Week and Months of the Year* for assistance with dates.

[5] Use *-lo* when speaking to or about a *male* and *-la* when speaking to or about a *female*.

[6] These sample anticipated responses have been included for you as a reference. You may also use them to confirm that you have understood the información as well. To do so, use the question *¿dijo + # + día(s)? [**dee**-hoh + # + **dee**-ah(s)]*. For example, you ask the question *¿Cuánto tiempo le queda hasta que se le arreste?* The speaker responds *Me quedan 3 días*. To confirm you heard the information correctly ask *¿Dijo 3 días?* to which the speaker will either say *sí* or provide the corrected response.

[7] In the case of *seguro*, a male speaker will use the *-o* ending and a female speaker will use the *-a* ending.

Practical Activities

A) ¿Hombre o mujer? (Male or female?)

Instructions: You will recall from past chapters, you learned how to make any phrase or expression written in the *YOU* form relate to the *He/Him* and *She/Her* forms as well. Remember too, that a proper name may be incorporated in such questions. Below, you have the names of two individuals whose gender has been indicated for absolute clarification. Underneath these names, appears a list of information you need to obtain from both persons. Using questions from this chapter, decide which ones you will use to obtain each piece of information. When you are sure of which questions you will use, practice saying each one aloud. You may wish to mark them in the text or write them on a separate sheet of paper. Do not forget to make any necessary modifications when addressing *Mario* as opposed to *Adela*. Lastly, review your questions with a partner, pointing out any changes you have made and why.

Mario (hombre)	*Adela (mujer)*
1. name 2. date of birth 3. marital status 4. mailing address 5. employment status 6. immigration status	

B) ¿Comprende? (Do You Understand?)

Instructions: Scan the following telephone conversation that takes place between a *paralegal (P)* and a *Spanish-speaking caller (SSC)* regarding a potential criminal charge. Read it several times for comprehension. Next, without the assistance of the text, transcribe the conversation into English line by line. Once you have finished your individual translation, compare it with at least two other classmates for peer correction and/or feedback. Only resort back to the text after all of you have had a chance to consult with one another and have exhausted each other as resources. ¡Atención!—Some phrases you need to check may be in previous chapters.

P—Buenos días. Soy la señorita Stone. Voy a atenderle pero hablo muy poco español. ¿Habla un poco de inglés?

_____.

SSC—Lo siento, no señorita.

_____.

P—No hay problema. Le necesito hacer unas preguntas. Por favor, hable clara y lentamente.

_____.

SSC—Cómo no, señorita. A sus órdenes.

_____.

P—¿Cuál es el mejor número de teléfono para usar si nos desconectamos?

_____.

SSC—El número de teléfono es el 789-555-9827.

_____.

P—Muchas gracias. ¿Llama Ud. de parte de sí mismo o de parte de otra persona?

SSC—Llamo de parte de mí mismo.

P—¿Cuál es su nombre completo y me lo puede deletrear lentamente, por favor?

SSC—Me llamo Carlos Álvarez Martínez—C-A-R-L-O-S Á-L-V-A-R-E-Z M-A-R-T-I-N-E-Z.

P—Sr. Álvarez, ¿Cuál es su dirección postal completa?

SSC—Mi dirección es 589 McFee Drive, Innsbrooke, Ohio, 48908.

P—¿Se le ha acusado de un delito recientemente?

SSC—Sí. Posesión de narcóticos.

P—¿Tiene copia de la acusación formal o el documento que enumera los cargos en su contra?

SSC—Sí señorita.

P—¿se ha indicado en la acusación formal dónde y cuándo debe presentarse?

SSC—Sí. El 26 de mayo a las 10 de la mañana en el tribunal del condado de Brunswick.

P—Gracias. ¿Quién es la persona en su familia con quien nos debemos comunicar referente a su caución si se le arresta?

SSC—Mi esposa, Carmen Álvarez García.

P—Está bien, señor. Le daré esta información a uno de nuestros abogados. Recibirá una llamada telefónica tan pronto como posible.

SSC—Muchas gracias.

P—De nada, señor Álvarez. Qué pase un buen día.

C) Preguntas y respuestas (Questions and Answers)

Instructions: Read each of the oral responses provided taking into account that none of the responses are related and are therefore, independent of one another. Then, try to recall and say aloud the question from the text that would elicit each response. If you would like, feel free to try writing out the question in the space provided. Do all of this first WITHOUT consulting the text. Next, consult with various classmates to compare your questions and/or ask for help in completing this task if you are unable to formulate questions to any of the responses yourself. Lastly, check your work by reviewing this chapter and making any necessary corrections.

1. ¿_____?
Sí. El abogado se llama Alfred Winstead.

2. ¿_____?
Sí, tengo la misma dirección que mi cónyuge.

3. ¿_____?
Es $2.500 y no es asegurada.

4. ¿_____?
El 15 de agosto a las 2 de la tarde en el tribunal del condado de Hayworth.

5. ¿_____?
No, no había testigos.

6. ¿_____?
Me quedan 3 o 4 días.

7. ¿_____?
En la cárcel del condado.

8. ¿_____?
Mi cónyuge se llama Diego Ponce Garza.

9. ¿_____?
Soy extranjera indocumentada.

10. ¿_____?
Sí. Tenemos 5 hijos.

D) Cyber-Investigation

The cultural and societal differences between the U.S. and Hispanic countries vary drastically. One example is the difference in the legal age of consent. Taking this into consideration, research what the legal age of consent is for five different Hispanic countries. Compare this with the legal age of consent in the U.S. What issues do you think arise from this difference? Find two examples on the internet where the legal age of consent in the United States caused legal issues for Hispanic adults. Summarize your findings for this assignment below.

Chapter 5

Immigration Law

Before You Begin

It should be understood that many Hispanics come to the U.S. with the belief that through diligence and hard work, they too, will be able to attain and provide a better life for themselves and their families. In addition to being able to provide the essentials, many also have aspirations of owning a home or even possibly a business at some time in the future. The less attractive side of this so-called *American Dream* is the negativity with which many of this people are greeted upon their arrival into the country. It is widely perpetuated that Hispanics come to U.S., rob American citizens of employment opportunities and become a societal burden. While it is true a U.S. citizen could occupy a position held by a Hispanic worker, the vast majority of the jobs are viewed as undesirable and are challenging, if not impossible, for many employers to otherwise fill. However, Hispanics are willing to accept such work and comply with the rigors that come along with the labor involved. Ranging from farm-workers and janitors to child-care providers and manual labor for hire, these positions are and will always be in high demand.

I. Personal Information

*een-fohr-mah-**see^ohn** payr-soh-**nahl***
Información personal

English	Pronunciation & Spanish
1. What is your full legal name?	*koo^ahl ays soo **nohm**-bray lay-**gahl** kohm-**play**-toh?* ¿Cuál es su nombre legal completo?[1]
2. Do you go by any other name?	***tee^ay**-nay ahl-**goon oh**-troh **nohm**-bray?* ¿Tiene algún otro nombre?[1]
3. Do you have any prior names?	*ah tay-**nee**-doh ahl-**goon oh**-troh **nohm**-bray ahn-tay-ree^ohr-**mayn**-tay?* ¿Ha tenido algún otro nombre anteriormente?
What was it?	*koo^ahl foo^ay?* ¿Cuál fue?[1]
4. What is your home address here in the U.S.?	*koo^ahl ays soo dee-rayk-**see^ohn** doh-mee-see-**lee^ah**-ree^ah ays-tah-doh-oo-nee-**dayn**-say?* ¿Cuál es su dirección domiciliaria estadounidense?[1, 2]
How long have you been at this address?	*pohr **koo^ahn**-toh **tee^aym**-poh ah rray-see-**dee**-doh ayn soo dee-rayk-**see^ohn** doh-mee-see-lee-**ah**-ree^ah?* ¿Por cuánto tiempo ha residido en su dirección domiciliaria?

one day	*oon **dee**-ah* un día[3]
(#) days	*(#) **dee**-ahs* (#) días[3]
one week	*oo-nah say-**mah**-nah* una semana[3]
(#) weeks	*(#) say-**mah**-nahs* (#) semanas[3]
one month	*oon mays* un mes[3]
(#) months	*(#) **may**-says* (#) meses[3]
one year	*oon **ahn**-yoh* un año[3]
(#) years	*(#) **ahn**-yohs* (#) años[3]
Are your home address and mailing address the same?	*sohn lahs **mees**-mahs soo dee-rayk-**see**^ohn doh-mee-cee-**lee**^**ah**-ree^ah ee soo dee-rayk-**see**^ohn pohs-tahl?* ¿Son las mismas su dirección domiciliaria y su dirección postal?
What is your mailing address here in the U.S.?	*koo^ahl ays soo dee-rayk-**see**^ohn pohs-**tahl** ays-tah-doh-oo-nee-**dayn**-say?* ¿Cuál es su dirección postal estadounidense?[1, 2]
5. Do you have a foreign address?	*tee^**ay**-nay dee-rayk-**see**^ohn ayn oh-troh pah-**ees**?* ¿Tiene dirección en otro país?
What is that address?	*koo^ahl ays **ay**-sah dee-rayk-**see**^ohn?* ¿Cuál es esa dirección?[1, 2]
6. What is your …	*koo^ahl ays soo …* ¿Cuál es su …
home phone number?	*noo-may-roh day tay-**lay**-foh-noh doh-mee-see-**lee**^**ah**-ree^oh?* número de teléfono domiciliario?[2]
work phone number?	*noo-may-roh day tay-**lay**-foh-noh dayl trah-**bah**-hoh?* número de teléfono del trabajo?[2]
cell phone number?	*noo-may-roh day tay-**lay**-foh-noh **moh**-beel?* número de teléfono móvil?[2]
email address?	*dee-rayk-**see**^ohn day koh-**rray**-oh ay-layk-**troh**-nee-koh?* dirección de correo electrónico?[1, 2, 4]
Please indicate how you wish to be contacted.	*pohr fah-**bohr**, een-**dee**-kay **koh**-moh pray-**fee**^**ay**-ray kay loh/lah kohn-tahk-**tay**-mohs.* Por favor, indique cómo prefiere que lo/la contactemos.[5]

7. What is your date of birth?

*koo^ahl ays soo **fay**-chah day nah-see-**mee^ayn**-toh?*
¿Cuál es su fecha de nacimiento?[6]

Where were you born?

***dohn**-day nah-**see^oh**?*
¿Dónde nació?[1]

Town?

***poo^ay**-bloh?*
¿Pueblo?[1]

City?

*see^oo-**dahd**?*
¿Ciudad?[1]

State?

*ays-**tah**-doh?*
¿Estado?[1]

Province?

*proh-**been**-see^ah?*
¿Provincia?[1]

Country?

*pah-**ees**?*
¿País?[1]

8. What is your nationality?

*koo^ahl ays soo nah-see^oh-nah-lee-**dahd**?*
¿Cuál es su nacionalidad?[7]

9. Do you have legal status to be in the country?

*ays-**tah** ah-**kee** lay-gahl-**mayn**-tay?*
¿Está aquí legalmente?

Are you ...

ays ...
¿Es ...

a legal resident?

*rray-see-**dayn**-tay lay-**gahl**?*
residente legal?

permanent resident?

*rray-see-**dayn**-tay payr-mah-**nayn**-tay?*
residente permanente?

What is your alien registration number?

*koo^ahl ays soo **noo**-may-roh day rray-**hees**-troh day een-mee-**grahn**-tay?*
¿Cuál es su número de registro de inmigrante?[2]

How long have you been a permanent resident?

*pohr **koo^ahn**-toh **tee^aym**-poh ah **see**-doh rray-see-**dayn**-tay payr-mah-**nayn**-tay?*
¿Por cuánto tiempo ha sido residente permanente?[1,2]

one day

*oon **dee**-ah*
un día[3]

(#) days

*(#) **dee**-ahs*
(#) días[3]

one week

***oo**-nah say-**mah**-nah*
una semana[3]

(#) weeks

*(#) say-**mah**-nahs*
(#) semanas[3]

one month

oon mays
un mes[3]

(#) months	*(#) **may**-says* (#) meses[3]
one year	*oon **ahn**-yoh* un año
(#) years	*(#) **ahn**-yohs* (#) años[3]
a U.S citizen?	*see^oo-dah-**dah**-noh/nah ays-tah-doh-oo-nee-**dayn**-say?* ciudadano/a estadounidense?[8]
a non-immigrant?	*ayks-trahn-**hay**-roh/rah noh een-mee-**grahn**-tay?* extranjero/a no inmigrante?[8]
10. Do you have proof of your immigration status?	***tee^ay**-nay **proo^ay**-bah day soo kohn-dee-**see^ohn** mee-grah-**toh**-ree^ah?* ¿Tiene prueba de su condición migratoria?
May I see it, please?	*pohr fah-**bohr**, lah **poo^ay**-doh bayr?* Por favor, ¿la puedo ver?
You will need to bring that with you (when you come to your appointment).	*nay-say-see-tah-**rah** trah-**ayr**-lah (**koo^ahn**-doh **bayn**-gah ah soo **see**-tah).* Necesitará traerla (cuando venga a su cita).
11. Do you have (photo) identification?	***tee^ay**-nay ee-dayn-tee-fee-kah-**see^ohn** (kohn **foh**-toh)?* ¿Tiene identificación (con foto)?
May I see it, please?	*pohr fah-**bohr**, lah **poo^ay**-doh bayr?* Por favor, ¿la puedo ver?
You will need to bring that with you (when you come to your appointment).	*nay-say-see-tah-**rah** trah-**ayr**-lah kohn-**see**-goh (**koo^ahn**-doh **bayn**-gah ah soo **see**-tah).* Necesitará traerla (cuando venga a su cita).
12. Do you have ...	***tee^ay**-nay ...* ¿Tiene ...
a driver's license?	*lee-**sayn**-see^ah **pah**-rah kohn-doo-**seer**?* licencia para conducir?
What is your driver's license number?	*koo^ahl ays soo **noo**-may-roh day lee-**sayn**-see^ah **pah**-rah kohn-doo-**seer**?* ¿Cuál es su número de licencia para conducir?[2]
From what state is it?	*day kay ays-**tah**-doh ays?* ¿De qué estado es?[1]
an immigration number?	***noo**-may-roh day een-mee-grah-**see^ohn**?* número de inmigración?
What is your immigration number?	*koo^ahl ays soo **noo**-may-roh day een-mee-grah-**see^ohn**?* ¿Cuál es su número de inmigración?[2]
a social security card?	*tahr-**hay**-tah day say-**goo**-roh soh-**see^ahl**?* tarjeta de seguro social?

What is your social security number?	*koo^ahl ays soo **noo**-may-roh day say-**goo**-roh soh-**see^ahl**?* ¿Cuál es su número de seguro social?[2]
a visa?	***bee**-sah?* visa?
What is your visa number?	*koo^ahl ays soo **noo**-may-roh day **bee**-sah?* ¿Cuál es su número de visa?[2]
Where is the consulate located that processed this visa?	***dohn**-day ays-**tah** ayl kohn-sol-**lah**-doh kay ayks-pee-**dee^oh** ays-tah **bee**-sah?* ¿Dónde está el consulado que expidió esta visa?[1,7]
a passport?	*pah-sah-**pohr**-tay?* pasaporte?
What is your passport number?	*koo^ahl ays soo **noo**-may-roh day pah-sah-**pohr**-tay?* ¿Cuál es su número de pasaporte?[2]
What was the date it was issued?	*ayn kay **fay**-chah foo^ay ayks-pay-**dee**-doh?* ¿En qué fecha fue expedido?[6]
What is the expiration date?	*koo^ahl ays lah **fay**-chah day bayn-see-**mee^ayn**-toh?* ¿Cuál es la fecha de vencimiento?[6]
From what country is it issued?	*kay pah-**ees** loh ayks-pee-**dee^oh**?* ¿Qué país lo expidió?[1,7]
You will need to bring your passport with you.	*nay-say-see-tah-**rah** trah-**ayr** soo pah-sah-**pohr**-tay.* Necesitará traer su pasaporte.
13. What is your form I-94 number?	*koo^ahl ays ayl **noo**-may-roh day soo fohr-moo-**lah**-ree^oh ee noh-**bayn**-tah ee **koo^ah**-troh?* ¿Cuál es el número de su formulario I-94?[2]
What is the expiration date of your form I-94?	*koo^ahl ays lah **fay**-chah day bayn-see-**mee^ayn**-toh day soo fohr-moo-**lah**-ree^oh ee noh-**bayn**-tah ee **koo^ah**-troh?* ¿Cuál es la fecha de vencimiento de su formulario I-94?[6]
14. What was your most recent date of entry to the U.S.?	*koo^ahl foo^ah lah **fay**-chah day soo ayn-**trah**-dah mahs rray-**see^ayn**-tay ayn lohs ays-**tah**-dohs oo-**nee**-dohs?* ¿Cuál fue la fecha de su entrada más reciente en los Estados Unidos?[6]
What was your port of entry?	*koo^ahl foo^ay soo **poon**-toh day ayn-**trah**-dah?* ¿Cuál fue su punto de entrada?[1]
Did you enter into the country ...	*ayn-**troh** ayn ayl pah-**ees** ...* ¿Entró en el país ...
by motor vehicle?	*ayn bay-**ee**-koo-loh moh-toh-ree-**sah**-doh?* en vehículo motorizado?
by boat?	*ayn **bahr**-koh?* en barco?

by plane?	*ayn ah-**bee**^ohn?* en avión?
on foot?	*ah pee^ay?* a pie?
by another means of transportation?	*ayn **oh**-troh **may**-dee^oh day trahns-pohr-tah-**see**^ohn?* en otro medio de transportación?
by pollero or coyote?	*kohn lah ah^ee-**yoo**-dah day poh-**yay**-roh oh koh^ee-**yoh**-tay?* con la ayuda de pollero o coyote?[9]
15. Do you have authorization to work in the U.S.?	*tee^ay-nay ah^oo-toh-ree-sah-**see**^ohn pah-rah trah-bah-**hahr** ayn lohs ays-**tah**-dohs oo-**nee**-dohs?* ¿Tiene autorización para trabajar en los Estados Unidos?
What is the expiration date of your work authorization?	*koo^ahl ays lah **fay**-chah day bayn-see-**mee**^ayn-toh day soo ah^oo-toh-ree-sah-**see**^ohn pah-rah trah-bah-**hahr**?* ¿Cuál es la fecha de vencimiento de su autorización para trabajar?[6]

II. Current Employment Information and Employment History

*een-fohr-mah-**see**^ohn ahk-**too**^ahl day aym-**play**-oh ee ahn-tay-say-**dayn**-tays lah-boh-**rah**-lays*
Información actual de empleo y antecedentes laborales

English	Pronunciation & Spanish
1. Are you currently employed?	*trah-**bah**-hah ahk-too^ahl-**mayn**-tay?* ¿Trabaja actualmente?
What is the name of your employer?	*koo^ahl ays ayl **nohm**-bray day soo aym-play-ah-**dohr**?* ¿Cuál es el nombre de su empleador?[1]
How do you spell that?	*koh-moh say ays-**kree**-bay **ay**-soh?* ¿Cómo se escribe eso?[1]
2. What was your date of hire?	*koo^ahl foo^ay soo **fay**-chah day kohn-trah-tah-**see**^ohn?* ¿Cuál fue su fecha de contratación?[6]
Is this position full-time or part-time?	*ays oon trah-**bah**-hoh day **tee**^aym-poh kohm-**play**-toh oh **tee**^aym-poh pahr-**see**^ahl?* ¿Es un trabajo de tiempo completo o tiempo parcial?
What is your current hourly wage?	*koo^ahn-toh **gah**-nah pohr **oh**-rah ahk-too^ahl-**mayn**-tay?* ¿Cuánto gana por hora actualmente?[2]
What is your monthly income?	*koo^ahl ays soo soo^ayl-doh mayn-**soo**^ahl?* ¿Cuál es su sueldo mensual?[2]
3. What is ... of your current employer?	*koo^ahl ays ... day soo aym-play-ah-**dohr** ahk-**too**^ahl?* ¿Cuál es ... de su empleador actual?
the address	*lah dee-rayk-**see**^ohn* la dirección[1, 2]

the phone number	*ayl **noo**-may-roh day tay-**lay**-foh-noh* el número de teléfono²
the fax number	*ayl **noo**-may-roh day fahks* el número de fax²
4. What is the name of your current supervisor?	***koh**-moh say **yah**-mah soo soo-payr-bee-**sohr** ahk-**too^ahl?*** ¿Cómo se llama su supervisor actual?¹
5. What is your profession?	*koo^ahl ays soo proh-fay-**see^ohn**?* ¿Cuál es su profesión?¹
How do you spell that?	***koh**-moh say ays-**kree**-bay **ay**-soh?* ¿Cómo se escribe eso?¹
6. Please make a list to give us that details your employment history for the last five years. You will need to include the following information for EACH employer: employer's name, complete address, your job title, month and year in which you were hired as well as the month and year in which you left.	*pohr fah-**bohr**, **ah**-gah **oo**-nah **lees**-tah **pah**-rah ayn-tray-**gahr**-nohs kay day-**tah**-yay soos ahn-tay-say-**dayn**-tays lah-boh-**rah**-lays pohr lohs **ool**-tee-mohs **seen**-koh **ahn**-yohs. day-bay-**rah** een-kloo-**eer** lah see-**ghee^ayn**-tay een-fohr-mah-**see^ohn** pah-rah **kah**-dah **oo**-noh day soos aym-play-ah-**doh**-rays: ayl **nohm**-bray dayl aym-play-ah-**dohr**, lah dee-rayk-**see^ohn** kohm-**play**-tah, ayl **tee**-too-loh day soo **poo^ays**-toh, ayl mays ee ayl **ahn**-yoh day soo kohn-trah-tah-**see^ohn** ah-see koh-moh ayl mays ee ayl **ahn**-yoh day soo pahr-**tee**-dah.* Por favor, haga una lista para entregarnos que detalla sus antecedentes laborales por los últimos cinco años. Deberá incluir la siguiente información para CADA uno de sus empleadores: el nombre del empleador, la dirección completa, el título de su puesto, el mes y el año de su contratación así como el mes y el año de su partida.

III. Education

*fohr-mah-**see^ohn** ah-kah-**day**-mee-kah*
Formación académica

English	Pronunciation & Spanish
1. Did you attend ... / Did you complete ...	*ah-sees-**tee^oh** a ... / kohm-play-**toh** ...* ¿Asistió a ... / ¿Completó ...
elementary school?	*lah pree-**mah**-ree^ah?* la primaria?
middle school/junior high?	*lah say-koon-**dah**-ree^ah?* la secundaria?
high school/senior high?	*lah pray-pah-rah-**toh**-ree^ah (ayl koh-**lay**-hee^oh)?* la preparatoria (el colegio)?¹⁰
vocational school?	*lah ays-**koo^ay**-lah boh-kah-see^oh-**nahl**?* la escuela vocacional?

college?	*lah oo-nee-bayr-see-**dahd**?* la universidad?
	*poh fah-**bohr**, **ah**-gah **oo**-nah **lees**-tah **pah**-rah ayn-tray-**gahr**-nohs kay een-**kloo**-yay lah see-**ghee^ayn**-tay een-fohr-mah-**see^ohn**: lohs **nohm**-brays day **toh**-dohs lohs ays-**koo^ay**-lahs ay eens-tee-**too**-tohs day ay-doo-kah-**see^ohn** ah-bahn-**sah**-dah ah lahs kay ah ah-sees-**tee**-doh, soo ays-pay-see^ah-lee-sah-**see^ohn** (see noh ays oon eens-tee-**too**-toh day ay-doo-kah-**see^ohn** ah-bahn-**sah**-dah, ays-**kree**-bah <ay-doo-kah-**see^ohn** hay-nay-**rahl**> **koh**-moh soo ays-pay-see^ah-lee-sah-**see^ohn**), lohs **tee**-too-lohs ee/oh sayr-tee-fee-**kah**-dohs kay say lay kohn-say-**dee^ay**-rohn ah-**see koh**-moh ayl **ahn**-yoh ayn ayl koo^ahl say lay kohn-fee-**ree^oh kah**-dah oo-noh. ·
Please make a list to give us that includes the following information: names of all schools attended, area of study (list "general education" if not an institute of higher learning), degrees and/or certificates awarded as well as the year each one was conferred.	Por favor, haga una lista para entregarnos que incluye la siguiente información: los nombres de todos los escuelas e institutos de educación avanzada a las que ha asistido, su especialización (si no es un instituto de educación avanzada, escriba <educación general> como su especialización), los títulos y/o certificados que se le concedieron así como el año en el cual se le confirió cada uno.

IV. Marital Status and Spousal Information

*ays-**tah**-doh see-**beel** ee **dah**-tohs day **kohn**-yoo-hay*
Estado civil y datos de cónyuge

English	Pronunciation & Spanish
1. Are you married?	*ays-**tah** kah-**sah**-doh/dah?* ¿Está casado/a?[8]
What was the date of the marriage?	*koo^ahl foo^ay lah **fay**-chah dayl mah-tree-**moh**-nee^oh?* ¿Cuál fue la fecha del matrimonio?[6]
Where did the marriage take place?	***dohn**-day say kah-**say**-rohn?* ¿Dónde se casaron?[1]
2. Are you divorced?	*ays-**tah** dee-boor-**see^ah**-doh/dah?* ¿Está divorciado/a?[8]
Have you been divorced before (including from your current spouse)?	*ah ays-**tah**-doh/dah dee-bohr-**see^ah**-doh/dah **ahn**-tays (een-kloo-**yayn**-doh soo **kohn**-yoo-hay ahk-**too^ahl**)?* ¿Ha estado divorciado/a antes (incluyendo su cónyuge actual)?[8]
How many times have you been divorced?	***koo^ahn**-tahs **bay**-says ah ays-**tah**-doh/dah dee-bohr-**see^ah**-doh/dah?* ¿Cuántas veces ha estado divorciado/a?[2, 8]
What was the date of that divorce?	*koo^ahl foo^ay lah **fay**-chah day **ay**-say dee-**bohr**-see^oh?* ¿Cuál fue la fecha de ese divorcio?[6]
What is the name of your former spouse?	***koh**-moh say **yah**-mah soo ahn-**tee**-goo^oh **kohn**-yoo-hay?* ¿Cómo se llama su antiguo/a cónyuge?[8]

Where were you married?	*dohn-day say kah-**sah**-rohn?* ¿Dónde se casaron?[1]
Where were you divorced?	*dohn-day say dee-bohr-**see^ah**-rohn?* ¿Dónde se divorciaron?[1]
3. Are you single?	*ays sohl-**tay**-roh/rah?* ¿Es soltero/a?[8]
4. Are you widowed?	*ays **bee^oo**-doh/dah?* ¿Es viudo/a?[8]
What was ...	*koo^ahl foo^ay ...* ¿Cuál fue ...
your spouse's date of birth?	*lah **fay**-chah day nah-see-**mee^ayn**-toh day soo **kohn**-yoo-hay?* la fecha de nacimiento de su cónyuge?[6]
Where was your spouse born?	*dohn-day nah-**see^oh** soo **kohn**-yoo-hay?* ¿Dónde nació su cónyuge?[1]
Town?	*poo^**ay**-bloh?* ¿Pueblo?[1]
City?	*see^oo-**dahd?*** ¿Ciudad?[1]
State?	*ays-**tah**-doh?* ¿Estado?[1]
Province?	*proh-**been**-see^ah?* ¿Provincia?[1]
Country?	*pah-**ees?*** ¿País?[1]
5. What is your spouse's name?	*koh-moh say **yay**-mah soo **kohn**-yoo-hay?* ¿Cómo se llama su cónyuge?[1]
6. Does your spouse go by any other name?	*tee^**ay**-nay soo **kohn**-yoo-hay ahl-**goon** oh-troh **nohm**-bray?* ¿Tiene su cónyuge algún otro nombre?
What is it?	*koo^ahl ays?* ¿Cuál es?[1]
7. Does your spouse have any prior names?	*ah tay-**nee**-doh soo **kohn**-yoo-hay ahl-**goon** oh-troh **nohm**-bray* *ahn-tay-ree^ohr-**mayn**-tay?* ¿Ha tenido su cónyuge algún otro nombre anteriormente?
What was it?	*koo^ahl foo^ay?* ¿Cuál fue?[1]
What was your spouse's maiden name?	*koo^ahl foo^ay ayl **nohm**-bray day sohl-**tay**-rah day soo **kohn**-yoo-hay?* ¿Cuál fue el nombre de soltera de su cónyuge?[1]
8. Is your spouse ...	*ays soo **koyn**-yoo-hay ...* ¿Es su cónyuge ...

a legal resident?	*rray-see-**dayn**-tay lay-**gahl**?* residente legal?
permanent resident?	*rray-see-**dayn**-tay payr-mah-**nayn**-tay?* residente permanente?
What is your spouse's alien registration number?	*koo^ahl ays ayl **noo**-may-roh day rray-**hees**-troh day een-mee-**grahn**-tay day soo **kohn**-yoo-hay?* ¿Cuál es el número de registro de inmigrante de su cónyuge?[2]
How long has your spouse been a permanent resident?	*pohr koo^**ahn**-toh **tee^aym**-poh ah **see**-doh soo **kohn**-yoo-hay rray-see-**dayn**-tay payr-mah-**nayn**-tay?* ¿Por cuánto tiempo ha sido su cónyuge residente permanente?
one day	*oon **dee**-ah* un día[3]
(#) days	*(#) **dee**-ahs* (#) días[3]
one week	***oo**-nah say-**mah**-nah* una semana[3]
(#) weeks	*(#) say-**mah**-nahs* (#) semanas[3]
one month	*oon mays* un mes[3]
(#) months	*(#) **may**-says* (#) meses[3]
one year	*oon **ahn**-yoh* un año[3]
(#) years	*(#) **ahn**-yohs* (#) años[3]
a U.S. citizen?	*see^oo-dah-**dah**-noh/nah ays-tah-doh-oo-nee-**dayn**-say?* ciudadano/a estadounidense?[8]
a non-immigrant?	*ayks-trahn-**hay**-roh/rah noh een-mee-**grahn**-tay?* extranjero/a no inmigrante?[8]
9. Does your spouse have a social security number?	***tee^ay**-nay soo **kohn**-yoo-hay oon **noo**-may-roh day say-**goo**-roh soh-**see^ahl**?* ¿Tiene su cónyuge un número de seguro social?
What is that number?	*koo^ahl ays **ay**-say **noo**-may-roh?* ¿Cuál es ese número?[2]
10. Can your spouse be reached by phone?	***oo**-noh say **poo^ay**-day koh-moo-nee-**kahr** kohn soo **kohn**-yoo-hay pohr tay-**lay**-foh-noh?* ¿Uno se puede comunicar con su cónyuge por teléfono?

What is your spouse's telephone number?	*koo^ahl ays ayl noo-may-roh day tay-lay-foh-noh day soo kohn-yoo-hay?* ¿Cuál es el número de teléfono de su cónyuge?[2]
11. Do you have the same address as your spouse?	*tee^ay-nay lah mees-mah dee-rayk-see^ohn kay soo kohn-yoo-hay?* ¿Tiene la misma dirección que su cónyuge?
What is your spouse's address?	*koo^ahl ays lah dee-rayk-see^ohn day soo kohn-yoo-hay?* ¿Cuál es la dirección de su cónyuge?[1,2]
12. What is your spouse's ...	*koo^ahl ays ...* ¿Cuál es ...
date of birth?	*lah fay-chah day nah-see-mee^ayn-toh day soo kohn-yoo-hay?* la fecha de nacimiento de su cónyuge?[6]
Where was your spouse born?	*dohn-day nah-see^oh soo kohn-yoo-hay?* ¿Dónde nació su cónyuge?[1]
Town?	*poo^ay-bloh?* ¿Pueblo?[1]
City?	*see^oo-dahd?* ¿Ciudad?[1]
State?	*ays-tah-doh?* ¿Estado?[1]
Province?	*proh-been-see^ah?* ¿Provincia?[1]
Country?	*pah-ees?* ¿País?[1]
13. Does your spouse have a passport?	*tee^ay-nay soo kohn-yoo-hay oon pah-sah-pohr-tay?* ¿Tiene su cónyuge un pasaporte?
What is your spouse's passport number?	*koo^ahl ays ayl noo-may-roh day pah-sah-pohr-tay day soo kohn-yoo-hay?* ¿Cuál es el número de pasaporte de su cónyuge?[2]
What was the date it was issued?	*ayn kay fay-chah foo^ay ayks-pay-dee-doh?* ¿En qué fecha fue expedido?[6]
What is the expiration date?	*koo^ahl ays lah fay-chah day bayn-see-mee^ayn-toh?* ¿Cuál es la fecha de vencimiento?[6]
From what country is it issued?	*kay pah-ees loh ayks-pee-dee^oh?* ¿Qué país lo expidió?[7]
14. When was the last time your spouse was in the U.S.? (month and year)	*koo^ahn-doh foo^ay lah ool-tee-mah bays kay soo kohn-yoo-hay ays-too-boh ayn los ays-tah-dohs oo-nee-dohs? (ayl mays y ayl ahn-yoh)* ¿Cuándo fue la última vez que su cónyuge estuvo en los Estados Unidos? (el mes y el año)[6]
What was your spouse's port of entry?	*koo^ahl foo^ay ayl poon-toh day ayn-trah-dah pah-rah soo kohn-yoo-hay?* ¿Cuál fue el punto de entrada para su cónyuge?[1]

15. Does your spouse have a visa?

*tee^ay-nay soo **kohn**-yoo-hay **oo**-nah **bee**-sah?*
¿Tiene su cónyuge una visa?

When does it expire? (month and year)

*koo^ahn-doh say **bayn**-say? (el mes y el año)*
¿Cuándo se vence? (el mes y el año)[6]

16. Has your spouse requested a visa?

*ah pay-**dee** soo **kohn**-yoo-hay **oo**-nah **bee**-sah?*
¿Ha pedido su cónyuge una visa?

17. Does your spouse work?

*trah-**bah**-hah soo **kohn**-yoo-hay?*
¿Trabaja su cónyuge?

What is your spouse's profession?

*koo^ahl ays lah proh-fay-**see^ohn** day soo **kohn**-yoo-hay?*
¿Cuál es la profesión de su cónyuge?[1]

How do you spell that?

*koh-moh say ays-**kree**-bay **ay**-soh?*
¿Cómo se escribe eso?[1]

18. Did your spouse attend ... / Did he/she complete ...

*ah-sees-**tee^oh** soo **kohn**-yoo-hay a ... / kohm-play-**toh** ...*
¿Asistió su cónyuge a ... / ¿Completó ...

elementary school?

*lah pree-**mah**-ree^ah?*
la primaria?

middle school/junior high?

*lah say-koon-**dah**-ree^ah?*
la secundaria?

high school/senior high?

*lah pray-pah-rah-**toh**-ree^ah (ayl koh-**lay**-hee^oh)?*
la preparatoria (el colegio)?[10]

vocational school?

*lah ays-**koo^ay**-lah boh-kah-see^oh-**nahl**?*
la escuela vocacional?

college?

*lah oo-nee-bayr-see-**dahd**?*
la universidad?

Please make a list to give us that includes the following information about your spouse: names of all schools attended, area of study (list "general education" if not an institute of higher learning), degrees and/or certificates awarded as well as the year each one was conferred.

*poh fah-**bohr**, **ah**-gah **oo**-nah lees-tah **pah**-rah ayn-tray-**gahr**-nohs kay een-**kloo**-yay lah see-**ghee^ayn**-tay een-fohr-mah-**see^ohn** soh-bray soo **kohn**-yoo-hay: lohs **nohm**-brays day **toh**-dohs lohs ays-**koo^ay**-lahs ay eens-tee-**too**-tohs day ay-doo-kah-**see^ohn** ah-bahn-**sah**-dah ah lahs kay ah ah-sees-**tee**-doh, soo ays-pay-see^ah-lee-sah-**see^ohn** (see noh ays oon eens-tee-**too**-toh day ay-doo-kah-**see^ohn** ah-bahn-**sah**-dah, ays-**kree**-bah <ay-doo-kah-**see^ohn** hay-nay-**rahl**> koh-moh soo ays-pay-see^ah-lee-sah-**see^ohn**), lohs **tee**-too-lohs ee/oh sayr-tee-fee-**kah**-dohs kay say lay kohn-say-**dee^ay**-rohn ah-**see** koh-moh ayl **ahn**-yoh ayn ayl koo^ahl say lay kohn-fee-**ree^oh** **kah**-dah **oo**-noh.*

Por favor, haga una lista para entregarnos que incluye la siguiente información sobre su cónyuge: los nombres de todos los escuelas e institutos de educación avanzada a las que ha asistido, su especialización (si no es un instituto de educación avanzada, escriba <educación general> como su especialización), los títulos y/o certificados que se le concedieron así como el año en el cual se le confirió cada uno.

19. Does your spouse have any relatives that live in the U.S.?

*tee^ay-nay soo **kohn**-yoo-hay ahl-**goo**-nohs pah-**ree^ayn**-tays kay **bee**-bayn ayn lohs ays-**tah**-dohs oo-**nee**-dohs?*

¿Tiene su cónyuge algunos parientes que viven en los Estados Unidos?

Please make a list to give us that includes the following information for each of your spouse's relatives that live in the U.S.: full name, relationship to your spouse, immigration status and address.

*pohr fah-**bohr**, **ah**-gah **oo**-nah lees-tah **pah**-rah ayn-tray-**gahr**-nohs kay een-**kloo**-yay lah see-**ghee^ayn**-tay een-fohr-mah-**see^ohn** pah-rah **kah**-dah **oo**-noh day lohs pah-**ree^ayn**-tays day soo **kohn**-yoo-hay kay **bee**-bay ayn lohs ays-**tah**-dohs oo-**nee**-dohs: **nohm**-bray kohm-**play**-toh, ayl pah-rayn-**tays**-koh kohn soo **kohn**-yoo-hay, soo kohn-dee-**see^ohn** mee-grah-**toh**-ree^ah ee soo dee-rayk-**see^ohn**.*

Por favor, haga una lista para entregarnos que incluye la siguiente información para cada uno de los parientes de su cónyuge que vive en los Estados Unidos: nombre completo, el parentesco con su cónyuge, su condición migratoria y su dirección.

V. Additional Family Information

*een-fohr-mah-**see^ohn** fah-mee-**lee^ahr** ah-dee-see^oh-**nahl***
Información familiar adicional

English	Pronunciation & Spanish
1. Do you have any children with your spouse and/or any other person?	*tee^**ay**-nay **ee**-hohs kohn soo **kohn**-yoo-hay ee/oh kohn ahl-**goo**-nah **oh**-trah payr-**soh**-nah?* ¿Tiene hijos con su cónyuge y/o con alguna otra persona?
Please make a list to give us that includes the following information about ANY children you have: full name, date of birth, country of birth and the name of the other individual with whom you had each child.	*poh fah-**bohr**, **ah**-gah **oo**-nah lees-tah **pah**-rah ayn-tray-**gahr**-nohs kay een-**kloo**-yay lah see-**ghee^ayn**-tay een-fohr-mah-**see^ohn** pah-rah **kah**-dah **ee**-hoh kay tee^**ay**-nay: **nohm**-bray kohm-**play**-toh, **fay**-chah day nah-see-**mee^ayn**-toh, pah-**ees** day nah-see-**mee^ayn**-toh ah-**see** koh-moh ayl **nohm**-bray dayl **oh**-tro een-dee-**bee**-doo^oh kohn kee^ayn **too**-boh **kah**-dah **ee**-hoh.* Por favor, haga una lista para entregarnos que incluye la siguiente información para CADA hijo que tiene: nombre completo, fecha de nacimiento, país de nacimiento así como el nombre del otro individuo con quien tuvo cada hijo.
2. Please make a list to give us of the following information regarding your father: full name, date of birth, city and country of birth, city and country of residence and if deceased, the date of death.	*pohr fah-**bohr**, **ah**-gah **oo**-nah lees-tah **pah**-rah ayn-tray-**gahr**-nohs kay een-**kloo**-yay lah see-**ghee^ayn**-tay een-fohr-mah-**see^ohn** soh-bray soo **pah**-dray: **nohm**-bray kohm-**play**-toh, **fay**-chah day nah-see-**mee^ayn**-toh, see^oo-**dahd** ee pah-**ees** day nah-see-**mee^ayn**-toh, see^oo-**dahd** ee pah-**ees** day rray-see-**dayn**-see^ah ee see ays-**tah** fah-yay-**see**-doh, lah **fay**-chah dayl fah-yay-see-**mee^ayn**-toh.* Por favor, haga una lista para entregarnos que incluye la siguiente información sobre su padre: nombre completo, fecha de nacimiento, ciudad y país de nacimiento, ciudad y país de residencia y si está fallecido, la fecha del fallecimiento.

3. Please make a list to give us of the following information regarding your mother: full name, maiden name, date of birth, city and country of birth, city and country of residence and if deceased, the date of death.	*pohr fah-**bohr**, **ah**-gah **oo**-nah **lees**-tah **pah**-rah ayn-tray-**gahr**-nohs kay een-**kloo**-yay lah see-**ghee^ayn**-tay een-fohr-mah-**see^ohn** soh-bray soo **mah**-dray: **nohm**-bray kohm-**play**-toh, **nohm**-bray day sohl-**tay**-rah, **fay**-chah day nah-see-**mee^ayn**-toh, see^oo-**dahd** ee pah-**ees** day nah-see-**mee^ayn**-toh, see^oo-**dahd** ee pah-**ees** day rray-see-**dayn**-see^ah ee see ays-**tah** fah-yay-**see**-dah, lah **fay**-chah dayl fah-yay-see-**mee^ayn**-toh.* Por favor, haga una lista para entregarnos que incluye la siguiente información sobre su madre: nombre completo, nombre de soltera, fecha de nacimiento, ciudad y país de nacimiento, ciudad y país de residencia y si está fallecida, la fecha del fallecimiento.
4. Do you have … that is a U.S. citizen or resident alien?	*tee^**ay**-nay … kay ays see^oo-dah-**dah**-noh/nah ays-tah-doh-oo-nee-**dayn**-say oh rray-see-**dayn**-tay ayks-trahn-**hay**-roh/rah?* ¿Tiene … que es ciudadano/a estadounidense o residente extranjero/a?[8]
a father	***pah**-dray* padre
How long has he had this status?	*koo^**ahn**-toh **tee^aym**-poh **ah**-say kay say lay kohn-say-**dee^oh** ays-tah kohn-dee-**see^ohn** mee-grah-**toh**-ree^ah?* ¿Cuánto tiempo hace que se le concedió esta condición migratoria?
one day	*ah-say oon **dee**-ah* hace un día[3]
(#) days	*ah-say (#) **dee**-ahs* hace (#) días[3]
one week	*ah-say **oo**-nah say-**mah**-nah* hace una semana[3]
(#) weeks	*ah-say (#) say-**mah**-nahs* hace (#) semanas[3]
one month	*ah-say oon mays* hace un mes[3]
(#) months	*ah-say (#) **may**-says* hace (#) meses[3]
one year	*ah-say oon **ahn**-yoh* hace un año[3]
(#) years	*ah-say (#) **ahn**-yohs* hace (#) años[3]
a mother	***mah**-dray* madre
How long has she had this status?	*koo^**ahn**-toh **tee^aym**-poh **ah**-say kay say lay kohn-say-**dee^oh** ays-tah kohn-dee-**see^ohn** mee-grah-**toh**-ree^ah?* ¿Cuánto tiempo hace que se le concedió esta condición migratoria?
a brother	*ayr-**mah**-noh* hermano

How long has he had this status?	*koo^ahn-toh tee^aym-poh ah-say kay say lay kohn-say-dee^oh ays-tah kohn-dee-see^ohn mee-grah-toh-ree^ah?* ¿Cuánto tiempo hace que se le concedió esta condición migratoria?
a sister	*ayr-mah-noh* hermana
How long has she had this status?	*koo^ahn-toh tee^aym-poh ah-say kay say lay kohn-say-dee^oh ays-tah kohn-dee-see^ohn mee-grah-toh-ree^ah?* ¿Cuánto tiempo hace que se le concedió esta condición migratoria?
a grandfather	*ah-boo^ay-loh* abuelo
How long has he had this status?	*koo^ahn-toh tee^aym-poh ah-say kay say lay kohn-say-dee^oh ays-tah kohn-dee-see^ohn mee-grah-toh-ree^ah?* ¿Cuánto tiempo hace que se le concedió esta condición migratoria?
a grandmother	*ah-boo^ay-loh* abuela
How long has she had this status?	*koo^ahn-toh tee^aym-poh ah-say kay say lay kohn-say-dee^oh ays-tah kohn-dee-see^ohn mee-grah-toh-ree^ah?* ¿Cuánto tiempo hace que se le concedió esta condición migratoria?

VI. Immigration History

ahn-tay-say-dayn-tays mee-grah-toh-ree^ohs
Antecedentes migratorios

English	Pronunciation & Spanish
1. Do you or any family members have any current petitions with the Immigration Service?	*ays kay oos-tayd oh ahl-goon mee^aym-broh fah-mee-lee^ayr tee^ay-nay oo-nah pay-tee-see^ohn payn-dee^ayn-tay kohn ayl sayr-bee-see^oh day een-mee-grah-see^ohn?* ¿Es que Ud. o algún miembro familiar tiene una petición pendiente con el servicio de inmigración?
Could you ... the name of the person who submitted the petition and when that was?	*poh-dree-ah ... ayl nohm-bray day lah payr-soh-nah kay soh-may-tee^oh lah pay-tee-see^ohn ee koo^ahn-doh foo^ay?* ¿Podría ... el nombre de la persona que sometió la petición y cuándo fue?
write down (here)	*ah-poon-tahr (ah-kee)* apuntar (aquí)
tell someone in Spanish / English	*day-seer-lay ah ahl-ghee^ayn ayn ays-pahn-yohl / een-glays* decirle a alguien en español / inglés

2. Has an application or petition ever been filed on your behalf with the U.S. Citizenship and Immigration Services or the Department of Labor?

*say lay ah soh-may-**tee**-doh **oo**-nah soh-lee-see-**tood** oh pay-tee-**see^ohn** day soo **pahr**-tay ahl sayr-**bee**-see^oh day see^oo-dah-dah-**nee**-ah ay een-mee-grah-**see^ohn** day ays-**tah**-dohs oo-**nee**-dohs oh ahl mee-nees-**tay**-ree^oh day trah-**bah**-hoh?*

¿Se le ha sometido una solicitud o petición de su parte al Servicio de Ciudadanía e Inmigración de Estados Unidos o al Ministerio de Trabajo?

Could you ... the name of the person who submitted the application or petition and when that was?

*poh-**dree**-ah ... ahl **nohm**-bray day lah payr-**soh**-nah kay soh-may-**tee^oh** lah pay-tee-**see^ohn** ee **koo^ahn**-doh foo^ay?*

¿Podría ... el nombre de la persona que sometió la solicitud o la petición y cuándo fue?

write down (here)

*ah-poon-**tahr** (ah-**kee**)*

apuntar (aquí)

tell someone in Spanish / English

*day-**seer**-lay ah **ahl**-ghee^ayn ayn ays-pahn-**yohl** / een-**glays***

decirle a alguien en español / inglés

3. Have you ever had any problems with Immigration, a U.S. Consulate or Port of Entry?

*ahl-**goo**-nah bays, ah tay-**nee**-doh proh-**blay**-mahs kohn lohs sayr-**bee**-see^ohs day een-mee-grah-**see^ohn**, oon kohn-soo-**lah**-doh ays-tah-doh-oo-nee-**dayn**-say oh oon **poon**-toh day ayn-**trah**-dah?*

Alguna vez, ¿ha tenido problemas con los servicios de inmigración, un consulado estadounidense o un punto de entrada?

Could you ... what occured and when each event happened?

*poh-**dree**-ah ... kay oh-koo-**rree^oh** ee **koo^ahn**-doh oo-boh **kah**-dah **kah**-soh?*

¿Podría ... qué ocurrió y cuándo hubo cada caso?

explain in writing

*ayks-plee-**kahr** pohr ays-**kree**-toh*

explicar por escrito

tell someone in Spanish / English

*day-**seer**-lay ah **ahl**-ghee^ayn ayn ays-pahn-**yohl** / een-**glays***

decirle a alguien en español / inglés

4. Please answer "yes" or "no" to the following questions.

*pohr fah-**bohr**, rrays-**pohn**-dah kohn <see> oh <noh> ah lahs see-**ghee^ayn**-tays pray-**goon**-tahs.*

Por favor, responda con <sí> o <no> a las siguientes preguntas.

Have you ever ...

*ahl-**goo**-nah bays, ah ...*

Alguna vez, ¿ha ...

had an exchange visitor visa?

*poh-say-**ee**-doh **oo**-nah **bee**-sah day bee-see-**tahn**-tay pohr een-tayr-**kahm**-bee^oh?*

poseído una visa de visitante por intercambio?

Could you ... how long ago that was and what it was for?

*poh-**dree**-ah ... **koo^ahn**-toh **tee^aym**-poh ah-say kay lah tay-**nee**-ah ee **pah**-rah kay foo^ay?*

¿Podría ... cuánto tiempo hace que la tenía y para qué fue?

write down (here)

*ah-poon-**tahr** (ah-**kee**)*

apuntar (aquí)

tell someone in Spanish / English	*day-seer-lay ah ahl-ghee^ayn ayn ays-pahn-yohl / een-glays* decirle a alguien en español / inglés
applied for a green card or any type of visa before?	*soh-lee-see-tah-doh ahn-tays oo-nah tahr-hay-tah day rray-see-dayn-see^ah oh oo-nah bee-sah day koo^ahl-kee^ayr klah-say* solicitado antes una tarjeta de residencia o una visa de cualquier clase?
Could you ... what was the result and when this happened?	*poh-dree-ah ... koo^ahl foo^ay ayl rray-sool-tah-doh ee koo^ahn-doh oo-boh?* ¿Podría ... cuál fue el resultado y cuándo hubo?
explain in writing	*ayks-plee-kahr pohr ays-kree-toh* explicar por escrito
tell someone in Spanish / English	*day-seer-lay ah ahl-ghee^ayn ayn ays-pahn-yohl / een-glays* decirle a alguien en español / inglés
been arrested?	*see-doh ah-rrays-tah-doh/dah?* sido arrestado/a?[8]
Could you ... what occured and when this happened?	*poh-dree-ah ... kay oh-koo-rree^oh ee koo^ahn-doh oo-boh?* ¿Podría ... qué ocurrió y cuándo hubo?
explain in writing	*ayks-plee-kahr pohr ays-kree-toh* explicar por escrito
tell someone in Spanish / English	*day-seer-lay ah ahl-ghee^ayn ayn ays-pahn-yohl / een-glays* decirle a alguien en español / inglés
had to appear before a U.S. immigration judge?	*kohm-pah-ray-see-doh ahn-tay oon hoo^ays mee-grah-toh-ree^oh ays-tah-doh-oo-nee-dayn-say?* comparecido ante un juez migratorio estadounidense?
Could you ... why and when this happened?	*poh-dree-ah ... pohr kay ee koo^ahn-doh oo-boh?* ¿Podría ... por qué y cuándo hubo?
explain in writing	*ayks-plee-kahr pohr ays-kree-toh* explicar por escrito
tell someone in Spanish / English	*day-seer-lay ah ahl-ghee^ayn ayn ays-pahn-yohl / een-glays* decirle a alguien en español / inglés
been deported from the U.S.?	*see-doh day-pohr-tah-doh/dah day lohs ays-tah-dohs oo-nee-dohs?* sido deportado/a de los Estados Unidos?[8]
Could you ... what occured and when this happened?	*poh-dree-ah ... kay oh-koo-rree^oh ee koo^ahn-doh oo-boh?* ¿Podría ... qué ocurrió y cuándo hubo?
explain in writing	*ayks-plee-kahr pohr ays-kree-toh* explicar por escrito
tell someone in Spanish / English	*day-seer-lay ah ahl-ghee^ayn ayn ays-pahn-yohl / een-glays* decirle a alguien en español / inglés

had to appear in court?	*kohm-pah-ray-**see**-doh ayn oon tree-boo-**nahl**?* comparecido en un tribunal?
Could you … what occured and when this happened?	*poh-**dree**-ah … kay oh-koo-**rree**^oh ee **koo**^ahn-doh **oo**-boh?* ¿Podría … qué ocurrió y cuándo hubo?
explain in writing	*ayks-plee-**kahr** pohr ays-**kree**-toh* explicar por escrito
tell someone in Spanish / English	*day-**seer**-lay ah **ahl**-ghee^ayn ayn ays-pahn-**yohl** / een-**glays*** decirle a alguien en español / inglés
had a job in the U.S. without authorization through INS?	*trah-bah-**hah**-doh ayn lohs ays-**tah**-dohs oo-**nee**-dohs seen lah ah^oo-toh-ree-sah-**see**^ohn dayl sayr-**bee**-see^oh day een-mee-grah-**see**^ohn ee nah-too-rah-lee-sah-**see**^ohn?* trabajado en los Estados Unidos sin la autorización del Servicio de Inmigración y Naturalización?
Could you … what the job was and what were your dates of employment?	*poh-**dree**-ah … kay **klah**-say day trah-**bah**-hoh tay-**nee**-ah ee **koo**^ah-lays **foo**^ay-rohn soos **fay**-chahs day aym-**play**-oh?* ¿Podría … qué clase de trabajo tenía y cuáles fueron sus fechas de empleo?
list (here)	*ah-**sayr oo**-nah **lees**-tah (ah-**kee**)* hacer una lista (aquí)
tell someone in Spanish / English	*day-**seer**-lay ah **ahl**-ghee^ayn ayn ays-pahn-**yohl** / een-**glays*** decirle a alguien en español / inglés
been denied entrance into the U.S.?	*see-doh day-nay-**gah**-doh/dah lah ayn-**trah**-dah ayn lohs ays-**tah**-dohs oo-**nee**-dohs?* sido denegado/a la entrada en los Estados Unidos?[8]
Could you … why and when this happened?	*poh-**dree**-ah … pohr kay ee **koo**^ahn-doh **oo**-boh?* ¿Podría … por qué y cuándo hubo?
explain in writing	*ayks-plee-**kahr** pohr ays-**kree**-toh* explicar por escrito
tell someone in Spanish / English	*day-**seer**-lay ah **ahl**-ghee^ayn ayn ays-pahn-**yohl** / een-**glays*** decirle a alguien en español / inglés

5. Please answer "yes" or "no" to the following questions. If you answer "yes" to any of these questions, you must be able to explain the issue in writing or get someone to help you put your explanation in writing.	*pohr fah-**bohr**, rrays-**pohn**-dah kohn <see> oh <noh> ah lahs see-**ghee**^ayn-tays pray-**goon**-tahs. see kohn-**tays**-tah kohn <see> a **koo**^ahl-**kee**^ayr day **ays**-tahs pray-**goon**-tahs, **day**-bay poh-**dayr** ayks-plee-**kahr** lah see-too^ah-**see**^ohn pohr ays-**kree**-toh oh ah-**sayr** kay **ahl**-ghee^ayn loh/lah ah^ee-**yoo**-day ah poh-**nayr** soo ayks-plee-kah-**see**^ohn por ays-**kree**-toh.* Por favor, responda con <sí> o <no> a las siguientes preguntas. Si contesta con <sí> a cualquier de estas preguntas, debe poder explicar la situación por escrito o hacer que alguien lo/la ayude a poner su explicación por escrito.

Do you have any special skills or training, including explosives and firearms?

*tee^ay-nay ahl-**goo**-nahs ah-bee-lee-**dah**-days oh kah-pah-see-tah-**see^oh**-nays ays-pay-**see^ah**-lays, een-kloo-**yayn**-doh ayn lohs **kahm**-pohs day ayks-ploh-**see**-bohs oh **ahr**-mahs day **foo^ay**-goh?*

¿Tiene algunas habilidades o capacitación especiales, incluyendo en los campos de explosivos o armas de fuego?

Have you ever been a drug addict or trafficked drugs into the U.S.?

*ah **see**-doh droh-gah-**deek**-toh/tah oh trah-fee-**kah**-doh **droh**-gahs ah lohs ays-**tah**-dohs oo-**nee**-dohs?*

¿Ha sido drogadicto/a o traficado drogas a los Estados Unidos?[8]

Have you ever had a communicable disease such as tuberculosis?

*ah tay-**nee**-doh **oo**-nah ayn-fayr-may-**dahd** kohn-tah-**hee^oh**-sah tahl **koh**-moh lah too-bayr-koo-**loh**-sees?*

¿Ha tenido una enfermedad contagiosa tal como la tuberculosis?

Have you ever been diagnosed with a mental disorder or physical disability?

*say lay ah dee^ahg-nohs-tee-**kah**-doh kohn oon trahs-**tohr**-noh mayn-**tahl** oh **oo**-nah dees-kah-pah-see-**dahd** fee-see-kah?*

¿Se le ha diagnosticado con un trastorno mental o una discapacidad física?

Have you ever recevied public benefits in the U.S. such as Medicare or welfare?

*ah rray-see-**bee**-doh bay-nay-**fee**-see^ohs **poo**-blee-kohs ayn lohs ays-**tah**-dohs oo-**nee**-dohs tahl **koh**-moh Medicare o lah ah-sees-**tayn**-see^ah **poo**-blee-kah?*

¿Ha recibido beneficios públicos en los Estados Unidos tal como Medicare o la asistencia pública?

Have you ever fraudulently misrepresented your immigration status in the U.S. for any reason including employment?

*ah rray-pray-sayn-**tah**-doh frah^oo-doo-layn-tah-**mayn**-tay soo kohn-dee-**see^ohn** mee-grah-**toh**-ree^ah ayn lohs ays-**tah**-dohs oo-**nee**-dohs pohr koo^ahl-**kee^ayr** rah-**sohn** een-kloo-**yayn**-doh **pah**-rah kohn-say-**gheer** aym-**play**-oh?*

¿Ha representado fraudulentamente su condición migratoria en los Estados Unidos por cualquier razón incluyendo para conseguir empleo?

Have you participated in any unlawful activity since entering the U.S.?

*ah pahr-tee-see-**pah**-doh ayn koo^ahl-**kee^ayr** ahk-tee-bee-**dahd** ee-**lee**-see-tah **days**-day kay ayn-**troh** ayn lohs ays-**tah**-dohs oo-**nee**-dohs?*

¿Ha participado en cualquier actividad ilícita desde que entró en los Estados Unidos?

Have you ever lost a passport or had one stolen?

*say lay ah payr-**dee**-doh oon pah-sah-**pohr**-tay oh say loh ahn rroh-**bah**-doh?*

¿Se le ha perdido un pasaporte o se lo han robado?

Have you ever been arrested, convicted or encarcerated for any reason anywhere in the world?

*ah **see**-doh ah-rrays-**tah**-doh/dah, hoos-**gah**-doh/dah kool-**pah**-blay oh ayn-kahr-say-**lah**-doh/dah pohr koo^ahl-**kee^ayr** rrah-**sohn** ayn koo^ahl-**kee^ayr** pahr-tay dayl **moon**-doh?*

¿Ha sido arrestado/a, juzgado/a culpable o encarcelado/a por cualquier razón en cualquier parte del mundo?[8]

Have you ever been the recipient of a rehabilitation decree, a pardon, amnesty or some other act of clemency?

*ah **see**-doh ayl/lah bay-nay-fee-**see^ah**-ree^oh/ah day oon day-**kray**-toh day rray-ah-bee-lee-tah-**see^ohn**, oon een-**dool**-toh, lah ahm-nays-**tee**-ah oh ahl-**goon** oh-troh **ahk**-toh day klay-**mayn**-see^ah?*

¿Ha sido el/la beneficiario/a de un decreto de rehabilitación, un indulto, la amnestía o algún otro acto de clemencia?[11]

	*ah fohr-**mah**-doh **pahr**-tay day oon pahr-**tee**-doh koh-moo-**nees**-tah oh toh-tah-lee-**tah**-ree^oh?*
Have you ever belonged to a communist or totalitarian party?	¿Ha formado parte de un partido comunista o totalitario?

	*ah pahr-tee-see-**pah**-doh day ahl-**goo**-nah mah-**nay**-rah ayn lah payr-say-koo-**see^ohn** day **oh**-trah payr-**soh**-nah pohr soo oh-pee-**nee^ohn** poh-**lee**-tee-kah, oh-**ree**-hayn nah-see^oh-**nahl**, **rrah**-sah oh kray-**ayn**-see^ahs rray-lee-**hee^oh**-sahs kohn-**fohr**-may ah lahs **ohr**-day-nays dayl goh-**bee^ayr**-noh naht-**sees**-tah day ah-lay-**mah**-nee^ah oh koo^ahl-**kee^ayr** ah-**lee^ah**-doh dayl **mees**-moh?*
Have you ever participated in any way in the persecution of another person due to his/her political opinion, national origin, race or religous beliefs as ordered by the Nazi Government of Germany or any Nazi Government of Germany ally?	¿Ha participado de alguna manera en la persecución de otra persona por su opinión política, origen nacional, raza o creencias religiosas conforme a las órdenes del gobierno nazista de Alemania o cualquier aliado del mismo?

	*ah pahr-tee-see-**pah**-doh ayn oon **ahk**-toh day hay-nay-**see**-dee^oh?*
Have you ever been a participant in any act of genocide?	¿Ha participado en un acto de genocidio?

	*ee soo **kohn**-yoo-hay …*
6. And your spouse …	Y su cónyuge …[12]

	*ee ahl-**goo**-noh day soos **ee**-hohs …*
7. And any of your children …	Y alguno de sus hijos …[12]

Notes

[1] Remember you can always ask that the caller spell the name, etc. by incorporating communication strategies and referencing *Chapter 12 — The Basics — I. The Alphabet*. Also, whenever possible during face-to-face encounters, allow the person with whom you are speaking to write down as much information for you.

[2] Reference *Chapter 12 — The Basics — II. Numbers*. Also, whenever possible during face-to-face encounters, allow the person with whom you are speaking to write down as much information for you as this will greatly facilitate communication and make utilizing numbers much easier since digits are represented the same in both languages.

[3] Anticipated responses have been included to assist you in comprehension as well as repeating responses back to a person should you wish to verify information you have heard. When you reach question 4 of the section *V. Additional Family Information*, the anticipated formulaic responses for a period or duration of time have been provided only once. However, it should be understood they apply to each family member listed for this questions when asking the question *¿Cuánto tiempo hace que se le condedió esta condición migratoria?*

[4] The symbol @ used in email addresses is called *arroba (ah-rroh-bah)* in Spanish.

[5] Use *-lo* when talking to or about a male; use *-la* when talking to or about a female.

[6] Reference *Chapter 13 — Telling Time the Easy Way — Days of the Week and Month of the Year*.

[7] Please see the APPENDIX for a list of countries and corresponding nationalities.

[8] Use the *-o* ending when talking to or about a *male*; use the *-a* ending when talking to or about a *female*.

[9] These two terms reference a person who is paid to smuggle people into a country illegally. Many times, the illegal immigrant or a family member of that illegal pays a hefty sum of money for this service which is not only illegal but dangerous as well.

[10] *Colegio* is another way to convey *preparatoria*. Be aware that *colegio* is NEVER used to mean *college*.

[11] Use *el beneficiario* when speaking to or about a *male*; use *la beneficiaria* when speaking to or about a *female*.

[12] To ask the same questions from **VI. Immigration History — 5**, use each of these phrases to preface your questions. Remember that in Spanish, the syntax (sentence structure) for *you (singular and formal)*, *he/him*, and *she/her* are grammatically identical. Therefore, you only need to verbalize clarification when changing or clarifying the person who is the focus of the question or phrase. It is not necessary to do so before EVERY question or phrase once you establish the context of the conversation.

Practical Activities

A) How long have you ...? (¿Cuánto tiempo hace que ...? / ¿Por cuánto tiempo ha ...?)

Part I—Instructions: There are quite a few questions in this chapter that request a period or duration of time as an anticipated response. This concept is expressed in a very formulaic fashion in Spanish and, with a little practice, can become exceptionally easy to identify and use. To get you accustomed to using these formulaic expressions, review this chapter and copy below two different phrases that begin with *¿Cuánto tiempo hace que ...* and two that begin with *¿Por cuánto tiempo ha....*

1. *¿Cuánto tiempo hace que* _____ ?

2. *¿Cuánto tiempo hace que* _____ ?

3. *¿Por cuánto tiempo ha* _____ ?

4. *¿Por cuánto tiempo ha* _____ ?

Next, study the formulaic anticipated response patterns that have been copied from the chapter. You may want to consult *Chapter 12—The Basics—II. Numbers* to help you.

one day **ah**-say oon **dee**-ah hace un día	one month **ah**-say oon mays hace un mes
(#) days **ah**-say (#) **dee**-ahs hace (#) días	(#) months **ah**-say (#) **may**-says hace (#) meses
one week **ah**-say **oo**-nah say-**mah**-nah hace una semana	one year **ah**-say oon **ahn**-yoh hace un año
(#) weeks **ah**-say (#) say-**mah**-nahs hace (#) semanas	(#) years **ah**-say (#) **ahn**-yohs hace (#) años

Part II—Instructions: Practice creating the following *anticipated responses* using the formulas you have just studied. You may do this aloud or write them down in the space provided. When reading this aloud, you may connect the last two items with the Spanish word *y (ee)*.
For example: *Hace 13 años, 9 meses y 3 semanas.*

1. 3 months / 1 day

_____.

2. 4 years / 6 months

_____.

3. 5 years / 1 week / 7 days

_____.

4. 1 year / 8 months / 2 weeks / 6 days

_____.

Lastly, form groups of two and designate one person A and the other B. Using the questions you completed in *Part I,* have person A ask his/her first question to which person B uses anticipated response number 1 provided above as the answer. B then asks A his/her first question from *Part I* to which A uses anticipated response number 1 again as the answer. Move onto question number 2, have both A and B repeat this process, both using anticipated response number 2 as the answer for both questions. Continue in this manner until all four questions have been asked and each anticipated response has been used twice. The purpose of using the same anticipated response as the answer for each pair of questions is to assist the learner in becoming accustomed to these examples to further assist them when formulating their own responses or comprehending those of a Spanish speaker.

Follow-up: Complete the following formulas with random but logical numbers.

1. _____ year(s) / _____ day(s)

2. _____ month(s) / _____ week(s) / _____ day(s)

3. _____ year(s) / _____ month(s) / _____ week(s)

4. _____ week(s) / _____ day(s)

Trade books with your partner. Then, say and/or write the four responses in Spanish he/she has created for numbers 1–4 above. When you are ready, say the four responses aloud to one another, peer correcting each other and making necessary changes as you go.

B) Los dos de Uds. (The two of you)

Part I—Instructions: In addition to asking a person directly for information—meaning the *you/your* forms—one may also need to ask information regarding a spouse—or the *he/him* or *she/her* forms. This activity will help you become more adept at handling such situations. The table below contains the information you will need to collect (12 pieces of information in all) from not only the client but also about the client's spouse. In order to avoid any confusion for the parties involved, ALWAYS complete the series of questions that deal directly with the client BEFORE moving on to any that relate to the client's spouse. Also, remember you have learned phrases to help you avoid such problems by clarifying with a simple expression such as those found in *Chapter 2—Collecting Basic Information In Person and By Phone—I. Personal Data.* In preparation for collecting the requisite information below, you may want to mark the appropriate questions in the chapter and/or write them out on a separate sheet of paper.

Ud.	su cónyuge
1. U.S. address	7. place of birth
2. foreign address	8. immigration status
3. home phone number	9. date of entry into the U.S.
4. email address	10. method of entry into the U.S.
5. communication preference	11. employment
6. date of birth	12. education

Part II—Instructions: Working with a partner, practice BOTH sets of questions you have just created as if one of you were the interviewer (legal professional) and the other, the interviewee (client). Make sure to indicate that you are first obtaining information from the client about the client. When you have finished the first set of interview questions, clarify that you now need to obtain information from the client about his/her spouse. Once one person has finished a complete interview regarding client and client's spouse, switch roles. Keep in mind, the client (interviewee) WILL SPEAK ONLY IN SPANISH AS WELL, utilizing the text to assist in the composition of responses and short answers.

Follow-up: Have one or two pairs present their interviews to the class. The members of the class, with no text or notes, will attempt to write down in English as much information as they can understand based on the dialogue to which they are listening. After each presentation, have the presenting pair ask questions from the interview and call on random classmates to respond according to what they have noted. The presenting pair will provide peer correction for the class.

C) Por favor, haga una lista ... (Please, make a list ...)

Instructions: In this chapter, you will notice requests for a client to create lists to assist you in obtaining information. This is an important communication strategy since it limits your oral production as a non-native speaker and allows the client the luxury of writing out this information saving both of you time and potential frustration. To facilitate this process, however, you may want to provide the client with a fill-in-the-blank table that will expedite this process. In this activity, you will create a sample table which you will ask a client to complete.

Reference *Section II—Current Employment Information and Employment History, question 6* of this chapter. Look at the English phrase first, notice you are requesting **five** pieces of information. Write each piece of information here below in ENGLISH in the FIRST blank provided.

1. _____ / _____
2. _____ / _____
3. _____ / _____
4. _____ / _____
5. _____ / _____

Next, read and study the corresponding SPANISH phrase. The information in the Spanish phrase appears in the same order as it is found in the ENGLISH phrase. Write the SPANISH version for each piece of information beside of its corresponding ENGLISH version above. Use punctuation marks and easily recognizable words to help you discern which SPANISH words are the ENGLISH translations. You may also choose to use an online bilingual dictionary to assist you.

Once you have completed the above assignment, create a blank, two-column by five-row table on a clean sheet of paper. Number each row on the left-hand side with numbers 1–5 and write ONLY the corresponding SPANISH words and/or phrases beside each number, leaving the column/rows on the right-hand side blank. Understand that if this were actually going to be given to a client, you would obviously want to create this table with a computer. This way, aside from being much more professional, you could begin to build a bank of tables labeled accordingly that could be printed off and used each time you needed to ask a new Spanish-speaking client for the same information.

Finally, trade tables with a classmate and without looking at the text, fill out the table by providing the requested information which may be real or fictitious. Once you have completed the table, return it to your classmate who will check to ensure all information requested has been provided and the table correctly completed. For example, to make sure that the information on the table given by the client for number one corresponds to your number one, review the first part of this activity in which you filled out both ENGLISH and SPANISH meanings for the pieces of information being requested. In this case, number one was **Employer's Name / el nombre del empleador**. Therefore, the first piece of information should state the employer's name.

Use this method when you come across such requests for creating any list, not only in this chapter, but in other future chapters as well. By first analyzing your request for the creation of a list, identifying in both SPANISH and ENGLISH the pieces of information you wish to obtain and placing them in a table format, the gathering of data will be much easier to manage.

D) Cyber-Investigation

To declare that immigrants have no place in the United States is an absurd and ignorant remark. As we are all aware, our country is built upon immigration. Aside from native Americans, all others, be it ourselves or our ancestors, were immigrants that were motivated to come to this country for a variety of reasons. Therefore, would it not be the case that Hispanics that have recently immigrated or attempt to immigrate into the U.S. do so for many of the same reasons that we or our ancestors once did? With this said, use the internet to research and discover what are the top five reasons Hispanics may decide to immigrate into the U.S. Next, search for a demographic breakdown of Hispanic immigrants that come into the U.S. on an annual basis. List the top five Spanish-speaking nationalities that make up this immigrant population. Find a description of the socio-economic backgrounds of these people as well as other issues such as their level of education, their professions in their home country and their average age—for both males and females. Do you notice any trends in which more males than females comprise the immigrant population? What might the reasons for this trend be? Find additional information that supports your findings. Summarize your research below.

Chapter 6

Personal Injuries

Before You Begin

A topic that greatly impacts the Hispanic community is the number of illegal Hispanic aliens involved in serious and/or fatal vehicular accidents each year. Nationwide, law enforcement reports that it commonly encounters illegals who are driving without a license, operating a vehicle belonging to a third or unknown party, operating a vehicle with false tags and most notably, driving without the requisite insurance for the vehicle. The fact that the majority of illegals do not speak or read English only serves to exacerbate these issues. Additionally, driving under the influence of alcohol occurs at a rate six times higher within the Hispanic population than in any other. Unfortunately, such reports perpetuate a tendency in the U.S. to villanize a population based on the sensationalized actions of a few. In the case of Hispanics, the controversial topic of illegal immigration has also resulted in Hispanics, including Hispanic-Americans, being targeted for discrimination, harassment and hate crimes.

I. General Questions

*pray-**goon**-tahs hay-nay-**rah**-lays*
Preguntas generales

English	Pronunciation & Spanish
1. Are you calling on behalf of yourself or someone else?	*yah-mah day **pahr**-tay day see **mees**-moh/mah oh day **oh**-trah payr-**soh**-nah?* ¿Llama de parte de sí mismo/a o de otra persona?[1]
Myself.	*mee **mees**-moh/mah.* Mí mismo/a.[1]
Someone else.	***oh**-trah payr-**soh**-nah.* Otra persona.
2. What is ...	*koo^ahl ays ...* ¿Cuál es ...
your name?	*ayl **nohm**-bray day oos-**tayd**?* el nombre de Ud.?[2]
the person's name?	*ayl **nohm**-bray day lah payr-**soh**-nah?* el nombre de la persona?[2]

3. Will you spell that for me (slowly) please?

*may loh day-lay-**tray**-ah (layn-tah-**mayn**-tay) pohr fah-**bohr**?*
¿Me lo deletrea (lentamente) por favor?[2]

4. Please respond with only "yes" or "no" to the following questions:

*pohr fah-**bohr** rrays-**pohn**-dah kohn **soh**-loh <see> oh <noh> ah lahs see-**ghee^ayn**-tays pray-**goon**-tahs:*
Por favor, responda con sólo <sí> o <no> a las siguientes preguntas:

5. Are the injuries related to …

*lahs lay-**see^oh**-nays **tee^ay**-nayn kay bayr kohn …*
¿Las lesiones tienen que ver con …

     an automobile accident?

*oon ahk-see-**dayn**-tay day **ah^oo**-toh?*
un accidente de auto?

     a product?

*ahl-**goon** proh-**dook**-toh?*
algún producto?

     medical malpractice?

*lah nay-glay-**hayn**-see^ah **may**-dee-kah?*
la negligencia médica?

     slip and fall?

*oon rrays-bah-**lohn** ee kah-**ee**-dah?*
un resbalón y caída?

6. When did the incident happen?

***koo^ahn**-doh **oo**-boh ayl een-see-**dayn**-tay?*
¿Cuándo hubo el incidente?[3, 4]

7. In reference to …

*rray-fay-**rayn**-tay ah …*
Referente a … [5]

     you …

*oos-**tayd** …*
Ud.…

     him …

ayl …
él …

     her …

***ay**-yah …*
ella …

     [insert name of person] …

8. Now, I'm going to ask you for some personal information:

*ah-**oh**-rah lay boh^ee ah pay-**deer oo**-nohs **dah**-tohs payr-soh-**nah**-lays:*
Ahora, le voy a pedir unos datos personales:

9. What is your date of birth?

*koo^ahl ays soo **fay**-chah day nah-see-**mee^ayn**-toh?*
¿Cuál es su fecha de nacimiento?[2, 3]

10. What is your driver's license number and what U.S. state is it from?

*koo^ahl ays soo **noo**-may-roh day lee-**sahn**-see^ah day kohn-doo-**seer** ee day kay ays-**tah**-doh ays-tah-doh-oo-nee-**dayn**-say ays soo lee-**sayn**-see^ah?*
¿Cuál es su número de licencia de conducir y de qué estado estadounidense es su licencia?[2, 3]

11. What is your home address?

*koo^ahl ays soo dee-rayk-**see^ohn** doh-mee-see-**lee^ah**-ree^ah?*
¿Cuál es su dirección domiciliaria?[2, 3]

Are your home address and mailing address the same?	*sohn lahs **mees**-mahs soo dee-rayk-**see^ohn** doh-mee-cee-**lee^ah**-ree^ah ee soo dee-rayk-**see^ohn** pohs-**tahl**?* ¿Son las mismas su dirección domiciliaria y su dirección postal?
What is your mailing address?	*koo^ahl ays soo dee-rayk-**see^ohn** pohs-**tahl**?* ¿Cuál es su dirección postal?[2, 3]

12. Are you employed?	*tee^**ay**-nay trah-**bah**-hoh ahk-too^ahl-**mayn**-tay?* ¿Tiene trabajo actualmente?
Where?	***dohn**-day trah-**bah**-hah?* ¿Dónde trabaja?[2]
What is the name of your employer?	*koo^ahl ays ayl **nohm**-bray day soo aym-play-ah-**dohr**?* ¿Cuál es el nombre de su empleador?[2]
What position do you hold?	*koo^ahl ays ayl **tee**-too-loh dayl **poo^ays**-toh kay oh-**koo**-pah?* ¿Cuál es el título del puesto que ocupa?[2]
Is that full-time or part-time?	*ays day **tee^aym**-poh kohm-**play**-toh oh pahr-**see^ahl**?* ¿Es de tiempo completo o parcial?
How many hours a week do you work approximately?	*ah-prohk-see-mah-dah-**mayn**-tay, **koo^ahn**-tahs **oh**-rahs trah-**bah**-hah ah lah say-**mah**-nah?* Aproximadamente, ¿cuántas horas trabaja a la semana?[3]
What is your salary?	*koo^ahl ays soo **soo^ayl**-doh?* ¿Cuál es su sueldo?[3]
What is your hourly wage?	*koo^**ahn**-toh **gah**-nah pohr **oh**-rah?* ¿Cuánto gana por hora?[3]
Did you miss any time from work as a result of the incident?	*payr-**dee^oh tee^aym**-poh ayn ayl trah-**bah**-hoh **koh**-moh rray-sool-**tah**-doh dayl een-see-**dayn**-tay?* ¿Perdió tiempo en el trabajo como resultado del incidente?
How much time?	*koo^**ahn**-toh **tee^aym**-poh payr-**dee^oh**?* ¿Cuánto tiempo perdió?[3]

13. Do you have medical insurance?	*tee^**ay**-nay say-**goo**-roh **may**-dee-koh?* ¿Tiene seguro médico?
What is the name of the insurer?	***koh**-moh say **yah**-mah soo proh-bay-ay-**dohr** day say-**goo**-roh **may**-dee-koh?* ¿Cómo se llama su proveedor de seguro médico?[2]
What is your policy number?	*koo^ahl ays ayl **noo**-may-roh day soo **poh**-lee-sah?* ¿Cuál es el número de su póliza?[3]

14. Are you married?	*ays-**tah** kah-**sah**-doh/dah?* ¿Está casado/a?[1]
What is the name of your spouse?	***koh**-moh say **yah**-mah soo **kohn**-yoo-hay?* ¿Cómo se llama su cónyuge?[2]

15. Do you have any children?

tee^ay-nay ee-hohs?
¿Tiene hijos?

How many?

koo^ayn-tohs?
¿Cuántos?[3]

What is the age of each one?

koo^ahl ays lah ay-dahd day kah-dah oo-noh?
¿Cuál es la edad de cada uno?[3]

---

16. Have either your spouse or your children been affected by your injuries?

ahn see-doh ah-fayk-tah-dohs soo kohn-yoo-hay oh soos ee-hohs pohr soos lay-see^oh-nays?
¿Han sido afectados su cónyuge o sus hijos por sus lesiones?

Have they taken on certain chores or helped around the house following the accident?

say ahn ayn-kahr-gah-doh day see^ayr-tahs tah-ray-ahs doh-may-stee-kahs oh ahn ah^ee-yoo-dah-doh ayn kah-sah days-day ayl ahk-see-dayn-tay?
¿Se han encargado de ciertas tareas domésticas o han ayudado en casa desde el accidente?

Could you describe to someone (in Spanish) how they have done that?

poh-dree-ah kohn-tahr-lay ah ahl-ghee^ayn (ayn ays-pahn-yohl) loh kay ahn ay-choh pah-rah ah^ee-yoo-dahr?
¿Podría contarle a alguien (en español) lo que han hecho para ayudar?

Can you tell me for about how long they have been helping since the accident?

poo^ay-day day-seer-may ah-prohk-see-mah-dah-mayn-tay koo^ahn-toh tee^aym-poh yay-bahn ay-yohs ah^ee-yoo-dahn-doh ayn kah-sah days-day ayl ahk-see-dayn-tay?
¿Puede decirme aproximadamente cuánto tiempo llevan ellos ayudando en casa desde el accidente?

one day

oon dee-ah
un día[8]

(#) days

(#) dee-ahs
(#) días[8]

one week

oo-nah say-mah-nah
una semana[8]

(#) weeks

(#) say-mah-nahs
(#) semanas[8]

one month

oon mays
un mes[8]

(#) months

(#) may-says
(#) meses[8]

one year

oon ahn-yoh
un año[8]

(#) years

(#) ahn-yohs
(#) años[8]

II. Automobile Accidents

*ahk-see-**dyan**-tays day **ah^oo**-toh*
Accidentes de auto

English	Pronunciation & Spanish
1. Were you involved in an automobile accident?	*ays-**too**-boh een-boh-loo-**krah**-doh/dah ayn oon ahk-see-**dayn**-tay day **ah^oo**-tohs?* ¿Estuvo involucrado/a en un accidente de autos?[1]
2. Were you the driver or a passenger?	***ay**-rah choh-**fayr** oh pah-sah-**hay**-roh/rah?* ¿Era chofer o pasajero/a?[1]
3. Do you have automobile insurance?	***tee^ay**-nay say-**goo**-roh day **ah^oo**-toh?* ¿Tiene seguro de auto?
What is the name of your insurer?	***koh**-moh say **yah**-mah soo proh-bay-ay-**dohr** day say-**goo**-roh day **ah^oo**-toh?* ¿Cómo se llama su proveedor de seguro de auto?[2]
What is your policy number?	*koo^ahl ays ayl **noo**-may-roh day soo **poh**-lee-sah?* ¿Cuál es el número de su póliza?[3]
4. What type of vehicle you were in?	*ayn kay **klah**-say day bay-**ee**-koo-loh ays-**tah**-bah?* ¿En qué clase de vehículo estaba?[2]
What was the ... of the vehicle?	*koo^ahl **ay**-rah ... dayl bay-**ee**-koo-loh?* ¿Cuál era ... del vehículo?
the make	*lah **mahr**-kah* la marca
the model	*ayl moh-**day**-loh* el modelo
the year	*ayl **ahn**-yoh day fah-bree-kah-**see^ohn*** el año de fabricación
5. Are you the owner of the vehicle?	*ays ayl **doo^ayn**-yoh/lah **doo^ayn**-yah dayl bay-**ee**-koo-loh?* ¿Es el dueño/la dueña del vehículo?[6]
Who is?	*kee^ayn ays?* ¿Quién es?[2]
What is your relationship with that person?	*koo^ahl ays soo pah-rayn-**tays**-koh kohn **ay**-sah payr-**soh**-nah?* ¿Cuál es su parentesco con esa persona?[2]
friend?	*ah-**mee**-goh/gah?* amigo/a?[1]
brother?	*ayr-**mah**-noh?* hermano?
sister?	*ayr-**mah**-nah?* hermana?

uncle?	*tee-oh?* tío?
aunt?	*tee-ah?* tía?
mother?	*mah-dray?* madre?
father?	*pah-dray?* padre?
boyfriend?	*noh-bee^oh?* novio?
girlfriend?	*noh-bee^ah?* novia?
cousin?	*pree-moh/mah?* primo/prima?[1]
other (relative)?	*oh-troh (pah-rayn-tays-koh fah-mee-lee^ahr)?* otro (parentesco familiar)?[2]

6. *(If borrowing the vehicle)* Did you have permission to borrow the vehicle?	*tay-nee-ah payr-mee-soh pah-rah oo-sahr ayl bay-ee-koo-loh?* ¿Tenía permiso para usar el vehículo?
7. What date did the accident occur?	*ayn kay fay-chah oo-boh ayl ahk-see-dayn-tay?* ¿En qué fecha hubo el accidente?[3, 4]
8. At approximately what time?	*a kay oh-rah mahs oh may-nohs?* ¿A qué hora más o menos?[7]
9. Where did the accident occur?	*dohn-day oo-boh ayl ahk-see-dayn-tay?* ¿Dónde hubo el accidente?[2]
10. Do you know in what city / county that is?	*sah-bay ayn kay see^oo-dahd / kohn-dah-doh ays-tah?* ¿Sabe en qué ciudad / condado está?[2]
Will you write that information here for me, please?	*may ays-kree-bay ay-sah een-fohr-mah-see^ohn ah-kee pohr fah-bohr?* ¿Me escribe esa información aquí, por favor?
11. Do you have the name of the other driver who was involved in the accident?	*tee^ay-nay ayl nohm-bray dayl oh-troh choh-fayr een-boh-loo-krah-doh ayn ayl ahk-see-dayn-tay?* ¿Tiene el nombre del otro chofer involucrado en el accidente?
What is that person's name?	*koh-moh say yah-mah ay-sah payr-soh-nah?* ¿Cómo se llama esa persona?[2]

12. Did you obtain his/her insurance information or address at the accident site?	*ohb-**too**-boh soo een-fohr-mah-**see^ohn** day say-**goo**-roh day **ah^oo**-toh oh soo dee-rayk-**see^ohn** ayn ayl **see**-tee^oh dayl ahk-see-**dayn**-tay?* ¿Obtuvo su información de seguro de auto o su dirección en el sitio del accidente?
13. Did the police respond?	*ah-koo-**dee^oh** ayl **see**-tee^oh lah poh-lee-**see**-ah?* ¿Acudió al sitio la policía?
14. Did the police cite anyone for causing the accident?	*mool-**toh** lah poh-lee-**see**-ah ah **ahl**-ghee^ayn pohr ah-**bayr** kah^oh-**sah**-doh ayl ahk-see-**dayn**-tay?* ¿Multó la policía a alguien por haber causado el accidente?
15. Do you think it was something you did or the other driver did that was the cause of the accident?	***kray**-ay kay foo^ay **ahl**-goh kay **ee**-soh oh kay ayl **oh**-troh choh-**fayr ee**-soh kay foo^ay lah **kah^oo**-sah dayl ahk-see-**dayn**-tay?* ¿Cree que fue algo que hizo o que el otro chofer hizo que fue la causa del accidente?
16. Did you notice anything funny or problematic about the vehicle you were in shortly before the accident?	*ohb-sayr-**boh ahl**-goh foo^**ay**-rah day loh nohr-**mahl** oh proh-blay-**mah**-tee-koh **soh**-bray ayl bay-**ee**-koo-loh ayn ayl koo^ahl ays-**tah**-bah **poh**-koh **ahn**-tays dayl ahk-see-**dayn**-tay?* ¿Observó algo fuera de lo normal o problemático sobre el vehículo en el cual estaba poco antes del accidente?
Any problems with the brakes?	*proh-**blay**-mahs kohn lohs **fray**-nohs?* ¿Problemas con los frenos?
Any mechanical problems?	*proh-**blay**-mahs may-**kah**-nee-kos?* ¿Problemas mecánicos?
17. How fast was the vehicle you were in traveling?	*ah kay bay-loh-see-**dahd ee**-bah ayl **ah^oo**-toh ayn ayl koo^ahl ays-**tah**-bah?* ¿A qué velocidad iba el auto en el cual estaba?
(#) miles an hour.	*ah (#) **mee**-yahs pohr **oh**-rah.* A (#) millas por hora.[3, 8]
(#) kilometers an hour.	*ah (#) kee-**loh**-may-trohs pohr **oh**-rah.* A (#) kilómetros por hora.[3, 8]
18. Do you have any idea about the speed …	***tee^ay**-nay ahl-**goo**-nah ee-**day**-ah **soh**-bray lah bay-loh-see-**dahd** …* ¿Tiene alguna idea sobre la velocidad …
of the other vehicle involved?	*dayl **oh**-troh bay-**ee**-koo-loh een-boh-loo-**krah**-doh?* del otro vehículo involucrado?[3]
of the other vehicles involved?	*day lohs **oh**-trohs bay-**ee**-koo-lohs en-boh-loo-**krah**-dohs?* de los otros vehículos involucrados?[3]
19. Did the police give you any number associated with the file / police report?	*lay dee^oh lah poh-lee-**see**-ah oon **noo**-may-roh ah-soh-**see^ah**-doh kohn ayl ayk-spay-**dee^ayn**-tay / een-fohr-may poh-lee-**see^ahl**?* ¿Le dio la policía un número asociado con el expediente / informe policial?

20. Do you have a copy of the police report?

*tee^ay-nay **oo**-nah **koh**-pee^ah dayl een-**fohr**-may poh-lee-**see^ahl**?*
¿Tiene una copia del informe policial?

---

21. Do you have a police report that you could fax me or provide to our office?

*tee^ay-nay oon een-**fohr**-may poh-lee-**see^ahl** kay may poh-**dree**-ah mahn-**dahr** pohr fahks oh trah-**ayr** ah **noo^ays**-troh boo-**fay**-tay?*
¿Tiene un informe policial que me podría mandar por FAX o traer a nuestro bufete?

We would like to review that immediately if at all possible.

*kee-see-**ay**-rah-mohs rray-bee-**sahr**-loh **koo^ahn**-toh **ahn**-tays see ays poh-**see**-blay.*
Quisiéramos revisarlo cuanto antes si es posible.

---

22. Were you injured in the accident?

*say lay-see^oh-**noh** ayn ayl ahk-see-**dayn**-tay?*
¿Se lesionó en el accidente?

Did you require medical attention at the accident scene?

*rray-see-**bee^oh** ah-tayn-**see^ohn** may-dee-kah ayn ayl **see**-tee^oh dayl ahk-see-**dayn**-tay?*
¿Recibió atención médica en el sitio del accidente?

---

23. Was anyone else in the car injured and treated at the hospital?

*ah-**bee**-ah ahl-**ghee^ayn** mahs ayn ayl **kah**-rroh kay say lahs-tee-**moh** ee foo^ay trah-**tah**-doh ayn ayl ohs-pee-**tahl**?*
¿Había alguien más en el carro que se lastimó y fue tratado en el hospital?[9, 5]

---

24. Did an ambulance or EMT respond?

*ah-koo-**dee^oh** oo-nah ahm-boo-**lahn**-see^ah oh **tayk**-nee-kohs day oor-**hayn**-see^ahs **may**-dee-kahs?*
¿Acudió una ambulancia o técnicos de urgencias médicas?

---

25. Were you taken to the hospital?

*loh/lah trahns-pohr-**tah**-rohn ahl ohs-pee-**tahl**?*
¿Lo/la transportaron al hospital?[10]

To which hospital were you taken?

*ah kay ohs-pee-**tahl** loh/lah trahns-pohr-**tah**-rohn?*
¿A qué hospital lo/la transportaron?[10]

Who took you?

*kee^ayn loh/lah trahns-pohr-**toh**?*
¿Quién lo/la transportó?[10]

Were you admitted overnight?

*too-boh kay pah-**sahr** lah **noh**-chay een-tayr-**nah**-doh/dah?*
¿Tuvo que pasar la noche internado/a?[6]

---

26. I'm going to ask you several questions regarding the injuries you suffered and the treatment you received at the hospital:

*boh^ee ah ah-**sayr**-lay **bah**-ree^ahs pray-**goon**-tahs **soh**-bray ayl trah-tah-**mee^ayn**-toh kay ray-see-**bee^oh** ayn ayl ohs-pee-**tahl** ee lahs lay-**see^oh**-nays kay soo-**free^oh**:*
Voy a hacerle varias preguntas sobre el tratamiento que recibió en el hospital y las lesiones que sufrió:

---

27. Did you suffer any broken bones?

*soo-**free^oh** ahl-**goo**-nohs **oo^ay**-sohs **roh**-tohs?*
¿Sufrió algunos huesos rotos?

What was broken?

*kay say lay rrohm-**pee^oh**?*
¿Qué se le rompió?[2, 11]

28. Did you suffer any lacerations?

*soo-free-**oh** ahl-**goo**-nahs lah-say-rah-**see^oh**-nays?*
¿Sufrió algunas laceraciones?

How many?

*koo^**ahn**-tahs?*
¿Cuántas?[3]

Can you point out where on your body?

*may **poo^ay**-day sayn-yah-**lahr dohn**-day en soo **koo^ayr**-poh?*
¿Me puede señalar dónde en su cuerpo?[11]

29. Did you require stitches?

*lay poo-**see^ay**-rohn **poon**-tohs?*
¿Le pusieron puntos?

Where?

dohn-day?
¿Dónde?[11]

30. Did you undergo …

*lay ee-**see^ay**-rohn …*
¿Le hicieron …

any x-rays?

*oo-nah rrah-dee^oh-grah-**fee**-ah?*
una radiografía?

CT scans?

*oo-nah toh-moh-grah-**fee**-ah kohm-poo-tay-ree-**sah**-dah?*
una tomografía computerizada?

MRIs?

*oo-nah ee-**mah**-hayn day rray-soh-**nahn**-see^ah mahg-**nay**-tee-kah?*
una imagen de resonancia magnética?

31. Were you given any medication at the hospital?

*lay ahd-mee-nees-**trah**-rohn ahl-**goon** may-dee-kah-**mayn**-toh ayn ayl ohs-pee-**tahl**?*
¿Le administraron algún medicamento en el hospital?

What is the name of the medication, if you know it?

*koo^ahl ays ayl **nohm**-bray dayl may-dee-kah-**mayn**-toh see loh **sah**-bay?*
¿Cuál es el nombre del medicamento si lo sabe?[2]

32. Were you admitted to the hospital following the emergency room visit or did they release you?

*loh/lah een-tayr-**nah**-rohn ayn ayl ohs-pee-**tahl** days-**poo^ays** day eer ah lah **sah**-lah day oor-**hayn**-see^ahs oh lay **dee^ay**-rohn day **ahl**-tah?*
¿Lo/la internaron en el hospital después de ir a la sala de urgencias o le dieron de alta?[10]

How long were you in the hospital after being admitted?

*pohr **koo^ayn**-toh **tee^aym**-poh ays-**too**-boh ayn ayl ohs-pee-**tahl** day-**spoo^ays** day sayr een-tayr-**nah**-doh/dah?*
¿Por cuánto tiempo estuvo en el hospital después de ser internado/a?[1, 3]

Did you undergo any other treatments or surgeries?

*say lay soh-may-**tee^oh** ah **oh**-trohs trah-tah-**mee^ayn**-tohs **may**-dee-kohs oh see-roo-**hee**-ahs?*
¿Se le sometió a otros tratamientos o cirugías?

Please make a list to give us of all treatments and/or surgeries you underwent.

*pohr fah-**bohr**, **ah**-gah **oo**-nah **lees**-tah **pah**-rah ayn-tray-**gahr**-nohs day **toh**-dohs lohs trah-tah-**mee^ayn**-tohs ee/oh see-roo-**gee**-ahs ah lohs kay loh/lah soh-may-**tee^ay**-rohn.*
Por favor, haga una lista para entregarnos de todos los tratamientos y/o cirugías a los que lo/la sometieron.[10]

33. When were you released?	*koo^ayn-doh lay **dee^ay**-rohn day **ahl**-tah?* ¿Cuándo le dieron de alta?[3, 4]
34. Did they give you any orders at discharge?	*lay **dee^ay**-rohn ahl-**goo**-nah **ohr**-dayn day **ahl**-tah?* ¿Le dieron alguna orden de alta?
Do you have a copy of those discharge orders?	*tee^ay-nay oo-nah **koh**-pee^ah day lah **ohr**-dayn day **ahl**-tah?* ¿Tiene una copia de la orden de alta?
35. Have you followed up with a physician since being released?	*oon **may**-dee-koh loh/lah ah ayk-sah-mee-**nah**-doh **days**-day kay lay **dee^ay**-rohn day **ahl**-tah?* ¿Un médico lo/la ha examinado desde que le dieron de alta?[10]
36. When was your last appointment?	*koo^ahn-doh foo^ay soo **ool**-tee-mah **see**-tah?* ¿Cuándo fue su última cita?[4]
37. When is your next appointment?	*koo^ayn-doh ays soo **prohk**-see-mah **see**-tah?* ¿Cuándo es su próxima cita?[4]
38. Can you provide us with a copy of the diagnosis?	*poo^ay-day proh-pohr-see^oh-**nahr**-nohs oo-nah **koh**-pee^ah dayl dee^ahg-**nohs**-tee-koh?* ¿Puede proporcionarnos una copia del diagnóstico?
39. If there was no trip to the hospital, have you seen a physician or other health care provider regarding your complaints / injuries?	*see noh nay-say-see-**tah**-bah eer ahl ohs-pee-**tahl**, ah **bee**-stoh ah oon **may**-dee-koh oo **oh**-troh proh-say-see^oh-**nahl** day sayr-bee-see^ohs day sah-**lood** rray-fay-**rahn**-tay ah soos doh-**layn**-see^ahs / lay-**see^oh**-nays?* Si no necesitaba ir al hospital, ¿ha visto a un médico u otro profesional de servicios de salud referente a sus dolencias / lesiones?
Who did you see?	*ah kee^ayn bee^oh?* ¿A quién vio?[12]
When was that?	*koo^ahn-doh foo^ay?* ¿Cuándo fue?[3, 4]
For what did they treat you?	*pah-rah kay loh/lah trah-**tah**-rohn?* ¿Para qué lo/la trataron?[10, 11]
Did they prescribe any medications for you to take?	*lay rray-say-**tah**-rohn ahl-**goon** may-dee-kah-**mayn**-toh?* ¿Le recetaron algún medicamento?
Did they prescribe any therapy?	*lay rray-say-**tah**-rohn tay-**rah**-pee^ah?* ¿Le recetaron terapia?[12]
What was that?	*koo^ahl foo^ay?* ¿Cuál fue?[11, 12]
40. Are you still following up for treatment and care for …	*ah-**oon** ays-**tah** rray-see-**bee^ayn**-doh trah-tah-**mee^ayn**-toh ee koo^ee-**dah**-doh may-dee-koh **pah**-rah …* ¿Aún está recibiendo tratamiento y cuidado médico para …

| this problem? | *ays*-tay proh-***blay***-mah?
este problema? |
| these problems? | *ays*-tohs proh-***blay***-mahs?
estos problemas? |

41. If your car was involved in the accident, have you spoken with the other driver's insurance carrier yet?

*see soo **kah**-rroh ays-**too**-boh een-boh-loo-**krah**-doh ayn ayl ahk-see-**dayn**-tay, say ah koh-moo-nee-**kah**-doh yah kohn ayl proh-bay-ay-**dohr** day say-**goo**-roh day **ah^oo**-toh dayl **oh**-troh choh-**fayr**?*

Si su carro estuvo involucrado en el accidente, ¿se ha comunicado ya con el proveedor de seguro de auto del otro chofer?

Could you ... what they told you?	*poh-**dree**-ah ... loh kay lay dee-**hay**-rohn?* ¿Podría ... lo que le dijeron?
put in writing	*poh-**nayr** pohr ays-**kree**-toh* poner por escrito
tell someone in Spanish	*day-**seer**-lay ah **ahl**-ghee^ayn ayn ays-pahn-**yohl*** decirle a alguien en español

42. Do you have any idea of the amount of property damage your car may have sustained?

*tee^**ay**-nay ahl-**goo**-nah ee-**day**-ah dayl **mohn**-toh day lohs **dahn**-yohs kay soo **kah**-roh ah soo-**free**-doh?*

¿Tiene alguna idea del monto de los daños que su carro ha sufrido?

Have you gotten any estimates for the repair of the damage?

*ah kohn-say-**ghee**-doh ahl-**goo**-nahs ays-tee-mah-**see^oh**-nays **pah**-rah lah rray-pah-rah-**see^ohn** day lohs **dahn**-yohs?*

¿Ha conseguido algunas estimaciones para la reparación de los daños?

Can you provide us with copies of those estimates?

*nohs **poo^ay**-day proh-pohr-see^oh-**nahr** koh-pee^ahs day **ay**-sahs ays-tee-mah-**see^oh**-nays?*

¿Nos puede proporcionar copias de esas estimaciones?

43. Have you ever been in an accident before?

*ah ays-**tah**-doh een-boh-loo-**krah**-doh/dah ayn oon ahk-see-**dayn**-tay **ahn**-tays?*

¿Ha estado involucrado/a en un accidente antes?[10]

Where?	***dohn**-day?* ¿Dónde?[12]
When?	*koo^**ayn**-doh?* ¿Cuándo?[3, 4]
Did you have any injuries?	*soo-**free^oh** ahl-**goo**-nahs lay-**see^oh**-nays?* ¿Sufrió algunas lesiones?
Was the other driver at fault?	*foo^ay lah **kool**-pah dayl **oh**-troh choh-**fayr**?* ¿Fue la culpa del otro chofer?
Did you sue in that case?	*day-mahn-**doh** ayn **ays**-tay **kah**-soh?* ¿Demandó en ese caso?
Did you settle the case?	*yay-**goh** ah oon ah-**koo^ayr**-doh ayn **ay**-say **kah**-soh?* ¿Llegó a un acuerdo en ese caso?

44. Have you ever been sued?

*ahl-**goo**-nah bays, say lay ah day-mahn-**dah**-doh?*
Alguna vez, ¿se le ha demandado?

Where?

__dohn__-day?
¿Dónde?[12]

Do you have a copy of the complaint?

*tee^**ay**-nay **koh**-pee^ah day lah day-**mahn**-dah?*
¿Tiene copia de la demanda?

Can you provide us with a copy of the complaint?

*nohs **poo^ay**-day proh-pohr-see^oh-**nahr koh**-pee^ah day lah day-**mahn**-dah?*
¿Nos puede proporcionar copia de la demanda?

---

45. Have you ever sued anyone else?

*ahl-**goo**-nah bays, ah day-mahn-**dah**-doh ah **ahl**-ghee^ayn?*
Alguna vez, ¿ha demandado a alguien?

Where?

__dohn__-day?
¿Dónde?[12]

Do you have a copy of the complaint?

*tee^**ay**-nay **koh**-pee^ah day lah day-**mahn**-dah?*
¿Tiene copia de la demanda?

Can you provide us with a copy of the complaint?

*nohs **poo^ay**-day proh-pohr-see^oh-**nahr koh**-pee^ah day lah day-**mahn**-dah?*
¿Nos puede proporcionar copia de la demanda?

---

46. Were there any witnesses to the accident?

*ah-**bee**-ah tays-**tee**-gohs ahl ahk-see-**dayn**-tay?*
¿Había testigos al accidente?

Do you know their names?

*__sah__-bay soos **nohm**-brays?*
¿Sabe sus nombres?

Do you have or did you get the addresses of the witnesses?

*tee^**ay**-nay oh kohn-see-**ghee^oh** lahs dee-rayk-**see^oh**-nays day lohs tays-**tee**-gohs?*
¿Tiene o consiguió las direcciones de los testigos?

Did you speak to them following the accident or at any time prior to talking to me now?

*ah-**bloh** kohn **ay**-yohs days-**poo^ays** dayl ahk-see-**dayn**-tay oh ayn ayn ahl-**goon** moh-**myn**-toh **ahn**-tays day ah-**blahr**-may ah-**oh**-rah?*
¿Habló con ellos después del accidente o en algún momento antes de hablarme ahora?

Could you ... what you spoke about?

*poh-**dree**-ah ... day loh kay ah-**bloh**?*
¿Podría ... de lo que habló?

put in writing

*poh-**nayr** pohr ays-**kree**-toh*
poner por escrito

tell someone in Spanish	*day-**seer**-lay ah **ahl**-ghee^ayn ayn ays-pahn-**yohl*** decirle a alguien en español
47. Did the driver or any other occupant of the other vehicle make any statement to you following the accident about either what happened or what they thought caused the accident?	***loo^ay**-goh dayl ahk-see-**dayn**-tay **mees**-moh, lay koh-mayn-**toh** ayl choh-**fayr** oh koo^ahl-**kee^ayr** oh-troh pah-say-**hay**-roh dayl **oh**-troh bay-**ee**-koo-loh koo^ahl-**kee^ayr** koh-sah **soh**-bray loh kay oh-pee-**nah**-bah ah-**bee**-ah oh-koo-**rree**-doh oh loh kay ah-**bee**-ah proh-boh-**kah**-doh ayl ahk-see-**dayn**-tay?* Luego del accidente mismo, ¿le comentó el chofer o cualquier otro pasajero del otro vehículo cualquier cosa sobre lo que opinaba había ocurrido o lo que había provocado el accidente?
48. Did the driver admit (s)he caused the accident?	*kohn-fay-**soh** ah-**bayr** proh-boh-**kah**-doh ahl ahk-see-**dayn**-tay lah payr-**soh**-nah kay mah-nay-**hah**-bah ayl **oh**-troh bay-ee-koo-loh?* ¿Confesó haber provocado al accidente la persona que manejaba el otro vehículo?
Do you remember exactly what was said?	*rray-**koo^ayr**-dah kohn ayk-sahk-tee-**tood** loh kay say **dee**-hoh?* ¿Recuerda con extactitud lo que se dijo?
Could you ... what was said?	*poh-**dree**-ah ... loh kay say **dee**-hoh?* ¿Podría ... lo que se dijo?
put in writing	*poh-**nayr** pohr ays-**kree**-toh* poner por escrito.
tell someone in Spanish	*day-**seer**-lay ah **ahl**-ghee^ayn ayn ays-pahn-**yohl*** decirle a alguien en español
49. Could you tell that information to someone (in Spanish) if necessary?	*poh-**dree**-ah kohn-**tahr**-lay **ay**-sah een-fohr-mah-**see^ohn** ah **ahl**-ghee^ayn (ayn ays-pahn-**yohl**) see ays nay-say-**sah**-ree^oh?* ¿Podría contarle esa información a alguien (en español) si es necesario?
50. Were there any witnesses to that information?	*ah-**bee**-ah tays-**tee**-gohs day **ay**-sah een-fohr-mah-**see^ohn**?* ¿Había testigos de esa información?
51. Did the other driver tell that same information to the police?	*lay kohn-**toh** lah payr-**soh**-nah kay mah-nay-**hah**-bah ayl **oh**-troh bay-ee-koo-loh **ays**-tah **mees**-mah een-fohr-mah-**see^ohn** ah lah poh-lee-**see**-ah?* ¿Le contó la persona que manejaba el otro vehículo esta misma información a la policía?
52. Do you have any written documentation regarding the accident?	***tee^ay**-nay ahl-**goo**-nah doh-koo-mayn-tah-**see^ohn** ays-**kree**-tah rray-fay-**rayn**-tay ah **ays**-tay ahk-see-**dayn**-tay?* ¿Tiene alguna documentación escrita referente a este accidente?
53. We may need to request medical and billing records from the hospital / providers that treated you.	***poo^ay**-day kay nohs **say**-ah may-nay-**stayr** pay-**deer**-lays soos rray-**hee**-strohs day fahk-too-rah-**see^ohn** ay ees-toh-**ree^ahl may**-dee-koh ah lohs ohs-pee-**tah**-lays / pro-bay-ay-**doh**-rays day-sayr-**bee**-see^ohs day sah-**lood** kay loh/lah trah-**tah**-rohn.* Puede que nos sea menester pedirles sus registros de facturación e historial médico a los hospitales / proveedores de servicios de salud que lo/la trataron.[10]

54. Can your provide us with your signature on an authorization if I give that to you so that we can request those?

*see lay doh^ee oon fohr-moo-**lah**-ree^oh day ah^oo-toh-ree-sah-**see^ohn**, nohs loh **poo^ay**-day feer-**mahr pah**-rah kay poh-**dah**-mohs pay-**deer ay**-sohs doh-koo-**mayn**-tohs?*

¿Si le doy un formulario de autorización, nos lo puede firmar para que podamos pedir esos documentos?[14]

---

55. As to your physical condition prior to the accident, do you have a primary care doctor that you see on a regular basis?

*kohn rrays-**payk**-toh ah soo kohn-dee-**see^ohn fee**-see-kah **pray**-bee^ah ahl ahk-see-**dayn**-tay, **tee^ay**-nay oon **may**-dee-koh day kah-bay-**say**-rah ah kee^ayn bah kohn fray-**koo^ayn**-see^ah?*

Con respecto a su condición física previa al accidente, ¿tiene un médico de cabecera a quién va con frecuencia?

What is the doctor's name?

koh-moh say yah-mah ayl may-dee-koh?

¿Cómo se llama el médico?[12]

What is the address of his/her office?

*koo^ahl ays lah dee-rrayk-**see^ohn** day soo kohn-sool-**toh**-ree^oh?*

¿Cuál es la dirección de su consultorio?[2, 3]

What is the phone number?

*koo^ahl ays soo **noo**-may-roh day tay-**lay**-foh-noh?*

¿Cuál es su número de teléfono?[3]

---

56. Prior to the accident, when was the last time you saw a doctor?

*ahn-tays dayl ahk-see-**dayn**-tay, **koo^ahn**-doh foo^ay lah **ool**-tee-mah bays kay foo^ay ahl **may**-dee-koh?*

Antes del accidente, ¿cuándo fue la última vez que fue al médico?[3]

one day ago

ah-say oon dee-ah

hace un día[8]

(#) days ago

ah-say (#) dee-ahs

hace (#) días[8]

one week ago

ah-say oo-nah say-mah-nah

hace una semana[8]

(#) weeks ago

ah-say (#) say-mah-nahs

hace (#) semanas[8]

one month ago

ah-say oon mays

hace un mes[8]

(#) months ago

ah-say (#) may-says

hace (#) meses[8]

one year ago

ah-say oon ahn-yoh

hace un año[8]

---

57. Can you write the reason for me here, please?

may poo^ay-day ays-kree-beer lah rrah-sohn ah-kee pohr fah-bohr?

¿Me puede escribir la razón aquí por favor?

III. Products Liability

*rrays-pohn-sah-bee-lee-**dahd** pohr lah fah-bree-kah-**see^ohn** day oon proh-**dook**-toh*
Responsabilidad por la fabricación de un producto

English	Pronunciation & Spanish
1. Was the product ...	*ayl proh-**dook**-toh foo^ay ...* ¿El producto fue ...
a piece of machinery?	*ahl-**goon tee**-poh day mah-kee-**nah**-ree^ah?* algún tipo de maquinaria?
an appliance?	*ahl-**goon** ay-layk-troh-doh-**mays**-tee-koh?* algún electrodoméstico?
a tool?	*ahl-**goo**-nah ay-rrah-**mee^ayn**-tah?* alguna herramienta?
a perishable food item?	*ahl-**goon** koh-mays-**tee**-blay pay-ray-say-**day**-roh?* algún comestible perecedero?
a non-perishable food item?	*ahl-**goon** koh-mays-**tee**-blay eem-pay-ray-say-**day**-roh?* algún comestible imperecedero?
a perishable non-food item?	*ahl-**goon** een-koh-mays-**tee**-blay pay-ray-say-**day**-roh?* algún incomestible perecedero?
a non-perishable non-food item?	*ahl-**goon** een-koh-mays-**tee**-blay eem-pay-ray-say-**day**-roh?* algún incomestible imperecedero?
for personal use?	***pah**-rah ayl **oo**-soh payr-soh-**nahl**?* para el uso personal?
for consumer use?	***pah**-rah ayl **oo**-soh dayl kohn-soo-mee-**dohr**?* para el uso del consumidor?
for professional use?	***pah**-rah ayl **oo**-soh proh-fay-**see^oh**-nahl?* para el uso profesional?
2. Do you know the name of the product?	***sah**-bay ayl **nohm**-bray dayl proh-**dook**-toh?* ¿Sabe el nombre del producto?
3. Will you spell that for me (slowly) please?	*may loh day-lay-**tray**-ah (days-**pah**-see^oh) pohr fah-**bohr**?* ¿Me lo deletrea (despacio) por favor?[2]
4. Will you write that for me here?	*may loh ays-**kree**-bay ah-**kee** pohr fah-**bohr**?* ¿Me lo escribe aquí por favor?[2]
5. Can you provide us with a picture or image of the product?	*nohs **poo^ay**-dah proh-pohr-see^oh-**nahr oo**-nah **foh**-toh oh ee-**mah**-hayn dayl proh-**dook**-toh?* ¿Nos puede proporcionar una foto o imagen del producto?
6. How long have you had the product?	***koo^ayn**-toh **tee^aym**-poh **ah**-say kay ah tay-**nee**-doh ayl proh-**dook**-toh?* ¿Cuánto tiempo hace que ha tenido el producto?[3]

one day	*oon **dee**-ah* un día[8]
(#) days	*(#) **dee**-ahs* (#) días[8]
one week	***oo**-nah say-**mah**-nah* una semana[8]
(#) weeks	*(#) say-**mah**-nahs* (#) semanas[8]
one month	*oon mays* un mes[8]
(#) months	*(#) **may**-says* (#) meses[8]
one year	*oon **ahn**-yoh* un año[8]
(#) years	*(#) **ahn**-hoys* (#) años

7. Is there an expiration date on the product?	*ah^ee **oo**-nah **fay**-chah day kah-doo-see-**dahd** ayn ayl proh-**dook**-toh?* ¿Hay una fecha de caducidad en el producto?[3]
8. Was the product being used only according to manufacturer's specifications?	*say oo-**sah**-bah ayl proh-**dook**-toh soh-lah-**mayn**-tay say-**goon** lahs een-dee-kah-**see^oh**-nays dayl fah-bree-**kahn**-tay?* ¿Se usaba el producto solamente según las indicaciones del fabricante?
9. Was the product leased or purchased?	*say ahl-kee-**loh** oh say kohm-**proh** ayl proh-**dook**-toh?* ¿Se alquiló o se compró el producto?
10. Was the product altered in any way?	*say moh-dee-fee-**koh** ayl proh-**dook**-toh day ahl-**goo**-nah mah-**nay**-rah?* ¿Se modificó el producto de alguna manera?
Could you ... how it was modified?	*poh-**dree**-ah ... **koh**-moh loh moh-dee-fee-**kah**-rohn?* ¿Podría ... cómo lo modificaron?
put in writing	*poh-**nayr** pohr ays-**kree**-toh* poner por escrito
tell someone in Spanish	*day-**seer**-lay ah **ahl**-ghee^ayn ayn ays-pahn-**yohl*** decirle a alguien en español
11. Did anyone fail to remove or attach a safety device?	*days-koo^ee-**doh** ahl-ghee^ayn kee-**tahr**-lay oh fee-**hahr**-lay oon dees-poh-see-**tee**-boh day say-goo-ree-**dahd** ahl proh-**dook**-toh?* ¿Descuidó alguien quitarle o fijarle un dispositivo de seguridad al producto?
12. Were you provided training on the proper use of the product?	*say lay kah-pah-see-**toh** ah oo-**sahr** ayl proh-**dook**-toh koh-rrayk-tah-**mayn**-tay?* ¿Se le capacitó a usar el producto correctamente?

English	Pronunciation & Spanish
13. Do you, your employer or a third party provide maintenance on this product?	*rray-ah-lee-**soh** oos-**tayd**, soo aym-play-ah-**dohr** oh **oo**-nah tayr-**say**-rah **pahr**-tay mahn-tay-nee-**mee^ayn**-toh ayn **ays**-tay proh-**dook**-toh?* ¿Realizó Ud., su empleador o una tercera parte mantenimiento en este producto?
14. When was maintenance last performed on this product?	***koo^ahn**-doh foo^ay lah **ool**-tee-mah bays kay say rray-ah-lee-**soh** mahn-tay-nee-**mee^ayn**-toh ayn **ays**-tay proh-**dook**-toh?* ¿Cuándo fue la última vez que se realizó mantenimiento en este producto?[3]
one day ago	*ah-say oon **dee**-ah* hace un día[8]
(#) days ago	*ah-say (#) **dee**-ahs* hace (#) días[8]
one week ago	*ah-say **oo**-nah say-**mah**-nah* hace una semana[8]
(#) weeks ago	*ah-say (#) say-**mah**-nahs* hace (#) semanas[8]
one month ago	*ah-say oon mays* hace un mes[8]
(#) months ago	*ah-say (#) **may**-says* hace (#) meses[8]
one year ago	*ah-say oon **ahn**-yoh* hace un año[8]
Who did it?	*kee^ayn loh rray-ah-lee-**soh**?* ¿Quién lo realizó?[2]
15. Were there any warnings regarding the use of this product of which you are aware?	*lay ee-**see^ay**-rohn sah-**bayr** see ah-**bee**-ah ahl-**goo**-nohs ah-**bee**-sohs **soh**-bray ayl **oo**-soh day **ays**-tay proh-**dook**-toh?* ¿Le hicieron saber si había algunos avisos sobre el uso de este producto?

IV. Medical Malpractice

*nay-glee-**hayn**-see^ah **may**-dee-kah*
Negligencia médica

English	Pronunciation & Spanish
1. What is the name of ... in question?	***koh**-moh say **yah**-mah ... ayn koo^ays-**tee^ohn**?* ¿Cómo se llama ... en cuestión?
the medical facility	*lah een-stah-lah-**see^ohn** **may**-dee-kah* la instalación médica[12]
the doctor	*ayl dohk-**tohr** el doctor[12]

2. When did you begin / end the medical treatment in question?	*koo^ahn-doh aym-pay-soh / tayr-mee-noh ayl trah-tah-mee^ayn-toh may-dee-koh ayn koo^ays-tee^ohn?* ¿Cuándo empezó / terminó el tratamiento médico en cuestión?[4]
3. Could you ... what makes you believe a health care professional did you harm?	*poh-dree-ah ... loh kay lay ah-say kray-ayr kay oon proh-fay-see^oh-nahl day sayr-bee-see^ohs day sah-lood lay ee-soh dahn-yoh?* ¿Podría ... lo que le hace creer que un profesional de servicios de salud le hizo daño?
describe in writing	*days-kree-beer pohr ays-kree-toh* describir por escrito
tell someone in Spanish	*day-seer-lay ah ahl-ghee^ayn ayn ays-pahn-yohl* decirle a alguien en español
4. Has any health care professional apologized for the results of your care?	*lay ah oh-fray-see-doh dees-kool-pahs ahl-goon proh-fay-see^oh-nahl day sayr-bee-see^ohs day sah-lood pohr lohs rray-sool-tah-dohs day soo ah-tayn-see^ohn may-dee-kah?* ¿Le ha ofrecido disculpas algún profesional de servicios de salud por los resultados de su atención médica?
5. Has anyone told you that the medical care you received caused you an injury?	*lay ah dee-choh ahl-ghee^ayn kay lah ah-tayn-see^ohn may-dee-kah kay rray-see-bee^oh lay proh-boh-koh oo-nah lay-see^ohn?* ¿Le ha dicho alguien que la atención médica que recibió le provocó una lesión?
6. Did anyone discuss the risks of the treatment or medication issue in question with you?	*lay ah-bee-ah koh-moo-nee-kah-doh ahl-ghee^ayn lohs rree^ays-gohs een-boh-loo-krah-dohs kohn ayl trah-tah-mee^ayn-toh oh lah may-dee-see-nah ayn koo^ays-tee^ohn?* ¿Le había comunicado alguien los riesgos involucrados con el tratamiento o la medicina en cuestión?
7. Did you sign any documents acknowledging you were aware of the risks of treatment or the medication?	*feer-moh ahl-goo-nohs doh-koo-mayn-tohs ayn lohs koo^ah-lays een-dee-koh kay say dah-bah koo^ayn-tah day lohs rree^ays-gohs ah-soh-see^ah-dohs kohn ayl trah-tah-mee^ayn-toh oh lah may-dee-see-nah?* ¿Firmó algunos documentos en los cuales indicó que se daba cuenta de los riesgos asociados con el tratamiento o la medicina?
8. Did you have a pre-existing relationship with the doctor in question?	*tay-nee-ah oo-nah rray-lah-see^ohn pray-ayk-sees-tayn-tay kohn ayl may-dee-koh/lah may-dee-kah ayn koo^ays-tee^ohn?* ¿Tenía una relación preexistente con el médico/la médica en cuestión?[13]
9. Was the physician in question assigned to you by a hospital?	*lay foo^ay ah-seeg-nah-doh/dah ayl may-dee-koh/lah may-dee-kah ayn koo^ays-tee^ohn pohr ayl ohs-pee-tahl?* ¿Le fue asignado/a el médico/la médica en cuestión por el hospital?[1]
10. Could you ... why you went to the hospital?	*poh-dree-ah ... pohr kay foo^ay ahl ohs-pee-tahl?* ¿Podría ... por qué fue al hospital?
describe in writing	*days-kree-beer pohr ays-kree-toh* describir por escrito

	tell someone in Spanish	*day-**seer**-lay ah **ahl**-ghee^ayn ayn ays-pahn-**yohl*** decirle a alguien en español
11. Could you … the current status of your condition?		*poh-**dree**-ah … ayl ays-**tah**-doh ahk-**too^ahl** day soo kohn-dee-**see^ohn**?* ¿Podría … el estado actual de su condición?
	describe in writing	*days-kree-**beer** pohr ays-**kree**-toh* describir por escrito
	tell someone in Spanish	*day-**seer**-lay ah **ahl**-ghee^ayn ayn ays-pahn-**yohl*** decirle a alguien en español
12. Could you … what your diagnosis was at that time?		*poh-**dree**-ah … koo^ahl foo^ay soo dee^ahg-**nohs**-tee-koh ayn ah-**kayl** moh-**mayn**-toh?* ¿Podría … cuál fue su diagnóstico en aquel momento?
	describe in writing	*days-kree-**beer** pohr ays-**kree**-toh* describir por escrito
	tell someone in Spanish	*day-**seer**-lay ah **ahl**-ghee^ayn ayn ays-pahn-**yohl*** decirle a alguien en español
13. Please list (here) the treatments you received and the results of those treatments.		*poh fah-**bohr**, ay-noo-**may**-ray (ah-**kee**) lohs trah-tah-**mee^ayn**-tohs kay ah rray-see-**bee**-doh ee lohs rray-sool-**tah**-dohs day **ay**-sohs trah-tah-**mee^ayn**-tohs.* Por favor, enumere (aquí) los tratamientos que ha recibido y los resultados de esos tratamientos.
14. Are you currently under a doctor's care?		*ahk-**too^ahl**-**mayn**-tay say ayn-**koo^ayn**-trah **bah**-hoh ayl koo^ee-**dah**-doh day oon **may**-dee-koh?* ¿Actualmente se encuentra bajo el cuidado de un médico?
	Please list (here) the reasons why.	*pohr fah-**bohr**, ay-noo-**may**-ray (ah-**kee**) lohs pohr-**kays**.* Por favor, enumere (aquí) los porqués.
15. Could you … what is your current diagnosis / prognosis?		*poh-**dree**-ah … koo^ahl ays soo dee^ahg-**nohs**-tee-koh / proh-**nohs**-tee-koh ahk-**too^ahl**?* ¿Podría … cuál es su diagnóstico / pronóstico actual?
	describe in writing	*days-kree-**beer** pohr ays-**kree**-toh* describir por escrito
	tell someone in Spanish	*day-**seer**-lay ah **ahl**-ghee^ayn ayn ays-pahn-**yohl*** decirle a alguien en español

V. Slip and Fall

*rrays-bah-**lohn** ee kah-**ee**-dah*
Resbalón y caída

English	Pronunciation & Spanish
	*koo^ahl ays ayl **nohm**-bray dayl nay-**goh**-see^oh **dohn**-day say kah^ee-**yoh**?*
1. What is the name of the business where you fell?	¿Cuál es el nombre del negocio donde se cayó?[12]
	*koo^ahl ays lah dee-rrayk-**see**^ohn kohm-**play**-tah dayl loo-**gahr dohn**-day say kah^ee-**yoh**?*
What is the complete address of the location where you fell?	¿Cuál es la dirección completa del lugar donde se cayó?[2, 3]
	*poh-**dree**-ah … ayn kay **pahr**-tay dayl ays-tab-lay-see-**mee**^ayn-toh ahs-**tah**-bah **koo**^ahn-doh say kah^ee-**yoh**?*
2. Could you … what part of the establishment you were in when you fell?	¿Podría … en que parte del establecimiento estaba cuando se cayó?
	*ah-poon-**tahr** ah-**kee***
write down here	apuntar aquí
	*day-**seer**-lay ah **ahl**-ghee^ayn ayn ays-pahn-**yohl***
tell someone in Spanish	decirle a alguien en español
	*ah-kah-**bah**-bah day yay-**gahr** koo^ayn-doh **ays**-toh oh-koo-**rree**^oh?*
3. Had you just arrived when this happened?	¿Acababa de llegar cuando esto ocurrió?
	*pohr koo^ayn-toh **tee**^aym-poh ah-**bee**-ah ays-**tah**-doh ah-**yee** koo^ahn-doh say kah^ee-**yoh**?*
4. How long had you been there when you fell?	¿Por cuánto tiempo había estado allí cuando se cayó?[3]
	*noh **moo**-choh **tee**^aym-poh*
not very long	no mucho tiempo[8]
	*oo-nohs **poh**-kohs mee-**noo**-tohs*
a few minutes	unos pocos minutos[8]
	*oon mee-**noo**-toh*
a minute	un minuto[8]
	*(#) mee-**noo**-tohs*
(#) minutes	(#) minutos[8]
	*oo-nahs **poh**-kahs **oh**-rahs*
a few hours	unas pocas horas[8]
	*oo-nah **oh**-rah*
an hour	una hora[8]
	*(#) **oh**-rahs*
(#) hours	(#) horas[8]

5. Were you leaving this location when this happened?

*ays-**tah**-bah sah-**lee^ayn**-doh day **ays**-tay loo-**gahr** koo^**ayn**-doh **ays**-toh oh-koo-**rree^oh**?*

¿Estaba saliendo de este lugar cuando esto ocurrió?

---

6. Were you with anyone else when you fell?

*ays-**tah**-bah kohn **oh**-trah payr-**soh**-nah koo^**ayn**-doh say kah^ee-**yoh**?*

¿Estaba con otra persona cuando se cayó?

Please list here their names, addresses and phone numbers.

*fah-**bohr** day ays-kree-**beer** ah-**kee** lohs **nohm**-brays, dee-rayk-**see^oh**-nays ee **noo**-may-rohs day tay-**lay**-foh-noh day **kah**-dah payr-**soh**-nah.*

Favor de escribir aquí los nombres, direcciones y números de teléfono de cada persona.

If you don't know this information, can you get it for us?

*see noh **sah**-bay **ays**-tah een-fohr-mah-**see^ohn**, nohs lah **poo^ay**-day kohn-say-**gheer**?*

Si no sabe esta información, ¿nos la puede conseguir?

---

7. Did the person(s) you were with witness the fall?

*lah/loh bee^oh kah-**ayr**-say lah(s) payr-**soh**-nah(s) kohn kee^**ayn** ays-**tah**-bah?*

¿La/lo vio caerse la(s) persona(s) con quién(es) estaba?[10]

---

8. Could you ... what you were doing before the fall?

*poh-**dree**-ah ... loh kay ah-**see**-ah ahn-tay-**ree^ohr** ah lah kah-**ee**-dah?*

¿Podría ... lo que hacía anterior a la caída?

describe in writing

*days-kree-**beer** pohr ays-**kree**-toh*

describir por escrito

tell someone in Spanish

*day-**seer**-lay ah **ahl**-ghee^ayn ayn ays-pahn-**yohl***

decirle a alguien en español

---

9. Did you see the condition or obstacle that caused the fall?

*bee^oh lah kohn-dee-**see^ohn** oh ayl ohb-**stah**-koo-loh kay proh-boh-**koh** lah kah-**ee**-dah?*

¿Vio la condición o el obstáculo que provocó la caída?

---

10. Did you see the condition or obstacle before you fell?

*bee^oh lah kohn-dee-**see^ohn** oh ayl ohb-**stah**-koo-loh **ahn**-tays day kah-**ayr**-say?*

¿Vio la condición o el obstáculo antes de caerse?

Could you ... what the condition or obstacle was like?

*poh-**dree**-ah ... **koh**-moh **ay**-rah lah kohn-dee-**see^ohn** oh ayl ohb-**stah**-koo-loh?*

¿Podría ... cómo era la condición o el obstáculo?

describe in writing

*days-kree-**beer** pohr ays-**kree**-toh*

describir por escrito

tell someone in Spanish

*day-**seer**-lay ah **ahl**-ghee^ayn ayn ays-pahn-**yohl***

decirle a alguien en español

---

11. Was the obstacle or condition obvious?

*ay-rah ay-bee-**dayn**-tay lah pray-**sayn**-see^ah dayl ohb-**stah**-koo-loh oh lah kohn-dee-**see^ohn**?*

¿Era evidente la presencia del obstáculo o la condición?

12. Were there any caution signs posted near the location of the obstacle or condition?

*ah-**bee**-ah fee-**hah**-doh ahl-**goo**-nohs lay-**tray**-rohs day ah-**bee**-soh **sayr**-kah dayl loo-**gahr** dayl ohbs-**tah**-koo-loh oh lah kohn-dee-**see^ohn**?*

¿Había fijado algunos letreros de aviso cerca del lugar del obstáculo o la condición?

13. Do you know the cause of the obstacle or condition?

*sah-bay lah **kah^oo**-sah dayl ohb-**stah**-koo-loh oh lah kohn-dee-**see^ohn**?*

¿Sabe la causa del obstáculo o la condición?

Could you ... what the cause was?

*poh-**dree**-ah ... koo^ahl foo^ay lah **kah^oo**-sah?*

¿Podría ... cuál fue la causa?

describe in writing

*days-kree-**beer** pohr ays-**kree**-toh*

describir por escrito

tell someone in Spanish

*day-**seer**-lay ah **ahl**-ghee^ayn ayn ays-pahn-**yohl***

decirle a alguien en español

14. Did you see any employees nearby when you fell?

*bee^oh ah ahl-**goo**-nohs aym-play-**ah**-dohs **sayr**-kah **koo^ahn**-doh say kah^ee-**yoh**?*

¿Vio a algunos empleados cerca cuando se cayó?

Did you get the name of each employee?

*ohb-**too**-boh ayl **nohm**-bray day **kah**-dah aym-play-**ah**-doh?*

¿Obtuvo el nombre de cada empleado?

Will you please make a list of that information to give us?

*pohr fah-**bohr**, nohs **ah**-say **oo**-nah **lees**-tah day **ay**-sah een-fohr-mah-**see^ohn** pah-rah ayn-tray-**gahr**-nohs?*

Por favor, ¿nos hace una lista de esa información para entregarnos?

15. Were there any employees that would have been able to see you when you fell?

*ah-**bee**-ah aym-play-**ah**-dohs kay oo-**bee^ay**-rahn poh-**dee**-doh **bayr**-loh/lah **koo^ahn**-doh say kah^ee-**yoh**?*

¿Había empleados que hubieran podido verlo/la cuando se cayó?[10]

16. Did any employee make any comments to you about the cause of your accident?

*lay **ee**-soh koh-mayn-**tah**-ree^ohs ahl-**goon** aym-play-**ah**-doh **soh**-bray lah **kah^oo**-sah day soo ahk-see-**dayn**-tay?*

¿Le hizo comentarios algún empleado sobre la causa de su accidente?

Could you identify the employee or employees that made these comments?

*poh-**dree**-ah ee-dayn-tee-fee-**kahr** ahl aym-play-**ah**-doh oh a lohs aym-play-**ah**-dohs kay lay ee-**see^ay**-rohn **ays**-tohs koh-mayn-**tah**-ree^ohs?*

¿Podría identificar al empleado o a los empleados que le hicieron estos comentarios?

Could you ... what each comment was?

*poh-**dree**-ah ... koo^ahl foo^ay ayl koh-mayn-**tah**-ree^oh day **kah**-dah oo-noh?*

¿Podría ... cuál fue el comentario de cada uno?

put in writing

*poh-**nayr** pohr ays-**kree**-toh*

poner por escrito

tell someone in Spanish

*day-**seer**-lay ah **ahl**-ghee^ayn ayn ays-pahn-**yohl***

decirle a alguien en español

	*lay koh-moo-nee-**koh** ayl ahk-see-**dayn**-tay ah ahl-**goon** soo-payr-bee-**sohr** oh ayn-kahr-**gah**-doh?*
17. Did you make a report about the accident to any one in charge?	¿Le comunicó el accidente a algún supervisor o encargado?
	*ah-**pahr**-tay day oon aym-play-**ah**-doh, lay ee-soh koh-mayn-**tah**-ree^ohs **oh**-trah payr-**soh**-nah **soh**-bray lah **kah^oo**-sah day soo ahk-see-**dayn**-tay?*
18. Did any one other than an employee make comments about the cause of your accident?	Aparte de un empleado, ¿le hizo comentarios otra persona sobre la causa de su accidente?
	*fah-**bohr** day ays-kree-**beer** ah-**kee** lohs **nohm**-brays, dee-rayk-**see^oh**-nays ee **noo**-may-rohs day tay-**lay**-foh-noh day **kah**-dah payr-**soh**-nah.*
Please list here their names, addresses and phone numbers.	Favor de escribir aquí los nombres, direcciones y números de teléfono de cada persona.
	*see noh **sah**-bay ays-tah een-fohr-mah-**see^ohn**, nohs lah **poo^ay**-day kohn-say-**gheer**?*
If you don't know this information, can you get it for us?	Si no sabe esta información, ¿nos la puede conseguir?
	*kay **tee**-poh day sah-**pah**-tohs yay-**bah**-bah **koo^ahn**-doh **oo**-boh ayl ahk-see-**dayn**-tay?*
19. What kind of shoes were you wearing at the time of the accident?	¿Qué tipo de zapatos llevaba cuando hubo el accidente?[2]
	*ah-**oon** tee^**ay**-nay **ay**-sohs sah-**pah**-tohs?*
Do you still have those shoes?	¿Aún tiene esos zapatos?
	*poh-**dree**-ah ... ayk-sahk-tah-**mayn**-tay **koh**-moh say kah^ee-**yoh**?*
20. Could you ... exactly how you fell?	¿Podría ... exactamente cómo se cayó?
	*days-kree-**beer** pohr ays-**kree**-toh*
describe in writing	describir por escrito
	*day-**seer**-lay ah **ahl**-ghee^ayn ayn ays-pahn-**yohl***
tell someone in Spanish	decirle a alguien en español
	*may **poo^ay**-day day-mohs-**trahr** kohn koo^ee-**dah**-doh ayk-sahk-tah-**mayn**-tay **koh**-moh say kah^ee-**yoh**?*
21. Can you carefully demonstrate for me exactly how you fell?	¿Me puede demostrar con cuidado exactamente cómo se cayó?
	*ah kohn-sool-**tah**-doh ah **oh**-troh ah-boh-**gah**-doh rray-fay-**rayn**-tay ah **ays**-tohs ah-**soon**-tohs?*
22. Have you spoken with any other attorneys about these issues?	¿Ha consultado a otro abogado referente a estos asuntos?
	*koo^**ahl** ays ayl **nohm**-bray kohm-**play**-toh dayl ah-boh-**gah**-doh?*
What is full name of the attorney?	¿Cuál es el nombre completo del abogado?[2]

*fah-**bohr** day ayn-tayn-**dayr** kay **ahs**-tah kay say rray-**see**-bah kohn-feer-mah-**see^ohn** day noh-**soh**-trohs kohn rrays-**payk**-toh ah **ays**-tay ah-**soon**-toh ayn lah koo^ahl say day-**tah**-yahn lohs **play**-sohs day **noo^ays**-troh ah-**koo^ayr**-doh **pah**-rah rray-pray-sayn-**tahr**-loh/lah, noh **soh**-mohs soo rray-pray-sayn-**tahn**-tay lay-**gahl pah**-ray **ays**-tay oh neen-**goon oh**-troh ah-**soon**-toh.*

23. Please understand that until you receive correspondence from us regarding this issue that details the terms of our agreement to represent you in this matter, we are not your legal representative on this or any other issue.

Favor de entender que hasta que se reciba confirmación mediante correspondencia de nosotros con respecto a este asunto en la cual se detallan los plazos de nuestro acuerdo para representarlo/la, no somos su representante legal para este o ningún otro asunto.[10]

Notes

[1] Use the *-o* ending when speaking to a *male*; use the *-a* ending when speaking to a *female*. Also, anticipated responses have been provided, in which case the speaker will use the necessary ending in his/her response.

[2] Reference *Chapter 12—The Basics—I. The Spanish Alphabet* to aid you in listening comprehension and spelling. Also, whenever possible, ask the speaker to write down the information for you.

[3] For questions where an address or phone number is requested, you may also need to reference *Chapter 12—The Basics—II. Numbers*. Whenever possible, ask the speaker to write down the information for you.

[4] Reference *Chapter 13—Telling Time the Easy Way—II. Days of the Week and Months of the Year* for formulaic formation of dates in Spanish. Once again, if you are meeting face-to-face with the speaker, allow him/her to write down responses to questions for you.

[5] In Spanish, the syntax (sentence structure) for *you (singular and formal), he/him,* and *she/her* are grammatically identical. Notice that ALL of the English questions and phrases in this chapter are written in the second person singular—*you*. Likewise, the vast majority of Spanish phrases in this book could be conveyed as *he/him* or *she/her* as well, though not noted in the English translation. If the person with whom you are speaking is the potential client, use the phrase *Referente a Ud. (In reference to you …)* to ensure the conversation is being conducted directly with that person. If the person with whom you are speaking is inquiring on behalf of someone else, then use either *Referente a él (In reference to him …)* or *Referente a ella (In reference to her …)* depending upon the sex of the individual on whose behalf the person is inquiring. At anytime you wish to change the focus of the question, simply insert the expression *Referente a Ud., él* or *ella …* before the phrase. For example, to change the focus to a female say *Referente a ella, ¿tiene trabajo actualmente? (In reference to her, is she currently employed?).* You may even insert the **proper name** of the person accordingly to maximize comprehension—*Referente a Carlos.* You only need to verbalize clarification when changing or clarifying the person who is the focus of the question or phrase. It is not necessary to do so before EVERY question or phrase once you establish the context of the conversation.

[6] Use *el dueño* for a *male* and *la dueña* for a *female.*

[7] Reference *Chapter 13—Telling Time the Easy Way—I. Time* for formulaic sentence structure regarding *time.*

[8] These phrases have been included as anticipated responses. You may also use them to repeat the information back to the person to ensure you have understood his/her response correctly.

[9] If the response is "YES" to question 23, repeat questions 24–40 AFTER interviewing the person with whom you are speaking. Use the communication strategy covered earlier in **NOTE 5** to reference a third person.

[10] Use *-lo* when talking to or about a *male* and use *-la* when talking to or about a *female.*

[11] You may wish to use the *Human Body* diagrams found in the APPENDIX. They are labeled both in English and Spanish.

[12] Remember to consult past chapters for phrases you may need in which you request necessary information or ask someone to repeat, spell, etc. as these are all part of effective communication strategies.

[13] This is another common way to say *doctor* in Spanish. They are presented as an alternative to familiarize you with optional vocabulary you may commonly encounter. Use *el médico* when referring to a *male* and use *la médica* when referring to a *female.*

[14] Reference *Chapter 11—Questions Related to Medical Issues—IV. Medical Information Consent Release Form* for a bilingual sample of this document. *Chapter 11* contains additional questions related to medical issues you may find to be beneficial.

Practical Activities

A) En contexto (In context)

Part I—Instructions: A series of Spanish questions and/or statements from this chapter have been listed below. WITHOUT LOOKING IN THE TEXT, determine if each question or statement is related to letter *A) Automobile Accident*, letter *B) Products Liability*, letter *C) Medical Malpractice* or letter *D) Slip and Fall*. Then, in the blank provided before each question or statement, write the corresponding letter (A, B, C or D). When you have finished, compare your responses with a classmate and make any necessary corrections. For extra practice, try writing the English translation of each phrase in the space provided under each Spanish question. Do this first WITHOUT consulting the text.

1. _____ ¿Le comunicó el accidente a algún supervisor o encargado?

2. _____ ¿Le contó la persona que manejaba el otro vehículo esta misma información a la policía?

3. _____ ¿Por cuánto tiempo había estado allí cuando se cayó?

4. _____ ¿Observó algo fuera de lo normal o problemático sobre el vehículo en el cual estaba poco antes del accidente?

5. _____ ¿Nos puede proporcionar una foto o imagen del producto?

6. _____ ¿Tiene alguna idea sobre la velocidad del otro vehículo involucrado?

7. _____ ¿Firmó algunos documentos en los cuales indicó que se daba cuenta de los riesgos del tratamiento o la medicina?

8. _____ ¿Realizó Ud., su empleador o una tercera parte mantenimiento en este producto?

9. _____ ¿Se le descuidó a alguien quitarle o fijarle un dispositivo de seguridad al producto?

10. _____ ¿Podría decirle a alguien en español el estado actual del obstáculo o la condición?

11. _____ ¿Le ha ofrecido disculpas algún profesional de servicios de salud por los resultados de su atención médica?

12. _____ ¿Había fijado algunos letreros de aviso cerca de la localización del accidente?

13. _____ ¿Podría describir por escrito cuál es su diagnóstico actual?

14. _____ ¿Qué tipo de zapatos llevaba cuando hubo el accidente?

15. _____ ¿Tiene alguna idea de cuánto daño a la propiedad su carro ha sufrido?

16. _____ ¿Se modificó el producto de alguna manera?

Part II—Instructions: Read the following brief explanation of a *cognate*.

*A **cognate** is a word that looks similar, sounds similar and has the same meaning in two different languages.*

With this explanation in mind, review the sixteen Spanish phrases/questions above. Read through EACH phrase and circle any SPANISH words that you believe are *cognates*. Then working with a partner, discuss what you believe the ENGLISH equivalent to be and write it above each circled word. After everyone has had a chance to do this with a partner, compare with other classmates to see how many cognates they believe they found. Share your findings together as a class starting with number one and point out the cognates that were found and their English meaning. Lastly, you may want to consult a bilingual dictionary to verify the meaning of each cognate. By recognizing cognates, you will be able to identify information you already know and add to your working knowledge of Spanish.

Part III—Instructions: Make a list below of ONLY the ENGLISH equivalents for the cognates you have identified. Working either individually, in pairs or as a group, say each English word aloud and try to say the SPANISH word from memory. If doing this in pairs or as a group, divide the list of cognates up so that each person has approximately the same number. Each person will then take turns quizzing his/her partner or group members by saying ONLY the ENGLISH equivalent of each word and relying on his/her partner or a member of the group to provide the SPANISH word. When necessary, assist each other before having to refer back to the phrases from Part I for assistance.

List COGNATES in this box. Numbers 1-10 have been typed out to get you started.

1.   8.

2.   9.

3.   10.

4.   etc.

5.

6.

7.

B) Collecting Basic Information

Instructions: Either individually or in pairs, use the following flowchart to assist you in practicing ALOUD the variations for the collection of common information you may come across based on the phrases and expressions in section *I. General Questions* of this chapter. As you follow the flowchart, you may want to reference that section of this chapter to find the appropriate question or phrase you would use to effectively communicate with a Spanish speaker. The information given in the flowchart is meant to serve as clues that will guide you to the Spanish questions and/or phrases you will need to incorporate. They are NOT intended as direct English translations of the questions and phrases you will need.

Where required, anticipated response options have been provided for some questions to assist with the flow of the conversation. Otherwise, responses must be invented.

Communication Flowchart

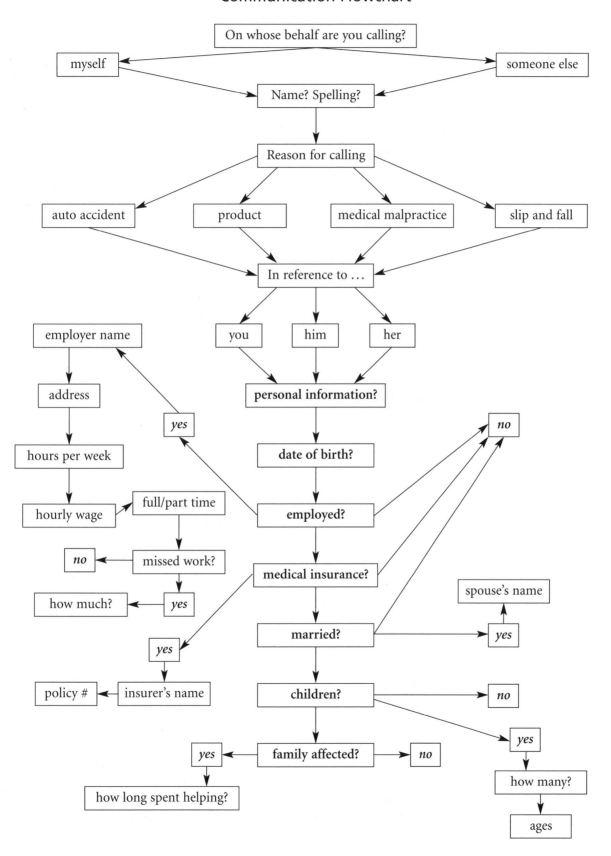

C) Collecting Specific Information

Instructions: Starting with block number one, read the responses that have been given. Then, WITHOUT consulting the text, try to recall the SPANISH question or expression that would be used to elicit each response provided. If you find you are unable to recall all of the necessary information, consult with various classmates before reviewing the text. After all of you have completed this task, practice the block as a dialogue, taking turns playing the roles of interviewer and interviewee. Remember to use the responses already provided as the answers to the interviewer's questions. Continue this process with ALL four blocks of information. In some cases, you may need to consult a bilingual dictionary for anticipated responses that are not easily identifiable.

BLOCK 1—
Accidentes de auto

1. Sí, estuve en un accidente.
2. El chofer.
3. No, no tengo seguro.
4. Es un Honda Civic.
5. Soy el dueño.
6. El 13 de junio a las 2 de la tarde.
7. Sí, la policía acudió.
8. No, nada fuera de lo normal.
9. Sí, tengo copia.
10. Sí, se lo mando por FAX.
11. No, no me lesioné.
12. No, es mi primer accidente.

BLOCK 2—
Responsabilidad por la fabricación de un producto

1. Fue un tipo de maquinaria.
2. No, no sé el nombre.
3. Sí, tengo foto del producto.
4. Hace 5 meses.
5. No sé si se usaba el producto según las indicaciones o no.
6. Se alquiló.
7. Sí, fue modificado.
8. Sí, puedo poner por escrito cómo lo modificaron.
9. Hace mucho tiempo.
10. Un compañero de trabajo lo realizó.

BLOCK 3—
Negligencia médica

1. Es el hospital Snyder Memorial.
2. El tratamiento empezó el 6 de enero, 2011.
3. No, nada de disculpas.
4. No, nada de riesgos tampoco.
5. No sé sobre los documentos.
6. Sí, tenía una relación profesional muy buena.
7. Sí, puedo decirle a alguien por qué fui.
8. Sí, puedo describir por escrito mi estado actual.
9. No, no tengo médico en este momento.

BLOCK 4—
Resbalón y caída

1. Es el Greenbrooke Mall en Mooresville.
2. 5478 Forest Hill Road.
3. No mucho tiempo, 15 minutos quizás.
4. Estaba con mi novio.
5. No, no era evidente.
6. No, ningún empleado estaba cerca.
7. Sí, se lo comuniqué al supervisor.
8. Llevaba unas sandalias.
9. Sí, aún las tengo.
10. No, ningún otro abogado.

D) Cyber-Investigation

We all know that Americans (those from the United States in this case) have been labeled litigious in nature but what about Hispanics? First, research to find out why we as Americans have become stereotyped as being litigious. Do you agree or disagree with what you find? Then, search to find out how such personal injury matters, such as those referenced in this chapter, would be handled by the judicial system in a Spanish-speaking,

Latin American country (for example—Mexico). Then read and consider the following question: What is the likelihood that a Hispanic would file a personal injury related complaint with regards to each of the four topics—Automobile Accidents, Products Liability, Medical Malpractice as well as Slip and Fall—in a U.S. court of law based on what you have discovered about the respective judicial system in a specific Spanish-speaking, Latin American country? In your opinion, would a Hispanic that has resided in the U.S. for some time be less reluctant to take such a matter to court than a recent arrival or a Hispanic that does not speak English? Summarize your findings below.

Chapter 7

Employment Law

Before You Begin

Between 1992 and 2006, Hispanic workers accounted for thirteen percent of job-related accidents. The construction industry alone, which is an extremely popular source of employment for this population, was responsible for one in every three deaths that happened on the job. Statistics from this period indicate that this is shockingly higher in comparison to job-related injuries and fatalities that occurred among Caucasians and African Americans. Moreover, these risks increased exponentially for foreign-born Hispanics who experienced a seventy percent higher risk for job-related accidents than those Hispanics that were born in the U.S. According to the CDC (Center for Disease Control), this was largely due to obstacles such as communication barriers as well as inadequate training and poor supervision.

Aside from the high rate of work-related injuries and fatalities, Hispanics report having experienced severe and frequent unfair treatment and discrimination in the workplace. The most common concerns they voiced include being overlooked for one's hard work, not receiving raises or bonuses, not having their concerns and opinions taken seriously, being passed over for promotions and being ignored when attempting to provide, what they genuinely felt to be, necessary feedback or suggestions.

I. General Questions

*pray-**goon**-tahs hay-nay-**rah**-lays*
Preguntas generales

English	Pronunciation & Spanish
1. I'm going to ask you a series of questions.	*lay boh^ee ah ah-**sayr** oo-nah **say**-ree^ay day pray-**goon**-tahs.* Le voy a hacer una serie de preguntas.
2. Please respond "yes" or "no" so I can determine the reason for your call.	*pohr fah-**bohr**, rrays-**pohn**-dah kohn \<see\> oh \<noh\> **pah**-rah kay **poo^ay**-dah ah-bay-ree-**goo^ahr** ayl proh-**poh**-see-toh day soo yah-**mah**-dah.* Por favor, responda con \<sí\> o \<no\> para que pueda averiguar el propósito de su llamada.
3. Is it an issue regarding …	*ays **soh**-bray …* ¿Es sobre …[1,2]
wrongful termination?	*ayl days-**pee**-doh een-**hoo**-stoh?* el despido injusto?
worker's compensation?	*lah een-daym-nee-sah-**see^ohn** lah-boh-**rahl**?* la indemnización laboral?

107

(sexual) discrimination?	*lah dees-kree-mee-nah-**see^ohn** (sayk-**soo^ahl**)?* la discriminación (sexual)?
age discrimination?	*lah dees-kree-mee-nah-**see^ohn** pohr ay-**dahd**?* la discriminación por edad?
(sexual) harassment?	*ayl ah-**koh**-soh (sayk-**soo^ahl**)?* el acoso (sexual)?
retaliation?	*lah rray-pray-**sah**-lee^ah?* la represalia?
wage and hour dispute?	***oo**-nah dees-**poo**-tah sah-lah-**ree^ahl** oh **soh**-bray lah **kahr**-gah oh-**rah**-ree^ah?* una disputa salarial o sobre la carga horaria?

II. Worker's Compensation

*een-daym-nee-sah-**see^ohn** lah-boh-**rahl***
Indemnización laboral

English	Pronunciation & Spanish
1. What was the date of the accident?	*koo^ahl foo^ay lah **fay**-chah dayl ahk-see-**dayn**-tay?* ¿Cuál fue la fecha del accidente?[3]
2. Where did the accident take place?	***dohn**-day **oo**-boh ayl ahk-see-**dayn**-tay?* ¿Dónde hubo el accidente?[4]
3. For what company / employer were you working at the time of the accident?	***pah**-rah kay kohm-pahn-**yee**-ah / aym-play-ah-**dohr** trah-bah-**hah**-bah **koo^ahn**-doh **oo**-boh ayl ahk-see-**dayn**-tay?* ¿Para qué compañía / empleador trabajaba cuando hubo el accidente?[4]
4. Who was your supervisor at the time of the accident?	*kee^ayn **ay**-rah soo soo-payr-bee-**sohr koo^ahn**-doh **oo**-boh ayl ahk-see-**dayn**-tay?* ¿Quién era su supervisor cuando hubo el accidente?
5. To whom was the accident reported?	*ah kee^ayn lay koh-moo-nee-**koh** ayl ahk-see-**dayn**-tay?* ¿A quién le comunicó el accidente?
6. When was the accident reported?	***koo^ahn**-doh say dee^oh **pahr**-tay dayl ahk-see-**dayn**-tay?* ¿Cuándo se dio parte del accidente?
7. What was your rate of pay per hour?	*koo^ahl **ay**-rah soo **tah**-sah day **pah**-goh pohr **oh**-rah?* ¿Cuál era su tasa de pago por hora?[5]
8. Did you receive overtime pay?	*rray-see-**bee^oh pah**-goh pohr **oh**-rahs **ayks**-trahs trah-bah-**hah**-dahs?* ¿Recibió pago por horas extras trabajadas?
9. Did you have health insurance benefits with the employer where you were injured?	*tay-**nee**-ah say-**goo**-roh **may**-dee-koh may-**dee^ahn**-tay lah kohm-pahn-**yee**-ah / ayl aym-play-ah-**dohr koo^ahn**-doh say lahs-stee-**moh** ayn ayl trah-**bah**-hoh?* ¿Tenía seguro médico mediante la compañía / el empleador cuando se lastimó en el trabajo?

10. I'm going to mail you a questionnaire in which you will need to detail how the accident happened.

boh^ee ah mahn-dahr-lay oon koo^ays-tee^oh-nah-ree^oh ayn ayl koo^ahl nay-say-see-tah-rah day-tah-yahr koh-moh oh-koo-rree^oh ayl ahks-ee-dayn-tay.

Voy a mandarle un cuestionario en el cual necesitará detallar cómo ocurrió el accidente.

---

11. You will need to make a list of injuries you sustained ...

nay-say-see-tah-rah ay-noo-may-rahr toh-dahs lahs lay-see^oh-nays kay ah soo-free^oh ...

Necesitará enumerar todas las lesiones que sufrió ...

here on this paper please.

ah-kee ayn ays-tay pah-payl pohr fah-bohr.

aquí en este papel por favor.

on the questionnaire I will mail to you.

ayn ayl koo^ays-tee^oh-nah-ree^oh kay lay ayn-bee^ah-ray pohr koh-rray-oh.

en el cuestionario que le enviaré por correo.

---

12. Are you currently working?

ays-tah trah-bah-hahn-doh ahk-too^ahl-mayn-tay?

¿Está trabajando actualmente?

Were you fired?

say lay days-pee-dee^ay-rohn?

¿Se le despidieron?

Did you quit?

day-hoh ayl trah-bah-hoh

¿Dejó el trabajo?

---

13. Are you currently receiving worker's compensation benefits?

ahk-too^ahl-mayn-tay, ays-tah rray-see-bee^ayn-doh lah een-daym-nee-sah-see^ohn lah-boh-rahl?

Actualmente, ¿está recibiendo la indemnización laboral?

---

14. Who has treated you for this injury?

kee^ayn lay ah trah-tah-doh ays-tah lay-see^ohn?

¿Quién le ha tratado esta lesión?

What is the name and phone number of this doctor?

koo^ahl ays ayl nohm-bray ee ayl noo-may-roh day tay-lay-foh-noh day ays-tay dohk-tohr?

¿Cuál es el nombre y el número de teléfono de este doctor?[4, 5]

---

15. Who is your worker's compensation treating physician now?

kee^ayn ays soo may-dee-koh day een-daym-nee-sah-see^ohn lah-boh-rahl ah-oh-rah?

¿Quién es su médico de indemnización laboral ahora?

What is the name and phone number of this doctor?

koo^ahl ays ayl nohm-bray ee ayl noo-may-roh day tay-lay-foh-noh day ays-tay dohk-tohr?

¿Cuál es el nombre y el número de teléfono de este doctor?[4, 5]

---

16. When was your last treatment?

koo^ahn-doh foo^ay soo ool-tee-moh trah-tah-mee^ayn-toh may-dee-koh?

¿Cuándo fue su último tratamiento médico?[3]

---

17. Has any other attorney represented you in this matter?

loh/lah ah rray-pray-sayn-tah-doh oh-troh ah-boh-gah-doh rrays-payk-toh ah ays-tay ah-soon-toh?

¿Lo/la ha representado otro abogado respecto a este asunto?[6]

	koh-moh say *yah*-mah ayl ah-boh-*gah*-doh?
What is the name of the attorney?	¿Cómo se llama el abogado?
18. Who referred you to our office?	*kee^ayn lay rray-koh-mayn-**doh noo^ays**-troh boo-**fay**-tay?* ¿Quién le recomendó nuestro bufete?
19. What type of business is your employer in?	*ah kay **klah**-say day nay-**goh**-see^oh say day-**dee**-kah soo aym-play-ah-**dohr**?* ¿A qué clase de negocio se dedica su empleador?[4]
20. Is this company based here?	*ays-**tah** oo-bee-**kah**-dah ah-**kee** lah **say**-day preen-see-**pahl** day lah kohm-pahn-**yee**-ah?* ¿Está ubicada aquí la sede principal de la compañía?
21. Does it have a headquarters in the state?	***tee^ay**-nay lah kohm-pahn-**yee**-ah **oo**-nah **say**-day ayn **ays**-tay ays-**tah**-doh?* ¿Tiene la compañía una sede en este estado?
22. Do you know where the headquarters is located?	***sah**-bah **dohn**-day ays-**tah** oo-bee-**kah**-dah lah **say**-day preen-see-**pahl** day lah kohm-pahn-**yee**-ah?* ¿Sabe dónde está ubicada la sede principal de la compañía?
In what …	*ayn kay …* ¿En qué …
state?	*ays-**tah**-doh?* estado?[4]
city?	*see^oo-**dahd**?* ciudad?[4]
23. What position did you hold there?	*kay **poo^ays**-toh oh-koo-**pah**-bah ah-**yee**?* ¿Qué puesto ocupaba allí?[4]
In what department did you work?	*ayn kay day-pahr-tah-**mayn**-toh trah-bah-**hah**-bah?* ¿En qué departamento trabajaba?[4]
24. How large was that department?	***koo^ahn**-tahs payr-**soh**-nahs trah-bah-**hah**-bahn ayn ayl day-pahr-tah-**mayn**-toh?* ¿Cuántas personas trabajaban en el departmento?[5]
25. How many co-workers did you have in …	***koo^ahn**-tohs kohm-pahn-**yay**-rohs day trah-**bah**-hoh tay-**nee**-ah ayn …* ¿Cuántos compañeros de trabajo tenía en …
that deparment?	***ay**-say day-pahr-tah-**mayn**-toh?* ese departamento?[5]
that office?	*ay-sah oh-fee-**see**-nah?* esa oficina?[5]
26. Has your job performance ever been evaluated by anyone at the company?	***ahl**-ghee^ayn day lay kohm-pahn-**yee**-ah ah ay-bah-**loo^ah**-doh soo day-saym-**payn**-yoh lah-boh-**rahl**?* ¿Alguien de la compañía ha evaluado su desempeño laboral?

	*ahl-**goo**-nah bays, ah rray-see-**bee**-doh **oo**-nah ay-bah-loo^ah-**see**^ohn day day-saym-**payn**-yoh lah-boh-**rahl** days-fah-boh-**rah**-blay?*
27. Have you ever received a poor performance review?	Alguna vez, ¿ha recibido una evaluación de desempeño laboral desfavorable?
	*ahl-**goo**-nah bays ah rray-see-**bee**-doh ah-moh-nays-tah-**see**^ohn pohr ays-**kree**-toh ayn ayl trah-**bah**-hoh?*
28. Have you ever been written up?	Alguna vez, ¿ha recibido amonestación por escrito en el trabajo?
	*koo^ahl day lahs see-**ghee**^**ayn**-tays rrah-**soh**-nays may-**hohr** days-**kree**-bay pohr kay rray-see-**bee**^oh ah-moh-nays-tah-**see**^ohn ayn ayl trah-**bah**-hoh?*
Which one of the following reasons best describes the reason why you were written up?	¿Cuál de las siguientes razones mejor describe por qué recibió amonestación por escrito en el trabajo?
	*ayl day-saym-**payn**-yoh lah-boh-**rahl**.*
job performance	el desempeño laboral
	*ayl ah^oo-sayn-**tees**-moh.*
absenteeism	el ausentismo
	*lay eem-poon-too^ahl-lee-**dahd**.*
tardiness	la impuntualidad
	*ayk-say-**see**-bahs soh-lee-see-**too**-days day ah^oo-**sayn**-see^ah.*
excessive leave requests	excesivas solicitudes de ausencia
	*ayl ahs-**payk**-toh **fee**-see-koh.*
appearance	el aspecto físico
	*ayl ee-**hee**^**ay**-nay.*
hygiene	el higiene
	*ayl kohm-pohr-tah-**mee**^**ayn**-toh.*
conduct	el comportamiento
	*lah een-soo-bohr-dee-nah-**see**^**ohn**.*
insubordination	la insubordinación
	*lay dee-**hay**-rohn kay see noh may-hoh-**rah**-rah say-**ree**-ah days-pay-**dee**-doh/dah?*
29. Were you told that if you did not improve that you would be terminated?	¿Le dijeron que si no mejorara sería despedido/a?[6]
	*ahl-**goo**-nah bays, say lay ah ah-sayn-**dee**-doh ayn ayl trah-**bah**-hoh?*
30. Have you ever been promoted?	Alguna vez, ¿se le ha ascendido en el trabajo?
	*ah kay **poo**^**ays**-toh foo^ay ayl ah-**sayn**-soh?*
To what position?	¿A qué puesto fue el ascenso?[4]
	*ahl-**goo**-nah bays, say lay ah nay-**gah**-doh oon ah-**sayn**-soh?*
31. Have you ever been denied a promotion?	Alguna vez, ¿se le ha negado un ascenso?
	*koo^**ahn**-doh **oo**-boh?*
When did this happen?	¿Cuándo hubo?[3]

What position were you denied?	*koo^ahl foo^ay ayl **poo^ays**-toh kay say lay nay-**goh**?* ¿Cuál fue el puesto que se le negó?[4]
Who informed you of the denial?	*kee^ayn lay koh-moo-nee-**koh** lah nay-gah-**see^ohn** dayl ah-**sayn**-soh?* ¿Quién le comunicó la negación del ascenso?
Do you recall the reason?	*say ah-**koo^ayr**-dah dayl pohr-**kay**?* ¿Se acuerda del porqué?
Could you … what that was?	*poh-**dree**-ah … ayl pohr-**kay**?* ¿Podría … el porqué?
put in writing	*poh-**nayr** pohr ays-**kree**-toh* poner por escrito
tell someone in Spanish / English	*day-**seer**-lay ah **ahl**-ghee^ayn ayn ays-pahn-**yohl** / een-**glays*** decirle a alguien en español / inglés
32. Did your employer ever provide you with written documents, such as policies and procedures manuals, employee handbooks, written memos, etc.?	*ayl aym-play-ah-**dohr** lay proh-pohr-see^oh-**noh** doh-koo-**mayn**-tohs ays-**kree**-tohs **tah**-lays **koh**-moh mah-**noo^ah**-lays day proh-say-dee-**mee^ayn**-tohs ee poh-**lee**-tee-kahs, oon mah-**noo^ahl** **pah**-rah aym-play-**ah**-dohs, rray-kohr-dah-**toh**-ree^ohs ays-**kree**-tohs, ayt-**say**-tay-rah?* ¿El empleador le proporcionó documentos escritos, tales como manuales de procedimientos y políticas, un manual para empleados, recordatorios escritos, etc.?
Do you still have these documents?	*ah^oon **tee^ay**-nay **ay**-sohs doh-koo-**mayn**-tohs?* ¿Aún tiene esos documentos?
Would you allow us to review those?	*nohs payr-mee-tee-**ree**-ah rray-bee-**sahr**-lohs?* ¿Nos permitiría revisarlos?
33. Were there any unions where you worked?	*ah-**bee**-ah seen-dee-**kah**-tohs lah-boh-**rah**-lays **dohn**-day trah-bah-**hah**-bah?* ¿Había sindicatos laborales donde trabajaba?
What is the name of each union?	*koh-moh say **yah**-mah **kah**-dah seen-dee-**kah**-toh lah-boh-**rahl**?* ¿Cómo se llama cada sindicato laboral?[4]
34. Did you belong to any union?	***ay**-rah **mee^aym**-broh day oon seen-dee-**kah**-toh?* ¿Era miembro de un sindicato?
35. When you were was hired, did you complete a job application?	*koo^ahn-doh loh/lah kohn-trah-**tah**-rohn, yay-**noh** oo-nah soh-lee-see-**tood** day aym-**play**-oh?* Cuando lo/la contrataron, ¿llenó una solicitud de empleo?[7]
36. When you were considered for a promotion, were you required to submit an application or resume?	*tay-**nee**-ah kay soh-may-**tayr** oo-nah soh-lee-see-**tood** oh oon koo-rree-koo-loom bee-**tah**-ay **koo^ahn**-doh say lay kohn-see-day-**rah**-bah **pah**-rah oon ah-**sayn**-soh ayn ayl trah-**bah**-hoh?* ¿Tenía que someter una solicitud o un currículum vitae cuando se le consideraba para un ascenso en el trabajo?
37. Do you know what the qualifications are for the position …	***sah**-bay **koo^ah**-lays sohn lohs rray-kee-**see**-tohs dayl **poo^ays**-toh …* ¿Sabe cuáles son los requisitos del puesto …

for which you were hired?	*pah-rah ayl koo^ahl say lay kohn-trah-toh?* para el cual se le contrató?
to which you were promoted?	*ahl kay say lay ah-sayn-dee^oh?* al que se le ascendió?
Could you … what they are?	*poh-dree-ah … koo^ah-lays sohn?* ¿Podría … cuáles son?
put in writing	*poh-nayr pohr ays-kree-toh* poner por escrito
tell someone in Spanish / English	*day-seer-lay ah ahl-ghee^ayn ayn ays-pahn-yohl / een-glays* decirle a alguien en español / inglés

III. (Sexual) Discrimination

dees-kree-mee-nah-see^ohn (sayk-soo^ahl)
Discriminación (sexual)

English	Pronunciation & Spanish
1. Do you believe you were discriminated against because of …	*kray-ay kay say lay dees-kree-mee-noh pohr …* ¿Cree que se le discriminó por …
age?	*lah ay-dahd?* la edad?
sex/gender?	*ayl sayk-soh?* el sexo?
ethnicity?	*lah ayt-nee-see-dahd?* la etnicidad?
race?	*lah rrah-sah?* la raza?
nationality?	*lah nah-see^oh-nah-lee-dahd?* la nacionalidad?
religious beliefs?	*lahs kray-ayn-see^ahs rray-lee-hee^oh-sahs?* las creencias religiosas?
sexual orientation?	*lah oh-ree^ayn-tah-see^ohn sayk-soo^ahl?* la orientación sexual?
physical disability?	*dees-kah-pah-see-dahd fee-see-kah?* discapacidad física?
mental disability?	*dees-kah-pah-see-dahd mayn-tahl?* discapacidad mental?
pregnancy?	*ayl aym-bah-rah-soh?* el embarazo?

2. What are the approximate ages of your co-workers?	*koo^ah-lays sohn lahs ay-**dah**-days ah-prohk-see-**mah**-dahs day soos kohm-pahn-**yay**-rohs day trah-**bah**-hoh?* ¿Cuáles son las edades aproximadas de sus compañeros de trabajo?⁵
3. What gender are the majority of your co-workers—men or women?	*koo^ahl ays ayl **sayk**-soh day lah mah-yoh-**ree**-ah day soos kohm-pahn-**yay**-rohs day trah-**bah**-hoh—**ohm**-brays oh moo-**hay**-rays?* ¿Cuál es el sexo de la mayoría de sus compañeros de trabajo—hombres o mujeres?
4. What is the approximate age of the person who was promoted?	*koo^ahl ays lah ay-**dahd** ah-prohk-see-**mah**-dah day lah payr-**soh**-nah kay ah-sayn-**dee^ay**-rohn?* ¿Cuál es la edad aproximada de la persona que ascendieron?⁵
5. What is the gender of the person who was promoted?	*koo^ahl ays ayl **sayk**-soh day lah payr-**soh**-nah kay ah-sayn-**dee^ay**-rohn?* ¿Cuál es el sexo de la persona que ascendieron?
6. Were any others your age terminated?	*days-pee-**dee^ay**-rohn ah oh-trahs payr-**soh**-nahs day lah **mees**-mah ay-**dahd**?* ¿Despidieron a otras personas de la misma edad?
7. Were other men / women terminated?	*days-pee-**dee^ay**-rohn ah oh-trohs **ohm**-brays / otrahs moo-**hay**-rays?* ¿Despidieron a otros hombres / otras mujeres?
8. Did you perceive a difference in treatment between the way that you were treated in your job as opposed to younger or older workers?	*noh-**tah**-bah **oo**-nah dee-fay-**rayn**-see^ah **ayn**-tray lah mah-**nay**-rah ayn lah koo^ahl loh/lah trah-**tah**-bahn ayn ayl trah-**bah**-hoh ayn kohn-**trah**-stay ah lohs trah-bah-hah-**doh**-rays may-**noh**-rays oh mah-**yoh**-rays?* ¿Notaba una diferencia entre la manera en la cual lo/la trataban en el trabajo en contraste a los trabajadores menores o mayores?⁷
9. Did you perceive a difference in treatment between the way that you were treated in your job as opposed to ...	*noh-**tah**-bah **oo**-nah dee-fay-**rayn**-see^ah ayn lah mah-**nay**-rah ayn lah koo^ahl loh/lah trah-**tah**-bahn ayn ayl trah-**bah**-hoh ayn kohn-**trahs**-tay ah ...* ¿Notaba una diferencia en la manera en la cual lo/la trataban en el trabajo en contraste a ... ⁷
other males?	*oh-trohs **ohm**-brays?* otros hombres?
other females?	*oh-trahs moo-**hay**-rays?* otras mujeres?
Could you ... how you were treated differently?	*poh-**dree**-ah ... **koh**-moh loh/lah trah-**tah**-bahn day **moh**-doh dees-**teen**-toh?* ¿Podría ... cómo lo/la trataban de modo distinto?⁷
put in writing	*poh-**nayr** por ays-**kree**-toh* poner por escrito
tell someone in Spanish / English	*day-**seer**-lay ah **ahl**-ghee^ayn ayn ays-pahn-**yohl** / een-**glays*** decirle a alguien en español / inglés

10. Could you ... an example of when this occurred?

*poh-**dree**-ah ... oon ay-**haym**-ploh day **koo^ahn**-doh **ays**-toh oh-koo-**rree^oh**?*
¿Podría ... un ejemplo de cuándo esto ocurrió?

    detail in writing

*day-tah-**yahr** por ays-**kree**-toh*
detallar por escrito

    describe to someone in Spanish / English

*days-kree-**beer**-lay ah **ahl**-ghee^ayn ayn ays-pahn-**yohl** / een-**glays***
describirle a alguien en español / inglés

11. Has anyone ever complained about the quality of your work?

*ahl-**goo**-nah bays, **ahl**-ghee^ayn say ah kay-**hah**-doh day soo day-saym-**payn**-yoh lah-boh-**rahl**?*
Alguna vez, ¿alguien se ha quejado de su desempeño laboral?

    Who complained?

*kee^ayn say kay-**hoh**?*
¿Quién se quejó?

    When did it happen?

*koo^**ayn**-doh **oo**-boh?*
¿Cuándo hubo?[3]

    Could you ... what it was about?

*poh-**dree**-ah ... day loh kay say trah-**tah**-bah?*
¿Podría ... de lo que se trataba?

    put in writing

*poh-**nayr** ayn ays-**kree**-toh*
poner por escrito

    tell someone in Spanish / English

*day-**seer**-lay ah **ahl**-ghee^ayn ayn ays-pahn-**yohl** / een-**glays***
decirle a alguien en español / inglés

12. Do you know if the employer had an Affirmative Action Plan in place?

***sah**-bay see ayl aym-play-ah-**dohr** ah-**bee**-ah eem-play-mayn-**tah**-doh oon plahn day ee-goo^ahl-**dahd** day oh-pohr-too-nay-**dah**-days ee ahk-**see^ohn** ah-feer-mah-**tee**-bah?*
¿Sabe si el empleador había implementado un plan de igualdad de oportunidades y acción afirmativa?

13. Do you know if there have ever been similar complaints regarding ...

***sah**-bay see ahl-**goo**-nah bays ah ah-**bee**-doh **kay**-hahs pah-ray-**see**-dahs rray-fay-**rayn**-tay ...*
¿Sabe si alguna vez ha habido quejas parececidas referente ...

    gender?

*ahl **sayk**-soh?*
al sexo?

    race?

*ah lah **rrah**-sah?*
a la raza?

    age?

*ah lah ay-**dahd**?*
a la edad?

    retaliation?

*ah lahs rray-pray-**sah**-lee^ahs?*
a las represalias?

    discrimination?

*a lah dees-kree-mee-nah-**see^ohn**?*
a la discriminación?

| harassment? | *ahl ah-**koh**-soh?*
al acoso? |

| 14. Do you know if the company has ever been sued by an employee for such things? | ***sah**-bay see ahl-**goo**-nah bays oon aym-play-**ah**-doh ah day-mahn-**dah**-doh ah lah kohm-pahn-**yee**-ah pohr **tah**-lays ah-feer-mah-**see^oh**-nays?*
¿Sabe si alguna vez un empleado ha demandado a la compañía por tales afirmaciones? |

IV. (Sexual) Harassment

*ah-**koh**-soh (sayk-**soo**^ahl)*
Acoso (sexual)

English	Pronunciation & Spanish
1. Do you recall specifically what actions you considered to be (sexually) harassing?	*rray-**koo**^ayr-dah ays-pay-see-fee-kah-**mayn**-tay kay ahk-**see^oh**-nays kohn-see-day-**rah**-bah ah-koh-sah-**doh**-rahs (sayk-soo^ahl-**mayn**-tay)?* ¿Recuerda específicamente qué acciones consideraba acosadoras (sexualmente)?
Would you be willing to tell someone about them in detail?	*ays-tah-**ree**-ah dees-**poo^ays**-toh ah kohn-**tahr**-say-lahs ah **ahl**-ghee^ayn ayn day-**tah**-yay?* ¿Estaría dispuesto/a a contárselas a alguien en detalle?[6]
2. Were there ever any witnesses to the harassment?	***sah**-bay see ah-**bee**-ah tays-**tee**-gohs day lohs ah-**koh**-sohs?* ¿Sabe si había testigos de los acosos?
3. Could you provide their names, job titles and contact information (if they no longer work there)?	*nohs **poo^ay**-day proh-pohr-see^oh-**nahr** soos **nohm**-brays, **tee**-too-lohs day **poo^ays**-toh ay een-fohr-mah-**see^ohn** day kohn-**tahk**-toh (see yah noh trah-**bah**-hahn ah-**yee**)?* ¿Nos puede proporcionar sus nombres, títulos de puesto e información de contacto (si ya no trabajan allí)?
Write them for me here, please.	*ays-**kree**-bah-may lah een-fohr-mah-**see^ohn** ah-**kee**, pahr fah-**bohr**.* Escríbame la información aquí, por favor.
4. Did you ever witness this type of harassment of other employees?	*ahl-**goo**-nah bays, ah-**bee**-ah ah-tays-tee-**goo^ah**-doh **ays**-tah **klah**-say day ah-**koh**-soh **kohn**-trah **oh**-trohs aym-play-**ah**-dohs?* Alguna vez, ¿había atestiguado esta clase de acoso contra otros empleados?
Against whom?	***kohn**-trah kee^ayn?* ¿Contra quién?
When did it happen?	***koo^ahn**-doh **oo**-boh?* ¿Cuándo hubo?
Could you ... what you witnessed?	*poh-**dree**-ah ... loh kay pray-sayn-**see^oh**?* ¿Podría ... lo que presenció?

	poh-**nayr** pohr ays-**kree**-toh
put in writing	poner por escrito
	day-**seer**-lay ah **ahl**-ghee^ayn ayn ays-pahn-**yohl** / een-**glays**
tell someone in Spanish / English	decirle a alguien en español / inglés

V. Retaliation

rray-pray-**sah**-lee^ah
Represalia

English	Pronunciation & Spanish
1. Could you … what makes you believe you were retaliated against?	poh-**dree**-ah … pohr kay ah-**lay**-gah kay say toh-**mah**-rohn rray-pray-**sah**-lee^ahs ayn soo **kohn**-trah? ¿Podría … por qué alega que se tomaron represalias en su contra?
put in writing	poh-**nayr** pohr ays-**kree**-toh poner por escrito
tell someone in Spanish / English	day-**seer**-lay ah **ahl**-ghee^ayn ayn ays-pahn-**yohl** / een-**glays** decirle a alguien en español / inglés
2. Has anyone ever said anything to you about the claim or complaint?	ahl-**goo**-nah bays, **ahl**-ghee^ayn lay ah koh-mayn-**tah**-doh **ahl**-goh **soh**-bray soo ah-feer-mah-**see^ohn** oh soo **kay**-hah? Alguna vez, ¿alguien le ha comentado algo sobre su afirmación o su queja?
Could you … what was said exactly?	poh-**dree**-ah … loh kay say lay **dee**-hoh ayk-sahk-tah-**mayn**-tay? ¿Podría … lo que se le dijo exactamente?
put in writing	poh-**nayr** pohr ays-**kree**-toh poner por escrito
tell someone in Spanish / English	day-**seer**-lay ah **ahl**-ghee^ayn ayn ays-pahn-**yohl** / een-**glays** decirle a alguien en español / inglés
3. After your complaint, …	**loo^ay**-goh day soo **kay**-hah, … Luego de su queja, …
were you demoted?	loh/lah bah-**hah**-rohn day **rahn**-goh? ¿lo/la bajaron de rango?[7]
were you given new responsibilites?	lay kohn-seeg-**nah**-rohn rray-spohn-sah-bee-lee-**dah**-days **noo^ay**-bahs? ¿le consignaron responsabilidades nuevas?
were you assigned different hours?	lay ah-seeg-**nah**-rohn oon oh-**rah**-ree^oh dee-fay-**rayn**-tay? ¿le asignaron un horario diferente?
were your hours cut?	lay rray-doo-**hay**-rohn soos **oh**-rahs day trah-**bah**-hoh? ¿le redujeron sus horas de trabajo?
was your salary cut?	lay rray-doo-**hay**-rohn soo **soo^ayl**-doh? ¿le redujeron su sueldo?[10]

	ayk-spay-ree-mayn-toh mahs dee-fee-kool-tah-days ayn trah-tahr kohn oh-trahs payr-soh-nahs ayn lah kohm-pah-yee-ah?
did you experience more difficulty in dealing with others in the company?	¿experimentó más dificultades en tratar con otras personas en la compañía?
	poh-dree-ah … loh kay ayks-pay-ree-mayn-toh ayk-sahk-tah-mayn-tay?
Could you … what you experienced exactly?	¿Podría … lo que experimentó exactamente?
	poh-nayr pohr ays-kree-toh
put in writing	poner por escrito
	day-seer-lay ah ahl-ghee^ayn ayn ays-pahn-yohl / een-glays
tell someone in Spanish / English	decirle a alguien en español / inglés

	ahl-goo-nah bays, lay ah ah-blah-doh a ahl-ghee^ayn soh-bray ays-tahs een-kee^ay-too-days?
4. Have you spoken to anyone regarding these concerns?	Alguna vez, ¿le ha hablado a alguien sobre estas inquietudes?
	kohn kee^ayn?
With whom?	¿Con quién?
	koo^ahn-doh?
When?	¿Cuándo?
	kay poo^ays-toh oh-koo-pah ays-tah payr-soh-nah?
What is this person's position?	¿Qué puesto ocupa esta persona?[4]
	poh-dree-ah … loh kay say lay dee-hoh ayk-sahk-tah-mayn-tay?
Could you … what was said to you exactly?	¿Podría … lo que se le dijo exactamente?
	poh-nayr pohr ays-kree-toh
put in writing	poner por escrito
	day-seer-lay ah ahl-ghee^ayn ayn ays-pahn-yohl / een-glays
tell someone in Spanish / English	decirle a alguien en español / inglés

	ah soo pah-ray-sayr, toh-moh lah kohm-pahn-yee-ah may-dee-dahs pah-rah pray-bay-neer ays-tahs rray-pray-sah-lee^ahs?
5. In your mind, did the company take any steps to prevent this retaliation?	A su parecer, ¿tomó la compañía medidas para prevenir estas represalias?
	poh-dree-ah … lahs may-dee-dahs kay toh-mah-rohn oh noh toh-mah-rohn?
Could you … what steps they did or did not take?	¿Podría … las medidas que tomaron o no tomaron?
	poh-nayr pohr ays-kree-toh
put in writing	poner por escrito
	day-seer-lay ah ahl-ghee^ayn ayn ays-pahn-yohl / een-glays
tell someone in Spanish / English	decirle a alguien en español / inglés

VI. Wage and Hour Dispute

*dees-**poo**-tah sah-lah-**ree^ahl** oh **soh**-bray lah **kahr**-gah oh-**rah**-ree^ah*
Disputa salarial o sobre la carga horaria

English	Pronunciation & Spanish
1. How much were you making at the time that you contend you were …	*koo^**ahn**-toh gah-**nah**-bah koo^**ahn**-doh ah-**feer**-mah kay …* ¿Cuánto ganaba cuando afirma que …[5]
terminated?	*say lay days-pee-**dee^oh?*** se le despidió?
discriminated against?	*say lay dees-kree-mee-**noh?*** se le discriminó?
retaliated against?	*say toh-**moh** rray-pray-**sah**-lee^ah ayn soo **kohn**-trah?* se tomó represalia en su contra?
demoted?	*say lay rray-lay-**goh** ah oon **poo^ays**-toh een-fay-**ree^ohr?*** se le relegó a un puesto inferior?
denied a promotion?	*say lay nay-**goh** oon ah-**sayn**-soh?* se le negó un ascenso?
harassed?	*say lay ah-koh-**soh?*** se le acosó?
2. Does that include overtime?	*__ays__-toh een-**kloo**-yay **oh**-rahs **ayks**-trahs trah-bah-**hah**-dahs?* ¿Esto incluye horas extras trabajadas?
3. Did you work overtime?	*trah-bah-**hoh oh**-rahs **ayk**-strahs?* ¿Trabajó horas extras?
4. Were you required to work overtime?	*lay **ay**-rah oh-blee-gah-**toh**-ree^oh trah-bah-**hahr oh**-rahs **ayks**-trahs?* ¿Le era obligatorio trabajar horas extras?
Did you ever have any problems doing that?	*ahl-**goo**-nah bays, tay-**nee**-ah proh-**blay**-mahs kohn trah-bah-**hahr oh**-rahs **ayks**-trahs?* Alguna vez, ¿tenía problemas con trabajar horas extras?
Could you … why you could not work the extra hours?	*poh-**dree**-ah … pohr-**kay** no poh-**dee**-ah trah-bah-**hahr oh**-rahs **ayks**-trahs?* ¿Podría … por qué no podía trabajar horas extras?
put in writing	*poh-**nayr** pohr ays-**kree**-toh* poner por escrito
tell someone in Spanish / English	*day-**seer**-lay ah **ahl**-ghee^ayn ayn ays-pahn-**yohl** / een-**glays*** decirle a alguien en español / inglés

VII. Promotion Denied

*nay-gah-**see**^ohn day ah-**sayn**-soh ayn ayl trah-**bah**-hoh*
Negación de ascenso en el trabajo

English	Pronunciation & Spanish
1. If you were denied a promotion or had a promotion rescinded, was your pay also affected?	*say bee^oh eem-pahk-**tah**-doh soo sah-**lah**-ree^oh **koh**-moh rray-sool-**tah**-doh day **oo**-nah nay-gah-**see**^ohn day **ah**-sayn-**soh** ayn ayl trah-**bah**-hoh oh lah ah-noo-lah-**see**^ohn day oon ah-**sayn**-soh?* ¿Se vio impactado su salario como resultado de una negación de ascenso en el trabajo o la anulación de un ascenso?
By how much?	*pohr **koo**^ayn-toh dee-**nay**-roh?* ¿Por cuánto dinero?[5]
2. Do you know who was promoted instead?	*sah-bay kee^ayn rray-see-**bee**^oh ayl ah-**sayn**-soh ayn soo loo-**gahr**?* ¿Sabe quién recibió el ascenso en su lugar?
Do you know the person's name?	*sah-bay **koh**-moh say **yah**-mah lah payr-**soh**-nah?* ¿Sabe cómo se llama la persona?[4]
3. How long had that person been with the company / employer?	*pohr **koo**^ayn-toh **tee**^aym-poh ah-**bee**-ah trah-bah-**hah**-doh **ays**-ah payr-**soh**-nah **pah**-rah lah kohm-pahn-**yee**-ah / ayl aym-play-ah-**dohr**?* ¿Por cuánto tiempo había trabajado esa persona para la compañía / el empleador?
one day	*oon **dee**-ah* un día[11]
(#) days	*(#) **dee**-ahs* (#) días[5, 11]
one week	***oo**-nah say-**mah**-nah* una semana[11]
(#) weeks	*(#) say-**mah**-nahs* (#) semanas[5, 11]
one month	*oon mays* un mes[5, 11]
(#) months	*(#) **may**-says* (#) meses[5, 11]
one year	*oon **ahn**-yoh* un año[5, 11]
(#) years	*(#) **ahn**-hoys* (#) años[11]
4. What is ... of the person (if known)?	*koo^ahl ays ... day lah payr-**soh**-nah (see say **sah**-bay)?* ¿Cuál es ... de la persona (si se sabe)?
gender	*ayl **sayk**-soh* el sexo

race	*lah **rrah**-sah* la raza[8]
approximate age	*lah ay-**dahd** ah-prohk-see-**mah**-dah* la edad aproximada[5]

VIII. Termination

*days-pay-**dee**-doh*
Despedido

English	Pronunciation & Spanish
1. Were you offered a severance package or pay?	*lay oh-fray-**see^ay**-rohn rray-gah-**lee**-ah oh een-daym-nee-sah-**see^ohn** pohr **say**-say day aym-**play**-oh?* ¿Le ofrecieron regalía o indemnización por cese de empleo?
2. Were you given anything in writing?	*lay **dee^ay**-rohn **ahl**-goh pohr ay-**skree**-toh* ¿Le dieron algo por escrito?
May we have a copy?	*nohs **poo^ay**-day proh-pohr-see^oh-**nahr** oo-nah **koh**-pee^ah?* ¿Nos puede proporcionar una copia?
3. Who terminated you?	*kee^ayn loh/lah day-spee-**dee^oh**?* ¿Quién lo/la despidió?[7]
4. Could you ... the reason they gave you for being terminated?	*poh-**dree**-ah ... lah rrah-**sohn** kay lay **dee^ay**-rohn **pah**-rah ayl days-pay-**dee**-doh?* ¿Podría ... la razón que le dieron para el despido?
put in writing	*poh-**nayr** pohr ays-**kree**-toh* poner por escrito
tell someone in Spanish / English	*day-**seer**-lay ah **ahl**-ghee^ayn ayn ays-pahn-**yohl** / een-**glays*** decirle a alguien en español / inglés
5. Do you know if anyone else was also terminated for the same reason?	***sah**-bay see day-spee-**dee^ay**-rohn ah **oh**-trah payr-**soh**-nah pohr lah **mees**-mah rrah-**sohn**?* ¿Sabe si despidieron a otra persona por la misma razón?
What is ... of the person (if known)?	*koo^ahl ays ... day lah payr-**soh**-nah (see say **sah**-bay)?* ¿Cuál es ... de la persona (si se sabe)?
gender	*ayl **sayk**-soh* el género
race	*lah **rrah**-sah* la raza[8]
approximate age	*lah ay-**dahd** ah-prohk-see-**mah**-dah* la edad aproximada[5]

IX. Wrongful Termination

*days-**pee**-doh een-**hoo**-stoh*
Despido injusto

English	Pronunciation & Spanish
1. What is the name and address of the employer that terminated you?	*koo^ahl-ays sohn ayl **nohm**-bray ee lah dee-rayk-**see^ohn** dayl aym-play-ah-**dohr** kay loh/lah days-pee-**dee^oh**?* ¿Cuáles son el nombre y la dirección del empleador que lo/la despidió?[4, 5, 7]
2. What is the phone number of your current employer?	*koo^ahl ays ayl **noo**-may-roh day tay-**lay**-foh-noh day soo aym-play-ah-**dohr** ahk-**too^ahl**?* ¿Cuál es el número de teléfono de su empleador actual?[5]
3. Are there any closely affiliated companies or parent companies that may also be liable?	*ah^ee ahl-**goo**-nah **oh**-trah kohm-pahn-**yee**-ah mah-**trees** oh ah-fee-**lee^ah**-dah kay tahm-**bee^ayn** poo^ay-day sayr rrays-pohn-**sah**-blay?* ¿Hay alguna otra compañía matriz o afiliada que también pueda ser responsable?
Will you be able to provide their names and addresses?	*nohs poh-**drah** proh-pohr-see^oh-**nahr** soos **nohm**-brays ee dee-rayk-**see^ohn**-nays?* ¿Nos podrá proporcionar sus nombres y direcciones?
Write that information for me here, please.	*ays-**kree**-bah-may **ay**-sah een-fohr-mah-**see^ohn** ah-**kee** pohr fah-**bohr**.* Escríbame esa información aquí, por favor.
4. What was the date of the termination?	*koo^ahl foo^ay lah **fay**-chah dayl days-**pee**-doh?* ¿Cuál fue la fecha del despido?[3]
5. What was the last date of active work for this employer?	*koo^ahl foo^ay lah **fay**-chah dayl **ool**-tee-moh **dee**-ah day trah-**bah**-hoh ahk-**tee**-boh kohn **ays**-tay aym-play-ah-**dohr**?* ¿Cuál fue la fecha del último día de trabajo activo con este empleador?[3]
6. Approximately what date were you first notified you were fired or would be fired?	*ah-prohk-see-mah-dah-**mayn**-tay, koo^ahl foo^ay lah **fay**-chah ayn lah koo^ahl rray-see-**bee^oh** noh-tee-fee-kah-**see^ohn** pohr bays pree-**may**-rah day kay foo^ay days-pay-**dee**-doh/dah oh **ee**-bah ah sayr days-pay-**dee**-doh/dah?* Aproximadamente, ¿cuál fue la fecha en la cual recibió notificación por vez primera de que fue despedido/a o iba a ser despedido/a?[3, 6]
7. Please respond with "yes" to any of the following statements that may apply:	*pohr fah-**bohr**, rrays-**pohn**-dah kohn <see> ah koo^ahl-ays-**kee^ayr** day lahs see-**ghee^ayn**-tays day-clah-rah-**see^oh**-nays kay ah-**plee**-kayn:* Por favor, responda con <sí> a cualesquier de las siguientes declaraciones que apliquen:
You were terminated for ...	*foo^ay days-pay-**dee**-doh/dah pohr ...* Fue despedido/a por ...[6]
performance.	*ayl day-saym-**payn**-yoh lah-boh-**rahl**.* el desempeño laboral.

absenteeism.

*ayl ah^oo-sayn-**tees**-moh.*
el ausentismo.

tardiness.

*lay eem-poon-too^ahl-lee-**dahd**.*
la impuntualidad.

excessive leave requests.

*ayk-say-**see**-bahs soh-lee-see-**too**-days day ah^oo-**sayn**-see^ah.*
excesivas solicitudes de ausencia.

appearance.

*ayl ahs-**payk**-toh **fee**-see-koh.*
el aspecto físico.

hygiene.

*ayl ee-**hee^ay**-nay.*
el higiene.

conduct.

*ayl kohm-pohr-tah-**mee^ayn**-toh.*
el comportamiento.

ethnicity.

*lah ayt-nee-see-**dahd**.*
la etnicidad.

religious beliefs.

*lahs kray-**ayn**-see^ahs rray-lee-**hee^oh**-sahs.*
las creencias religiosas.

sexual orientation.

*lah oh-ree^ayn-tah-**see^ohn** sayk-**soo^ahl**.*
la orientación sexual.

company economic problems.

*proh-**blay**-mahs ay-koh-**noh**-mee-kohs day lah kohm-pahn-**yee**-ah.*
problemas económicos de la compañía.

other reason.

***oh**-trah rrah-**sohn**.*
otra razón.

---

8. Did you receive anything in writing from the employer about the termination?

*rray-see-**bee^oh** ahl-goh pohr ays-**kree**-toh dayl aym-play-ah-**dohr soh**-bray ayl days-**pee**-doh?*
¿Recibió algo por escrito del empleador sobre el despido?

Can you provide our office with a copy?

*nohs **poo^ay**-day proh-pohr-see^oh-**nahr** oo-nah **koh**-pee^ah?*
¿Nos puede proporcionar una copia?

---

9. How much were you earning (an hour) at the time of termination?

***koo^ahn**-toh gah-**nah**-bah (pohr **oh**-rah) ayn ayl moh-**mayn**-toh dayl days-**pee**-doh?*
¿Cuánto ganaba (por hora) en el momento del despido?[5]

---

10. Did the company offer bonuses?

*pah-**gah**-bah lah kohm-pahn-**yee**-ah boh-nee-fee-kah-**see^oh**-nays oh soh-bray-**soo^ayl**-doh?*
¿Pagaba la compañía bonificaciones o sobresueldo?

---

11. How much overtime did you work?

***koo^ahn**-tahs **oh**-rahs **ayks**-trahs trah-bah-**hoh**?*
¿Cuántas horas extras trabajó?[5]

---

12. How much overtime were you working on average?

***koo^ahn**-tahs **oh**-rahs **ayks**-trahs trah-bah-**hah**-bah ayn proh-**may**-dee^oh?*
¿Cuántas horas extras trabajaba en promedio?[5]

koo^ahn-toh gah-noh pohr lahs oh-rahs ayks-trahs trah-bah-hah-dahs?

13. How much did you earn in overtime pay? ¿Cuánto ganó por las horas extras trabajadas?[5]

---

koo^ahl foo^ay soo soo^ayl-doh broo-toh pah-rah ayl ahn-yoh kah-layn-dah-ree^oh pah-sah-doh?

14. What was your gross annual income for the last calendar year? ¿Cuál fue su sueldo bruto para el año calendario pasado?[5]

---

gah-noh toh-doh ays-toh mee^ayn-trahs trah-bah-hah-bah pah-rah ayl aym-play-ah-dohr kay loh/lah days-pee-dee^oh oh day ahl-goo-nah oh-trah foo^ayn-tay?

15. Was all of this earned at the employer that terminated you or from some other source? ¿Ganó todo esto mientras trabajaba para el empleador que lo/la despidió o de alguna otra fuente?[7]

---

tee^ay-nay koh-pee^ah day ...

16. Do you have a copy of your ... ¿Tiene copia de ...

soo ool-tee-moh kohm-proh-bahn-tay day sah-lah-ree^ohs ay eem-poo^ay-stohs day ays-tay aym-play-ah-dohr?

last W-2 provided by this employer? su último comprobante de salarios e impuestos de este empleador?

soos tah-loh-nays day chay-kay day ays-tay aym-play-ah-dohr?

paystubs from this employer? sus talones de cheque de este empleador?

nohs poo^ay-day proh-pohr-see^ah-nahr koh-pee^ahs day ays-tohs doh-koo-mayn-tohs?

Can you provide us with copies of these documents? ¿Nos puede proporcionar copias de estos documentos?

---

soo aym-play-ay-dohr ahn-tay-ree^ohr lay proh-porh-see^oh-noh ...

17. Did your past employer provide you with ... ¿Su empleador anterior le proporcionó ...

ayl say-goo-roh dayn-tahl?

dental insurance? el seguro dental?

een-dee-bee-doo^ahl oh fah-mee-lee^ahr?

Individual or family? ¿Individual o familiar?

ayl say-goo-roh day sah-lood?

medical insurance? el seguro de salud?

een-dee-bee-doo^ahl oh fah-mee-lee^ahr?

Individual or family? ¿Individual o familiar?

ayl say-goo-roh day bees-tah?

vision insurance? el seguro de vista?

een-dee-bee-doo^ahl oh fah-mee-lee^ahr?

Individual or family? ¿Individual o familiar?

oon plahn day payn-see^oh-nays?

pension plan? un plan de pensiones?

lah pahr-tee-see-pah-see^ohn ayn lahs oo-tee-lee-dah-days?

profit sharing plan? la participación en las utilidades?

stock options?	*lah* **kohm**-*prah ohp-see^oh-***nahl** *day ahk-***see^oh**-*nays?* la compra opcional de acciones?
other benefits?	**oh**-*trohs bay-nay-***fee**-*see^ohs mahr-hee-***nah**-*lays?* otros beneficios marginales?
18. Did you receive severance pay?	*rray-see-***bee^oh** *een-daym-nee-sah-***see^ohn** *pohr days-***pee**-*doh?* ¿Recibió indemnización por despido?
How much severance did you receive?	*koo^***ahn**-*toh dee-***nay**-*roh lay pah-***gah**-*rohn day een-daym-nee-sah-***see^ohn***?* ¿Cuánto dinero le pagaron de indemnización?[5]
19. What were the name and home address of your immediate supervisor at the time of termination?	*koo^***ahl**-*ays* **ay**-*rahn ayl* **nohm**-*bray ee lah dee-rayk-***see^ohn** *day soo soo-payr-bee-***sohr** *een-may-***dee^ah**-*toh ahl moh-***mayn**-*toh day soo days-***pee**-*doh?* ¿Cuáles eran el nombre y la dirección domiciliaria de su supervisor inmediato al momento de su despido?[4, 5]
20. Was your relationship with your immediate supervisor positive or negative?	*lah rray-lah-***see^ohn** *kay tay-***nee**-*ah kohn soo soo-payr-bee-***sohr** *een-may-***dee^ah**-*toh ay-rah poh-see-***tee**-*bah oh nay-gah-***tee**-*bah?* ¿La relación que tenía con su supervisor inmediato era positiva o negativa?
21. Could you provide the names and titles of supervisors or key employees above and below you?	*nohs poh-***dree**-*ah proh-pohr-see^oh-***nahr** *lohs* **nohm**-*brays ee lohs* **tee**-*too-lohs dayl* **poo^ays**-*toh dayl trah-***bah**-*hoh pah-*rah *lohs soo-payr-bee-***soh**-*rays oh aym-play-***ah**-*dohs* **klah**-*bay kay oh-koo-***pah**-*bahn oon* **poo^ays**-*toh een-fay-***ree^ohr** *o soo-pay-***ree^ohr** *ahl* **soo**-*yoh?* ¿Nos podría proporcionar los nombres y los títulos del puesto de trabajo para los supervisores o empleados clave que ocupaban un puesto inferior o superior al suyo?
Write that information for me here, please.	*ays-***kree**-*bah-may* **ay**-*sah een-fohr-mah-***see^ohn** *ah-***kee** *pohr fah-***bohr**. Escríbame esa información aquí, por favor.

X. Questions Regarding Spouse and Children

*pray-***goon**-*tahs* **soh**-*bray* **kohn**-*yoo-hay ay* **ee**-*hohs*
Preguntas sobre cónyuge e hijos

English	**Pronunciation & Spanish**
1. Do you have any children?	**tee^***ay*-*nay* **ee**-*hohs?* ¿Tiene hijos?
How many children do you have?	*koo^***ahn**-*tohs* **ee**-*hohs* **tee^***ay*-*nay?* ¿Cuántos hijos tiene?[5, 12]
How many male children and how many female children?	*koo^***ahn**-*tohs* **ee**-*hohs ee koo^***ahn**-*tahs* **ee**-*hahs?* ¿Cuántos hijos y cuántas hijas tiene?[5]

What is the name of each one?	*koo^ahl ays ayl **nohm**-bray day **kah**-dah **oo**-noh?* ¿Cuál es el nombre de cada uno?[4]
What is the age of each one?	***koo^ahl** ays lah ay-**dahd** day **kah**-dah **oo**-noh?* ¿Cuál es la edad de cada uno?[5]
Can you write (all of) that information for me here, please?	*may **poo^ay**-day ays-kree-**beer** (**toh**-dah) ay-sah een-fohr-mah-**see^ohn** ah-**kee**, pohr fah-**bohr**?* ¿Me puede escribir (toda) esa información aquí, por favor?
2. Do any of the children work?	*ahl-**goo**-nohs day lohs **ee**-hohs trah-**bah**-hahn?* ¿Algunos de los hijos trabajan?
3. How many children live at home?	***koo^ahn**-tohs **ee**-hohs **bee**-bayn ayn **kah**-sah?* ¿Cuántos hijos viven en casa?[5]
4. Does your spouse work?	*trah-**bah**-hah soo **kohn**-yoo-hay?* ¿Trabaja su cónyuge?
5. Where does your spouse work?	***dohn**-day trah-**bah**-hah soo **kohn**-yoo-hay?* ¿Dónde trabaja su cónyuge?[4]
6. What type of work does your spouse do?	*ah kay say day-**dee**-kah soo **kohn**-yoo-hah?* ¿A qué se dedica su cónyuge?[4]
7. Does your spouse receive a salary or is paid by the hour?	*rray-**see**-bay soo **kohn**-yoo-hay oon **soo^ayl**-doh oh say lay **pah**-gah ah la **oh**-rah?* ¿Recibe su cónyuge un sueldo o se le paga a la hora?
8. How much does your spouse earn (hourly)?	***koo^ahn**-toh **gah**-nah soo **kohn**-yoo-hah (ah lah **oh**-rah)?* ¿Cuánto gana su cónyuge (a la hora)?[5]

XI. Education, Military Experience and Work History

*ay-doo-kah-**see^ohn**, ayks-pay-ree-**^ayn**-see-^ah mee-lee-**tahr** ee ahn-tay-say-**dayn**-tays lah-boh-**rah**-lays*
Educación, experiencia militar y antecedentes laborales

English	Pronunciation & Spanish
1. Did you attend ... / Did you complete ...	*ah-sees-**tee^oh** a ... / kohm-play-**toh** ...* ¿Asistió a ... / ¿Completó ...
elementary school?	*lah pree-**mah**-ree^ah?* la primaria?
middle school/junior high?	*lah say-koon-**dah**-ree^ah?* la secundaria?
high school/senior high?	*lah pray-pah-rah-**toh**-ree^ah?* la preparatoria?
vocational school?	*lah ays-**koo^ay**-lah boh-kah-see^oh-**nahl**?* la escuela vocacional?

college?	*lah oo-nee-bayr-see-**dahd**?* la universidad?
2. Have you served in the armed forces?	*ah sayr-**bee**-doh ayn lahs **foo^ayr**-sahs ahr-**mah**-dahs?* ¿Ha servido en las fuerzas armadas?
3. Are you presently in the armed forces / the reserves?	*ays-**tah** seer-**bee^ayn**-doh ahk-too^ahl-**mayn**-tay ayn lahs **foo^ayr**-sahs ahr-**mah**-dahs / lahs rray-**sayr**-bahs mee-lee-**tah**-rays?* ¿Está sirviendo actualmente en las fuerzas armadas / las reservas militares?
4. How many total employers have you had?	*koo^**ahn**-tohs aym-play-ah-**doh**-rays ah tay-**nee**-doh ayn toh-**tahl**?* ¿Cuántos empleadores ha tenido en total?
5. How long did you work with the … employer?	*pohr koo^**ahn**-toh **tee^aym**-poh trah-bah-**hoh pah**-rah soo … aym-play-ah-**dohr**?* ¿Por cuánto tiempo trabajó para su … empleador?[9, 13]
first	*pree-**mayr*** primer
second	*say-**goon**-doh* segundo
third	*tayr-**sayr*** tercer
fourth	*koo^**ahr**-toh* cuarto
fifth	*keen-toh* quinto
sixth	*sayks-toh* sexto
seventh	*sayp-tee-moh* séptimo
eighth	*ohk-**tah**-boh* octavo
ninth	*noh-**bay**-noh* noveno
tenth	*day-see-moh* décimo
Could you … the type of work performed, the reason for leaving and the dates of your employment with each employer?	*poh-**dree**-ah … ayl **tee**-poh day trah-**bah**-hoh day-saym-payn-**yah**-doh, lah rrah-**sohn pah**-rah day-**hahr**-loh ee lahs **fay**-chahs day soo aym-**play**-oh kohn **kah**-dah aym-play-ah-**dohr**?* ¿Podría … el tipo de trabajo desempeñado, la razón para dejarlo y las fechas de su empleo con cada empleador?

put in writing	*poh-**nayr** pohr ays-**kree**-toh* poner por escrito
tell someone in Spanish / English	*day-**seer**-lay ah **ahl**-ghee^ayn ayn ays-pahn-**yohl** / een-**glays*** decirle a alguien en español / inglés
6. Were you provided with a written job description?	*say lay dee^oh **oo**-nah days-kreep-**see^ohn** ays-kree-tah dayl trah-**bah**-hoh?* ¿Se le dio una descripción escrita del trabajo?
Can you provide us with a copy?	*nohs **poo^ay**-day proh-pohr-see^oh-**nahr** oo-nah **koh**-pee^ah?* ¿Nos puede proporcionar una copia?
7. Have you ever been hospitalized or treated for …	*ah **see**-doh ohs-pee-tah-lee-**sah**-doh/dah oh trah-**tah**-doh/dah pohr …* ¿Ha sido hospitalizado/a o tratado/a por …[6]
mental illness?	*oon trahs-**tohr**-noh mayn-**tahl**?* un trastorno mental?
alcoholism?	*ayl ahl-koh-oh-**lees**-moh?* el alcoholismo?
drugs?	***droh**-gahs?* drogas?
other health problems?	***oh**-trohs proh-**blay**-mahs day sah-**lood**?* otros problemas de salud?
8. Have you ever been involuntarily terminated before?	*ah **see**-doh/dah days-pay-**dee**-doh/dah een-boh-loon-tah-ree^ah-**mayn**-tay **ahn**-tays?* ¿Ha sido despedido/a involuntariamente antes?[6]
9. Have you ever given false information on an employment application before?	*ah proh-pohr-see^oh-**nah**-doh een-fohr-mah-**see^ohn** fahl-sah ayn oo-nah soh-lee-see-**tood** day trah-**bah**-hoh **ahn**-tays?* ¿Ha proporcionado información falsa en una solicitud de trabajo antes?

XII. Litigation History

*ahn-tay-say-**dayn**-tays day lee-**tee**-hee^oh*
Antecedentes de litigio

English	Pronunciation & Spanish
1. Have you ever been involved in other lawsuits or other litigation before?	*ah ay-**stah**-doh een-boh-loo-**krah**-doh/dah ayn **oh**-trohs play^ee-tohs oh proh-**say**-sohs hoo-dee-**see^ah**-lays **ahn**-tays?* ¿Ha estado involucrado/a en otros pleitos o procesos judiciales antes?[6]
2. Are you involved in any other lawsuits or other litigation currently?	*say ayn-**koo^ayn**-trah een-boh-loo-**krah**-doh/dah ayn **oh**-trohs play^ee-tohs oh proh-**say**-sohs hoo-dee-**see^ah**-lays ahk-too^ahl-**mayn**-tay?* ¿Se encuentra involucrado/a en otros pleitos o procesos judiciales actualmente?[6]

3. Is the legal proceeding related to …
*say **trah**-tah ayl **play**^ee-toh day …*
¿Se trata el pleito de …

unemployment compensation?
*lah kohm-payn-sah-**see**^ohn pohr days-aym-**play**-oh?*
la compensación por desempleo?

worker's compensation?
*lah een-daym-nee-sah-**see**^ohn lah-boh-**rahl**?*
la indemnización laboral?

the Equal Employment Opportunity Commission?
*lah koh-mee-**see**^ohn day ee-goo^ahl-**dahd** day oh-pohr-too-nee-**dah**-days day day-saym-**play**-oh?*
la Comisión de Igualdad de Oportunidades de Empleo?

the National Labor Relations Board?
*lah **hoon**-tah nah-see^oh-**nahl** day rray-lah-**see**^oh-nays dayl trah-**bah**-hoh?*
la Junta Nacional de Relaciones del Trabajo?

OSHA?
*lah ahd-mee-nees-trah-**see**^ohn day lah say-goo-ree-**dahd** ee lah sah-**lood** oh-koo-pah-see^oh-**nah**-lays?*
la Administración de la Seguridad y la Salud Ocupacionales?

a state or local civil rights agency?
***oo**-nah ah-**hayn**-see^ah ays-tah-**tahl** oh loh-**kahl** day day-**ray**-chohs see-**bee**-lays?*
una agencia estatal o local de derechos civiles?

bankruptcy?
*lah bahn-kah-**rroh**-tah?*
la bancarrota?

other?
***oh**-troh **tay**-mah?*
otro tema?

4. Do you have any criminal convictions?
***tee**^ay-nay ahn-tay-say-**dayn**-tays pay-**nah**-lays?*
¿Tiene antecedentes penales?

5. Are there any pending criminal cases against you?
*ah^ee **kah**-sohs pay-**nah**-lays payn-**dee**^ayn-tays ayn soo **kohn**-trah?*
¿Hay casos penales pendientes en su contra?

6. Have you spoken with …
*ah ah-**blah**-doh kohn …*
¿Ha hablado con …

any other attorney?
***oh**-troh ah-boh-**gah**-doh?*
otro abogado?

another law firm?
***oh**-troh boo-**fay**-tay day ah-boh-**gah**-dohs?*
otro bufete de abogados?

Did you share this same information?
*kohm-pahr-**tee**^oh ay-stah **mees**-mah een-fohr-mah-**see**^ohn?*
¿Compartió esta misma información?

Please write down for me the names and telephone numbers of attorneys with whom you have already spoken.
*pohr fah-**bohr**, ah-**poon**-tay-may lohs **nohm**-brays ee lohs **noo**-may-rohs day tay-**lay**-foh-noh day lohs ah-boh-**gah**-dohs kohn **kee**^ay-nays yah say ah koh-moo-nee-**kah**-doh.*
Por favor, apúnteme los nombres y los números de teléfono de los abogados con quienes ya se ha comunicado.   .

7. Are you presently represented by ...

*yah say ayn-**koo**^**ayn**-trah rray-pray-sayn-**tah**-doh/dah pohr ...*
¿Ya se encuentra representado/a por ...[6]

another attorney?

*oh-troh ah-boh-**gah**-doh?*
otro abogado?

another law firm?

*oh-troh boo-**fay**-tay day ah-boh-**gah**-dohs?*
otro bufete de abogados?

I'm afraid we are unable to speak with you any further.

*lah-**mayn**-toh noh poh-**dayr** ah-**blahr**-lay mahs day **ays**-tay ah-**soon**-toh.*
Lamento no poder hablarle más de este asunto.

8. Have you filed a complaint with ...

*ah pray-sayn-**tah**-doh oo-nah day-**mahn**-dah kohn ...*
¿Ha presentado una demanda con ...

the EEOC?

*lah koh-mee-**see**^**ohn** day ee-goo^ahl-**dahd** day oh-pohr-too-nee-**dah**-days day aym-**play**-oh?*
la Comisión de Igualdad de Oportunidades de Empleo?

another agency?

*oh-trah ah-**hayn**-see^ah?*
otra agencia?

With what entity?

*kohn kay ayn-tee-**dahd**?*
¿Con qué entidad?[4]

With whom?

kohn kee^ayn?
¿Con quién?[4]

What is that individual's phone number?

*koo^ahl ays ayl **noo**-may-roh day tay-**lay**-foh-noh day **ay**-say een-dee-**bee**-doo^oh?*
¿Cuál es el número de teléfono de ese individuo?[5]

When did you file the complaint?

*koo^**ahn**-doh*
¿Cuándo presentó la demanda?[3]

Where did you file the complaint?

dohn-day?
¿Dónde presentó la demanda?[4]

9. Was it a written complaint?

*ayn-tray-**goh** lah day-**mahn**-dah pohr ays-**kree**-toh?*
¿Entregó la demanda por escrito?

Can you provide us with a copy?

*nohs **poo**^**ay**-day proh-pohr-see^oh-**nahr** oo-nah **koh**-pee^ah?*
¿Nos puede proporcionar una copia?

XIII. Disciplinary Actions and Job Appraisals

*ahk-**see^oh**-nays dee-see-plee-**nah**-ree^ahs ee ay-bah-loo^ah-**see^oh**-nays dayl days-aym-**payn**-yoh*
Acciones disciplinarias y evaluaciones del desempeño laboral

English	Pronunciation & Spanish
1. Were you terminated from this job or did you quit voluntarily?	*lo/lah days-pee-**dee^ay**-rohn day **ays**-tay trah-**bah**-hoh oh loh day-**hoh** boh-loon-tah-ree^ah-**mayn**-tay?* ¿Lo/la despidieron de este trabajo o lo dejó voluntariamente?[7]
Were you ever given any warnings or reprimands—formal, informal, written or verbal—prior to the termination?	*say lay dee^oh ahl-**goon** ah-**bee**-soh oh rray-pree-**mayn**-dah—**say**-ah fohr-**mahl**, een-fohr-**mahl**, ays-**kree**-toh oh bayr-**bahl**—**ahn**-tays dayl days-**pee**-doh?* ¿Se le dio algún aviso o reprimenda—sea formal, informal, escrito o verbal—antes del despido?
Please provide the dates, the content and from whom they were given.	*pohr fah-**bohr**, ays-**kree**-bah ah-**kee** lahs **fah**-chahs ee ayl kohn-tay-**nee**-doh day **kah**-dah ah-**bee**-soh oh rray-pray-**mayn**-dah ee day kee^ayn oh-ree-hee-**noh**.* Por favor, escriba aquí las fechas y el contenido de cada aviso o reprimenda y de quién originó.
2. Have you experienced any other prior discipline on the job before?	*ah ayk-spay-ree-mayn-**tah**-doh ahl-**goo**-nah oh-trah **klah**-say day dee-see-**plee**-nah ayn ayl trah-**bah**-hoh ahn-tay-ree^ohr-**mayn**-tay?* ¿Ha experimentado alguna otra clase de disciplina en el trabajo anteriormente?
Could you … the disciplinary measures that were taken?	*poh-**dree**-ah … lahs may-**dee**-dahs dee-see-plee-**nah**-ree^ahs kay say toh-**mah**-rohn?* ¿Podría … las medidas disciplinarias que se tomaron?
put in writing	*poh-**nayr** pohr ays-**kree**-toh* poner por escrito
tell someone in Spanish / English	*day-**seer**-lay ah **ahl**-ghee^ayn ayn ays-pahn-**yohl** / een-**glays*** decirle a alguien en español / inglés
3. Were you ever made aware that your job was in jeopardy?	*ayn ahl-**goon** moh-**mayn**-toh, lay ee-**see^ay**-rohn sah-**bayr** kay koh-**rree**-ah ayl **ree^ays**-goh day payr-**dayr** ayl trah-**bah**-hoh?* En algún momento, ¿le hicieron saber que corría el riesgo de perder el trabajo?
4. Did you ever recieve … from supervisors for going above and beyond the duties of your job?	***oo**-boh ahl-**goon** moh-**mayn**-toh **koo^ahn**-doh rray-see-**bee^oh** … day soo-payr-bee-**soh**-rays pohr eer **moo**-choh mahs ah-**yah** day lohs day-**bay**-rays nohr-**mah**-lays day soo trah-**bah**-hoh?* ¿Hubo algún momento cuando recibió … de supervisores por ir mucho más allá de los deberes normales de su trabajo?
awards	***pray**-mee^ohs* premios
compliments	*ay-**loh**-hee^ohs* elogios

other types of recognition	*oh-troh **tee**-poh day rray-koh-noh-see-**mee^ayn**-toh* otro tipo de reconocimiento

---

5. Were you ever given any written appraisals of your job performance?	*rray-see-**bee^oh** ay-bah-loo^ah-**see^oh**-nays ays-**kree**-tahs day soo days-aym-**payn**-yoh lah-boh-**rahl**?* ¿Recibió evaluaciones escritas de su desempeño laboral?
Can you provide us with copies of these written appraisals?	*nohs **poo^ay**-day proh-pohr-see^oh-**nahr koh**-pee^ahs day **ays**-tahs ay-bah-loo^ah-**see^oh**-nays ays-**kree**-tahs?* ¿Nos puede proporcionar copias de estas evaluaciones escritas?

---

6. Can you describe your job history at the company that terminated you in a written questionnaire?	*nohs **poo^ay**-day day-tah-**yahr** ayn oon koo^ays-tee^oh-**nah**-ree^oh soo ayn-tay-say-**dayn**-tay lah-boh-**rahl** kohn lah kohm-pahn-**yee**-ah kay loh/lah days-pee-**dee^oh**?* ¿Nos puede detallar en un cuestionario su antecedente laboral con la compañía que lo/la despidió?[7]

---

7. We will need you to make us a list with the names, addresses and home telephone numbers for ... who have knowledge of your work history and that would say favorable things about your performance.	*nay-say-see-**tah**-mohs kay nohs **ah**-gah **oo**-nah **lees**-tah day lohs **nohm**-brays, dee-rayk-**see^oh**-nays ee **noo**-may-rohs day tay-**lay**-foh-noh doh-mee-see-**lee^ah**-ree^ohs day ... kay **tee^ay**-nayn koh-noh-see-**mee^ayn**-toh day soos ahn-tay-say-**dayn**-tays lah-boh-**rah**-lays ee kay ah-**ree**-ahn koh-mayn-**tah**-ree^ohs fah-boh-**rah**-blays **soh**-bray soo day-saym-**payn**-yoh lah-boh-**rahl**.* Necesitamos que nos haga una lista de los nombres, direcciones y números de teléfono domiciliarios de ... que tienen conocimiento de sus antecedentes laborales y que harían comentarios favorables sobre su desempeño laboral.
supervisors ...	*soo-payr-bee-**soh**-rays ...* supervisores ...
formen ...	*kah-pah-**tah**-says ...* capataces ...
co-workers ...	*kohm-pahn-**yay**-rohs day trah-**bah**-hoh ...* compañeros de trabajo ...
other employees ...	***oh**-trohs aym-play-**ah**-dohs ...* otros empleados ...
all co-workers ...	***toh**-dohs lohs kohm-pahn-**yay**-rohs day trah-**bah**-hoh ...* todos los compañeros de trabajo ...

---

8. Do you know the company president, chief officer or personnel director?	*koh-**noh**-say ahl pray-say-**dayn**-tay day lah kohm-pahn-**yee**-ah, ahl hay-**rayn**-tay preen-see-**pahl** oh ahl **hay**-fay day rray-**koor**-sohs oo-**mah**-nohs?* ¿Conoce al presidente de la compañía, al gerente principal o al jefe de recursos humanos?

---

9. Have you appealed or protested the termination to any of them?	*ah ah-pay-**lah**-doh oh proh-tays-**tah**-doh ayl days-**pee**-doh ah ahl-**goo**-noh day **ay**-yohs?* ¿Ha apelado o protestado el despido a alguno de ellos?

10. Were there witnesses to the incident(s) in question?	*ah-**bee**-ah tays-**tee**-gohs ah lohs een-see-**dayn**-tays ayn koo^ays-**tee^ohn**?* ¿Había testigos a los incidentes en cuestión?
Please make a list of their names, addresses and home telephone numbers to give us.	*pohr fah-**bohr**, **ah**-gah **oo**-nah **lees**-tah day soos **nohm**-brays, dee-rayk-**see^oh**-nays ee **noo**-may-rohs day tay-**lay**-foh-noh doh-mee-see-**lee^ah**-ree^ohs **pah**-rah ayn-tray-**gahr**-nohs.* Por favor, haga una lista de sus nombres, direcciones y números de teléfono domiciliarios para entregarnos.
11. Are there other persons who might have helpful information regarding the termination, such as neighbors, doctors, lawyers, police or government officials?	*ah^ee **oh**-trahs payr-**soh**-nahs kay **poo^ay**-dahn tay-**nayr** een-fohr-mah-**see^ohn** oo-teel rrays-**payk**-toh ahl days-pay-**dee**-doh **tah**-lays **koh**-moh bay-**see**-nohs, **may**-dee-kohs, ah-boh-**gah**-dohs, oh-fee-**see^ah**-lays day poh-lee-**see**-ah oo oh-fee-**see^ah**-lays goo-bayr-nah-mayn-**tah**-lays?* ¿Hay otras personas que puedan tener información útil respecto al despido tales como vecinos, médicos, abogados, oficiales de policía u oficiales gubernamentales?
Please make a list of their names, addresses and home telephone numbers to give us.	*pohr fah-**bohr**, **ah**-gah oo-nah **lees**-tah day soos **nohm**-brays, dee-rayk-**see^oh**-nays ee **noo**-may-rohs day tay-**lay**-foh-noh doh-mee-see-**lee^ah**-ree^ohs **pah**-rah ayn-tray-**gahr**-nohs.* Por favor, haga una lista de sus nombres, direcciones y números de teléfono domiciliarios para entregarnos.

XIV. Current Employment Status

*see-too^ah-**see^ohn** lah-boh-**rahl** ahk-**too^ahl***
Situación laboral actual

English	Pronunciation & Spanish
1. Have you been job hunting since the termination?	*ah ays-**tah**-doh boos-**kahn**-doh trah-**bah**-hoh **days**-day ayl days-pay-**dee**-doh?* ¿Ha estado buscando trabajo desde el despido?
Please make a list of the names and addresses of the employers and the dates they were contacted to give us.	*pohr fah-**bohr**, **ah**-gah oo-nah **lees**-tah day lohs **nohm**-brays ee dee-rayk-**see^oh**-nays day lohs aym-play-ah-**doh**-rays kohn kay ah kohn-tahk-**tah**-doh ee lahs **fay**-chahs day **ays**-tah koh-moo-nee-kah-**see^ohn** **pah**-rah ayn-tray-**gahr**-nohs.* Por favor, haga una lista de los nombres y direcciones de los empleadores con que ha contactado y las fechas de esta comunicación para entregarnos.
2. Have you rejected recent job offers?	*ah nay-**gah**-doh oh-**fayr**-tahs day aym-**play**-oh rray-**see^ayn**-tays?* ¿Ha negado ofertas de empleo recientes?
Could you ... why the job offer was rejected?	*poh-**dree**-ah ... pohr kay say rray-chah-**soh** lah oh-**fayr**-tah day aym-**play**-oh?* ¿Podría ... por qué se rechazó la oferta de empleo?
explain in writing	*ayks-plee-**kahr** pohr ays-**kree**-toh* explicar por escrito

tell someone in Spanish / English	*day-**seer**-lay ah **ahl**-ghee^ayn ayn ays-pahn-**yohl** / een-**glays***
	decirle a alguien en español / inglés

3. Do you have a resumé or summary of your job history?

*tee^**ay**-nay oon koo-**rree**-koo-loom bee-**tah**-eh oh oon rray-**soo**-mayn day soos ahn-tay-say-**dayn**-tays lah-boh-**rah**-lays?*

¿Tiene un currículum vitae o un resumen de sus antecedentes laborales?

Please provide us with a copy of that.

*Por fah-**bohr**, proh-pohr-**see^oh**-nay-nohs oo-nah **koh**-pee^ay day **ay**-say.*

Por favor, proporciónenos una copia de ese.

4. Please make a list that includes the following information: jobs you have had since the termination, the names of those employers and the dates in which you worked for each employer.

*pohr fah-**bohr**, **ah**-gah **oo**-nah **lees**-tah kay een-**kloo**-yay lah see-**ghee^ayn**-tay een-fohr-mah-**see^ohn**: lohs trah-**bah**-hohs kay ah tay-**nee**-doh **days**-day ayl days-**pee**-doh, lohs **nohm**-brays day **ay**-sohs aym-play-ay-**doh**-rays ee lahs **fay**-chahs ayn lahs kay trah-bah-**hoh pah**-rah **kah**-dah aym-play-ah-**dohr**.*

Por favor, haga una lista que incluye la siguiente información: los trabajos que ha tenido desde el despido, los nombres de esos empleadores y las fechas en las que trabajó para cada empleador.

5. What is your ...

koo^ahl ays soo ...

¿Cuál es su ...

  current pay rate?

*tah-sah day **pah**-goh ahk-**too^ahl**?*

tasa de pago actual?[5]

  annual income?

*een-**gray**-soh ah-**noo^ahl**?*

ingreso anual?[5]

  overtime pay?

*kohm-payn-sah-**see^ohn pah**-rah lahs **oh**-rahs **ayks**-trahs trah-bah-**hah**-dahs?*

compensación para las horas extras trabajadas?[5]

6. Are you currently employed?

*ays-**tah** aym-play-**ah**-doh/dah ahk-too^ahl-**mayn**-tay?*

¿Está empleado/a actualmente?[6]

  What is the name of your present employer?

***koh**-moh say **yah**-mah soo aym-play-ah-**dohr** ahk-**too^ahl**?*

¿Cómo se llama su empleador actual?[4]

7. What is the title of your job/position with the employer?

*koo^ahl ays soo **tee**-too-loh dayl **poo^ays**-toh **dohn**-day trah-**bah**-hah?*

¿Cuál es su título del puesto donde trabaja?[4]

8. Does the current employer provide you with ...

*soo aym-play-ah-**dohr** ahk-**too^ahl** lay proh-pohr-**see^oh**-nah ...*

¿Su empleador actual le proporciona ...

  dental insurance?

*ayl say-**goo**-roh dayn-**tahl**?*

el seguro dental?

  Individual or family?

*een-dee-bee-**doo^ahl** oh fah-mee-**lee^ahr**?*

¿Individual o familiar?

  medical insurance?

*ayl say-**goo**-roh day sah-**lood**?*

el seguro de salud?

Individual or family?	*een-dee-bee-**doo**^ahl oh fah-mee-**lee**^ahr?* ¿Individual o familiar?
vision insurance?	*ayl say-**goo**-roh day **bees**-tah?* el seguro de vista?
Individual or family?	*een-dee-bee-**doo**^ahl oh fah-mee-**lee**^ahr?* ¿Individual o familiar?
pension plan?	*oon plahn day payn-**see**^oh-nays?* un plan de pensiones?
profit sharing plan?	*lah pahr-tee-see-pah-**see**^ohn ayn lahs oo-tee-lee-**dah**-days?* la participación en las utilidades?
stock options?	*lah **kohm**-prah ohp-see^oh-**nahl** day ahk-**see**^oh-nays?* la compra opcional de acciones?
other benefits?	***oh**-trohs bay-nay-**fee**-see^ohs mahr-hee-**nah**-lays?* otros beneficios marginales?

XV. Termination Documentation and Assessment

*dees-kree-mee-nah-**see**^ohn ee ay-bah-loo^ah-**see**^ohn dayl days-**pee**-doh*
Discriminación y evaluación del despido

English	Pronunciation & Spanish
1. Is there reason to believe the company that terminated you has important documents about your time there and your termination?	*ah^ee rrah-**sohn pah**-rah kray-**ayr** kay lah kohm-pahn-**yee**-ah kay loh/lah days-pee-**dee**^oh tee^**ay**-nay doh-koo-**mayn**-tohs eem-pohr-**tahn**-tays **soh**-bray soo **tee**^**aym**-poh kay trah-bah-**hoh** ah-**yee** ee soo days-pee-doh?* ¿Hay razón para creer que la compañía que lo/la despidió tiene documentos importantes sobre su tiempo que trabajó allí y su despido?[7]
2. Do those documents include …	***ays**-tohs doh-koo-**mayn**-tohs een-**kloo**-yayn …* ¿Estos documentos incluyen …
medical records?	*ees-toh-**ree**^**ah**-lays **may**-dee-kohs?* historiales médicos?
personnel files?	*ees-toh-**ree**^**ah**-lays dayl aym-play-**ah**-doh?* historiales del empleado?
evaluations and appraisals?	*ay-bah-loo^ah-**see**^**oh**-nays day soo day-saym-**payn**-yoh lah-boh-**rahl**?* evaluaciones de su desempeño laboral?
memos regarding the termination?	*may-moh-**rahn**-doom **soh**-bray ayl days-**pee**-doh?* memorándum sobre el despido?
3. Are there other employees that have committed similar offenses and have not been terminated?	*ah^ee **oh**-trohs aym-play-**ah**-dohs kay ahn koh-may-**tee**-doh een-frahk-**see**^**oh**-nays pah-ray-**see**-dahs **pay**-roh noh **foo**^**ay**-rohn days-pay-**dee**-dohs?* ¿Hay otros empleados que han cometido infracciones parecidas pero no fueron despedidos?

	*pohr fah-**bohr**, **ah**-gah **oo**-nah **lees**-tah **pah**-rah ayn-tray-**gahr**-nohs day lohs **nohm**-brays day tays-**tee**-gohs poh-tayn-**see^ah**-lays kohn koh-noh-see-**mee^ayn**-toh dee-**rayk**-toh day **oh**-trohs aym-play-**ah**-dohs kay no days-pee-**dee^ay**-rohn .*
Please make a list of names to give to us of potential witnesses with direct knowledge of the other employees who were not terminated.	Por favor, haga una lista para entregarnos de los nombres de testigos potenciales con conocimiento directo de otros empleados que no despidieron.
	*ahn-tay-**ree^ohr** ahl days-**pee**-doh, loh/lah trah-**tah**-rohn day **oo**-nah mah-**nay**-rah dees-**teen**-tah kay ah lohs **oh**-trohs aym-play-**ah**-dohs kay ah-**bee**-ahn koh-may-**tee**-doh een-frahk-**see^oh**-nays pah-ray-**see**-dahs?*
4. Prior to termination, were you treated differently than others that had committed similar offenses?	Anterior al despido, ¿lo/la trataron de una manera distinta que a los otros empleados que habían cometido infracciones parecidas?[7]
	*ah pah-day-**see**-doh day ahl-**goo**-nohs day lohs see-**ghee^ayn**-tays proh-**blay**-mahs day sah-**lood days**-day ayl days-**pee**-doh?*
5. Have you experienced any of the following health problems since the termination?	¿Ha padecido de algunos de los siguientes problemas de salud desde el despido?
	*lah een-kee^ay-**tood** ay-moh-see^oh-**nahl**?*
emotional distress?	¿la inquietud emocional?
	*lah nayr-bee^oh-see-**dahd**?*
nervousness?	¿la nerviosidad?
	*lah ahn-see^ay-**dahd**?*
anxiety?	¿la ansiedad?
	*lah ee-rree-tah-bee-lee-**dahd**?*
irritability?	¿la irritabilidad?
	*lah oo-mee-yah-**see^ohn**?*
humiliation?	¿la humillación?
	*lah **fahl**-tah day bah-**lohr** payr-soh-**nahl**?*
feelings of worthlessness?	¿la falta de valor personal?
	*lah een-fay-ree^oh-ree-**dahd**?*
feelings of inferiority?	¿la inferioridad?
	*lah day-pray-**see^ohn**?*
depression?	¿la depresión?
	*payn-sah-**mee^ayn**-tohs day soo^ee-**see**-dee^oh?*
thoughts of suicide?	¿pensamientos de suicidio?
	*ayl rray-trah^ee-**mee^ayn**-toh day ah-**mee**-gohs ee fah-**mee**-lee^ah?*
withdrawal from friends and family?	¿el retraimiento de amigos y familia?
	*ayl rray-trah^ee-**mee^ayn**-toh day lahs ahk-tee-bee-**dah**-days nohr-**mah**-lays?*
withdrawal from normal activities?	¿el retraimiento de las actividades normales?
	*lah **fahl**-tah day kohn-sayn-trah-**see^ohn**?*
lack of concentration?	¿la falta de concentración?

increased drinking?	*oon ah^oo-**mayn**-toh dayl kohn-**soo**-moh day ahl-koh-**ohl**?* ¿un aumento del consumo de alcohol?
increased smoking?	*oon ah^oo-**mayn**-toh ayn foo-**mahr**?* ¿un aumento de fumar?
loss of self-esteem?	*lah **payr**-dee-dah day lah ah^oo-toh-ays-**tee**-mah?* ¿la pérdida de la autoestima?
loss of confidence?	***oo**-nah dees-mee-noo-**see^ohn** ayn lah kohn-**fee^ahn**-sah?* ¿una disminución en la confianza?
loss of pride?	*lah **payr**-dee-dah dayl ohr-**goo**-yoh?* ¿la pérdida del orgullo?
embarrassment?	*lah bayr-**goo^ayn**-sah?* ¿la vergüenza?
stomach aches and pains?	*ayl doh-**lohr** ays-toh-mah-**kahl**?* ¿el dolor estomacal?
insomnia?	*ayl een-**sohm**-nee^oh?* ¿el insomnio?
nightmares?	*pay-sah-**dee**-yahs?* ¿pesadillas?
irregular sleep patterns?	***pah^oo**-tahs day **soo^ayn**-yoh ee-rray-goo-**lah**-rays?* ¿pautas de sueño irregulares?
loss of appetite?	*lah **payr**-dee-dah dayl ah-pay-**tee**-toh?* ¿la pérdida del apetito?
increase in appetite?	*oon ah^oo-**mayn**-toh dayl ah-pay-**tee**-toh?* ¿un aumento del apetito?
headaches?	*ayl doh-**lohr** day kah-**bay**-sah?* ¿el dolor de cabeza?
lifestyle changes?	***kahm**-bee^ohs ayn soo ays-**tee**-loh day **bee**-dah?* ¿cambios en su estilo de vida?
marital problems?	*proh-**blay**-mahs mah-tree-moh-**nee^ah**-lays?* ¿problemas matrimoniales?
relationship problems?	*proh-**blay**-mahs day rray-lah-**see^oh**-nays?* ¿problemas de relaciones?
sexual problems?	*proh-**blay**-mahs sayk-**soo^ah**-lays?* ¿problemas sexuales?
other problems?	***oh**-trohs proh-**blay**-mahs?* ¿otros problemas?

6. Has your spouse suffered ...	*ah soo-**free**-doh soo **kohn**-yoo-hay ...* ¿Ha sufrido su cónyuge ...
emotional distress?	*lah een-kee^ay-**tood** ay-moh-see^oh-**nahl**?* ¿la inquietud emocional?

mental anxiety?	*day lah ahn-see^ay-**dahd** mayn-**tahl**?* de la ansiedad mental?
other problems?	***oh**-trohs proh-**blay**-mahs?* otros problemas?

7. Were pension benefits affected by the termination?	*ah-fayk-**toh** ayl days-**pee**-doh soos prays-tah-**see^oh**-nays day hoo-bee-lah-**see^ohn**?* ¿Afectó el despido sus prestaciones de jubilación?

8. Have you suffered financial damages as a result of the termination?	*ah ayks-pay-ree-mayn-**tah**-doh ahl-**goon dahn**-yoh fee-nahn-**see^ay**-roh **koh**-moh rray-sool-**tah**-doh dayl days-**pee**-doh?* ¿Ha experimentado algún daño financiero como resultado del despido?

9. What is the best estimate of these financial damages?	*koo^ahl ays soo may-**hohr** ays-tee-mah-**see^ohn** day **ays**-tohs **dahn**-yohs fee-nahn-**see^ay**-rohs?* ¿Cuál es su mejor estimación de estos daños financieros?[5]
Could you ... basis of the calculations of this estimate?	*poh-**dree**-ah ... lah foon-dah-**see^ohn** day lahs kahl-koo-lah-**see^oh**-nays day **ays**-tah ays-tee-mah-**see^ohn**?* ¿Podría ... la fundación de las calculaciones de esta estimación?
explain in writing	*ayks-plee-**kahr** pohr ays-**kree**-toh* explicar por escrito
tell someone in Spanish / English	*day-**seer**-lay ah **ahl**-ghee^ayn ayn ays-pahn-**yohl** / een-**glays*** decirle a alguien en español / inglés

10. I'm going to mail you a questionnaire in which you will need to detail some of the information about which I have asked during this interview.	*boh^ee ah mahn-**dahr**-lay oon koo^ays-tee^oh-**nah**-ree^oh ayn ayl koo^ahl nay-say-see-tah-**rah** day-tah-**yahr** ahl-**goo**-nah day lah een-fohr-mah-**see^ohn** soh-bray lah koo^ahl lay ay pray-goon-**tah**-doh doo-**rahn**-tay **ays**-tah ayn-tray-**bees**-tah.* Voy a mandarle un cuestionario en el cual necesitará detallar alguna de la información sobre la cual le he preguntado durante esta entrevista.

11. If you are unable to complete the questionnaire alone, someone will need to assist you.	*see noh **poo^ay**-day kohm-play-**tahr** ayl koo^ays-tee^oh-**nah**-ree^oh **soh**-loh/lah, **ahl**-ghee^ayn nay-say-see-tah-**rah** ah^ee-yoo-**dahr**-loh/lah.* Si no puede completar el cuestionario solo/a, alguien necesitará ayudarlo/la.[7]

12. It is necessary to have this detailed information in order to proceed in the assessment of your potential case.	*ays may-nays-**tayr** tay-**nayr ays**-tah een-fohr-mah-**see^ohn** day-tah-**yah**-dah **pah**-rah proh-say-**gheer** kohn lah ay-bah-loo^ah-**see^ohn** day soo **kah**-soh poh-tayn-**see^ahl**.* Es menester tener esta información detallada para proseguir con la evaluación de su caso potencial.

13. After receiving and completing the questionnaire, please mail it back to us as soon as possible.	*days-**poo^ays** day rray-see-**beer** ee kohm-play-**tahr** ayl koo^ays-tee^oh-**nah**-ree^oh, pohr fah-**bohr mahn**-day-nohs-loh ayn say-**ghee**-dah.* Después de recibir y completar el cuestionario, por favor, mándenoslo en seguida.

	*ahl-ghee^ayn rray-bee-sah-**rah** soos rrays-**poo^ay**-stahs ee lah een-fohr-mah-**see^ohn** day-tah-**yah**-dah ee **loo^ay**-goh loh/lah kohn-tahk-tah-**rah**.*
14. Someone will review your responses and detailed information and will then contact you.	Alguien revisará sus respuestas y la información detallada y luego lo/la contactará.[7]

	*say ah koh-moo-nee-**kah**-doh kohn **oh**-troh ah-boh-**gah**-doh rray-fay-**rayn**-tay ah **ays**-tohs ah-**soon**-tohs?*
15. Have you spoken with any other attorneys about these issues?	¿Se ha comunicado con otro abogado referente a estos asuntos?
	*koo^ahl ays ayl **nohm**-bray kohm-**play**-toh dayl ah-boh-**gah**-doh?*
What is the full name of the attorney?	¿Cuál es el nombre completo del abogado?[4]

	*fah-**bohr** day ayn-tayn-**dayr** kay **ahs**-tah kay say rray-**see**-bah kohn-feer-mah-**see^ohn** day noh-**soh**-trohs kohn rrays-**payk**-toh ah **ays**-tay ah-**soon**-toh ayn lah koo^ahl say day-**tah**-yahn lahs kohn-dee-**see^oh**-nays day **noo^ays**-troh ah-**koo^ayr**-doh **pah**-rah rray-pray-sayn-**tahr**-loh/lah, noh **soh**-mohs soo rray-pray-sayn-**tahn**-tay lay-**gahl pah**-ray **ays**-tay nee neen-**goon oh**-troh ah-**soon**-toh.*
16. Please understand that until you receive correspondence from us regarding this issue that details the conditions of our agreement to represent you in this matter, we are not your legal representative on this or any other issue.	Favor de entender que hasta que se reciba confirmación mediante correspondencia de nosotros con respecto a este asunto en la cual se detallan las condiciones de nuestro acuerdo para representarlo/la, no somos su representante legal para este ni ningún otro asunto.[7]

Notes

[1] Once you find out the inquiry for the call, locate the respective questions for that section in this chapter and begin your interview of the caller.

[2] Questions regarding denial of promotions have been included at the end of this chapter as the last section since it may tie into several of the issues addressed in Employment Law.

[3] Reference *Chapter 13—Telling Time the Easy Way—II. Days of the Week and Months of the Year.* This will assist you with comprehension as well as oral production.

[4] Remember you can always ask that the caller spell the name, etc. by incorporating communication strategies from *Chapter 2—Collecting Basic Information In Person and By Phones* and referencing *Chapter 12—The Basics—I. The Alphabet.*

[5] Reference *Chapter 12—The Basics—II. Numbers.*

[6] Use the *-o* ending when talking to or about a *male*; use the *-a* ending when talking to or about a *female.*

[7] Use *-lo* when speaking to or about a *male* and use *-la* when speaking to or about a *female.*

[8] See the *Appendix* for a listing of races with their pronunciation in Spanish.

[9] After *tenth (décimo)* use cardinal numbers rather than ordinal numbers. For example, *your eleventh employer* would be *su once empleador.*

[10] An alternative word for *sueldo* is *salario (sah-**lah**-ree^oh).*

[11] These short phrases have been included to assist you with understanding common anticipated responses. You may also use them to repeat the information you hear back to the individual to make sure you have correctly recorded the information you requested.

[12] In Spanish, whenever a mixed group is referenced (meaning males and females), the grammatical form defers to the plural masculine. For this reason, additional questioning may be necessary to obtain correct information. For example, *hijos* means not only *male children* (or *sons*) but also *male and female children* (mixed group—*sons and daughters*). Therefore, you will notice follow-up questions that ask *how many male children* and *how many female children* have been included.

[13] Reference this chapter, section *VII.—Promotion Denied*—phrase 4 for anticipated responses to this question.

Practical Activities

A) Matching

Instructions: Match the beginning of each question or phrase with its proper ending. Attempt to complete as much of this activity WITHOUT consulting the text. After you have matched all phrases successfully, reference the pronunciation guide for each one and practice the phrase aloud. Concentrate on meaning while doing so.

1. ¿Cree que …	a. un plan de igualdad de oportunidades y acción afirmativa?
2. ¿Sabe si había …	b. cada sindicato laboral?
3. Luego de su queja, …	c. indemnización por cese de empleo?
4. ¿Quién es su médico …	d. de la persona que ascendieron?
5. A su parecer, …	e. pagaron de indemnización?
6. ¿Cuánto ganaba cuando …	f. cuando hubo el accidente?
7. ¿Cómo se llama …	g. su último comprobante de salarios e impuestos de este empleador?
8. ¿Le ofrecieron regalía o …	h. ¿alguien se ha quejado de su desempeño laboral?
9. ¿Cuál es el sexo …	i. ¿le asignaron un horario diferente?
10. ¿Cuánto dinero le …	j. último día de trabajo activo con este empleador?
11. ¿Sabe si el empleador había implementado …	k. de indemnización laboral?
12. ¿Tiene copia de …	l. ¿tomó la compañía medidas para prevenir estas represalias?
13. ¿Quién era su supervisor …	m. afirma que se tomó represalia en su contra?
14. ¿Cuál fue la fecha del …	n. se le discriminó por la raza?
15. Alguna vez, …	o. testigos de los acosos?

B) Diálogo (Dialogue)

Instructions: For this activity you will definitely need to recall information from *Chapter 1—Getting Started* and *Chapter 2—Collecting Basic Information in Person and by Phone*. You will also need to implement the communication strategy of switching between direct and indirect speech (*you* as opposed to *he/him* or *she/her*). Reference *Chapter 6—Personal Injuries—I. General Questions—phrase 7* or *Chapter 2—Collecting Basic Information in Person and by Phone—I. Personal Data—phrase 7* to assist you with this.

Study the following dialogue that occurs between you and a Spanish-speaking caller. Then, working SECTION BY SECTION, prepare in SPANISH the discourse taking place between the two speakers. The dialogue has been broken into sections to make it more manageable. Only, go onto to the next section AFTER you have successfully prepared the one before it. Notice that ALL of the dialogue is written in ENGLISH. Once you have prepared ALL sections of the dialogue, you and a partner will RECREATE it in its entirety speaking ONLY SPANISH.

NOTE: This dialogue portrays a female calling for another female.

Section 1

entrevistador/a (interviewer)	entrevistado/a (interviewee)
Good afternoon. Thank you for calling McMillan and Associates.	Hello, my name is Silvia Montoyo. (mohn-**toh**^ee-yoh)
Are you calling on behalf of yourself or someone else, Ms. Montoyo?	On behalf of someone else.
Fine. Is that person male or female?	Female.
Do you speak any English, Ms. Montoyo?	I'm sorry, no.
No problem. I need to ask you some questions about her. Please speak slowly and clearly. I only speak a little Spanish.	Of course.
What is her full name?	Anita Vásquez. (**bahs**-kays)
How old is she?	40.
What is her birthdate?	August 26, 1970.
Where was she born?	Santa Cruz, México.
What is her marital status?	Single.
What is her current address?	489 Rosebush Way, Huntsboro, Georgia, 34290.
What is her current telephone number?	470-555-3735.
Is she a legal resident?	Yes.
Is she currently working?	No.

Section 2

entrevistador/a (interviewer)	entrevistado/a (interviewee)
Please respond with yes or no so I can determine the reason for your call.	Okay.
Is it an issue regarding wrongful termination?	No.
Worker's compensation?	No.
Sexual or age discrimination?	No.
Sexual harassment?	Yes.
Does she recall what actions she considered to be sexually harassing?	Yes.
Would she be willing to tell someone about them in detail?	Yes.
Were there any witnesses to the harassment?	I don't know.

Section 3

entrevistador/a (interviewer)	entrevistado/a (interviewee)
Does she have any children?	No.
Did she attend or complete elementary school?	Yes.
Middle school?	Yes.
High school?	No.
How many total employers has she had?	3.
How long did she work with the first employer?	8 months.
The second employer?	2 years 3 months.
The third employer?	6 weeks.
Could she put in writing the type of work performed, the reason for leaving and the dates of employment with each employer?	Yes.

Section 4

entrevistador/a (interviewer)	entrevistado/a (interviewee)
Has she ever been involved in other lawsuits or other litigation before?	I'm not sure.
Does she have any criminal convictions?	No.
Has she filed a complaint with the EEOC?	No.
Another agency?	No.
Was she ever given any written appraisals of her job performance?	Yes.
Can she provide us with copies of these written appraisals?	No problem.
We will need her to make a list with the names, addresses and home telephone numbers for all co-workers who have knowledge of her work history and that would have favorable things to say about her performance.	Okay.
Was she fired from this job or did she quit voluntarily?	She quit it.

C) Conclusión del diálogo (Dialogue conclusion)

Instructions: You probably noticed the above dialogue ended abruptly. This is because the SPANISH version of the conclusion has been provided below. Read through it several times, looking for words and phrases you can easily recognize. Then, in the space provided, translate the Spanish version into English. Rely on classmates to assist you if you have trouble. Only refer to the text if you are unable to complete the translation after conferring with various peers. Do not forget, you are still talking to the caller ABOUT another person. This should be reflected in your translation where necessary.

"Voy a mandarle un cuestionario en el cual necesitará detallar alguna de la información sobre la cual le he preguntado durante la entrevista. Es menester tener esta información detallada para proseguir con la evaluación de su caso potencial. Después de recibir y completar el cuestionario, por favor, mándenoslo en seguida. Alguien revisará sus respuestas y la información detallada y luego la contactará. Favor de entender que hasta que se reciba confirmación mediante correspondencia de nosotros con respecto a este asunto en la cual se detallan las condiciones de nuestro acuerdo para representarlo/la, no somos su representante legal para este ni ningún otro asunto".

_____

_____

_____

_____

_____

_____

_____

D) Dialogue Creation

Part I—Instructions: Using the dialogue and its conclusion as presented in B and C above as a model, create your own using the text to assist you. However, rather than composing one lengthy conversation, you will be composing three short ones based on different topics. The topics of each dialogue are written above each table. Therefore, consult the respective section from this chapter when composing your dialogue. Also, consider the logical flow of information to ensure your interaction with the interviewee sounds as realistic as possible. Remember, for this part of the activity you are writing in ENGLISH. Lastly, you may omit a personal introduction and assume that part of the dialogue has already taken place.

NOTE: Include a minimum of eight lines of dialogue per person. Also note,
the interviewee MAY be calling on someone else's behalf.

Topic—Litigation History (male calling for himself)

entrevistador/a (interviewer)	entrevistado/a (interviewee)

Topic — Termination Documentation and Assessment (female calling for her son)

entrevistador/a (interviewer)	entrevistado/a (interviewee)

Topic — Wrongful Termination (male calling for female friend)

entrevistador/a (interviewer)	entrevistado/a (interviewee)

Part II — Instructions: Now pair up with a classmate and recreate each of the English conversations you just created in Spanish. Try to do this without consulting the text unless you absolutely have to do so. You may even wish to switch roles and recreate the conversations in Spanish a second time.

E) Cyber-Investigation

Gender equality in the workplace has always been an issue here in the United State. Though some will argue males continue to receive preferential treatment to a certain degree, females in the workplace have gained considerable ground over the past thirty-plus years. In contrast, the Hispanic culture is male-dominated and therefore, Hispanic females may not realize when their rights in the workplace are being violated due to what they may perceive as acceptable behavior and treatment according to cultural norms. Taking this into consideration, research the concept of *machismo*. How do you define this concept? Are there positive as well as negative aspects to this cultural phenomenon? How might Hispanic females misinterpret or completely overlook personal violations as serious as sexual harassment and gender discrimination on the job because of this element of the Hispanic culture? How might employers educate their female Hispanic employees on the topics of sexual harassment and gender discrimination? Summarize your findings below.

Chapter 8

Family Law

Before You Begin

When asked about their perception of the Hispanic family, many non-Hispanics responded that they view it as a complex social structure in which multiple generations reside together for the greater good of the family. While this may still be true to some extent, it has been noted that as the Hispanic population in the U.S. has increased, so has the number of single-family homes, especially among second-generation and American-born Hispanics. Conversely, when compared with the current condition of the typical American family, two-parent Hispanic families continue to remain disproportionately higher. Interestingly enough, the potential for separations and/or divorces between married foreign-born Hispanics tends to increase the longer they remain in the U.S. as opposed to those Hispanics of the same demographic make-up that remain in their country of origin.

I. Personal Information

*een-fohr-mah-**see^ohn** payr-soh-**nahl***
Información personal

English	Pronunciation & Spanish
1. What is your full legal name?	*koo^ahl ays soo **nohm**-bray lay-**gahl** kohm-**play**-toh?* ¿Cuál es su nombre legal completo?[1]
2. Do you go by any other name?	***tee^ay**-nay ahl-**goon oh**-troh **nohm**-bray?* ¿Tiene algún otro nombre?
What is it?	*koo^ahl ays?* ¿Cuál es?[1]
3. Do you have any prior names?	*ah tay-**nee**-doh ahl-**goon oh**-troh **nohm**-bray ahn-tay-ree^ohr-**mayn**-tay?* ¿Ha tenido algún otro nombre anteriormente?
What was it?	*koo^ahl foo^ay?* ¿Cuál fue?[1]
4. What is your ...	*koo^ahl ays soo ...* ¿Cuál es su ...
date of birth?	***fay**-chah day nah-see-**mee^ayn**-toh?* fecha de nacimiento?[2]
social security number?	***noo**-may-roh day say-**goo**-roh soh-**see^ahl**?* número de seguro social?[3]

147

5. What is your driver's license number and what U.S. state is it from?

*koo^ahl ays soo **noo**-may-roh day lee-**sahn**-see^ah day kohn-doo-**seer** ee day kay ays-**tah**-doh ays-tah-doh-oo-nee-**dayn**-say ays soo lee-**sayn**-see^ah?*

¿Cuál es su número de licencia de conducir y de qué estado estadounidense es su licencia?[1, 3]

6. What is your home address?

*koo^ahl ays soo dee-rayk-**see^ohn** doh-mee-see-lee^ah-ree^ah?*

¿Cuál es su dirección domiciliaria?[1, 3]

How long have you been at this address?

*poh **koo^ahn**-toh **tee^aym**-poh bee-**bee**-doh ayn soo dee-rayk-**see^ohn** doh-mee-see-lee-**ay**-ree^ay?[3]*

¿Por cuánto tiempo ha vivido en su dirección domiciliaria?

one day

*oon **dee**-ah*

un día[4]

(#) days

*(#) **dee**-ahs*

(#) días[3, 4]

one week

***oo**-nah say-**mah**-nah*

una semana[4]

(#) weeks

*(#) say-**mah**-nahs*

(#) semanas[3, 4]

one month

oon mays

un mes[4]

(#) months

*(#) **may**-says*

(#) meses[3, 4]

one year

*oon **ahn**-yoh*

un año[4]

(#) years

*#) **ahn**-yohs*

(#) años[3, 4]

Are your home address and mailing address the same?

*sohn lahs **mees**-mahs soo dee-rayk-**see^ohn** doh-mee-cee-lee^ah-ree^ah ee soo dee-rayk-**see^ohn** pohs-tahl?*

¿Son las mismas su dirección domiciliaria y su dirección postal?

What is your mailing address?

*koo^ahl ays soo dee-rayk-**see^ohn** pohs-tahl?*

¿Cuál es su dirección postal?[1, 3]

7. What is your ...

koo^ahl ays soo ...

¿Cuál es su ...

home phone number?

***noo**-may-roh day tay-**lay**-foh-noh doh-mee-see-**lee^ah**-ree^oh?*

número de teléfono domiciliario?[3]

work phone number?

***noo**-may-roh day tay-**lay**-foh-noh ayn ayl trah-**bah**-hoh?*

número de teléfono en el trabajo?[3]

cell phone number?

***noo**-may-roh day tay-**lay**-foh-noh **moh**-beel?*

número de teléfono móvil?[3]

8. What is ... of your employer?

*koo^ahl ays ... day soo aym-play-ah-**dohr**?*
¿Cuál es ... de su empleador?

   the name

*ayl **nohm**-bray*
el nombre[1]

   the address

*lah dee-rayk-**see^ohn***
la dirección[1, 3]

   the phone number

*ayl **noo**-may-roh day tay-**lay**-foh-noh*
el número de teléfono[3]

What is the title of your position?

*koo^ahl ays ayl **tee**-too-loh day soo **poo^ays**-toh?*
¿Cuál es el título de su puesto?[1]

Are you ...

*trah-**bah**-hah day ...*
¿Trabaja de ...

   full-time?

***tee^aym**-poh kohm-**play**-toh?*
tiempo completo?

   part-time?

***tee^aym**-poh pahr-**see^ahl**?*
tiempo parcial?

How many hours a week do you work?

*koo^**ahn**-tahs **oh**-rahs trah-**bah**-hah ah lah say-**mah**-nah?*
¿Cuántas horas trabaja a la semana?[3]

9. Please list your educational experience and vocational training including the number of years you attended high school, community college, continuing education programs, etc.

*pohr fah-**bohr**, ay-noo-**may**-ray soo ayks-pay-**ree^ayn**-see^ah ah-kah-**day**-mee-kah ee soo kah-pah-see-tah-**see^ohn** boh-kah-see^oh-**nahl** een-kloo-**yayn**-doh **koo^ahn**-tohs **ahn**-yohs ah-sees-**tee^oh** ahl koh-**lay**-hee^oh, <community college>, proh-**grah**-mahs day ay-doo-kah-**see^ohn** kohn-**tee**-noo^ah, ayt-**say**-tay-rah.*
Por favor, enumere su experiencia académica y su capacitación vocacional incluyendo cuántos años asistió al colegio, <community college>, programas de educación contínua, etc.[5]

10. Do you have an email address?

*tee^**ay**-nay dee-rayk-**see^ohn** day koh-**rray**-oh ay-layk-**troh**-nee-koh?*
¿Tiene dirección de correo electrónico?

Do you prefer to communicate with us via email or telephone?

*pray-**fee^ay**-ray koh-moo-nee-**kahr**-say kohn noh-**soh**-trohs pohr koh-**rray**-oh ay-layk-**troh**-nee-koh oh pohr tay-**lay**-foh-noh?*
¿Prefiere comunicarse con nosotros por correo electrónico o por teléfono?

What is your email address?

*koo^ahl ays soo dee-rayk-**see^ohn** day koh-**rray**-oh ay-layk-**troh**-nee-koh?*
¿Cuál es su dirección de correo electrónico?[1, 3, 6]

II. Marriage Information

*een-fohr-mah-**see^ohn** mah-tree-moh-**nee^ahl***
Información matrimonial

English	Pronunciation & Spanish
1. What was the date of your current marriage?	*koo^ahl foo^ay lah **fay**-chah day soo mah-tree-**moh**-nee^oh ahk-**too^ahl**?* ¿Cuál fue la fecha de su matrimonio actual?[2]
2. Is there a prenuptial, premarital or marital property agreement in existence?	*ayks-**ees**-tay oon ah-**koo^ayr**-doh day proh-pee^ay-**dahd** pray-noop-**see^ahl**, pray-mah-tree-moh-**nee^ahl** oh mah-tree-moh-**nee^ahl**?* ¿Existe un acuerdo de propiedad prenupcial, prematrimonial o matrimonial?
3. In what city and state did you get married?	*ayn kay see^oo-**dahd** ee ays-**tah**-doh say kah-**soh**?* ¿En qué ciudad y estado se casó?[1]
4. Are you currently living with your spouse?	***bee**-bay kohn soo **kohn**-yoo-hay ah-**oh**-rah?* ¿Vive con su cónyuge ahora?
What was the date of your separation?	*koo^ahl foo^ay lah **fay**-chah day soo say-pah-rah-**see^ohn**?* ¿Cuál fue la fecha de su separación?[2]
5. When was the last time you had sexual relations with your spouse?	*koo^**ahn**-doh foo^ay lah **ool**-tee-mah bays kay **too**-boh rray-lah-**see^oh**-nays sayk-**soo^ah**-lays kohn soo **kohn**-yoo-hay?* ¿Cuándo fue la última vez que tuvo relaciones sexuales con su cónyuge?
one day	***ah**-say oon **dee**-ah* hace un día[4]
(#) days	***ah**-say (#) **dee**-ahs* hace (#) días[3, 4]
one week	***ah**-say **oo**-nah say-**mah**-nah* hace una semana[4]
(#) weeks	***ah**-say (#) say-**mah**-nahs* hace (#) semanas[3, 4]
one month	***ah**-say oon mays* hace un mes[4]
(#) months	***ah**-say (#) **may**-says* hace (#) meses[3, 4]
one year	***ah**-say oon **ahn**-yoh* hace un año[4]
(#) years	***ah**-say (#) **ahn**-yohs* hace (#) años[3, 4]

6. Including this marriage, how many times …

*see say een-**kloo**-yay **ays**-tay mah-tree-**moh**-nee^oh, **koo^ahn**-tahs **bay**-says …*
Si se incluye este matrimonio, ¿cuántas veces …[3]

have you been married?

*ah ays-**stah**-doh kah-**sah**-doh/dah?*
ha estado casado/a?[7]

has your spouse been married?

*ah ays-**tah**-doh kah-**sah**-doh/dah soo **kohn**-yoo-hay?*
ha estado casado/a su cónyuge?[7]

7. Have you been divorced before (including from your current spouse)?

*ah ays-**tah**-doh/dah dee-bohr-**see^ah**-doh/dah **ahn**-tays (een-kloo-**yayn**-doh soo **kohn**-yoo-hay ahk-**too^ahl**)?*
¿Ha estado divorciado/a antes (incluyendo su cónyuge actual)?[7]

How many times have you been divorced?

*koo^ahn-tahs bay-says ah ays-**tah**-doh/dah dee-bohr-**see^ah**-doh/dah?*
¿Cuántas veces ha estado divorciado/a?[3, 7]

What was the date of the divorce?

*koo^ahl foo^ay lah **fay**-chah dayl dee-**bohr**-see^oh?*
¿Cuál fue la fecha del divorcio?[1, 8]

What is the name of your former spouse?

*koh-moh say **yah**-mah soo ahn-**tee**-goo^oh **kohn**-yoo-hay?*
¿Cómo se llama su antiguo/a cónyuge?[1, 7, 8]

What was the name of the court in which you were divorced?

*koh-moh say **yah**-mah ayl tree-boo-**nahl dohn**-day say fohr-mah-lee-**soh** soo dee-**bohr**-see^oh?*
¿Cómo se llama el tribunal dónde se formalizó su divorcio?[1, 8]

In which county and state is it located?

*ayn kay kohn-**dah**-doh ee ays-**tah**-doh ays-**tah** see-too-**ah**-doh?*
¿En qué condado y estado está situado?[1, 8]

8. Has your spouse been divorced before?

*ah ays-**tah**-doh dee-bohr-**see^ah**-doh/dah **ahn**-tays soo **kohn**-yoo-hay?*
¿Ha estado divorciado/a antes su cónyuge?[7]

9. Please answer with "yes" or "no" to the reasons for which you are seeking divorce from your spouse:

*pohr fah-**bohr**, kohn-**tays**-tay kohn <see> oh <noh> ah lahs rrah-**soh**-nays pohr lahs **koo^ah**-lays ah day-see-**dee**-doh dee-bohr-**see^ayr**-say day soo **kohn**-yoo-hay:*
Por favor, conteste con <sí> o <no> a las razones por las cuales ha decidido divorciarse de su cónyuge:

adultery?

*lah een-fee-day-lee-**dahd**?*
la infidelidad?

incarceration of your spouse?

*ayl ayn-kahr-say-lah-**mee^ayn**-toh day soo **kohn**-yoo-hay?*
el encarcelamiento de su cónyuge?

physical abuse from spouse?

*ayl ah-**boo**-soh **fee**-see-koh koh-may-**tee**-doh pohr soo **kohn**-yoo-hay?*
el abuso físico cometido por su cónyuge?

mental abuse from spouse?

*ayl ah-**boo**-soh mayn-**tahl** koh-may-**tee**-doh day soo **kohn**-yoo-hay?*
el abuso mental cometido por su cónyuge?

abandonment?

*ayl ah-bahn-**doh**-noh?*
el abandono?

spouse has drug problems?	*lohs proh-**blay**-mahs kay **tee^ay**-nay soo **kohn**-yoo-hay kohn **droh**-gahs?* los problemas que tiene su cónyuge con drogas?
spouse has drinking problems?	*lohs proh-**blay**-mahs kay **tee^ay**-nay soo **kohn**-yoo-hay kohn ahl-koh-**ohl**?* los problemas que tiene su cónyuge con alcohol?
10. If applicable, would you like to return to using your maiden name?	*see proh-**say**-day, kee-**see^ay**-rah bohl-**bayr** ah oo-**sahr** soo **nohm**-bray day sohl-**tay**-rah?* Si procede, ¿quisiera volver a usar su nombre de soltera?
Are you currently pregnant?	*ahk-too^ahl-**mayn**-tay, ays-**tah** aym-bah-rah-**sah**-dah?* Actualmente, ¿está embarazada?
11. Are you interested in reconciliation?	*lay een-tay-**ray**-sah lah rray-kohn-see-lee^ah-**see^ohn**?* ¿Le interesa la reconciliación?
12. Has your spouse expressed interest in reconciliation?	*lay een-tay-**ray**-sah ah soo **kohn**-yoo-hay lah rray-kohn-see-lee^ah-**see^ohn**?* ¿Le interesa a su cónyuge la reconciliación?
13. Have you and your spouse tried marriage counseling?	*ah proh-**bah**-doh say-**see^oh**-nays day kohn-say-hay-**ree**-ah mah-tree-moh-**nee^ahl** kohn soo **kohn**-yoo-hay?* ¿Ha probado sesiones de consejería matrimonial con su cónyuge?
Please make a list to give us of the name and location of each counselor and the date of the first counseling appointment with each one.	*pohr fah-**bohr**, **ah**-gah **oo**-nah **lees**-tah **pah**-ray ayn-tray-**gahr**-nohs kay een-**kloo**-yay ayl **nohm**-bray ee lah oo-bee-kah-**see^ohn** day **kah**-dah kohn-say-**hay**-roh kohn kee^ayn ah-**blah**-rohn ah-**see** koh-moh lah **fay**-chah day lah pree-**may**-rah **see**-tah day kohn-say-hay-**ree**-ah kohn **kah**-dah **oo**-noh.* Por favor, haga una lista para entregarnos que incluye el nombre y la ubicación de cada consejero con quien hablaron así como la fecha de la primera cita de consejería con cada uno.
14. Have you been involved in legal or other proceedings with your current spouse?	*ah ays-**tah**-doh een-boh-loo-**krah**-doh/dah ayn ahk-**see^oh**-nays lay-**gah**-lays oh noh lay-**gah**-lays kohn soo **kohn**-yoo-hay ahk-**too^ahl**?* ¿Ha estado involucrado/a en acciones legales o no legales con su cónyuge actual?[7]
Could you explain the details of that situation …	*poh-**dree**-ah ayks-plee-**kahr** lohs day-**tah**-yays day ah-**kay**-yah see-too^ah-**see^ohn** …* ¿Podría explicar los detalles de aquella situación …
in writing (in English / Spanish)?	*pohr ays-**kree**-toh (ayn een-**glays** / ays-pahn-**yohl**)?* por escrito (en inglés / español)?
in Spanish with an interpreter present?	*ayn ays-pahn-**yohl** kohn oon een-**tayr**-pray-tay pray-**sayn**-tay?* en español con un intérprete presente?

III. Children

ee-hohs
Hijos

English	Pronunciation & Spanish
	*tee^ay-nay ahl-**goo**-nohs **ee**-hohs — **say**-ahn lay-**hee**-tee-mohs oh ah-dohp-**tah**-dohs — day **ays**-tay mah-tree-**moh**-nee^oh?*
1. Do you have any children — legitimate or adopted — from this marriage?	¿Tiene algunos hijos — sean legítimos o adoptados — de este matrimonio?
	*pohr fah-**bohr**, **ah**-gah oo-nah **lees**-tah **pah**-rah ayn-tray-**gahr**-nohs kay een-**kloo**-yay ayl **nohm**-bray kohm-**play**-toh lay-**gahl** ee lah **fay**-chah day nah-see-**mee^ayn**-toh day **kah**-dah **ee**-hoh.*
Please make a list to give us with the full legal name and date of birth for each of your children.	Por favor, haga una lista para entregarnos que incluye el nombre completo legal y la fecha de nacimiento de cada hijo.
	*see proh-**say**-day, ah-**poon**-tay ayl **noo**-may-roh day say-**goo**-roh soh-**see^ahl** day **kah**-dah oo-noh ahl **lah**-doh dayl **nohm**-bray rrays-payk-**tee**-boh.*
If applicable, provide the social security number of each child beside the child's name.	Si procede, apunte el número de seguro social de cada uno al lado del nombre respectivo.
	*days-**poo^ays** day **kah**-dah ah-noh-tah-**see^ohn**, ays-**kree**-bah ayl **nohm**-bray day lah payr-**soh**-nah kohn kee^ayn **bee**-bay **kah**-dah **ee**-hoh.*
After each entry, write the name of the person with whom each child lives.	Después de cada anotación, escriba el nombre de la persona con quién vive cada hijo.
	*pohr fah-**bohr**, rray-ays-**kree**-bah ayl **nohm**-bray day **kah**-dah **ee**-hoh ee **ah**-gah oo-nah **lees**-tah ayn kay say een-**dee**-kah kohn kee^ayn **kah**-dah oo-noh ah bee-**bee**-doh doo-**rahn**-tay lohs **seen**-koh **ool**-tee-mohs **ahn**-yohs.*
Please rewrite the name of each child and list where and with whom each child has lived in the past five years.	Por favor, reescriba el nombre de cada hijo y haga una lista en que se indica con quién cada uno ha vivido durante los cinco últimos años.
	*ah-say-**goo**-ray-say day een-**kloo^eer** lahs **fay**-chahs kay een-**dee**-kahn lah doo-rah-**see^ohn** day **tee^aym**-poh pah-**sah**-dah ayn **kah**-dah doh-mee-**see**-lee^oh.*
Be sure to include dates showing the duration spent at each residence.	Asegúrese de incluir las fechas que indican la duración de tiempo pasada en cada domicilio.
	*(een-**kloo**-yay lohs **nohm**-brays day **kah**-dah payr-**soh**-nah kay ah-bee-**tah**-bah **kah**-dah rray-see-**dayn**-see^ah **dohn**-day bee-**bee**-ah **kah**-dah **ee**-hoh ahn-tay-ree^ohr-**mayn**-tay.)*
(Include the names of ALL persons that resided at each location where the child previously lived.)	(Incluya los nombres de cada persona que habitaba cada residencia donde vivía cada hijo anteriormente.)
	*tee^ay-nay ahl-**goo**-nohs **ee**-hohs — lay-**gee**-tee-mohs oh ah-dohp-**tah**-dohs — day oo-nah rray-lah-**see^ohn** ahn-tay-**ree^ohr**?*
2. Do you have any children — legitimate or adopted — from a previous relationship?	¿Tiene algunos hijos — legítimos o adoptados — de una relación anterior?

Please make a list to give us with the full legal name and date of birth for each of your children.	*pohr fah-**bohr**, **ah**-gah **oo**-nah **lees**-tah **pah**-rah ayn-tray-**gahr**-nohs kay een-**kloo**-yay ayl **nohm**-bray kohm-**play**-toh lay-**gahl** ee lah **fay**-chah day nah-see-**mee^ayn**-toh day **kah**-dah **ee**-hoh.* Por favor, haga una lista para entregarnos que incluye el nombre completo legal y la fecha de nacimiento de cada hijo.
After each entry, write with whom each child resides.	*days-**poo^ays** day **kah**-dah ah-noh-tah-**see^ohn**, ays-**kree**-bah kohn **kee^ayn** **bee**-bay ayl **ee**-hoh.* Después de cada anotación, escriba con quién vive el hijo.

3. Does your spouse have any children—legitimate or adopted—from a previous relationship?	*tee^**ay**-nay soo **kohn**-yoo-hay ahl-**goo**-nohs **ee**-hohs—lay-**gee**-tee-mohs oh ah-dohp-**tah**-dohs—day **oo**-nah rray-lah-**see^ohn** ahn-tay-**ree^ohr**?* ¿Tiene su cónyuge algunos hijos—legítimos o adoptados—de una relación anterior?
Please make a list to give us with the full legal name and date of birth for each of the children.	*pohr fah-**bohr**, **ah**-gah **oo**-nah **lees**-tah **pah**-rah ayn-tray-**gahr**-nohs kay een-**kloo**-yay ayl **nohm**-bray kohm-**play**-toh lay-**gahl** ee lah **fay**-chah day nah-see-**mee^ayn**-toh day **kah**-dah **ee**-hoh.* Por favor, haga una lista para entregarnos que incluye el nombre completo legal y la fecha de nacimiento de cada hijo.
After each entry, write with whom each child resides.	*days-**poo^ays** day **kah**-dah ah-noh-tah-**see^ohn**, ays-**kree**-bah kohn **kee^ayn** **bee**-bay ayl **ee**-hoh.* Después de cada anotación, escriba con quién vive el hijo.

4. Do any of your children (from your current marriage) have any physical problems or other issues that may be a factor in this case?	*ays kay ahl-**goo**-noh day lohs **ee**-hohs (day soo mah-tree-**moh**-nee^oh ahk-**too^ahl**) **soo**-fray day proh-**blay**-mahs **fee**-see-kohs oo **oh**-trahs dee-fee-koo-**tah**-days kay **poo^ay**-dayn eem-pahk-**tahr** ays-tay **kah**-soh?* ¿Es que alguno de los hijos (de su matrimonio actual) sufre de problemas físicos u otras dificultades que pueden impactar este caso?
Please indicate which child by pointing to the name on the list of children you have just completed.	*poh fah-**bohr**, een-**dee**-kay kay **ee**-hoh ahl sayn-yah-**lahr** soo **nohm**-bray ayn lah **lees**-tah kay ah-**kah**-bah day kohm-play-**tahr**.* Por favor, indique qué hijo al señalar su nombre en la lista que acaba de completar.
Does the child suffer from …	***soo**-fray ayl **ee**-hoh / lah **ee**-hah day …* ¿Sufre el hijo/la hija de …?[7]
a physical disability?	***oo**-nah dees-kah-pah-see-**dahd** **fee**-see-kah?* una discapacidad física?
a mental disability?	*oon trahs-**tohr**-noh mayn-**tahl**?* un trastorno mental?
a learning disability?	***oo**-nah dee-fee-kool-**tahd** day ah-prayn-dee-**sah**-hay?* una dificultad de aprendizaje?
a terminal disease?	***oo**-nah ayn-fayr-mee-**dahd** een-koo-**rah**-blay?* una enfermedad incurable?

a life-threatening disease?	*oo-nah ayn-fayr-may-**dahd** kay ah-may-**nah**-sah lah **bee**-dah?* una enfermedad que amenaza la vida?
a birth defect?	*oon day-**fayk**-toh day nah-see-**mee^ayn**-toh?* un defecto de nacimiento?
5. Do you anticipate a dispute regarding custody of your child (children)?	*ahn-tee-**see**-pah **oo**-nah dis-**poo**-tah kohn rrays-**payk**-toh ah lah koos-**toh**-dee^ah day soo(s) ee-hoh(s)?* ¿Anticipa una disputa con respecto a la custodia de su(s) hijo(s)?
Regarding … do you want sole custody or shared?	*rray-fay-**rayn**-tay ah … kee-**see^ay**-rah lah koos-**toh**-dee^ah ayks-kloo-**see**-bah oh kohm-pahr-**tee**-dah?* Referente a … quisiera la custodia exclusiva o compartida?
physical custody,	*lah koos-**toh**-dee^ah **fee**-see-kah,* la custodia física,
legal custody,	*lah koos-**toh**-dee^ah lay-**gahl**,* la custodia legal,
6. Have any of the children of this marriage been the subject of …	*ays kay ahl-**goo**-nohs day lohs **ee**-hohs day **ays**-tay mah-tree-**moh**-nee^oh ahn **see**-doh ayl ayn-**foh**-kay day …* ¿Es qué algunos de los hijos de este matrimonio han sido el enfoque de …
social security investigations?	*een-bays-tee-gah-**see^oh**-nays day say-**goo**-roh soh-**see^ahl**?* investigaciones de seguro social?
neglect or delinquency proceedings?	*ahk-too^ah-**see^oh**-nays lay-**gah**-lays day nay-glee-**hayn**-see^ah oh day-leen-**koo^ayn**-see^ah?* actuaciones legales de negligencia o delincuencia?
adoption?	*ah-dohp-**see^ohn**?* adopción?
grandparental rights proceedings?	*ahk-too^ah-**see^oh**-nays lay-**gah**-lays **soh**-bray lohs day-**ray**-chohs day ah-**boo^ay**-lohs?* actuaciones legales sobre los derechos de abuelos?
personal injury actions?	***kah**-sohs day lay-**see^oh**-nays payr-soh-**nah**-lays?* casos de lesiones personales?
any other legal proceedings?	*oh-trahs ahk-too^ah-**see^oh**-nays lay-**gah**-lays?* otras actuaciones legales?
Could you explain the details of that situation …	*poh-**dree**-ah ayks-plee-**kahr** lohs day-**tah**-yays day ah-**kay**-yah see-too^ah-**see^ohn** …* ¿Podría explicar los detalles de aquella situación …
in writing (in English / Spanish)?	*pohr ays-**kree**-toh (ayn een-**glays** / ays-pahn-**yohl**)?* por escrito (en inglés / español)?
in Spanish with an interpreter present?	*ayn ays-pahn-**yohl** kohn oon een-**tayr**-pray-tay pray-**sayn**-tay?* en español con un intérprete presente?

English	Pronunciation & Spanish
7. Are there any cases pending regarding possession of or access to any child of this marriage?	*ah^ee ahl-**goo**-nohs **kah**-sohs payn-**dee^ayn**-tays kohn rrays-**payk**-toh ah lah koos-**toh**-dee^ah day oh ayl ahk-**say**-soh ah oon **ee**-hoh day **ays**-tay mah-tree-**moh**-nee^oh?* ¿Hay algunos casos pendientes con respecto a la custodia de o el acceso a un hijo de este matrimonio?
Please make a list to give us of the name of the state and the county where each case is pending.	*pohr fah-**bohr**, **ah**-gah **oo**-nah **lees**-tah **pah**-rah ayn-tray-**gahr**-nohs kay een-**kloo**-yay lohs **nohm**-brays dayl ays-**tah**-doh ee dayl kohn-**dah**-doh **dohn**-day **kah**-dah **kah**-soh ays-**tah** payn-**dee^ayn**-tay.* Por favor, haga una lista para entregarnos que incluye los nombres del estado y del condado donde cada caso está pendiente.
Also, provide the date the case was filed and each case number.	*tahm-**bee^ayn**, ah-**poon**-tay lah **fay**-chah ayn lah koo^ahl say pray-sayn-**toh** ayl **kah**-soh ee ayl **noo**-may-roh day **kah**-soh day **kah**-dah **oo**-noh.* También, apunte la fecha en la cual se presentó el caso y el número de caso de cada uno.
8. Does any child from this marriage own any property of notable value?	*ays kay ahl-**goon** ee-hoh day **ays**-tay mah-tree-**moh**-nee^oh ays proh-pee^ay-**tah**-ree^oh day **oo**-nah proh-pee^ay-**dahd** day bah-**lohr** noh-**tah**-blay?* ¿Es que algún hijo de este matrimonio es propietario de una propiedad de valor notable?
Please make a list to give us that tells what type of property it is, where it is located and the approximate value.	*pohr fah-**bohr**, **ah**-gah **oo**-nah **lees**-tah **pah**-rah ayn-tray-**gahr**-nohs kay een-**kloo**-yay lah **klah**-say day proh-pee^ay-**dahd** kay ays, **dohn**-day ays-**tah** oo-bee-**kah**-dah ee ayl bah-**lohr** aprohk-see-**mah**-doh.* Por favor, haga una lista para entregarnos que incluye la clase de propiedad que es, dónde está ubicada y el valor aproximado.

IV. Property Information

*pahr-tee-koo-**lah**-rays day proh-pee^ay-**dahd***
Particulares de propiedad

English	Pronunciation & Spanish
1. What is the address of the primary residence of marriage?	*koo^ahl ays lah dee-rayk-**see^ohn** dayl doh-mee-**see**-lee^oh preen-see-**pahl** day **ays**-tay mah-tree-**moh**-nee^oh?* ¿Cuál es la dirección del domicilio principal de este matrimonio?[1, 3]
What is the current market value of that residence?	*koo^ahl ays ayl bah-**lohr** day mayr-**kah**-doh ahk-**too^ahl** day **ay**-say doh-mee-**see**-lee^oh?* ¿Cuál es el valor de mercado actual de ese domicilio?[1, 3]
What is the outstanding mortgage balance of that residence?	*koo^ahl ays ayl **sahl**-doh day lah ee-poh-**tay**-kah payn-**dee^ayn**-tay **pah**-rah **ay**-say doh-mee-**see**-lee^oh?* ¿Cuál es el saldo de la hipoteca pendiente para ese domicilio?[1, 3]
2. Do you own ...	***tee^ay**-nay ...* ¿Tiene ...

Does your spouse own ...	*tee^ay-nay soo **kohn**-yoo-hay ...* ¿Tiene su cónyuge ...
Do you both own ...	*tee^ay-nayn **hoon**-tohs ...* ¿Tienen juntos ...
any secondary residences?	*doh-mee-**see**-lee^ohs say-koon-**dah**-ree^ohs?* domicilios secundarios?
any vacation homes?	*kah-sahs de **kahm**-poh oh day bay-ran-**nay**-oh?* casas de campo o de veraneo?
Please make a list to give us that includes the address of each property, the current market value and the outstanding mortgage balance for each entry.	*pohr fah-**bohr**, ah-gah **oo**-nah **lees**-tah **pah**-rah ayn-tray-**gahr**-nohs kay een-**kloo**-yay lah dee-rayk-**see^ohn**, ayl bah-**lohr** koh-mayr-**see^ahl** ahk-**too^ahl** ee ayl **sahl**-doh day lah ee-poh-**tay**-kah payn-**dee^ayn**-tay day **kah**-dah proh-pee^ay-**dahd**.* Por favor, haga una lista para entregarnos que incluye la dirección, el valor comercial actual y el saldo de la hipoteca pendiente de cada propiedad.
3. Do you own ...	*tee^ay-nay ...* ¿Tiene ...
Does your spouse own ...	*tee^ay-nay soo **kohn**-yoo-hay ...* ¿Tiene su cónyuge ...
Do you both own ...	*tee^ay-nayn **hoon**-tohs ...* ¿Tienen juntos ...
any vehicles?	*ahl-**goo**-nohs bay-ee-koo-lohs?* algunos vehículos?
Please make a list of those vehicles to give us that includes the make, model, VIN number, current market value, outstanding debt and by whom each vehicle is driven.	*por fah-**bohr**, ah-gah **oo**-nah **lees**-tah day ay-sohs bay-ee-koo-lohs **pah**-rah ayn-tray-**gahr**-nohs kay een-**kloo**-yay lah see-**ghee^ayn**-tay een-fohr-mah-**see^ohn**: lah **mahr**-kah, ayl moh-**day**-loh, ayl **noo**-may-roh day ee-dayn-tee-fee-kah-**see^ohn** day bay-ee-koo-loh, ayl bah-**lohr** day mayr-**kah**-doh ahk-**too^ahl**, ayl **sahl**-doh dayl pah-gah-**ray** day **ah^oo**-toh ee kee^ayn loh kohn-**doo**-say.* Por favor, haga una lista de esos vehículos para entregarnos que incluye la siguiente información: la marca, el modelo, el número de identificación de vehículo, el valor de mercado actual, el saldo del pagaré de auto y quién lo maneja.
4. Please make a list to give us of any ...	*pohr fah-**bohr**, ah-gah **oo**-nah **lees**-tah **pah**-rah ayn-tray-**gahr**-nohs day ...* Por favor, haga una lista para entregarnos de ...
that you have.	*kay **tee^ay**-nay.* que tiene.
your spouse has.	*kay **tee^ay**-nay soo **kohn**-yoo-hay.* que tiene su cónyuge.
both of you have together.	*kay **tee^ay**-nayn **hoon**-tohs.* que tienen juntos.
banking and investment accounts ...	*koo^ayn-tahs bahn-**kah**-ree^ahs ee day een-bayr-**see^oh**-nays ...* cuentas bancararias y de inversiones ...

	*een-**kloo**-yah lah see-**ghee^ayn**-tay een-fohr-mah-**see^ohn**: lah **klah**-say day **koo^ayn**-tah kay ays, ayl **nohm**-bray ee lah oo-bee-kah-**see^ohn** day lah ayn-tee-**dahd** fee-nahn-**see^ay**-rah kay lah **goo^ahr**-dah, (lahs **koo^ah**-troh **ool**-tee-mahs **see**-frahs dayl) ayl **noo**-may-roh day **koo^ayn**-tah ee ayl **mohn**-toh ahk-**too^ahl** day **kah**-dah oo-nah.*
Include the type of account, the financial institute where it is located, the (last four digits of the) account number, and the amount of each one.	Incluya la siguiente información: la clase de cuenta que es, el nombre y la ubicación de la entidad financiera que la guarda, (las cuatro últimas cifras del) el número de cuenta y el monto actual de cada una.
	*ahk-**see^oh**-nays, **boh**-nohs ee **fohn**-dohs day een-bayr-**see^ohn** …*
stocks, bonds, and mutual funds …	acciones, bonos y fondos de inversión …
	*een-**kloo**-yah lah see-**ghee^ayn**-tay een-fohr-mah-**see^ohn**: lah **klah**-say day een-bayr-**see^ohn** kay ays, lah kahn-tee-**dahd** day ahk-**see^oh**-nays poh-say-**ee**-dahs, lohs **nohm**-brays kay ah-pah-**ray**-sayn ayn ayl sayr-tee-fee-**kah**-doh ahk-see^oh-**nah**-ree^oh ee ayl bah-**lohr** day **kah**-dah oo-nah.*
Include the type of investment, the number of shares, the names on the certificate, and the value of each one.	Incluya la siguiente información: la clase de inversión que es, la cantidad de acciones poseídas, los nombres que aparecen en el certificado accionario y el valor de cada una.
	*plah-nays day payn-**see^oh**-nays …*
retirement accounts …	planes de pensiones …
	*een-**kloo**-yah lah see-**ghee^ayn**-tay een-fohr-mah-**see^ohn**: lah **klay**-say dayl plahn kay ays, lah oo-bee-kah-**see^ohn** oh ayl **nohm**-bray dayl aym-play-ah-**dohr** kay ays ayl tay-nay-**dohr** dayl plahn, lohs **nohm**-brays ayn **kah**-dah plahn ee ayl bah-**lohr** ah-prohk-see-**mah**-doh day **kah**-dah oo-noh.*
Include the type of account, the location or name of the employer through whom the account is held, the names on each account, and the approximate value of each account.	Incluya la siguiente información: la clase de plan que es, la ubicación o el nombre del empleador que es el tenedor del plan, los nombres en cada plan y el valor aproximado de cada uno.
	*poh-lee-sahs day say-**goo**-roh day pohr **bee**-dah …*
life insurance policies …	pólizas de seguro de por vida …
	*een-**kloo**-yah lah see-**ghee^ayn**-tay een-fohr-mah-**see^ohn**: lah **klah**-say day **poh**-lee-sah kay ays, ayl **nohm**-bray day lah kohm-pahn-**yee**-ah day say-**goo**-roh, ayl bah-**lohr** noh-mee-**nahl** ee ayl bah-**lohr** ay-fayk-**tee**-boh.*
Include the type of insurance police it is, the name of the insurance company, the name of the insured, the face, and the cash value.	Incluya la siguiente información: la clase de póliza que es, el nombre de la compañía de seguro, el valor nominal y el valor efectivo.
	*pohr fah-**bohr**, ays-**kree**-bah lohs **nohm**-brays day **toh**-dohs lohs bay-nay-fee-**see^ay**-ree^ohs day **kah**-dah **poh**-lee-sah.*
Please write the names of any beneficiaries for each policy.	Por favor, escriba los nombres de todos los beneficiarios de cada póliza.
	*pohr fah-**bohr**, **ah**-gah oo-nah **lees**-tah **pah**-rah ayn-tray-**gahr**-nohs day koo^ah-lays-**kee^ayr** oh-trohs ahk-**tee**-bohs seeg-nee-fee-kah-**tee**-bohs **tah**-lays koh-moh **bahr**-kahs, **oh**-brahs day **ahr**-tay, ahn-tee-goo^ay-**dah**-days, koh-layk-**see^oh**-nays, ayt-**say**-tay-rah ee ayl bah-**lohr** ah-prohk-see-**mah**-doh day **kah**-dah oo-noh.*
5. Please make a list to give us of any other significant assets such as boats, artwork, jewelry, antiques, collections, etc. and the approximate value of each.	Por favor, haga una lista para entregarnos de cualesquier otros activos significativos tales como barcas, obras de arte, antigüedades, colecciones, etc. y el valor aproximado de cada uno.

6. Have you received any property as a gift or inheritance during the marriage?

ah rray-see-__bee__-doh proh-pee^ay-__dahd koh__-moh rray-__gah__-loh oh ay-__rayn__-see^ah doo-__rahn__-tay ayl mah-tree-__moh__-nee^oh?

¿Ha recibido propiedad como regalo o herencia durante el matrimonio?

Please make a list to give us of all gifts and properties as well as the current fair market value for each one.

pohr fah-__bohr__, __ah__-gah __oo__-nah __lees__-tah __pah__-rah ayn-tray-__gahr__-nohs day __toh__-dohs __ays__-tohs rray-__gah__-lohs ee proh-pee^ay-__dah__-days ah-__see koh__-moh ayl bah-__lohr__ koh-mayr-__see^ahl__ ahk-__too^ahl pah__-rah __kah__-dah __oo__-noh.

Por favor, haga una lista para entregarnos de todos estos regalos y propiedades así como el valor comercial actual para cada uno.

7. Has your spouse received any property as a gift or inheritance during the marriage?

ah rray-see-__bee__-doh soo __kohn__-yoo-hay proh-pee^ay-__dahd koh__-moh rray-__gah__-loh oh ay-__rayn__-see^ah doo-__rahn__-tay ayl mah-tree-__moh__-nee^oh?

¿Ha recibido su cónyuge propiedad como regalo o herencia durante el matrimonio?

Please make a list to give us of all gifts and properties as well as the current fair market value for each one.

pohr fah-__bohr__, __ah__-gah __oo__-nah __lees__-tah __pah__-rah ayn-tray-__gahr__-nohs day __toh__-dohs __ays__-tohs rray-__gah__-lohs ee proh-pee^ay-__dah__-days ah-__see koh__-moh ayl bah-__lohr__ koh-mayr-__see^ahl__ ahk-__too^ahl pah__-rah __kah__-dah ah-noh-tah-__see^ohn__.

Por favor, haga una lista para entregarnos de todos estos regalos y propiedades así como el valor comercial actual para cada anotación.

V. Debts

__day^oo__-dahs
Deudas

English	Pronunciation & Spanish
1. Please make a list to give us of ALL debts that …	*pohr fah-__bohr__, __ah__-gah __oo__-nah __lees__-tah __pah__-rah ayn-tray-__gahr__-nohs day __toh__-dahs lahs __day^oo__-dahs kay …* Por favor, haga una lista para entregarnos de todas las deudas que …
you have.	*tee^__ay__-nay.* tiene.
your spouse has.	*tee^__ay__-nay soo __kohn__-yoo-hay.* tiene su cónyuge.
Include the following information: name of creditor, names on each account, the outstanding balance of each, and the last 4 digits of each account number.	*een-__kloo__-yah lah een-fohr-mah-__see^ohn__ see-__ghee^ayn__-tay: ayl __nohm__-bray dayl ah-kray-ay-__dohr__, lohs __nohm__-brays kay ah-pah-__ray__-sayn ayn __kah__-dah __koo^ayn__-tah, ayl __sahl__-doh payn-__dee^ayn__-tay day __kah__-dah __koo^ayn__-tah ee lahs __koo^ah__-troh __ool__-tee-mahs __see__-frahs day __kah__-dah __noo__-may-roh day __koo^ayn__-tah.* Incluya la información siguiente: el nombre del acreedor, los nombres que aparecen en cada cuenta, el saldo pendiente de cada cuenta y las cuatro últimas cifras de cada número de cuenta.

VI. Mediation

*may-dee^ah-**see^ohn***
Mediación

English	Pronunciation & Spanish
1. Would you like to participate in mediation?	*kee-**see^ay**-rah pahr-tee-see-**pahr** ayn lah may-dee^ah-**see^ohn**?* ¿Quisiera participar en la mediación?
2. Have you participated in mediation in the past two years?	*ah pahr-tee-see-**pah**-doh ayn lah may-dee^ah-**see^ohn** doo-**rahn**-tay lohs dohs **ool**-tee-mohs **ahn**-yohs?* ¿Ha participado en la mediación durante los dos últimos años?
3. If the court orders mediation, do you agree to split the costs with your spouse?	*see ayl hoo^ays ohr-**day**-nah lah may-dee^ah-**see^ohn**, ah-**koo^ayr**-dah pah-**gahr** lah mee-**tahd** day lohs **kohs**-tohs see soo **kohn**-yoo-hay **pah**-gah lah **oh**-trah?* Si el juez ordena la mediación, ¿acuerda pagar la mitad de los costos si su cónyuge paga la otra?
4. Do you feel your case is inappropriate to be mediated due to domestic violence, aggression or other factors?	*day-**bee**-doh ah lah bee^oh-**layn**-see^ah doh-**mays**-tee-kah, lah ah-gray-**see^ohn** oo **oh**-trohs fahk-**toh**-rays, **see^ayn**-tay kay say-**ree**-ah een-ah-proh-**pee^ah**-doh soh-may-**tayr** soo **kah**-soh ah lah may-dee^ah-**see^ohn**?* Debido a la violencia doméstica, la agresión u otros factores, ¿siente que sería inapropiado someter su caso a la mediación?
Could you explain … why you feel this way?	*poh-**dree**-ah ayks-plee-**kahr** … pohr kay say **see^ayn**-tay ah-**see**?* ¿Podría explicar … por qué se siente así?
in writing (in English / Spanish)?	*pohr ays-**kree**-toh (ayn een-**glays** / ays-pahn-**yohl**)?* por escrito (en inglés / español)?
in Spanish with an interpreter present?	*ayn ays-pahn-**yohl** kohn oon een-**tayr**-pray-tay pray-**sayn**-tay?* en español con un intérprete presente?
5. If you are unable to pay for mediation would you be willing to have a court appointed mediator mediate your case?	*ays-tah-**ree**-ah dees-**poo^ays**-toh/tah ah payr-mee-**teer** kay oon may-dee^ah-**dohr** day-seeg-**nah**-doh pohr ayl tree-boo-**nahl may**-dee^ay soo **kah**-soh see noh **poo^ay**-day kohs-tay-**ahr** lah may-dee^ah-**see^ohn**?* ¿Estaría dispuesto/a a permitir que un mediador desginado por el tribunal medie su caso si no puede costear la mediación?[7]
6. Please respond with "yes" to any of the issues you feel must be mediated:	*pohr fah-**bohr**, rray-**spohn**-dah kohn <see> ah koo^ah-lays-**kee^ayr** day lohs ah-**soon**-tohs see-**ghee^ayn**-tays kay nay-say-**see**-tahn day may-dee^ah-**see^ohn**:* Por favor, responda con <sí> a cualesquier de los asuntos siguientes que necesitan de mediación:
custody	*lah koos-**toh**-dee^ah* la custodia

bill payments	*ayl pah-goh de koo^ayn-tahs* el pago de cuentas
exclusive use of marital residence	*lah oh-koo-pah-see^ohn ayks-kloo-see-bah dayl doh-mee-see-lee^oh mah-tree-moh-nee^ahl* la ocupación exclusiva del domicilio matrimonial
personal belongings	*lohs ay-fayk-tohs payr-soh-nah-lays* los efectos personales
spousal support	*lah mah-noo-tayn-see^ohn kohn-yoo-gahl* la manutención conyugal
division of property	*lah dee-bee-see^ohn day proh-pee^ay-dahd* la división de propiedad
parenting time	*ayl tee^aym-poh dees-poh-nee-blay pah-rah pah-sahr kohn lohs ee-hohs* el tiempo disponible para pasar con los hijos
real estate	*lohs bee^ay-nays rrah-ee-says* los bienes raíces
retirement savings	*lohs ah-oh-rrohs day hoo-bee-lah-see^ohn* los ahorros de jubilación
Please make a list to give us of any other issues you feel must be mediated.	*pohr fah-bohr, ah-gah oo-nah lees-tah pah-rah ayn-tray-gahr-nohs day koo^ah-lays-kee^ayr oh-trohs ah-soon-tohs kay nay-say-see-tayn day may-dee^ah-see^ohn ah soo pah-ray-sayr.* Por favor, haga una lista para entregarnos de cualesquier otros asuntos que necesiten de mediación a su parecer.
7. Have you spoken with any other attorneys about these issues?	*lay ah ah-blah-doh kohn oh-troh ah-boh-gah-doh rray-fay-rayn-tay ah ays-tohs ah-soon-tohs?* ¿Le ha hablado con otro abogado referente a estos asuntos?
What is the full name of the attorney?	*koo^ahl ays ayl nohm-bray kohm-play-toh dayl ah-boh-gah-doh?* ¿Cuál es el nombre completo del abogado?[1]
8. Please understand that until you receive correspondence from us regarding this issue that details the terms of our agreement to represent you in this matter, we are not your legal representative on this or any other issue.	*fah-bohr day ayn-tayn-dayr kay ahs-tah kay say rray-see-bah kohn-feer-mah-see^ohn day noh-soh-trohs kohn rrays-payk-toh ah ays-tay ah-soon-toh ayn lah koo^ahl say day-tah-yahn lohs play-sohs day noo^ays-troh ah-koo^ayr-doh pah-rah rray-pray-sayn-tahr-loh/lah, noh soh-mohs soo rray-pray-sayn-tahn-tay lay-gahl pah-ray ays-tay nee neen-goon oh-troh ah-soon-toh.* Favor de entender que hasta que se reciba confirmación mediante correspondencia de nosotros con respecto a este asunto en la cual se detallan los plazos de nuestro acuerdo para representarlo/la, no somos su representante legal para este ni ningún otro asunto.

Notes

[1] Remember you can always ask that the caller spell the name, etc. by incorporating communication strategies from *Chapter 2—Collecting Basic Information in Person and by Phone* and referencing *Chapter 12—The Basics—I. The Alphabet.*

[2] Reference *Chapter 13—Telling Time the Easy Way—II. Days of the Week and Months of the Year.* This will assist you with comprehension as well as oral production.

[3] Reference *Chapter 12—The Basics—II. Numbers.*

[4] These short phrases have been included to assist you with understanding common anticipated responses. You may also use them to repeat the information you hear back to the individual to make sure you have correctly recorded the information you requested.

[5] Repeat questions 8 and 9 for the spouse by preceding the questions with *<Y su cónyuge ...> (ee soo **kohn**-yoo-hay).* This will switch the subject from *you* to *your spouse.*

[6] The symbol @ used in email addresses is called *arroba (ah-**rroh**-bah)* in Spanish.

[7] Use the *-o* ending when talking to or about a male; use the *-a* ending when talking to or about a female.

[8] Repeat each of these questions for each divorce the individual has had.

Practical Activities

A) Oral Practice

Instructions: As with all chapters, this one begins with the collection of personal information*—a task you should be rather skilled at by this time. Therefore, rather than begin this activity with the collection of personal data, assume this has already been done and go directly into asking the Spanish-speaker topic specific questions. Clues regarding the information you are to obtain are provided below in SPANISH. Using what you have learned about recognizing cognates and anticipated responses, use this knowledge to interpret the given responses. This will assist you in locating the necessary question/phrase. Compare your findings with a classmate then practice saying aloud together the question/phrase and the response all in SPANISH. You may wish to mark the respective phrases in the book or write them out in the space provided under each SPANISH response.

[* *Please review Chapter 2—Collecting Basic Information in Person and by Phone if you would like to review this process.*]

Información matrimonial

1. La fecha del matrimonio fue el 13 de noviembre, 2001.

   _____

2. Hace 4 días que tuvimos *(too-bee-mohs)* relaciones sexuales.

   _____

3. He *(ay)* estado casada 2 veces.

   _____

4. Por el abuso físico cometido por mi cónyuge.

   _____

5. No, no hemos *(ay-mohs)* probado sesiones de consejería.

   _____

Hijos

1. Sí, tengo *(tayn-goh)* tres hijos de este matrimonio.

   _____

2. No, no tengo *(tayn-goh)* hijos de una relación anterior.

   _____

3. Mi cónyuge tiene una hija *(ee-hah)* de una relación anterior.

   _____

4. No, ningún *(neen-goon)* problema físico u otra dificultad.

   _____

5. No, ninguna *(neen-goo-nah)* disputa con respecto a la custodia de mis hijos.

   _____

Particulares de propiedad

1. Sí, tenemos *(tay-nay-mohs)* una casa de veraneo.

   _____

2. Tengo un Ford Mustang.

   _____

3. Mi cónyuge tiene acciones y bonos pero ningún *(neen-goon)* fondo de inversión.

   _____

4. Tenemos *(tay-nay-mohs)* planes de pensiones.

   _____

5. Yo no, pero mi cónyuge ha recibido dinero como herencia durante el matrimonio.

   _____

Mediación

1. Sí, quisiera participar.

   _____

2. Sí, acuerdo *(ah-koo^ayr-doh)* pagar la mitad de los costos.

   _____

3. Sí—el pago de cuentas y la manutención conyugal.

   _____

4. No, no sería inapropiado someter mi caso a la mediación.

   _____

5. No, ningún *(neen-goon)* otro abogado.

   _____

Follow-up: With a partner, recreate each set of questions and answers in the form of a dialogue. After one of you have gone through all four sets asking the questions while you partner reads the Spanish responses aloud, switch roles and go through them one more time. You will notice that most of the words in the responses come from the chapter with some minor changes, therefore only a limited pronunciation key is provided here.

B) Por favor, haga una lista ... (Please, make a list ...)

Part I—Instructions: This chapter contains more requests for a client to create a list to assist you in obtaining information. Once again, remember that this is an important communication strategy that will save both of you time and potential frustration. To facilitate this process, however, you may want to provide the client with a fill-in-the-blank table that will expedite this process. In this activity, you will create another sample table which you will ask a client to complete.

Reference *Section IV—Property Information, question 3* of this chapter. After the "yes" and "no" questions, you will see an English phrase that starts *Please make a list....* Notice you are requesting **six** pieces of information. Write each piece of information here below in ENGLISH in the FIRST blank provided.

A. _____ / _____

B. _____ / _____

C. _____ / _____

D. _____ / _____

E. _____ / _____

F. _____ / _____

Next, read and study the corresponding SPANISH phrase. The information in the Spanish phrase appears in the same order as it is found in the ENGLISH phrase. Write the SPANISH version for each piece of information beside of its corresponding ENGLISH version above. Use punctuation marks and easily recognizable words to help you discern which SPANISH words are the ENGLISH translations. You may also choose to use an online bilingual dictionary to assist you.

Once you have completed the above assignment, create a blank, six-column table on a clean sheet of paper using the entire size of the paper itself. Starting with the first column, write *A* and ONLY the corresponding SPANISH word and/or phrase that you wrote above. Continue doing this with letters *B–F* until you have lettered and labeled each column according to your notes above. Understand that if this were actually going to be giving to a client, you would obviously want to create this table with a computer. This way, aside from being much more professional, you could begin to build a bank of tables labeled accordingly that could be printed off and used each time you needed to ask a new Spanish-speaking client for the same information.

Part II—Instructions: Now that you have worked through the above process to assist you in creating tables clients will use to prepare lists of information, repeat this process for *Section IV—Property Information, question 4—banking and investment accounts; stocks, bonds, and mutual funds; retirement accounts; life insurance policies.* Be sure to go through the steps outlined in PART I to make sure you are accurately locating and labeling the information. When you have finished, you will have four additional tables. Lastly, trade all five of your tables with a partner and have him/her go back to the chapter and check your work against the phrases from the text. Make any necessary changes or corrections. Do not forget, the number of columns depends upon the number of pieces of information you are collecting.

Use this method when you come across such requests for creating any list, not only in this chapter, but in future chapters as well. By first analyzing your request for the creation of a list, identifying in both SPANISH and ENGLISH the pieces of information you wish to obtain and placing them in a table format, the gathering of data will be much easier to manage.

C) Cyber-Investigation

In BEFORE YOU BEGIN, you read some general information about the Hispanic family and how non-Hispanics typically perceive them. However, how do Hispanics conceptualize their relationships with family members? Search on the internet to find information that deals with Hispanics and their concept of family. Then, look for information that explains how Americans (non-Hispanics) describe this same concept. What are the similarities? What are the differences? Does one population place more emphasis on the importance of family than the other? Next, research the term *familismo*. What exactly does it entail? Is this an essential element of the Hispanic population? Why or why not? Finally, taking into consideration what you have learned about family and its meaning to the Hispanic population, do you think Hispanics would be more likely or less likely to seek out the services of a family law attorney for these personal matters? Find at least one online source to support your opinion and summarize your findings below.

Chapter 9

Real Estate Law and Probate

Before You Begin

According to a study conducted by HUD (Housing and Urban Development), Hispanics continue to experience housing discrimination on a number of levels. From being quoted higher rental prices than other ethnic groups, to receiving less than fair and equal treatment from real estate and rental agents when applying for a loan or submitting a credit check, this population is still faced with a challenge to attain something as basic yet essential as a place to live. While similar situations have improved for other minorities over the past twenty plus years, Hispanics continue to face discrimination comparable to that which they experienced in 1989. On the flip side of this issue, while Hispanics that legally reside in the U.S. have the right to report and take action against such acts of discrimination, others without this status do not. Those who are here illegally, aside from facing discrimination, also deal with exploitation since landlords know that illegals will not file a report or make a complaint. This results in deplorable living conditions for which tenants are overpaying and/or repairs and maintenance that are never performed—not to mention threats of being reported to immigration services for not complying with the payment of rent or unfair rent increases.

I. General Information

*een-fohr-mah-**see^ohn** hay-nay-**rahl***
Información general

English	Pronunciation & Spanish
1. What is your name?	*koh-moh say **yah**-mah?* ¿Cómo se llama?[1]
2. What is the best phone number to use in case we are disconnected?	*kay **noo**-may-roh day tay-**lay**-foh-noh ays may-**hohr** oo-**sahr** see nohs days-koh-nayk-**tah**-mohs?* ¿Qué número de teléfono es mejor usar si nos desconectamos?[2]
3. Are you calling on behalf of yourself or someone else?	***yah**-mah oos-**tayd** day **pahr**-tay day see **mees**-moh/mah oh day **pahr**-tay day **oh**-trah payr-**soh**-nah?* ¿Llama Ud. de parte de sí mismo/a o de parte de otra persona?[3]
4. I'm calling on behalf of ...	***yah**-moh day **pahr**-tay day ...* Llamo de parte de ...
myself.	*mee **mees**-moh.* mí mismo/a.[3]

167

	*day **oh**-trah payr-**soh**-nah.*
another person.	de otra persona.

	*lay nay-say-**see**-toh ah-**sayr** oo-nahs pray-**goon**-tahs.*
5. I need to ask you some questions.	Le necesito hacer unas preguntas.

	*lay nay-say-**see**-toh ah-**sayr** oo-nahs pray-**goon**-tahs **soh**-bray ayl / **ay**-yah.*
6. I need to ask you some questions about him / her.	Le necesito hacer unas preguntas sobre él / ella.

	*lah payr-**soh**-nah ays **ohm**-bray oh moo-**hayr**?*
7. Is the person male or female?	¿La persona es hombre o mujer?

	*rray-fay-**rayn**-tay ah …*
8. In reference to …	Referente a … [4]

	*oos-**tayd** …*
you …	Ud.…

	ayl …
him …	él …

	***ay**-yah …*
her …	ella …

[insert name of person] …

	*ays kay **ay**-sah payr-**soh**-nah ays soo …*
9. Is that person your …	¿Es que esa persona es su …

	***kohn**-yoo-hay?*
spouse?	cónyuge?

	*ah-**mee**-goh/gah?*
friend?	amigo/a? [3]

	***pah**-dray?*
father?	padre?

	***mah**-dray?*
mother?	madre?

	*ayr-**mah**-noh?*
brother?	hermano?

	*ayr-**mah**-nah?*
sister?	hermana?

	***ee**-hoh?*
son?	hijo?

	***ee**-hoh?*
daughter?	hija?

	*pah-**ree**^**ayn**-tay?*
relative?	pariente?

acquaintance?	*ah-**mee**-goh/gah day **pah**-soh?* amigo/a de paso?[3]
10. What is your full legal name?	*koo^ahl ays soo **nohm**-bray lay-**gahl** kohm-**play**-toh?* ¿Cuál es su nombre legal completo?
11. Do you go by any other name?	***tee^ay**-nay ahl-**goon** oh-troh **nohm**-bray?* ¿Tiene algún otro nombre?
12. What is your …	*koo^ahl ays soo …* ¿Cuál es su …
paternal last name / father's last name?	*ah-pay-**yee**-doh pah-**tayr**-noh?* apellido paterno?[1]
maternal last name / mother's maiden name?	*ah-pay-**yee**-doh mah-**tayr**-noh?* apellido materno?[1]
13. What is your …	*koo^ahl ays soo …* ¿Cuál es su …
date of birth?	***fay**-chah day nah-see-**mee^ayn**-toh?* fecha de nacimiento?[5]
social security number?	***noo**-may-roh day say-**goo**-roh soh-**see^ahl**?* número de seguro social?[2]
14. Are you a U.S. citizen?	*ays see^oo-dah-**dah**-noh/nah ays-tah-doh-oo-nee-**dayn**-say?* ¿Es ciudadano/a estadounidense?[3]
15. What's your …	*koo^ahl ays soo …* ¿Cuál es su …
citizenship number?	***noo**-may-roh day see^oo-dah-dah-**nee**-ah?* número de ciudadanía?[2]
alien registration number?	***noo**-may-roh day rray-**hees**-stroh day een-mee-**grahn**-tay?* número de registro de inmigrante?[2]
16. What is your current address?	*koo^ahl ays soo dee-rayk-**see^ohn** ahk-**too^ahl**?* ¿Cuál es su dirección actual?[1,2]
17. What is your current telephone number?	*koo^ahl ays soo **noo**-may-roh day tay-**lay**-foh-noh ahk-**too^ahl**?* ¿Cuál es su número de teléfono actual?[3]
18. What is the best number to reach you?	*koo^ahl ays ayl may-**hohr noo**-may-roh day tay-**lay**-foh-noh **pah**-ray kohn-tahk-**tahr**-loh/lah?* ¿Cuál es el mejor número de teléfono para contactarlo/la?[6]
19. Do you have a job?	***tee^ay**-nay trah-**bah**-hoh?* ¿Tiene trabajo?
Where?	***dohn**-day?* ¿Dónde?

What do you do?	*ah kay say day-**dee**-kah?* ¿A qué se dedica?[1]
20. Can you spell that for me (slowly)?	*may loh **poo^ay**-day day-lay-tray-**ahr** (layn-tah-**mayn**-tay)?* ¿Me lo puede deletrear (lentamente)?[1]
21. Do you prefer to receive communication from our office by …	*pray-**fee^ay**-ray rray-see-**beer** koh-moo-nee-kah-**see^ohn** day **noo^ays**-troh boo-**fay**-tay pohr …* ¿Prefiere recibir comunicación de nuestro bufete por …
phone?	*tay-**lay**-foh-noh?* teléfono?
email?	*koh-**rray**-oh ay-layk-**troh**-nee-koh?* correo electrónico?
mail?	*koh-**rray**-oh?* correo?
22. What is …	*koo^ahl ays …* ¿Cuál es …
the e-mail address?	*lah dee-rayk-**see^ohn** day koh-**rray**-oh ay-layk-**troh**-nee-koh?* la dirección de correo electrónico?[1, 7]
the phone number you prefer to use?	*ayl **noo**-may-roh day tay-**lay**-foh-noh kay pray-**fee^ay**-ray oo-**sahr**?* el número de teléfono que prefiere usar?[2]
May we leave you messages?	*poh-**day**-mohs day-**hahr**-lay mayn-**sah**-hays?* ¿Podemos dejarle mensajes?
the address you prefer to use to receive corrrespondence?	*lah dee-rayk-**see^ohn** kay pray-**fee^ay**-ray oo-**sahr** **pah**-rah rray-see-**beer** koh-rray-spohn-**dayn**-see^ah?* la dirección que prefiere usar para recibir correspondencia?[1, 2]

II. Landlord and Tenant Disputes

*dees-**poo**-tahs **ayn**-tray proh-pee^ay-**tah**-ree^oh ay een-kee-**lee**-noh*
Disputas entre propietario e inquilino

A. Tenant Discrimination

*dees-kree-mee-nah-**see**^ohn **kohn**-trah een-kee-**lee**-nohs*
Discriminación contra inquilinos

English	Pronunciation & Spanish
1. Are you the head of your household?	*ays kah-**bay**-sah de **kah**-sah?* ¿Es cabeza de casa?
2. Please respond with "yes" to the ethnicity that applies to you:	*pohr fah-**bohr**, rray-**spohn**-day kohn \<see\> ah la ayt-nee-see-**dahd** kay lay koh-rrays-**pohn**-day:* Por favor, responda con \<sí\> a la etnicidad que le corresponde:
Hispanic or Latino	*ees-**pah**-noh oh lah-**tee**-noh* hispano o latino
Non Hispanic or Latino	*noh ees-**pah**-noh nee lah-**tee**-noh* no hispano ni latino
3. Please respond with "yes" to all racial categories that apply to you:	*pohr fah-**bohr**, rray-**spohn**-dah kohn \<see\> ah toh-dahs lahs kah-tay-goh-**ree**-ahs rrah-**see**^ah-lays kay koh-rrays-**pohn**-dayn:* Por favor, responda con \<sí\> a todas las categorías raciales que le corresponden:
American Indian	***een**-dee^oh nohr-tay-ah-may-ree-**kah**-noh* indio norteamericano
Native Alaskan	*een-**dee**-hay-nah day ah-**lahs**-kah* indígena de Alaska
White	***blahn**-koh, kah^oo-**kah**-see-koh* blanco, caucásico
Black or African American	***nay**-groh, ah-froh-ah-may-ree-**kah**-noh* negro, afroamericano
Asian	*ah-**see**^ah-tee-koh* asiático
Native Hawaiian	*ah-wah^ee-**yah**-noh* hawaiano
Hawaiian Pacific Islander	*een-**dee**-hay-nah day lah poh-lee-**nay**-see^ah* indígena de la Polinesia
4. How many reside in your household?	***koo**^ahn-tahs payr-**soh**-nahs **bee**-bayn ayn soo **kah**-sah?* ¿Cuántas personas viven en su casa?[2]

5. What is the collective monthly income for your household?

*koo^ah-lays sohn lohs een-**gray**-sohs mayn-**soo^ah**-lays koh-layk-**tee**-bohs day lahs payr-**soh**-nahs kay **bee**-bayn ayn soo **kah**-sah?*
¿Cuáles son los ingresos mensuales colectivos de las personas que viven en su casa?[2]

6. What was the exact date that you took physical occupation of the dwelling?

*koo^ahl foo^ay lah **fay**-chah ayk-**sahk**-tah ayn lah koo^ahl aym-pay-**soh** ah ah-bee-**tahr** lah bee-**bee^ayn**-dah?*
¿Cuál fue la fecha exacta en la cual empezó a habitar la vivienda?[5]

7. Do you have a written rental agreement for the dwelling?

*tee^**ayn**-nay oon kohn-**trah**-toh ays-**kree**-toh day ah-rrayn-dah-**mee^ayn**-toh **pah**-rah lah bee-**bee^ayn**-dah?*
¿Tiene un contrato escrito de arrendamiento para la vivienda?

Is the rental agreement a fixed-term lease or a month-to-month lease?

*ays kay ayl kohn-**trah**-toh day ah-rrayn-dah-**mee^ayn**-toh ays ah **plah**-soh **fee**-hoh oh day mays ah mays?*
¿Es que el contrato de arrendamiento es a plazo fijo o de mes a mes?

8. Have you filed a complaint of any type with any other agency?

*ah pray-sayn-**tah**-doh oo-nah day-**noon**-see^ah day koo^ahl-**kee^ayr klah**-say kohn ahl-**goo**-nah **oh**-trah ah-**hayn**-see^ah?*
¿Ha presentado una denuncia de cualquier clase con alguna otra agencia?

What is the name of the agency?

*koh-moh say **yah**-mah lah ah-**hayn**-see^ah?*
¿Cómo se llama la agencia?[1]

What was the date of the filing?

*koo^ahl foo^ay lah **fay**-chah day lah pray-sayn-tah-**see^ohn**?*
¿Cuál fue la fecha de la presentación?[5]

Was the complaint for ...

*say trah-**tah**-bah lah day-**noon**-see^ah ...*
¿Se trataba la denuncia ...

sexual harassment?

*dayl ah-**koh**-soh sayk-**soo^ahl**?*
del acoso sexual?

habitability of a dwelling?

*day lah ah-bee-tah-bee-lee-**dahd** day lah bee-**bee^ayn**-dah?*
de la habitabilidad de la vivienda?

employment discrimination?

*day lah dees-kree-mee-nah-**see^ohn** lah-boh-**rahl**?*
de la discriminación laboral?

housing discrimination?

*day lah dees-kree-mee-nah-**see^ohn** ayn mah-**tay**-ree^ah day bee-**bee^ayn**-dah?*
de la discriminación en materia de vivienda?

discrimination in public accommodations?

*day lah dees-kree-mee-nah-**see^ohn** ayn mah-**tay**-ree^ah day bee-**bee^ayn**-dah **poo**-blee-kah?*
de la discriminación en materia de vivienda pública?

personal injury?

*day **oo**-nah lay-**see^ohn** payr-soh-**nahl**?*
de una lesión personal?

9. Is your rent subsidized?

*rray-**see**-bay oon soob-**see**-dee^oh day ah-rrayn-dah-**mee^ayn**-toh?*
¿Recibe un subsidio de arrendamiento?

Do you live in ...	*bee-bay ayn ...* ¿Vive en ...
public housing (owned by the city or county)?	*oo-nah bee-**bee^ayn**-dah **poo**-blee-kah (day lah koo^ahl lah see^oo-**dahd** oh ayl kohn-**dah**-doh ays **doo^ayn**-yoh)?* una vivienda pública (de la cual la ciudad o el condado es dueño)?
low income housing (owned by the city or county)?	*oo-nah bee-**bee^ayn**-day **pah**-rah payr-**soh**-nahs day **bah**-hohs een-**gray**-sohs (day lah koo^ahl lah see^oo-**dahd** oh ayl kohn-**dah**-doh ays **doo^ayn**-yoh)?* una vivienda para personas de bajos ingresos (de la cual la ciudad o el condado es dueño)?
Is it ...	*ays ...* ¿Es ...
section 8 housing?	*oo-nah bee-**bee^ayn**-dah day sayk-**see^ohn** oh-choh?* una vivienda de sección ocho?
a project-based community?	*oon kohm-**play**-hoh day bee-**bee^ayn**-dahs soo-bayn-see^oh-**nah**-dahs?* un complejo de viviendas subvencionadas?
bond program housing?	*oo-nah bee-**bee^ayn**-dah **koo**-yah kohn-strook-**see^ohn** foo^ay fee-nahn-**see^ah**-dah ah trah-**bays** day oon proh-**grah**-mah day **boh**-noh?* una vivienda cuya construcción fue financiada a través de un programa de bono?
10. Is the individual who discriminated against you ...	*ays kay ayl een-dee-**bee**-doo^oh kay dees-kree-mee-**noh** ayn soo **kohn**-trah ays ...* ¿Es que el individuo que discriminó en su contra es ...
the property owner?	*ayl **doo^ayn**-yoh day lah proh-pee^ay-**dahd**?* el dueño de la propiedad?
the property manager?	*ayl ahd-mee-nees-trah-**dohr** day lah proh-pee^ay-**dah**?* el administrador de la propiedad?
a leasing agent?	*oon ah-**hayn**-tay day ah-rrayn-dah-**mee^ayn**-toh?* un agente de arrendamiento?
a maintenance worker?	*oon trah-bah-hah-**dohr** day mahn-tay-nee-**mee^ayn**-toh?* un trabajador de mantenimiento?
another employee of the property?	*oh-troh aym-play-**ah**-doh day lah proh-pee^ay-**dahd**?* otro empleado de la propiedad?
11. What is the address of the location where the discrimination took place?	*koo^ahl ays lah dee-rayk-**see^ohn** day lah oo-bee-kah-**see^ohn** **dohn**-day toh-**moh** loo-gahr ayl **ahk**-toh day dees-kree-mee-nah-**see^ohn**?* ¿Cuál es la dirección de la ubicación donde tomó lugar el acto de discriminación?[1, 2]
Is this ...	*ays ...* ¿Es ...
a single family home?	*oo-nah bee-**bee^ayn**-dah oo-nee-fah-mee-**lee^ahr**?* una vivienda unifamiliar?

a duplex?	*oo-nah **kah**-sah fohr-**mah**-dah pohr dohs bee-**bee^ayn**-dahs een-day-payn-**dee^ayn**-tays?* una casa formada por dos viviendas independientes?
an apartment complex?	*oon kohm-**play**-hoh day day-pahr-tah-**mayn**-tohs?* un complejo de departamentos?
a trailer park?	*oon **pahr**-kay day rray-**mohl**-kays?* un parque de remolques?
What is the owner's name?	*koh-moh say yah-mah ayl **doo^ayn**-yoh?* ¿Cómo se llama el dueño?[1]
Who is the property management company?	*koh-moh say yah-mah lah kohm-pahn-**yee**-ah day ahd-mee-nee-strah-**see^ohn** day lah proh-pee^ay-**dahd**?* ¿Cómo se llama la compañía de administración de la propiedad?[1]
Who is the property manager?	*koh-moh say yah-mah ayl ahd-mee-nee-strah-**dohr** day lah proh-pee^ay-**dahd**?* ¿Cómo se llama el administrador de la propiedad?[1]

12. Respond with "yes" to any of the following reasons for which you feel you were …	*rray-**spohn**-dah kohn <see> ah koo^ah-lays-**kee^ayr** day lahs see-**ghee^ayn**-tahs rrah-**soh**-nahs pohr lahs **koo^ah**-lays oh-**pee**-nah kay …* Responda con <sí> a cualesquier de las siguientes razones por las cuales opina que …
discriminated against:	*dees-kree-mee-**nah**-rohn ayn soo **kohn**-trah:* discriminaron en su contra:
harassed:	*loh/lah ah-koh-**sah**-rohn:* lo/la acosaron:[6]
age	*lah ay-**dahd*** la edad
ethnicity	*lah ayt-nee-see-**dahd*** la etnicidad
sex	*ayl **sayk**-soh* el sexo
religion	*lah rray-lee-**hee^ohn*** la religión
race	*lah **rrah**-sah* la raza
sexual orientation	*lah oh-ree^ayn-tah-**see^ohn** sayk-**soo^ahl*** la orientación sexual
income source	*lah **foo^ayn**-tay day soos een-**gray**-sohs* la fuente de sus ingresos
national origin	*ayl oh-**ree**-hayn nah-see^oh-**nahl*** el origen nacional

mental disability	*lah dees-kah-pah-see-**dahd** mayn-**tahl**?* la discapacidad mental
physical disability	*lah dees-kah-pah-see-**dahd** fee-see-kah?* la discapacidad física
you have children	***tee^ay**-nay ee-hohs* tiene hijos
you are a single parent	*ays **mah**-dray / **pah**-dray seen pah-**ray**-hah* es madre / padre sin pareja[8]
other reason	***oh**-trah rrah-**sohn*** otra razón

---

13. Based on your previous response(s), what was the name of the person who ...

*bah-**sah**-doh ayn soo(s) rrays-**poo^ays**-tah(s) ahn-tay-**ree^ohr**(-ays), **koh**-moh say **yah**-mah lah payr-**soh**-nah kay ...*

Basado en su(s) respuesta(s) anterior(es), ¿cómo se llama la persona que ...

made the hateful, discriminatory remarks?	*ee-soh **ays**-tohs koh-mayn-**tah**-ree^ohs oh-**dee^oh**-sohs ee dees-kree-mee-nah-**toh**-ree^ohs?* hizo estos comentarios odiosos y discriminatorios?[1]
harassed you?	*loh/lah ah-koh-**soh**?* lo/la acosó?[6]

Could you ... what was specifically said to you?

*poh-**dree**-ah ... loh kay say lay **dee**-hoh ays-pay-see-fee-kah-**mayn**-tay?*

¿Podría ... lo que se le dijo específicamente?

explain to someone (in Spanish)	*ayks-plee-**kahr**-lay ah **ahl**-ghee^ayn (ayn ays-pahn-**yohl**)* explicarle a alguien (en español)
describe in writing (in Spanish)	*days-kree-**beer** pohr ays-**kree**-toh (ayn ays-pahn-**yohl**)* describir por escrito (en español)

What was the date (month, day and year) of ...

*koo^ahl foo^ay lah **fay**-chah (mays, **dee**-ah ee **ahn**-yoh) dayl ...*

¿Cuál fue la fecha (mes, día y año) del ...

the harassment?	*ah-**koh**-soh?* acoso?[5]
the discrimination?	***ahk**-toh day dees-kree-mee-nah-**see^ohn**?* acto de discriminación?[5]

---

14. Were you treated differently from other tenants not of your racial and ethnic background?

*loh/lah trah-**tah**-rohn dee-fay-**ryan**-tay kay ah lohs **oh**-trohs een-kee-**lee**-nohs kay noh sohn day soo **rrah**-sah nee soo ayt-nee-see-**dahd**?*

¿Lo/la trataron diferente que a los otros inquilinos que no son de su raza ni su etnicidad?[6]

Was this regarding ...	*say trah-**tah**-bah ...* ¿Se trataba ...

use of community ammenities (pool, playground, etc.)?	*dayl oo-soh day lohs sayr-**bee**-see^ohs koh-moo-nee-**tah**-ree^ohs (lah pee-**see**-nah, ayl **pah**-tee^oh day rray-**kray**-oh, ayt-**say**-tay-rah)* del uso de los servicios comunitarios (la piscina, el patio de recreo, etc.)
use of laundry facilities?	*dayl oo-soh day lah lah-bayn-dah-**ree**-ah koh-moo-nee-**tah**-ree^ah?* del uso de la lavandería comunitaria?
parking privileges?	*day lohs pree-bee-**lay**-hee^ohs day ays-tah-see^oh-nah-**mee^ayn**-toh?* de los privilegios de estacionamiento?
guidelines regarding guests?	*day lahs **nohr**-mahs **pah**-rah een-bee-**tah**-dohs?* de las normas para invitados?
complaints from neighbors about the people in your dwelling?	*day lahs **kay**-hahs prah-sayn-**tah**-dahs pohr bay-**see**-nohs **soh**-bray lahs payr-**soh**-nahs day soo bee-**bee^ayn**-dah?* de las quejas presentadas por vecinos sobre las personas de su vivienda?
complaints from you and your family about neighbors?	*day soos **kay**-hahs oh lahs day soos **mee^aym**-brohs fah-mee-**lee^ah**-rays **soh**-bray lohs bay-**see**-nohs?* de sus quejas o las de sus miembros familiares sobre los vecinos?
maintenance requests for the interior of your dwelling?	*day lohs pay-**dee**-dohs day mahn-tay-nee-**mee^ayn**-toh **pah**-rah ayl een-tay-**ree^ohr** day soo bee-**bee^ayn**-dah?* de los pedidos de mantenimiento para el interior de su vivienda?
maintenance requests for the exterior of your dwelling?	*day lohs pay-**dee**-dohs day mahn-tay-nee-**mee^ayn**-toh **pah**-rah ayl ayks-tay-**ree^ohr** day soo bee-**bee^ayn**-dah?* de los pedidos de mantenimiento para el exterior de su vivienda?
Could you ... the details of the situation?	*poh-**dree**-ah ... lohs day-**tah**-yays day lah see-too^ah-**see^ohn**?* ¿Podría ... los detalles de la situación?
explain to someone (in Spanish)	*ayks-plee-**kahr**-lay ah **ahl**-ghee^ayn (ayn ays-pahn-**yohl**)* explicarle a alguien (en español)
describe in writing (in Spanish)	*days-kree-**beer** pohr ays-**kree**-toh (ayn ays-pahn-**yohl**)* describir por escrito (en español)
15. Were you given any explanation for the reasons you were treated this way?	*lay oh-fray-**see^ay**-rohn ahl-**goo**-nah ayks-plee-kah-**see^ohn** day lahs rrah-**soh**-nays pohr lahs koo^ah-lays loh/lah trah-**tah**-rohn ah-**see**?* ¿Le ofrecieron alguna explicación de las razones por las cuales lo/la trataron así?[6]
Could you ... what was specifically said to you?	*poh-**dree**-ah ... loh kay say lay **dee**-hoh ays-pay-see-fee-kah-**mayn**-tay?* ¿Podría ... lo que se le dijo específicamente?
explain to someone (in Spanish)	*ayks-plee-**kahr**-lay ah **ahl**-ghee^ayn (ayn ays-pahn-**yohl**)* explicarle a alguien (en español)
describe in writing (in Spanish / English)	*days-kree-**beer** pohr ays-**kree**-toh (ayn ays-pahn-**yohl** / een-**glays**)* describir por escrito (en español / inglés)

16. Were you refused housing?

*lay nay-**gah**-rohn bee-**bee**^**ayn**-dah?*
¿Le negaron vivienda?

On what date (month, day and year) were you refused housing?

*koo^ahl foo^ay lah **fay**-chah (mays, **dee**-ah, **ahn**-yoh) ayn lah koo^ahl lay nay-**gah**-rohn bee-**bee**^**ayn**-dah?*
¿Cuál fue la fecha (mes, día y año) en la cual le negaron vivienda?[5]

---

17. Did you receive ... notice to vacate the premises?

*rray-see-**bee**^**oh** ah-**bee**-soh ... **pah**-rah days-oh-koo-**pahr** lah proh-pee^ay-**dahd**?*
¿Recibió aviso ... para desocupar la propiedad?

    written

*ays-**kree**-toh*
escrito

    verbal

*bayr-**bahl***
verbal

    written and verbal

*ays-**kree**-toh ee bayr-**bahl***
escrito y verbal

How many days notice did you receive to vacate the premises?

*koo^**ahn**-tohs **dee**-ahs day ah-**bee**-soh lay **dee**^**ay**-rohn **pah**-rah days-oh-koo-**pahr** lah proh-pee^ay-**dahd**?*
¿Cuántos días de aviso le dieron para desocupar la propiedad?[2]

Was it a notice to ...

*foo^ay oon ah-**bee**-soh day ...*
¿Fue un aviso de ...

    pay or quit?

*pah-goh oh day-sah-**loh**-hoh?*
pago o desalojo?

How much were you to pay?

*koo^**ahn** say kay-**ree**-ah kay pah-**gah**-rah?*
¿Cuánto se quería que pagara?[2]

    perform or quit?

*koom-plee-**mee**^**ayn**-toh oh day-sah-**loh**-hoh?*
cumplimiento o desalojo?

Did you perform the obligation specified?

*koom-**plee**^**oh** kohn lah oh-blee-gah-**see**^**ohn** ays-pay-see-fee-**kah**-dah?*
¿Cumplió con la obligación especificada?

Could you ... what the obligation you were to perform was?

*poh-**dree**-ah ... koo^ahl **ay**-rah lah oh-blee-gah-**see**^**ohn** kay ah-**bee**-ah day rray-ah-lee-**sahr**?*
¿Podría ... cuál era la obligación que había de realizar?

    explain to someone (in Spanish)

*ayks-plee-**kahr**-lay ah **ahl**-ghee^ayn (ayn ays-pahn-**yohl**)*
explicarle a alguien (en español)

    describe in writing (in Spanish / English)

*days-kree-**beer** pohr ays-**kree**-toh (ayn ays-pahn-**yohl** / een-**glays**)*
describir por escrito (en español / inglés)

    quit only?

*day-sah-**loh**-hoh **koh**-moh lah **oo**-nee-kah ohp-**see**^**ohn**?*
desalojo como la única opción?

English	Pronunciation & Spanish
18. Please make a list to give us of the names and telephone numbers of any witnesses to the situation you told me about.	*pohr fah-bohr, ah-gah oo-nah lees-tah pah-rah ayn-tray-gahr-nohs day lohs nohm-brays ee lohs noo-may-rohs day tay-lay-foh-noh day koo^ah-lays-kee^ayr tays-tee-gohs kay pray-sayn-see^ah-rohn ayl een-see-dayn-tay kay may ah days-kree-toh.* Por favor, haga una lista para entregarnos de los nombres y los números de teléfono de cualesquier testigos que prensenciaron el incidente que me ha descrito.
19. Please make a list to give us of the names and telephone numbers of any other persons that have had similar experiences where you live.	*pohr fah-bohr, ah-gah oo-nah lees-tah pah-rah ayn-tray-gahr-nohs day lohs nohm-brays ee lohs noo-may-rohs day tay-lah-foh-noh pah-rah koo^ah-lays-kee^ayr payr-soh-nahs kay ahn tay-nee-doh ayk-spay-ree^ayn-see^ahs pah-ray-see-dahs dohn-day bee-bay.* Por favor, haga una lista para entregarnos de los nombres y los números de teléfono para cualesquier personas que han tenido experiencias parecidas donde vive.
20. Do you feel you were harmed … by this incident?	*kray-ay kay ays-tay een-see-dayn-tay lay ee-soh dahn-yoh …* ¿Cree que este incidente le hizo daño …
financially	*fee-nahn-see^ay-roh?* financiero?
mentally	*mayn-tahl?* mental?
physically	*fee-see-koh?* físico?
emotional	*ay-moh-see^oh-nahl?* emocional?

B. Landlord—Evictions

proh-pee^ay-tah-ree^oh — days-ah-oo-see^ohs
Propietario—desahucios

English	Pronunciation & Spanish
1. What is the complete address of the property about which you are filing this complaint?	*koo^ahl ays lah dee-rray-see^ohn kohm-play-tah day la proh-pee^ay-dahd soh-bray lah koo^ahl ays-tah pray-sayn-tahn-doh ays-tah kay-hah?* ¿Cuál es la dirección completa de la propiedad sobre la cual está presentando esta queja?[1, 2]
2. Was the rental agreement individual or joint?	*foo^ay oon kohn-trah-toh day ah-rrayn-dah-mee^ayn-toh een-dee-bee-doo^ahl oh kohn-hoon-toh?* ¿Fue un contrato de arrendamiento individual o conjunto?
3. What is the full name of the tenant who appears on the rental agreement for this property?	*koo^ahl ays ayl nohm-bray kohm-play-toh dayl een-kee-lee-noh koo-yoh nohm-bray ah-pah-ray-say ayn ayl kohn-trah-toh day ah-rrayn-dah-mee^ayn-toh pah-rah ays-tah proh-pee^ay-dahd?* ¿Cuál es el nombre completo del inquilino cuyo nombre aparece en el contrato de arrendamiento para esta propiedad?[1]

4. What are the full names of the tenants who appear on the rental agreement for this property?

*koo^ah-lays sohn lohs **nohm**-brays kohm-**play**-tohs day lohs een-kee-**lee**-nohs koo-yohs **nohm**-brays ah-pah-**ray**-sayn ayn ayl kohn-**trah**-toh day ah-rrayn-dah-**mee^ayn**-toh **pah**-rah **ays**-tah proh-pee^ay-**dahd**?*

¿Cuáles son los nombres completos de los inquilinos cuyos nombres aparecen en el contrato de arrendamiento para esta propiedad?[1]

5. Has a tenant of this property recently complained either verbally or in writing about the condition of the premises?

*say ah kay-**hah**-doh rray-see^ayn-tay-**mayn**-tay oon een-kee-**lee**-noh day **ays**-tah proh-pee^ay-**dahd** day lahs kohn-dee-**see^oh**-nays dayl loh-**kahl** **say**-ah bayr-bahl-**mayn**-tay oh pohr ays-**kree**-toh?*

¿Se ha quejado recientemente un inquilino de esta propiedad de las condiciones del local sea verbalmente o por escrito?

Does the complaint deal with ...

*say **trah**-tah lah **kay**-hah day ...*

¿Se trata la queja de ...

a maintenance request?

*oon pay-**dee**-doh day mahn-tay-nee-**mee^ayn**-toh?*

un pedido de mantenimiento?

unsuitable living conditions?

*kohn-dee-**see^oh**-nays een-ah-day-**koo^ah**-dahs day bee-**bee^ayn**-dah?*

condiciones inadecuadas de vivienda?

a community ordinance?

***oo**-nah ohr-day-**nahn**-sah koh-moo-nee-**tah**-ree^ah?*

una ordenanza comunitaria?

6. Has a tenant complained about the condition of the premises within the last ...

*say ah kay-**hah**-doh oon een-kee-**lee**-noh **soh**-bray lahs kohn-dee-**see^oh**-nays dayl loh-**kahl dayn**-troh day lohs **ool**-tee-mohs ...*

¿Se ha quejado un inquilino sobre las condiciones del local dentro de los últimos ...

90 days?

*noh-**bayn**-tah **dee**-ahs?*

noventa días?

180 days?

***see^ayn**-toh oh-**chayn**-tah **dee**-ahs?*

ciento ochenta días?

7. Did you send your tenant(s) a notice of right to terminate tenancy?

*lay(s) mahn-**doh** a soo(s) een-kee-**lee**-noh(s) oon ah-**bee**-soh day day-**ray**-choh day kahn-say-**lahr** soo kohn-**trah**-toh day ah-rrayn-dah-**mee^ayn**-toh?*

¿Le(s) mandó a su(s) inquilino(s) un aviso de derecho de cancelar su contrato de arrendamiento?[9]

8. Has the tenant ...

*ays kay ayl een-kee-**lee**-noh ah ...*

¿Es que el inquilino ha ...

Have the tenants ...

*ays kay lohs een-kee-**lee**-nohs ahn ...*

¿Es que los inquilinos han ...

violated or is/are currently violating any provision set forth in the written rental agreement?

*een-freen-**hee**-doh oh ahk-too^ahl-**mayn**-tay ays-**tah(n)** een-freen-**hee^ayn**-doh ahl-**goo**-nah ays-tee-poo-lah-**see^ohn** ays-tah-blay-**see**-dah pohr ays-**kree**-toh ayn ayl kohn-**trah**-toh day ah-rrayn-dee-**mee^ayn**-toh?*

infringido o actualmente está(n) infringiendo alguna estipulación establecida por escrito en el contrato de arrendamiento?

Does the violation deal with ...

*say **trah**-tah lah een-frahk-**see^ohn** ...*

¿Se trata la infracción ...

late rent payments?	*day lohs **pah**-gohs ah-trah-**sah**-dohs day ah-rrayn-dah-**mee**^ayn-toh?* de los pagos atrasados de arrendamiento?
cessation of rent payments?	*day lah say-sah-**see**^ohn day **pah**-gohs day ah-rrayn-dah-**mee**^ayn-toh?* de la cesación de pagos de arrendamiento?
destruction of property?	*day lah days-trook-**see**^ohn day proh-pee^ay-**dahd**?* de la destrucción de propiedad?
unauthorized tenancy?	*day lay oh-koo-pah-**see**^ohn noh ah^oo-toh-ree-**sah**-dah day lah bee-**bee**^ayn-dah?* de la ocupación no autorizada de la vivienda?
illegal use of dwelling?	*dayl **oo**-soh ee-lay-**gahl** day lah bee-**bee**^ayn-dah?* del uso ilegal de la vivienda?
9. Have you received any complaints or warnings from the Health Department or city/county code enforcement?	*ah rray-see-**bee**-doh ahl-**goo**-nahs **kay**-hahs oh ah-**bee**-sohs dayl day-pahr-tah-**mayn**-toh day sah-**lood poo**-blee-kah oh dayl day-pahr-tah-**mayn**-toh day ah-plee-kah-**see**^ohn day **koh**-dee-gohs moo-nee-see-**pah**-lays oh dayl kohn-**dah**-doh?* ¿Ha recibido algunas quejas o avisos del departamento de salud pública o del departamento de aplicación de códigos municipales o del condado?
Do you have a copy of this complaint or warning?	*tee^**ay**-nay **oo**-nah **koh**-pee^ah day lah **kay**-hah oh ayl ah-**bee**-soh?* ¿Tiene una copia de la queja o el aviso?
Can you provide us with a copy of the complaint or warning?	*nohs **poo**^ay-day proh-pohr-see^oh-**nahr oo**-nah **koh**-pee^ah day lah **kay**-hah oh ayl ah-**bee**-soh?* ¿Nos puede proporcionar una copia de la queja o el aviso?
10. Are any of the (authorized) tenants of this property members of the armed forces?	*sohn **mee**^aym-brohs day lahs **foo**^ayr-sahs ahr-**mah**-dahs ahl-**goo**-nohs day lohs een-kee-**lee**-nohs (ah^oo-toh-ree-**sah**-dohs) day **ays**-tah proh-pee^ay-**dahd**?* ¿Son miembros de las fuerzas armadas algunos de los inquilinos (autorizados) de esta propiedad?
11. Do you have reason to believe persons other than those whose names appear on the rental agreement are residing on the premises?	***kray**-ay kay ah^**ee**-yah payr-**soh**-nahs **koo**-yohs **nohm**-brays noh ah-pah-**ray**-sayn ayn ayl kohn-**trah**-toh day ah-rrayn-dah-**mee**^ayn-toh oh-koo-**pahn**-doh ayl loh-**kahl**?* ¿Cree que haya personas cuyos nombres no aparecen en el contrato de arrendamiento ocupando el local?
Do you know the names of those individuals?	***sah**-bay lohs **nohm**-brays day ah-**kay**-yohs een-dee-**bee**-doo^ohs?* ¿Sabe los nombres de aquellos individuos?
Please make a list of the names to give us.	*pohr fah-**bohr**, **ah**-gah **oo**-nah **lees**-tah day lohs **nohm**-brays **pah**-rah ayn-tray-**gahr**-nohs .* Por favor, haga una lista de los nombres para entregarnos.

12. What is the amount of the monthly rental payment as stipulated in the rental agreement?

koo^ayn-toh ays ayl pah-goh mayn-soo^ahl day ah-rrayn-dah-mee^ayn-toh say-goon loh ays-tee-poo-lah-doh pohr ayl kohn-trah-toh day ah-rree^ayn-doh?

¿Cuánto es el pago mensual de arrendamiento según lo estipulado por el contrato de arriendo?[2]

13. What is the outstanding amount owed to you for rental of the property?

koo^ahl ays ayl mohn-toh payn-dee^ayn-tay kay say lay day-bah pohr ayl ah-rrayn-dah-mee^ayn-toh day lah proh-pee^ay-dahd?

¿Cuál es el monto pendiente que se le debe por el arrendamiento de la propiedad?[2]

14. Is tenancy of the property subject to rent control or an eviction control ordinance?

say bay lah oh-koo-pah-see^ohn day lah proh-pee^ay-dahd soo-hay-tah ahl kohn-trohl day ah-rrayn-dah-mee^ayn-toh oh ah oo-nah ohr-day-nahn-sah day kohn-trohl day days-ah-loh-hoh?

¿Se ve la ocupación de la propiedad sujeta al control de arrendamiento o a una ordenanza de control de desalojo?

15. Please respond with "yes" to the applicable responses:

pohr fah-bohr, rrays-pohn-dah kohn <see> ah lahs rray-plee-kahs kay koh-rrays-pohn-dayn:

Por favor, responda con <sí> a las réplicas que corresponden:

Did the rental agreement indicate the property to be rented on a ...

say ays-tee-poo-lah-bah ayn ayl kohn-trah-toh day ah-rrayn-dah-mee^ayn-toh kay say ah-rrayn-dah-ree-ah lah proh-pee^ay-dahd ...

¿Se estipulaba en el contrato de arrendamiento que se arrendaría la propiedad ...

month-to-month basis?

soh-bray oo-nah bah-say day mays ah mays?

sobre una base de mes a mes?

period of six months?

pohr oon pay-ree-oh-doh day say^ees may-says?

por un período de seis meses?

one-year period?

pohr oon pay-ree-oh-doh day oohn ahn-yoh?

por un período de un año?

period of 18 months?

pohr oon pay-ree-oh-doh day dee^ays ee oh-choh may-says?

por un periódo de diez y ocho meses?

two-year period?

pohr oon pay-ree-oh-doh day dohs ahn-yohs?

por un período de dos años?

Did the rental agreement require the tenant(s) to submit a ...

say-goon ayl kohn-trah-toh day ah-rrayn-dah-mee^ayn-toh, say rray-kay-ree-ah kay ayl een-kee-lee-noh (lohs een-kee-lee-nohs) ayn-tray-gah-rah(n) ...

Según el contrato de arrendamiento, ¿se requería que el inquilino (los inquilinos) entregara(n) ...

30-day vacancy notice?

oo-nah noh-tee-fee-kah-see^ohn day lah een-tayn-see^ohn day days-oh-koo-pahr lah bee-bee^ayn-dah kohn tray^een-tah dee-ahs day ahn-tay-lah-see^ohn?

una notificación de la intención de desocupar la vivienda con treinta días de antelación?

90-day vacancy notice?

oo-nah noh-tee-fee-kah-see^ohn day lah een-tayn-see^ohn day days-oh-koo-pahr lah bee-bee^ayn-dah kohn noh-bayn-tah dee-ahs day ahn-tay-lah-see^ohn?

una notificación de la intención de desocupar la vivienda con noventa días de antelación?

16. By what day of the month did the rental agreement require rent payment to be submitted?

say-goon ayl kohn-trah-toh day ah-rrayn-day-mee^ayn-toh, koo^ahl ay-rah lah fay-chah lee-mee-tay pah-rah lah koo^ahl say day-bee-ah rray-mee-teer ayl pah-goh day ah-rrayn-dah-mee^ayn-toh?

Según el contrato de arrendamiento, ¿cuál era la fecha límite para la cual se debía remitir el pago de arrendamiento?[5]

What is the amount of any late fees for the collection of late rent payment?

koo^ahn-toh sohn lohs kahr-gohs ah-dee-see^oh-nah-lays pohr lohs pah-gohs ah-trah-sah-dohs?

¿Cuánto son los cargos adicionales por pagos de arrendamiento atrasados?[2]

17. Were the terms and conditions of the rental contract explained and/or expressly provided ...

lay(s) ayks-plee-kah-rohn ee/oh lay(s) proh-pohr-see^oh-nah-rohn ayks-pray-sah-mayn-tay lohs plah-sohs ee kohn-dee-see^oh-nays dayl kohn-trah-toh day ah-rrayn-dah-mee^ayn-toh ...

¿Le(s) explicaron y/o le(s) proporcionaron expresamente los plazos y condiciones del contrato de arrendamiento ...[9]

to the authorized tenant?

ahl een-kee-lee-noh ah^oo-toh-ree-sah-doh?

al inquilino autorizado?

to the authorized tenants?

ah lohs een-kee-lee-nohs ah^oo-toh-ree-sah-dohs?

a los inquilinos autorizados?

18. Were any alterations made to the original rental agreement after ...

lay ee-see^ay-rohn kahm-bee^ohs ahl kohn-trah-toh day ah-rrayn-dah-mee^ayn-toh days-poo^ays day kay ...

¿Le hicieron cambios al contrato de arrendamiento original después de que ...

the authorized tenant had signed it?

ayl een-kee-lee-noh ah^oo-toh-ree-sah-doh loh feer-moh?

el inquilino autorizado lo firmó?

the authorized tenants had signed it?

lohs een-kee-lee-nohs ah^oo-toh-ree-sah-dohs loh feer-mah-rohn?

los inquilinos autorizados lo firmaron?

Were you aware of these changes?

sah-bee-ah day ays-tohs kahm-bee^ohs?

¿Sabía de estos cambios?

Were the tenants aware of these changes?

sah-bee-ahn lohs een-kee-lee-nohs day ays-tohs kahm-bee^ohs?

¿Sabían los inquilinos de estos cambios?

Did you have the ... an amended rental contract in which these changes were set forth?

ee-soh kay ... oon kohn-trah-toh day ah-rrayn-day-mee^ayn-toh ayn-mayn-dah-doh ayn ayl koo^ahl say ays-tee-poo-lah-bahn lohs kahm-bee^ohs?

¿Hizo que ... un contrato de arrendamiento enmendado en el cual se estipulaban los cambios?

the tenant sign ...

ayl een-kee-lee-noh feer-mah-rah ...

el inquilino firmara ...

the tenants sign ...

lohs een-kee-lee-nohs feer-mah-rahn ...

los inquilinos firmaran ...

Can you provide us with a copy of both the original and the amended rental contracts?	*nohs **poo^ay**-day proh-pohr-see^oh-**nahr oo**-nah **koh**-pee^ah dayl kohn-**trah**-toh day ah-rrayn-dee-**mee^ayn**-toh oh-ree-hee-**nahl** ah-**see koh**-moh dayl ayn-mayn-**dah**-doh?* ¿Nos puede proporcionar una copia del contrato de arrendamiento original así como del enmendado?

19. Did you provide ... notice to vacate the premises?	*proh-pohr-see^oh-**noh** oon ah-**bee**-soh ... **pah**-rah days-oh-koo-**pahr** ayl loh-**kahl**?* ¿Proporcionó un aviso ... para desocupar el local?
written	*ays-**kree**-toh* escrito
verbal	*bayr-**bahl*** verbal
written and verbal	*ays-**kree**-toh ee bayr-**bahl*** escrito y verbal
How many days notice did you allow to vacate the premises?	***koo^ahn**-tohs **dee**-ahs day pray-ah-**bee**-soh say payr-mee-**tee^ay**-rohn **pah**-rah days-oh-koo-**pahr** ayl loh-**kahl**?* ¿Cuántos días de preaviso se permitieron para desocupar el local?[2]
Was it a notice to ...	*foo^ay oon ah-**bee**-soh day ...* ¿Fue un aviso de ...
pay or quit?	***pah**-goh oh day-sah-**loh**-hoh?* pago o desalojo?
How much did you request be paid?	***koo^ahn**-toh say kay-**ree**-ah kay pah-**gah**-rah?* ¿Cuánto se quería que pagara?[2]
perform or quit?	*koom-plee-**mee^ayn**-toh oh day-sah-**loh**-hoh?* cumplimiento o desalojo?
Did you perform the obligation specified?	*koom-**plee^oh** kohn lah oh-blee-gah-**see^ohn** ays-pay-see-fee-**kah**-dah?* ¿Cumplió con la obligación especificada?
Could you ... what the obligation you were to perform was?	*poh-**dree**-ah ... koo^ahl **ay**-rah lah oh-blee-gah-**see^ohn** kay ah-**bee**-ah day rray-ah-lee-**sahr**?* ¿Podría ... cuál era la obligación que había de realizar?
explain to someone (in Spanish / English)	*ayks-plee-**kahr**-lay ah **ahl**-ghee^ayn (ayn ays-pahn-**yohl** / een-**glays**)* explicarle a alguien (en español / inglés)
put in writing	*poh-**nahr** pohr ays-**kree**-toh* poner por escrito
quit only?	*day-sah-**loh**-hoh **koh**-moh lah **oo**-nee-kah ohp-**see^ohn**?* desalojo como la única opción?

Can you provide us with a copy of this notice?	*nohs poo^ay-day proh-pohr-see^oh-nahr koh-pee^ah day ays-tay ah-bee-soh?* ¿Nos puede proporcionar copia de este aviso?

---

20. Was a copy of the notice ...	*oo-nah koh-pee^ah dayl ah-bee-soh ...* ¿Una copia del aviso ...
given directly to the tenant?	*say lay dee^oh dee-rayk-tah-mayn-tay ahl een-kee-lee-noh?* se le dio directamente al inquilino?
given directly to the tenants?	*say lays dee^oh dee-rayk-tah-mayn-tay ah lohs een-kee-lee-nohs?* se les dio directamente a los inquilinos?
left with an individual at the property?	*say lay ayn-tray-goh ah oon een-dee-bee-doo^oh ayn ayl loh-kahl?* se le entregó a un individuo en el local?
What is the name of the person with whom you left the notice?	*koh-moh say yah-mah lah payr-soh-nah ah kee^ayn say lay ayn-tray-goh ayl ah-bee-soh* ¿Cómo se llama la persona a quien se le entregó el aviso?[1]
posted on the premises?	*say fee-hoh ayn ayl loh-kahl?* se fijó en el local?
mailed to the tenant via certified or registered mail?	*say lay mahn-doh ahl een-kee-lee-noh pohr koh-rray-oh sayr-tee-fee-kah-doh oh rray-hees-trah-doh?* se le mandó al inquilino por correo certificado o registrado?
mailed to the tenants via certified or registered mail?	*say lays mahn-doh ah lohs een-kee-lee-nohs pohr koh-rray-oh sayr-tee-fee-kah-doh oh rray-hees-trah-doh?* se les mandó a los inquilinos por correo certificado o registrado?
mailed to where to the tenant is employed?	*say lay mahn-doh ahl een-kee-lee-noh ayn soo loo-gahr day trah-bah-hoh?* se le mandó al inquilino en su lugar de trabajo?
mailed to to where the tenants are employed?	*say lays mahn-doh ahl een-kee-lee-nohs ayn soo loo-gahr day trah-bah-hoh?* se les mandó a los inquilinos en su lugar de trabajo?
Do you have some sort of proof of the delivery of such notice?	*tee^ay-nay ahl-goo-nah mah-nay-rah day kohm-proh-bahr lah ayn-tray-gah day tahl ah-bee-soh?* ¿Tiene alguna manera de comprobar la entrega de tal aviso?
Would that be ...	*say-ree-ah* ¿Sería ...
a signature of the person with whom you left the notice?	*lah feer-mah day lah payr-soh-nah ah kee^ayn lay ayn-tray-goh ayl ah-bee-soh?* la firma de la persona a quien le entregó el aviso?

physical verification of delivery sent to you by the postal service?	*bay-ree-fee-kah-see^ohn fee-see-kah kay say rray-see-bee^oh day lohs sayr-bee-see^ohs pohs-tah-lays day lah ayn-tray-gah dayl ah-bee-soh?* verificación física que se recibió de los servicios postales de la entrega del aviso?
post dated returned mail ...	*koh-rray-oh day-boo^ayl-toh pohs-fay-chah-doh kay ...* correo devuelto posfechado que ...
the tenant refused?	*ayl een-kee-lee-noh rray-chah-soh ah-sayp-tahr?* el inquilino rechazó aceptar?
the tenants refused?	*lohs een-kee-lee-nohs rray-chah-sah-rohn ah-sayp-tahr?* los inquilinos rechazaron aceptar?
Can you provide us with a copy of this proof?	*nohs poo^ay-day proh-pohr-see^oh-nahr koh-pee^ah day ays-tah proo^ay-bah?* ¿Nos puede proporcionar copia de esta prueba?

21. Are there any damages to the property for which you feel ...	*ah^ee ahl-goo-nohs dahn-yohs ah lah proh-pee^ay-dahd pohr lohs koo^ah-lays ah-lay-gah kay ...* ¿Hay algunos daños a la propiedad por los cuales alega que ...
the tenant is responsible?	*ayl een-kee-lee-noh ays rrays-pohn-sah-blay?* el inquilino es responsable?
the tenants are responsible?	*lohs een-kee-lee-nohs sohn rrays-pohn-sah-blays?* los inquilinos son responsables?
Please make a list of those to give us and write the estimated amount you believe it will cost to repair those damages beside each entry.	*pohr fah-bohr, ah-gah oo-nah lees-tah day ays-tohs dahn-yohs pah-rah ayn-tray-gahr-nohs ee loo^ay-goh day kah-dah ah-noh-tah-see^ohn, ays-kree-bah koo^ahn-toh kohs-tah-ree-ah ah-sayr kah-dah rray-pah-rah-see^ohn.* Por favor, haga una lista de estos daños para entregarnos y luego de cada anotación, escriba cuánto costaría hacer cada reparación.

C. Tenant—Evictions

een-kee-lee-noh—days-ah-oo-see^ohs
Inquilino—desahucios

English	Pronunciation & Spanish
1. What is the complete address of the property about which you are filing this complaint?	*koo^ahl ays lah dee-rray-see^ohn kohm-play-tah day la proh-pee^ay-dahd soh-bray lah koo^ahl ays-tah pray-sayn-tahn-doh ays-tah kay-hah?* ¿Cuál es la dirección completa de la propieadad sobre la cual está presentando esta queja?[1, 2]
2. Was the rental agreement individual or joint?	*foo^ay oon kohn-trah-toh day ah-rrayn-dah-mee^ayn-toh een-dee-bee-doo^ahl oh kohn-hoon-toh?* ¿Fue un contrato de arrendamiento individual o conjunto?

3. What is the full name of ... that appears on the rental agreement for this property?

*koo^ahl ays ayl **nohm**-bray kohm-**play**-toh dayl ... **koo**-yoh **nohm**-bray ah-pah-**ray**-say ayn ayl kohn-**trah**-toh day ah-rrayn-dah-**mee^ayn**-toh **pah**-rah **ays**-tah proh-pee^ay-**dahd**?*

¿Cuál es el nombre completo ... cuyo nombre aparece en el contrato de arrendamiento para esta propiedad?[1]

the owner

*dayl proh-pee^ay-**tah**-ree^oh*

del propietario

the rental company

*day lah kohm-pahn-**yee**-ah day ah-rrayn-dah-**mee^ayn**-toh*

de la compañía de arrendamiento

the property management company

*day lah kohm-pahn-**yee**-ah day hays-**tee^ohn** een-moh-bee-**lee^ah**-ree^ah*

de la compañía de gestión inmobiliaria

4. What are the full names of the tenants who appear on the rental agreement for this property?

***koo^ah**-lays sohn lohs **nohm**-brays kohm-**play**-tohs day lohs een-kee-**lee**-nohs **koo**-yohs **nohm**-brays ah-pah-**ray**-sayn ayn ayl kohn-**trah**-toh day ah-rrayn-dah-**mee^ayn**-toh **pah**-rah **ays**-tah proh-pee^ay-**dahd**?*

¿Cuáles son los nombres completos de los inquilinos cuyos nombres aparecen en el contrato de arrendamiento para esta propiedad?[1]

5. Have you recently complained either verbally or in writing about the condition of the premises?

*say ah kay-**hah**-doh rray-see^ayn-tay-**mayn**-tay day lahs kohn-dee-**see^oh**-nays dayl loh-**kahl say**-ah bayr-bahl-**mayn**-tay oh pohr ays-**kree**-toh?*

¿Se ha quejado recientemente de las condiciones del local sea verbalmente o por escrito?

Does the complaint deal with ...

*say **trah**-tah lah **kay**-hah day ...*

¿Se trata la queja de ...

a maintenance request?

*oon pay-**dee**-doh day mahn-tay-nee-**mee^ayn**-toh?*

un pedido de mantenimiento?

unsuitable living conditions?

*kohn-dee-**see^oh**-nays een-ah-day-**koo^ah**-dahs day bee-**bee^ayn**-dah?*

condiciones inadecuadas de vivienda?

a community ordinance?

***oo**-nah ohr-day-**nahn**-sah koh-moo-nee-**tah**-ree^ah?*

una ordenanza comunitaria?

6. Have you complained about the condition of the premises within the last ...

*say ah kay-**hah**-doh **soh**-bray lahs kohn-dee-**see^oh**-nays dayl loh-**kahl dayn**-troh day lohs **ool**-tee-**mohs** ...*

¿Se ha quejado sobre las condiciones del local dentro de los últimos ...

90 days?

*noh-**bayn**-tah **dee**-ahs?*

noventa días?

180 days?

***see^ayn**-toh oh-**chayn**-tah **dee**-ahs?*

ciento ochenta días?

7. Did you receive a notice of right to terminate tenancy?

*rray-see-**bee^oh** oon ah-**bee**-soh day day-**ray**-choh day kahn-say-**lahr** soo kohn-**trah**-toh day ah-rrayn-dah-**mee^ayn**-toh?*

¿Recibió un aviso de derecho de cancelar su contrato de arrendamiento?

	*nohs **poo^ay**-day proh-pohr-see^oh-**nahr** oo-nah **koh**-pee^ah day **ay**-say ah-**bee**-soh?*
Can you provide us with a copy of that notice?	¿Nos puede proporcionar una copia de ese aviso?
	*ah een-freen-**hee**-doh oh ahk-too^ahl-**mayn**-tay ays-**tah** een-freen-**hee^ayn**-doh ahl-**goo**-nah ays-tee-poo-lah-**see^ohn** ays-tah-blay-**see**-dah pohr ays-**kree**-toh ayn ayl kohn-**trah**-toh day ah-rrayn-dah-**mee^ayn**-toh?*
8. Have you or are you currently violating any provision set forth in the written rental agreement?	¿Ha infringido o actualmente está infringiendo alguna estipulación establecida por escrito en el contrato de arrendamiento?
	*ays kay lohs **oh**-trohs een-kee-lee-nohs day **ays**-tah bee-**bee^ayn**-dah ahn ah een-freen-**hee**-doh oh ahk-too^ahl-**mayn**-tay ays-**tahn** een-freen-**hee^ayn**-doh ahl-**goo**-nah ays-tee-poo-lah-**see^ohn** ays-tah-blay-**see**-dah pohr ays-**kree**-toh ayn ayl kohn-**trah**-toh day ah-rrayn-dah-**mee^ayn**-toh?*
Have the other tenants of this dwelling violated or are they currently violating any provision set forth in the written rental agreement?	¿Es que los otros inquilinos de esta vivienda han infringido o actualmente están infringiendo alguna estipulación establecida por escrito en el contrato de arrendamiento?
	*say **trah**-tah lah een-frahk-**see^ohn** …*
Does the violation deal with …	¿Se trata la infracción …
	*day lohs **pah**-gohs ah-trah-**sah**-dohs day ah-rrayn-dah-**mee^ayn**-toh?*
late rent payments?	de los pagos atrasados de arrendamiento?
	*day lah say-sah-**see^ohn** day **pah**-gohs day ah-rrayn-dah-**mee^ayn**-toh?*
cessation of rent payments?	de la cesación de pagos de arrendamiento?
	*day lah days-trook-**see^ohn** day proh-pee^ay-**dahd**?*
destruction of property?	de la destrucción de propiedad?
	*day lay oh-koo-pah-**see^ohn** noh ah^oo-toh-ree-**sah**-dah day lah bee-**bee^ayn**-dah?*
unauthorized tenancy?	de la ocupación no autorizada de la vivienda?
	*dayl **oo**-soh ee-lay-**gahl** day lah bee-**bee^ayn**-dah?*
illegal use of dwelling?	del uso ilegal de la vivienda?
	*say-bay see ayl proh-pee^ay-**tah**-ree^oh ah rray-see-**bee**-doh ahl-**goo**-nahs **kay**-hahs oh ah-**bee**-sohs dayl day-pahr-tah-**mayn**-toh day sah-**lood** **poo**-blee-kah oh dayl day-pahr-tah-**mayn**-toh ah-plee-kah-**see^ohn** day **koh**-dee-gohs moo-nee-see-**pah**-lays oh dayl kohn-**dah**-doh?*
9. Do you know if the owner has received any complaints or warnings from the Health Department or city/county code enforcement?	¿Sabe si el propietario ha recibido algunas quejas o avisos del departamento de salud pública o del departamento de aplicación de códigos municipales o del condado?
	*tee^ay-nay oo-nah **koh**-pee^ah day lah **kay**-hah oh ayl ah-**bee**-soh?*
Do you have a copy of this complaint or warning?	¿Tiene una copia de la queja o el aviso?
	*nohs **poo^ay**-day proh-pohr-see^oh-**nahr** oo-nah **koh**-pee^ah day lah **kay**-hah oh ayl ah-**bee**-soh?*
Can you provide us with a copy of the complaint or warning?	¿Nos puede proporcionar una copia de la queja o el aviso?

10. Are any of the (authorized) tenants of this property members of the armed forces?

sohn mee^aym-brohs day lahs foo^ayr-sahs ahr-mah-dahs ahl-goo-nohs day lohs een-kee-lee-nohs (ah^oo-toh-ree-sah-dohs) day ays-tah proh-pee^ay-dahd?

¿Son miembros de las fuerzas armadas algunos de los inquilinos (autorizados) de esta propiedad?

11. Are persons other than those whose names appear on the rental agreement residing on the premises?

ays kay payr-soh-nahs koo-yohs nohm-brays noh ah-pah-ray-sayn ayn ayl kohn-trah-toh day ah-rrayn-dah-mee^ayn-toh ays-tahn oh-koo-pahn-doh ayl loh-kahl?

¿Es que personas cuyos nombres no aparecen en el contrato de arrendamiento están ocupando el local?

What are the names of those individuals?

koo^ah-lays sohn lohs nohm-brays day ah-kay-yohs een-dee-bee-doo^ohs?

¿Cuáles son los nombres de aquellos individuos?[1]

Please make a list to give us of the names.

pohr fah-bohr, ah-gah oo-nah lees-tah day lohs nohm-brays pah-rah ayn-tray-gahr-nohs.

Por favor, haga una lista de los nombres para entregarnos.

12. What is the amount of the monthly rental payment as stipulated in the rental agreement?

koo^ayn-toh ays ayl pah-goh mayn-soo^ahl day ah-rrayn-dah-mee^ayn-toh say-goon loh ays-tee-poo-lah-doh pohr ayl kohn-trah-toh day ah-rree^ayn-doh?

¿Cuánto es el pago mensual de arrendamiento según lo estipulado por el contrato de arriendo?[2]

13. What is the outstanding amount you owe for rental of the property?

koo^ahl ays ayl mohn-toh payn-dee^ayn-tay kay say day-bay pohr ayl ah-rrayn-dah-mee^ayn-toh day lah proh-pee^ay-dahd?

¿Cuál es el monto pendiente que se debe por el arrendamiento de la propiedad?[2]

14. Is tenancy of the property subject to rent control or an eviction control ordinance?

say bay lah oh-koo-pah-see^ohn day lah proh-pee^ay-dahd soo-hay-tah ahl kohn-trohl day ah-rrayn-dah-mee^ayn-toh oh ah oo-nah ohr-day-nahn-sah day kohn-trohl day days-ah-loh-hoh?

¿Se ve la ocupación de la propiedad sujeta al control de arrendamiento o a una ordenanza de control de desalojo?

15. Please respond with "yes" to the applicable responses:

pohr fah-bohr, rrays-spohn-dah kohn <see> ah lahs rrays-poo^ays-tahs kay koh-rrays-pohn-dayn:

Por favor, responda con <sí> a las respuestas que corresponden:

Did the rental agreement indicate the property to be rented on a ...

say ays-tee-poo-lah-bah ayn ayl kohn-trah-toh day ah-rrayn-dah-mee^ayn-toh kay say ah-rrayn-dah-ree-ah lah proh-pee^ay-dahd ...

¿Se estipulaba en el contrato de arrendamiento que se arrendaría la propiedad ...

month-to-month basis?

soh-bray oo-nah bah-say day mays ah mays?

sobre una base de mes a mes?

period of six months?

pohr oon pay-ree-oh-doh day say^ees may-says?

por un período de seis meses?

one-year period?

pohr oon pay-ree-oh-doh day oohn ahn-yoh?

por un período de un año?

period of 18 months?	*pohr oon pay-**ree**-oh-doh day dee^ays ee **oh**-choh **may**-says?* por un período de diez y ocho meses?
two-year period?	*pohr oon pay-**ree**-oh-doh day dohs **ahn**-yohs?* por un período de dos años?
Did the rental agreement require you to submit a ...	*say-**goon** ayl kohn-**trah**-toh day ah-rrayn-dah-**mee^ayn**-toh, say rray-kay-**ree**-ah kay ayn-tray-**gah**-rah oos-**tayd** ...* Según el contrato de arrendamiento, ¿se requería que entregara Ud....
30-day vacancy notice?	***oo**-nah noh-tee-fee-kah-**see^ohn** day lah een-tayn-**see^ohn** day days-oh-koo-**pahr** lah bee-**bee^ayn**-dah kohn **tray^een**-tah **dee**-ahs day ahn-tay-lah-**see^ohn**?* una notificación de la intención de desocupar la vivienda con treinta días de antelación?
90-day vacancy notice?	***oo**-nah noh-tee-fee-kah-**see^ohn** day lah een-tayn-**see^ohn** day days-oh-koo-**pahr** lah bee-**bee^ayn**-dah kohn noh-**bayn**-tah **dee**-ahs day ahn-tay-lah-**see^ohn**?* una notificación de la intención de desocupar la vivienda con noventa días de antelación?
16. By what day of the month did the rental agreement require rent payment to be submitted?	*say-**goon** ayl kohn-**trah**-toh day ah-rrayn-day-**mee^ayn**-toh, koo^ahl **ay**-rah lah **fay**-chah **lee**-mee-tay **pah**-rah lah koo^ahl say day-**bee**-ah rray-mee-**teer** ayl **pah**-goh day ah-rrayn-dah-**mee^ayn**-toh?* Según el contrato de arrendamiento, ¿cuál era la fecha límite para la cual se debía remitir el pago de arrendamiento?
What is the amount of any late fees for the collection of late rent payment?	***koo^ahn**-toh sohn lohs **kahr**-gohs ah-dee-see^oh-**nah**-lays pohr lohs **pah**-gohs ah-trah-**sah**-dohs?* ¿Cuánto son los cargos adicionales por pagos de arrendamiento atrasados?[2]
17. Were the terms and conditions of the rental contract explained and/or expressly provided ...	*lay(s) ayks-plee-**kah**-rohn ee/oh lay(s) proh-pohr-see^oh-**nah**-rohn ayks-pray-sah-**mayn**-tay lohs **plah**-sohs ee kohn-dee-**see^oh**-nays dayl kohn-**trah**-toh day ah-rrayn-dah-**mee^ayn**-toh ...* ¿Le(s) explicaron y/o le(s) proporcionaron expresamente los plazos y condiciones del contrato de arrendamiento ... [9]
to you?	*ah oos-**tayd**?* a Ud.?
to the other authorized tenants?	*ah lohs **oh**-trohs een-kee-**lee**-nohs ah^oo-toh-ree-**sah**-dohs?* a los otros inquilinos autorizados?
18. Were any alterations made to the original rental agreement after ...	*lay ee-**see^ay**-rohn **kahm**-bee^ohs ahl kohn-**trah**-toh day ah-rrayn-dah-**mee^ayn**-toh days-**poo^ays** day kay ...* ¿Le hicieron cambios al contrato de arrendamiento original después de que ...
you had signed it?	*loh feer-**moh**?* lo firmó?
the other authorized tenants had signed it?	*lohs **oh**-trohs een-kee-**lee**-nohs ah^oo-toh-ree-**sah**-dohs loh feer-**mah**-rohn?* los otros inquilinos autorizados lo firmaron?

Were you aware of these changes?	*sah-**bee**-ah day **ays**-tohs **kahm**-bee^ohs?* ¿Sabía de estos cambios?
Were the other tenants aware of these changes?	*sah-**bee**-ahn lohs **oh**-trohs een-kee-**lee**-nohs day **ays**-tohs kahm-bee^ohs?* ¿Sabían los otros inquilinos de estos cambios?
Did they have … an ammended rental contract in which these changes were set forth?	*ee-**see**^ay-rohn kay … oon kohn-**trah**-toh day ah-rrayn-day-**mee**^ayn-toh ayn-mayn-**dah**-doh ayn ayl koo^ahl say ays-tee-poo-**lah**-bahn lohs **kahm**-bee^ohs?* ¿Hicieron que … un contrato de arrendamiento enmendado en el cual se estipulaban los cambios?
you sign …	*oos-**tayd** feer-**mah**-rah …* Ud. firmara …
the other tenants sign …	*lohs **oh**-trohs een-kee-**lee**-nohs feer-**mah**-rahn …* los otros inquilinos firmaran …
Can you provide us with a copy of both the original and the ammended rental contracts?	*nohs **poo**^ay-day proh-pohr-see^oh-**nahr** oo-nah **koh**-pee^ah dayl kohn-**trah**-toh day ah-rrayn-dee-**mee**^ayn-toh oh-ree-hee-**nahl** ah-**see** **koh**-moh dayl ayn-mayn-**dah**-doh?* ¿Nos puede proporcionar una copia del contrato de arrendamiento original así como del enmendado?

19. Were you given … notice to vacate the premises?	*lay proh-pohr-see^oh-**nah**-rohn oon ah-**bee**-soh … **pah**-rah days-oh-koo-**pahr** ayl loh-**kahl**?* ¿Le proporcionaron un aviso … para desocupar el local?
written	*ays-**kree**-toh* escrito
verbal	*bayr-**bahl*** verbal
written and verbal	*ays-**kree**-toh ee bayr-**bahl*** escrito y verbal
How many days notice were you allowed to vacate the premises?	***koo**^ahn-tohs **dee**-ahs day pray-ah-**bee**-soh lay payr-mee-**tee**^ay-rohn **pah**-rah days-oh-koo-**pahr** ayl loh-**kahl**?* ¿Cuántos días de preaviso le permitieron para desocupar el local?[2]
Was it a notice to …	*foo^ay oon ah-**bee**-soh day …* ¿Fue un aviso de …
pay or quit?	***pah**-goh oh day-sah-**loh**-hoh?* pago o desalojo?
How much were you to pay?	***koo**^ahn-toh say kay-**ree**-ah kay pah-**gah**-rah?* ¿Cuánto se quería que pagara?[2]
perform or quit?	*koom-plee-**mee**^ayn-toh oh day-sah-**loh**-hoh?* cumplimiento o desalojo?

Did you perform the obligation specified?	*koom-**plee^oh** kohn lah oh-blee-gah-**see^ohn** ays-pay-see-fee-**kah**-dah?* ¿Cumplió con la obligación especificada?
Could you ... what the obligation you were to perform was?	*poh-**dree**-ah ... koo^ahl **ay**-rah lah oh-blee-gah-**see^ohn** kay ah-**bee**-ah day rray-ah-lee-**sahr**?* ¿Podría ... cuál era la obligación que había de realizar?
explain to someone (in Spanish / English)	*ayks-plee-**kahr**-lay ah **ahl**-ghee^ayn (ayn ays-pahn-**yohl** / een-**glays**)* explicarle a alguien (en español / inglés)
put in writing	*poh-**nahr** pohr ays-**kree**-toh* poner por escrito
Can you provide us with a copy of this notice?	*nohs **poo^ay**-day proh-pohr-see^oh-**nahr** oo-nah **koh**-pee^ah day **ays**-tay ah-**bee**-soh?* ¿Nos puede proporcionar copia de este aviso?

20. Was a copy of the notice ...	***oo**-nah **koh**-pee^ah dayl ah-**bee**-soh ...* ¿Una copia del aviso ...
given directly to you?	*say lay dee^oh dee-rayk-tah-**mayn**-tay ah oos-**tayd**?* se le dio directamente a Ud.?
given directly to the other tenants?	*say lays dee^oh dee-rayk-tah-**mayn**-tay ah lohs **oh**-trohs een-kee-**lee**-nohs?* se les dio directamente a los otros inquilinos?
left with an individual at the property?	*say lay ayn-tray-**goh** ah oon een-dee-**bee**-doo^oh ayn ayl loh-**kahl**?* se le entregó a un individuo en el local?
What is the name of the person with whom notice was left?	***koh**-moh say **yah**-mah lah payr-**soh**-nah ah kee^ayn say lay ayn-tray-**goh** ayl ah-**bee**-soh* ¿Cómo se llama la persona a quien se le entregó el aviso?[1]
posted on the premises?	*say fee-**hoh** ayn ayl loh-**kahl**?* se fijó en el local?
mailed to you via certified or registered mail?	*say lay mahn-**doh** ah oos-**tayd** pohr koh-**rray**-oh sayr-tee-fee-**kah**-doh oh rray-hees-**trah**-doh?* se le mandó a Ud. por correo certificado o registrado?
mailed to the other tenants via certified or registered mail?	*say lays mahn-**doh** ah lohs **oh**-trohs een-kee-**lee**-nohs pohr koh-**rray**-oh sayr-tee-fee-**kah**-doh oh rray-hees-**trah**-doh?* se les mandó a los otros inquilinos por correo certificado o registrado?
mailed to where you are employed?	*say lay **mahn**-doh ah oos-**tayd** ayn soo loo-**gahr** day trah-**bah**-hoh?* se le mandó a Ud. en su lugar de trabajo?

mailed to where the other tenants are employed?	*say lays **mahn**-doh ah lohs **oh**-trohs een-kee-**lee**-nohs ayn soo loo-**gahr** day trah-**bah**-hoh?* se les mandó a los otros inquilinos en su lugar de trabajo?
21. Are there any damages to the property for which you feel ... but the owner says otherwise?	*ah^ee ahl-**goo**-nohs **dahn**-yohs ah lah proh-pee^ay-**dahd** pohr lohs **koo^ah**-lays ... **pay**-roh ayl proh-pee^ay-**tah**-ree^oh oh-**pee**-nah loh kohn-**trah**-ree^oh?* ¿Hay algunos daños a la propiedad por los cuales ... pero el propietario opina lo contrario?
you are not responsible	*oos-**tayd** noh ays rrays-pohn-**sah**-blay* Ud. no es responsable
the other tenants are not responsible	*lohs **oh**-trohs een-kee-**lee**-nohs noh sohn rrays-pohn-**sah**-blays* los otros inquilinos no son responsables
Please make a list of those damages to give us and write the estimated amount you believe it will cost to repair them beside each entry.	*pohr fah-**bohr**, **ah**-gah **oo**-nah **lees**-tah day **ays**-tohs **dahn**-yohs pah-rah ayn-tray-**gahr**-nohs ee **loo^ay**-goh day **kah**-dah ah-noh-tah-**see^ohn**, ays-**kree**-bah **koo^ahn**-toh oh-**pee**-nah kay kohs-tah-**ree**-ah ah-**sayr kah**-dah rray-pah-rah-**see^ohn**.* Por favor, haga una lista de estos daños para entregarnos y luego de cada anotación, escriba cuánto opina que costaría hacer cada reparación.

III. Probate

*bah-lee-dah-**see^ohn** tays-tah-mayn-**tah**-ree^ah*
Validación testamentaria

English	Pronunciation & Spanish
1. What is your relationship to the decedent?	*koo^ahl ays soo rray-lah-**see^ohn** kohn ayl ohk-**see**-soh/lah ohk-**see**-sah?* ¿Cuál es su relación con el occiso/la occisa?[10]
friend?	*ah-**mee**-goh/gah?* amigo/a?[1]
brother?	*ayr-**mah**-noh?* hermano?
sister?	*ayr-**mah**-nah?* hermana?
uncle?	***tee**-oh?* tío?
aunt?	***tee**-ah?* tía?
mother?	***mah**-dray?* madre?

father?	*pah-dray?* padre?
boyfriend?	*noh-bee^oh?* novio?
girlfriend?	*noh-bee^ah?* novia?
cousin?	*pree-moh/mah?* primo/prima?[1]
other (relative)?	*oh-troh (pah-rayn-tays-koh fah-mee-lee^ahr)?* otro (parentesco familiar)?

2. What is …	*koo^ahl ays …* ¿Cuál es …
the decedent's full name?	*ayl nohm-bray kohm-play-toh dayl ohk-see-soh/day lah ohk-see-sah?* el nombre completo del occiso/de la occisa?[1, 10]
the decedent's current address?	*lah dee-rayk-see^ohn ahk-too^ahl dayl ohk-see-soh/day lah ohk-see-sah?* la dirección actual del occiso/de la occisa?[1, 2, 10]

3. Does the decedent have a mailing address different from the current address?	*tee^ay-nay ayl ohk-see-soh/lah ohk-see-sah oo-nah dee-rayk-see^ohn pohs-tahl dee-fay-rayn-tay day lah dee-rayk-see^ohn ahk-too^ahl?* ¿Tiene el occiso/la occisa una dirección postal diferente de la dirección actual?[10]
What is the decedent's mailing address?	*koo^ahl ays lah dee-rayk-see^ohn pohs-tahl dayl ohk-see-soh/day lah ohk-see-sah?* ¿Cuál es la dirección postal del occiso/de la occisa?[1, 10]

4. Is the decendent a citizen of the United States?	*ays ayl ohk-see-soh/lah ohk-see-sah oon/oo-nah see^oo-dah-dah-noh/nah day lohs ays-tah-dohs oo-nee-dohs?* ¿Es el occiso/la occisa un/a ciudadano/a de los Estados Unidos?[3, 10]
What is the decedent's …	*koo^ahl ays ayl noo-may-roh day …* ¿Cuál es el número de …
citizenship number?	*see^oo-dah-dah-nee-ah dayl ohk-see-soh/day lah ohk-see-sah?* ciudadanía del occiso/de la occisa?[2, 10]
alien registration number?	*day rray-hees-troh day een-mee-grahn-tay dayl ohk-see-soh/day lah onk-see-sah?* de registro de inmigrante del occiso/de la occisa?[2, 10]

5. What was …	*koo^ahl foo^ay …* ¿Cuál fue …
the decedent's date of death?	*lah fay-chah dayl fah-yay-see-mee^ayn-toh dayl ohk-see-soh/day lah ohk-see-sah?* la fecha del fallecimiento del occiso/de la occisa?[5, 10]
the decedent's place of death — for example a hospital and its location?	*ayl loo-gahr dayl fah-yay-see-mee^ayn-toh dayl ohk-see-soh/day lah ohk-see-sah—pohr ay-haym-ploh oon ohs-pee-tahl ee lah oo-bee-kah-see^ohn dayl mees-moh?* el lugar del fallecimiento del occiso/de la occisa— por ejemplo un hospital y la ubicación del mismo?[1, 10]

	nohs **poo^ay**-*day proh-pohr-see^oh-***nahr oo**-*nah* **koh**-*pee^ah dayl sayr-tee-fee-***kah**-*doh day fah-yay-see-***mee^aynb**-*toh?*
6. Can you provide us with a copy of the death certificate?	¿Nos puede proporcionar una copia del certificado de fallecimiento?
	*koo^ahl day lahs see-***ghee^ayn**-*tays ohp-***see^oh**-*nays days-***kree**-*bay ayl ays-***tah**-*doh see-***beel** *dayl ohk-***see**-*soh/day lah ohk-***see**-*sah ayn ayl moh-***mayn**-*toh dayl fah-yay-see-***mee^ayn**-*toh:*
7. Which of the following describes the decedent's marital status at the time of death?	¿Cuál de las siguientes opciones describe el estado civil del occiso/de la occisa en el momento del fallecimiento?[10]
	*kah-***sah**-*doh/dah*
married	casado/a[3]
	*ays-***tah** *bee-bah lah pah-***ray**-*hah dayl ohk-***see**-*soh/day lah ohk-***see**-*sah?*
Is the decedent's spouse still alive?	¿Está viva la pareja del occiso/de la occisa?
	koh-*moh say* **yah**-*mah lah pah-***ray**-*hah dayl ohk-***see**-*soh/day lah ohk-***see**-*sah?*
What is the name of the decedent's spouse?	¿Cómo se llama la pareja del occiso/de la occisa?[10]
	*sohl-***tay**-*roh/rah*
single	soltero/a[3]
	*dee-bohr-***see^ah**-*doh/dah*
divorced	divorciado/a[3]
	koo^ahl foo^ay lah **fay**-*chah dayl dee-***bohr**-*see^oh?*
What was the date of the divorce?	¿Cuál fue la fecha del divorcio?[5]
	*ays-***tah** *bee-bah lah ayks-pah-***ray**-*hah dayl ohk-***see**-*soh/day lah ohk-***see**-*sah?*
Is the decedent's ex-spouse still alive?	¿Está viva la ex-pareja del occiso/de la occisa?[10]
	koh-*moh say* **yah**-*mah lah ayks-pah-***ray**-*hah dayl ohk-***see**-*soh/day lah ohk-***see**-*sah?*
What is the name of the decedent's ex-spouse?	¿Cómo se llama la ex-pareja del occiso/de la occisa?[1, 10]
	*say-pay-***rah**-*doh/dah*
separated	separado/a[3]
	bee^oo-*doh/dah*
widow(er)	viudo/a[3]
	*pah-***ray**-*hah day pohr* **bee**-*dah*
life partner	pareja de por vida
	*ays-***tah** *bee-bah lah pah-***ray**-*hah day pohr* **bee**-*dah dayl ohk-***see**-*soh/day lah ohk-***see**-*sah?[10]*
Is the decedent's life partner still alive?	¿Está viva la pareja de por vida del occiso/de la occisa?
	koh-*moh say* **yah**-*mah lah pah-***ray**-*hah day pohr* **bee**-*dah dayl ohk-***see**-*soh/day lah ohk-***see**-*sah?*
What is the name of the decedent's life partner?	¿Cómo se llama la pareja de por vida del occiso/de la occisa?[10]

	*pohr fah-**bohr**, **ah**-gah **oo**-nah **lees**-tah **pah**-rah ayn-tray-**gahr**-nohs kay een-**kloo**-yay lah see-**ghee^ayn**-tay een-fohr-mah-**see^ohn** pah-rah **toh**-dohs lohs **ee**-hohs soh-bray-bee-**bee^ayn**-tays dayl ohk-**see**-soh/day lah ohk-**see**-sah: **nohm**-bray kohm-**play**-toh, **fay**-chah day nah-see-**mee^ayn**-toh, dee-rayk-**see^ohn** ahk-**too^ahl**, **noo**-may-roh day tay-**lay**-foh-noh ee see say **sah**-bay, dee-rayk-**see^ohn** day koh-**rray**-oh ay-layk-**trohn**-nee-koh.*
8. Please make a list to give us of the following information for ALL of the decedent's surviving children: full name, date of birth, current address, telephone number and email address if known.	Por favor, haga una lista para entregarnos que incluye la siguiente información para TODOS los hijos sobrevivientes del occiso/de la occisa: nombre completo, fecha de nacimiento, dirección actual, número de teléfono y si se sabe, dirección de correo electrónico.[10]
	*pohr fah-**bohr**, **ah**-gah **oo**-nah **lees**-tah **pah**-rah ayn-tray-**gahr**-nohs kay een-**kloo**-yay lah see-**ghee^ayn**-tay een-fohr-mah-**see^ohn** pah-rah **toh**-dohs lohs **ee**-hohs fah-yay-**see**-dohs dayl ohk-**see**-soh/day lah ohk-**see**-sah: **nohm**-bray kohm-**play**-toh, **fay**-chah day nah-see-**mee^ayn**-toh, dee-rrayk-**see^ohn** ayn ayl moh-**mayn**-toh dayl fah-yay-see-**mee^ayn**-toh ee lah **fay**-chah day fah-yay-see-**mee^ayn**-toh.*
9. Please make a list to give us that includes the following information for ALL of the decedent's deceased children: full name, date of birth, address at time of death and date of death.	Por favor, haga una lista para entregarnos que incluye la siguiente información para TODOS los hijos fallecidos del occiso/de la occisa: nombre completo, fecha de nacimiento, dirección en el momento del fallecimiento y fecha de fallecimiento.[10]
	*pohr fah-**bohr**, **ah**-gah **oo**-nah **lees**-tah **pah**-rah ayn-tray-**gahr**-nohs kay een-**kloo**-yay lah see-**ghee^ayn**-tay een-fohr-mah-**see^ohn** pah-rah **toh**-dohs lohs **nee^ay**-hohs soh-bray-bee-**bee^ayn**-tays dayl ohk-**see**-soh/day lah ohk-**see**-sah: **nohm**-bray kohm-**play**-toh, **fay**-chah day nah-see-**mee^ayn**-toh, dee-rayk-**see^ohn** ahk-**too^ahl**, **noo**-may-roh day tay-**lay**-foh-noh ee see say **sah**-bay, dee-rayk-**see^ohn** day koh-**rray**-oh ay-layk-**trohn**-nee-koh.*
10. Please make a list to give us that includes the following information for ALL of the decedent's surviving grandchildren: full name, date of birth, current address, telephone number and email address if known.	Por favor, haga una lista para entregarnos que incluye la siguiente información para TODOS los nietos sobrevivientes del occiso/de la occisa: nombre completo, fecha de nacimiento, dirección actual, número de teléfono y si se sabe, dirección de correo electrónico.[10]
	*pohr fah-**bohr**, **ah**-gah **oo**-nah **lees**-tah **pah**-rah ayn-tray-**gahr**-nohs kay een-**kloo**-yay lah see-**ghee^ayn**-tay een-fohr-mah-**see^ohn** pah-rah **toh**-dohs lohs **nee^ay**-tohs fah-yay-**see**-dohs dayl ohk-**see**-soh/day lah ohk-**see**-sah: **nohm**-bray kohm-**play**-toh, **fay**-chah day nah-see-**mee^ayn**-toh, dee-rrayk-**see^ohn** ayn ayl moh-**mayn**-toh dayl fah-yay-see-**mee^ayn**-toh ee lah **fay**-chah day fah-yay-see-**mee^ayn**-toh.*
11. Please make a list to give us that includes the following information for ALL of the decedent's deceased grandchildren: full name, date of birth, address at time of death and date of death.	Por favor, haga una lista para entregarnos que incluye la siguiente información para TODOS los nietos fallecidos del occiso/de la occisa: nombre completo, fecha de nacimiento, dirección en el momento del fallecimiento y fecha de fallecimiento.[10]
	***dah**-doh kay ayl ohk-**see**-soh/lah ohk-**see**-sah noh **tee^ay**-nay neen-**goon** **ee**-hoh nee **nee^ay**-toh (soh-bray-bee-**bee^ayn**-tay), pohr fah-**bohr**, ays-**kree**-bah ah-**kee** lohs **nohm**-brahs kohm-**play**-tohs day lohs **pah**-drays dayl ohk-**see**-soh/day lah ohk-**see**-sah.*
12. Since the decedent does not have any surviving children or grandchildren, please write the full names of the decedent's parents here.	Dado que el occiso/la occisa no tiene ningún hijo ni nieto (sobreviviente), por favor, escriba aquí los nombres completos de los padres del occiso/de la occisa.[10]

	*koo^ahl ays lah dee-rayk-**see^ohn** day lohs **pah**-drays dayl ohk-**see**-soh/day lah ohk-**see**-sah?*
What is the address of the decedent's parents?	¿Cuál es la dirección de los padres del occiso/de la occisa?[1, 2, 10]

	*pohr fah-**bohr**, **ah**-gah **oo**-nah **lees**-tah **pah**-ray ayn-tray-**gahr**-nohs kay een-**kloo**-yay lah see-**ghee^ayn**-tay een-fohr-mah-**see^ohn** **pah**-rah **toh**-dohs lohs ayr-**mah**-nohs soh-bray-bee-**bee^ayn**-tays dayl ohk-**see**-soh/day lah ohk-**see**-sah: **nohm**-bray kohm-**play**-toh, **fay**-chah day nah-see-**mee^ayn**-toh, dee-rayk-**see^ohn** ahk-**too^ahl**, **noo**-may-roh day tay-**lay**-foh-noh ee see say **sah**-bay, dee-rayk-**see^ohn** day koh-**rray**-oh ay-layk-**trohn**-nee-koh.*
13. Please make a list to give us that includes the following information for ALL of the decedent's surviving siblings: full name, date of birth, current address, telephone number and email address if known.	Por favor, haga una lista para entregarnos que incluye la siguiente información para TODOS los hermanos sobrevivientes del occiso/de la occisa: nombre completo, fecha de nacimiento, dirección actual, número de teléfono y si se sabe, dirección de correo electrónico.[10]

	*pohr fah-**bohr**, **ah**-gah **oo**-nah **lees**-tah **pah**-rah ayn-tray-**gahr**-nohs kay een-**kloo**-yay lah see-**ghee^ayn**-tay een-fohr-mah-**see^ohn** **pah**-rah **toh**-dohs lohs ayr-**mah**-nohs fah-yay-**see**-dohs dayl ohk-**see**-soh/day lah ohk-**see**-sah: **nohm**-bray kohm-**play**-toh, **fay**-chah day nah-see-**mee^ayn**-toh, dee-rrayk-**see^ohn** ayn ayl moh-**mayn**-toh dayl fah-yay-see-**mee^ayn**-toh ee lah **fay**-chah day fah-yay-see-**mee^ayn**-toh.*
14. Please make a list to give us that includes the following information for ALL of the decedent's deceased siblings: full name, date of birth, address at time of death and date of death.	Por favor, haga una lista para entregarnos que incluye la siguiente información para TODOS los hermanos fallecidos del occiso/de la occisa: nombre completo, fecha de nacimiento, dirección en el momento del fallecimiento y fecha de fallecimiento.[10]

	*pohr fah-**bohr**, **ah**-gah **oo**-nah **lees**-tah **pah**-rah ayn-tray-**gahr**-nohs kay een-**kloo**-yay lah see-**ghee^ayn**-tay een-fohr-mah-**see^ohn** **pah**-rah **toh**-dohs lahs payr-**soh**-nahs nohm-**brah**-dahs **koh**-moh bay-nay-fee-**see^ah**-ree^ahs en ayl **ahk**-tah day **ool**-tee-mah boh-loon-**tahd** dayl ohk-**see**-soh/day lah ohk-**see**-sah: **nohm**-bray kohm-**play**-toh, **fay**-chah day nah-see-**mee^ayn**-toh, dee-rayk-**see^ohn** ahk-**too^ahl**, **noo**-may-roh day tay-**lay**-foh-noh ee see say **sah**-bay, dee-rayk-**see^ohn** day koh-**rray**-oh ay-layk-**trohn**-nee-koh.*
15. Please make a list to give us that includes the following information for ALL persons named as beneficiaries in the decedent's will: full name, date of birth, current address, telephone number and email address if known.	Por favor, haga una lista para entregarnos que incluye la siguiente información para TODAS las personas nombradas como beneficiarias en el acta de última voluntad del occiso/de la occisa: nombre completo, fecha de nacimiento, dirección actual, número de teléfono y si se sabe, dirección de correo electrónico.[10]

	*pah-ray **kah**-dah bay-nay-fee-**see^ah**-ree^oh yah fah-yay-**see**-doh, pohr-fah-**bohr**, **ah**-gah **oo**-nah **lees**-tah **pah**-ray ayn-tray-**gahr**-nohs kay een-**kloo**-yay lah see-**ghee^ayn**-tay een-fohr-mah-**see^ohn** **pah**-rah lah **pah-ray**-hah ee **kah**-dah **oo**-noh day lohs **ee**-hohs soh-bray-bee-**bee^ayn**-tays dayl bay-nay-fee-**see^ah**-ree^oh dee-**foon**-toh: **nohm**-bray kohm-**play**-toh, **fay**-chah day nah-see-**mee^ayn**-toh, dee-rayk-**see^ohn** ahk-**too^ahl**, **noo**-may-roh day tay-**lay**-foh-noh ee see say **sah**-bay, dee-rayk-**see^ohn** day koh-**rray**-oh ay-layk-**trohn**-nee-koh.*
For any beneficiary that is now deceased, please make a list to give us that includes the following information for the deceased beneficiaries surviving spouse and children: full name, date of birth, current address, telephone number and email address if known.	Para cada beneficiario ya fallecido, por favor, haga una lista de la siguiente información para la pareja y cada uno de los hijos sobrevivientes del beneficiario difunto: nombre completo, fecha de nacimiento, dirección actual, número de teléfono y si se sabe, dirección de correo electrónico.

*pohr fah-**bohr**, ah-gah **oo**-nah **lees**-tah **pah**-rah ayn-tray-**gahr**-nohs kay een-**kloo**-yay lah see-**ghee^ayn**-tay een-fohr-mah-**see^ohn** pah-rah **toh**-dohs lohs rray-pray-sayn-**tahn**-tays day lah proh-pee^ay-**dahd** dayl ohk-**see**-soh/day lah ohk-**see**-sah: **nohm**-bray kohm-**play**-toh, ah-**poh**-doh oh **nohm**-bray day sohl-**tay**-rah, **fay**-chah day nah-see-**mee^ayn**-toh, **noo**-may-roh day say-**goo**-roh soh-**see^ahl**, **noo**-may-roh day see^oo-dah-dah-**nee**-ah oh day rray-**hees**-troh day een-mee-**grahn**-tay see noh ays see^oo-dah-**dah**-noh/nah ays-tah-doh-oo-nee-**dayn**-say, dee-rayk-**see^ohn** ahk-**too^ahl**, **noo**-may-rohs day tay-**lay**-foh-noh ayn **kah**-sah ee dayl say-loo-**lahr**, dee-rayk-**see^ohn** day koh-**rray**-oh ay-layk-**trohn**-nee-koh, lah rray-lah-**see^ohn** dayl rray-pray-sayn-**tahn**-tay kohn ayl ohk-**see**-soh/lah ohk-**see**-sah ee see say ah hoos-**gah**-doh koohl-**pah**-blay ah **ays**-tah payr-**soh**-nah day oon day-**lee**-toh mah-**yohr** oh see **ays**-tah **mees**-mah say ah day-klah-**rah**-doh ayn bahn-kah-**rroh**-tah.*

16. Please make a list to give us that includes the following information for ALL representatives of the decedent's estate: full name, nickname or maiden name, date of birth, social security number, citizenship and alien registration number if not a U.S. citizen, current address, home phone and cell phone numbers, email address, the resprevative's relationship to the decedent and if this person has ever been convicted of a felony or has filed bankruptcy.

Por favor, haga una lista para entregarnos que incluye la siguiente información para TODOS los representantes de la propiedad del occiso/de la occisa: nombre completo, apodo o nombre de soltera, fecha de nacimiento, número de seguro social, número de ciudadanía o de registro de inmigrante si no es ciudadano/a estadounidense, dirección actual, números de teléfono en casa y del celular, dirección de correo electrónico, la relación del representante con el occiso/la occisa y si se ha juzgado culpable a esta persona de un delito mayor o si esta misma se ha declarado en bancarrota.[10]

*pohr fah-**bohr**, ah-gah **oo**-nah **lees**-tah **pah**-rah ayn-tray-**gahr**-nohs kay een-**kloo**-yay lah see-**ghee^ayn**-tay een-fohr-mah-**see^ohn** pah-rah **toh**-dohs lohs rray-pray-sayn-**tahn**-tays ahl-tayr-nah-**tee**-bohs day lah proh-pee^ay-**dahd** dayl ohk-**see**-soh/day lah ohk-**see**-sah: **nohm**-bray kohm-**play**-toh, ah-**poh**-doh oh **nohm**-bray day sohl-**tay**-rah, **fay**-chah day nah-see-**mee^ayn**-toh, **noo**-may-roh day say-**goo**-roh soh-**see^ahl**, **noo**-may-roh day see^oo-dah-dah-**nee**-ah oh day rray-**hees**-troh day een-mee-**grahn**-tay see noh ays see^oo-dah-**dah**-noh/nah ays-tah-doh-oo-nee-**dayn**-say, dee-rayk-**see^ohn** ahk-**too^ahl**, **noo**-may-rohs day tay-**lay**-foh-noh ayn **kah**-sah ee dayl say-loo-**lahr**, dee-rayk-**see^ohn** day koh-**rray**-oh ay-layk-**trohn**-nee-koh, lah rray-lah-**see^ohn** dayl rray-pray-sayn-**tahn**-tay kohn ayl ohk-**see**-soh/lah ohk-**see**-sah ee see say ah hoos-**gah**-doh koohl-**pah**-blay ah **ays**-tah payr-**soh**-nah day oon day-**lee**-toh mah-**yohr** oh see **ays**-tah **mees**-mah say ah day-klah-**rah**-doh ayn bahn-kah-**rroh**-tah.*

17. Please make a list to give us that includes the following information for ALL alternative representatives of the decedent's estate: full name, nickname or maiden name, date of birth, social security number, citizenship or alien registration number if not a U.S. citizen, current address, home phone and cell phone numbers, email address, the representative's relationship to the decedent and if this person has ever been convicted of a felony or has filed bankruptcy.

Por favor, haga una lista para entregarnos que incluye la siguiente información para TODOS los representantes alternativos de la propiedad del occiso/de la occisa: nombre completo, apodo o nombre de soltera, fecha de nacimiento, número de seguro social, número de ciudadanía o de registro de inmigrante si no es ciudadano/a estadounidense, dirección actual, números de teléfono en casa y del celular, dirección de correo electrónico, la relación del representante con el occiso/la occisa y si se ha juzgado culpable a esta persona de un delito mayor o esta misma se ha declarado en bancarrota.[10]

18. Are there any trusts?

*ayk-**sees**-tayn ahl-**goo**-nohs fee-day^ee-koh-**mee**-sohs?*
¿Existen algunos fideicomisos?

What is the name of each trust?

*koh-moh say **yah**-mah **kah**-dah fee-day^ee-koh-**mee**-soh?*
¿Cómo se llama cada fideicomiso?[1]

	*koo^ahl foo^ay lah **fay**-chah day kray-ah-**see^ohn** day **kah**-dah fee-day^ee-koh-**mee**-soh?*
What is the creation date for each trust?	¿Cuál fue la fecha de creación de cada fideicomiso?[5]
	*pohr fah-**bohr**, **ah**-gah **oo**-nah **lees**-tah **pah**-rah ayn-tray-**gahr**-nohs kay een-**kloo**-yay lah see-**ghee^ayn**-tay een-fohr-mah-**see^ohn pah**-rah **kah**-dah fee-day^ee-koh-**mee**-soh: ayl **nohm**-bray, lah dee-rayk-**see^ohn** ee ayl **noo**-may-roh day tay-**lah**-foh-noh day **kah**-dah fee-day^ee-koh-mee-**sah**-ree^oh.*
Please make a list to give us that includes the following information for each trust: the name, the address and the telephone number of each trustee.	Por favor, haga una lista para entregarnos que incluye la siguiente información para cada fideicomiso: el nombre, la dirección y el número de teléfono de cada fideicomisario.
	*ayk-**sees**-tayn ahl-**goo**-nahs **poh**-lee-sahs day say-**goo**-roh day pohr **bee**-dah?*
19. Are there any life insurance policies?	¿Existen algunas pólizas de seguro de por vida?
	*koo^ahl ays ayl **noo**-may-roh day **poh**-lee-sah **pah**-rah **kah**-dah **oo**-nah?*
What is the policy number of each policy?	¿Cuál es el número de póliza para cada una?[2]
	*koo^ahl ays lah **fay**-chah day ay-mee-**see^ohn** day **kah**-dah **poh**-lee-sah?*
What is the date of issue of each policy?	¿Cuál es la fecha de emisión de cada póliza?[5]
	*koo^ahl ays ayl bah-**lohr** day **kah**-dah **poh**-lee-sah?*
What is the value of each policy?	¿Cuál es el valor de cada póliza?[3]
	*koo^ahl ays ayl **nohm**-bray day lah kohm-pahn-**yee**-ah kay **tee^ay**-nay **kah**-dah **poh**-lee-sah?*
What is the name of the company that holds each policy?	¿Cuál es el nombre de la compañía que tiene cada póliza?[1]
	***tee^ay**-nay **koh**-pee^ah day **kah**-dah **poh**-lee-sah?*
Do you have a copy of each policy?	¿Tiene copia de cada póliza?
	*nohs **poo^ay**-day proh-pohr-see^oh-**nahr oo**-nah **koh**-pee^ah day **kah**-dah **poh**-lee-sah?*
Can you provide us with a copy of the policy?	¿Nos puede proporcionar una copia de cada póliza?
	*ayk-**sees**-tay say-**goo**-roh day ayn-**tee^ay**-rroh pray-pah-**gah**-doh oh oon plahn day ayn-**tee^ay**-rroh pray-pah-**gah**-doh?*
20. Is there a prepaid burial plan or burial insurance?	¿Existe seguro de entierro prepagado o un plan de entierro prepagado?
	*koo^ahl ays ayl **noo**-may-roh day lah **poh**-lee-sah / dayl plahn?*
What is the policy / plan number?	¿Cuál es el número de la póliza / del plan?[2]
	*koo^ahl ays lah **fay**-chah day ay-mee-**see^ohn**?*
What is the date of issue ?	¿Cuál es la fecha de emisión?[5]
	*koo^ahl ays ayl bah-**lohr**?*
What is the value?	¿Cuál es el valor?[5]
	*ayk-**sees**-tay **oo**-nah **kah**-hah day say-goo-ree-**dahd**?*
21. Is there a safety deposit box?	¿Existe una caja de seguridad?

What is the box number?	*koo^ahl ays ayl **noo**-may-roh day lah **kah**-hah?* ¿Cuál es el número de la caja?[5]
What is the bank's name?	*koo^ahl ays ayl **nohm**-bray dayl **bahn**-koh **dohn**-day ays-**tah** oo-bee-**kah**-dah?* ¿Cuál es el nombre del banco donde está ubicada?[1]
What is the bank's address?	*koo^ahl ays lah dee-rayk-**see^ohn** dayl **bahn**-koh?* ¿Cuál es la dirección del banco?[1, 2]
Who has possession of the key to the box?	*kee^ayn **tee^ay**-nay lah **yah**-bay ah lah **kah**-hah?* ¿Quién tiene la llave a la caja?
Who has access to the box?	*kee^ayn **tee^ay**-nay ahk-**say**-soh ah lah **kah**-hah?* ¿Quién tiene acceso a la caja?[1]

22. Are there any real estate assets?	*ayk-**sees**-tayn **oh**-trohs **bee^ay**-nays een-**moo^ay**-blays?* ¿Existen otros bienes inmuebles?
What is the name of each individual on the deed?	***koh**-moh say **yah**-mah **kah**-dah een-dee-**bee**-doo^oh **koo**-yoh **nohm**-bray ah-pah-**ray**-say ayn lah ays-kree-**too**-rah?* ¿Cómo se llama cada individuo cuyo nombre aparece en la escritura?[1]
What is the estimated value of each property?	*koo^ahl ays ayl bah-**lohr** ays-tee-**mah**-doh day **kah**-dah proh-pee^ay-**dahd**?* ¿Cuál es el valor estimado de cada propiedad?[5]
Is the property commercial or residential?	*ays lah proh-pee^ay-**dahd** **pah**-rah ayl **oo**-soh koh-mayr-**see^ahl** oh rray-see-dayn-**see^ahl**?* ¿Es la propiedad para el uso comercial o residencial?
Please list the physical location of each deed.	*pohr fah-**bohr**, ah-**poon**-tay **dohn**-day say ayn-**koo^ayn**-trah lah ays-kree-**too**-rah **pah**-rah **kah**-dah proh-pee^ay-**dahd**.* Por favor, apunte dónde se encuentra la escritura para cada propiedad.
Which property was the decedent's primary residence?	*koo^ahl day lahs proh-pee^ay-**dah**-days foo^ay ayl doh-mee-**see**-lee^oh preen-see-**pahl** dayl ohk-**see**-soh/day lah ohk-**see**-sah?* ¿Cuál de las propiedades fue el domicilio principal del occiso/de la occisa?[10]

23. Are there any ...	*ayk-**sees**-tayn ...* ¿Existen ...
checking accounts?	***koo^ayn**-tahs koh-**rree^ayn**-tays?* cuentas corrientes?
savings accounts?	***koo^ayn**-tahs day ah-**oh**-rroh?* cuentas de ahorro?
certificate of deposit accounts?	***koo^ayn**-tahs day sayr-tee-fee-**kah**-doh day day-**poh**-see-toh?* cuentas de certificado de depósito?

*pohr fah-**bohr**, **ah**-gah **oo**-nah **lees**-tah **pah**-rah ayn-tray-**gahr**-nohs kay een-**kloo**-yay lah see-**ghee^ayn**-tay een-fohr-mah-**see^ohn** pah-rah **kah**-dah **koo^ayn**-tah: lah **klah**-say day **koo^ayn**-tah kay ays, ayl **nohm**-bray dayl **doo^ayn**-yoh day lah **koo^ayn**-tah, ayl **sahl**-doh ays-tee-**mah**-doh, ayl **nohm**-bray dayl **bahn**-koh, lah dee-rayk-**see^ohn** ee ayl **noo**-may-roh day tay-**lay**-foh-noh dayl **bahn**-koh.*

Please make a list to give us that includes the following information for each account: the type of account, the owner, the estimated balance, the bank name, the bank address and the bank telephone number.	Por favor, haga una lista para entregarnos que incluye la siguiente información para cada cuenta: la clase de cuenta que es, el nombre del dueño de la cuenta, el saldo estimado, el nombre del banco, la dirección y el número de teléfono del banco.

*say-goo-ree-**dah**-days fee-nahn-**see^ay**-rahs?*

financial securities?	seguridades financieras?

*pohr fah-**bohr**, **ah**-gah oo-nah **lees**-tah **pah**-rah ayn-tray-**gahr**-nohs kay een-**kloo**-yay lah see-**ghee^ayn**-tay een-fohr-mah-**see^ohn** pah-rah **kah**-dah say-goo-ree-**dahd**: lah **klah**-say day say-goo-ree-**dahd** kah ays, ayl **doo^ayn**-yoh day lah say-goo-ree-**dahd**, ayl **sahl**-doh ays-tee-**mah**-doh, ayl **nohm**-bray dayl koh-rray-**dohr**, lah dee-rayk-**see^ohn** ee ayl **noo**-may-roh day tay-**lay**-foh-noh dayl koh-rray-**dohr**.*

Please make a list to give us that includes the following information for each security: the type of security, the owner, the estimated balance, the broker name, the broker address and the broker telephone number.	Por favor, haga una lista para entregarnos que incluye la siguiente información para cada seguridad: la clase de seguridad que es, el dueño de la seguridad, el saldo estimado, el nombre del corredor, la dirección y el número de teléfono del corredor.

*ayk-**sees**-tayn ahl-**goo**-nahs …*

24. Are there any …	¿Existen algunas …

*ee-poh-**tay**-kahs payn-**dee^ayn**-tays:*

outstanding mortgages?	hipotecas pendientes?

*pohr fah-**bohr**, **ah**-gah oo-nah **lees**-tah **pah**-rah ayn-tray-**gahr**-nohs kay een-**kloo**-yay lah see-**ghee^ayn**-tay een-fohr-mah-**see^ohn** pah-rah **kah**-dah ee-poh-**tay**-kah payn-**dee^ayn**-tay: see ays **oo**-nah ee-poh-**tay**-kah koh-mayr-**see^ahl** oh rray-see-dayn-**see^ahl**, ayl **sahl**-doh ays-tee-**mah**-doh, ayl **nohm**-bray dayl day^oo-**dohr**, **dohn**-day say ayn-**koo^ayn**-trahn lohs doh-koo-**mayn**-tohs ee-poh-tay-**kah**-ree^ohs, ayl **nohm**-bray day lah kohm-pahn-**yee**-ah ee-poh-tay-kah-ree^ah, ayl **nohm**-bray day oon rray-pray-sayn-**tahn**-tay day lah kohm-pahn-**yee**-ah ee-poh-tay-kah-ree^ah, lah dee-rayk-**see^ohn** ee ayl **noo**-may-roh day tay-**lay**-foh-noh day lah kohm-pahn-**yee**-ah ee-poh-tay-**kah**-ree^ah ah-**see** koh-moh ayl **noo**-may-roh day lah **koo^ayn**-tah ee-poh-tay-**kay**-ree^ah.*

Please make a list to give us that includes the following information for each outstanding mortgage: if the mortgage is residential or commercial, the estimated balance, the name of the debtor, the location of the mortgage documents, the name of the mortgage company, the name of a contact with the mortgage company, the address and telephone number of the mortgage company as well as the account number.	Por favor, haga una lista para entregarnos que incluye la siguiente información para cada hipoteca pendiente: si es una hipoteca comercial o residencial, el saldo estimado, el nombre de deudor, dónde se encuentran los documentos hipotecarios, el nombre de la compañía hipotecaria, el nombre de un representante de la compañía hipotecaria, la dirección y el número de teléfono de la compañía hipotecaria así como el número de la cuenta hipotecaria.

***koo^ayn**-tahs payn-**dee^ayn**-tays pohr koh-**brahr**?*

outstanding accounts receivable?	cuentas pendientes por cobrar?

*pohr fah-**bohr**, **ah**-gah **oo**-nah **lees**-tah **pah**-rah ayn-tray-**gahr**-nohs kay een-**kloo**-yay lah see-**ghee^ayn**-tay een-fohr-mah-**see^ohn pah**-rah **kah**-dah **koo^ayn**-tah payn-**dee^ayn**-tay: ayl **sahl**-doh ays-tee-**mah**-doh, ayl **nohm**-bray dayl day^oo-**dohr**, lah dee-rayk-**see^ohn** ee ayl **noo**-may-roh day tay-**lay**-foh-noh dayl day^oo-**dohr** ah-**see koh**-moh ayl **noo**-may-roh day lah **koo^ayn**-tah.*

Please make a list to give us that includes the following information for each outstanding accounts receivable: the estimated balance, the name of the debtor, the address and telephone number of the debtor as well as the account number.	Por favor, haga una lista para entregarnos que incluye la siguiente información para cada cuenta pendiente por cobrar: el saldo estimado, el nombre del deudor, la dirección y el número de teléfono del deudor así como el número de la cuenta.

---

25. Are there any ...

*ayk-**sees**-tayn ...*
¿Existen ...

    retirement accounts?

*ahl-**goo**-nahs **koo^ayn**-tahs day hoo-bee-lah-**see^ohn**?*
algunas cuentas de jubilación?

    IRAs?

*koo^ayn-tahs payr-soh-**nah**-lays day ah-**oh**-rroh hoo-bee-lah-**toh**-ree^oh?*
cuentas personales de ahorro jubilatorio?

    KEOGHs?

*plah-nays day payn-**see^oh**-nays **pah**-rah proh-fay-see^oh-**nah**-lays ah^oo-**toh**-noh-mohs?*
planes de pensiones para profesionales autónomos?

    SEPPs?

*pah-gohs ee-**goo^ah**-lays **ay**-chohs ah ee-**goo^ah**-lays een-tayr-**bah**-lohs day **tee^aym**-poh?*
pagos iguales hechos a iguales intervalos de tiempo?

    pensions?

*payn-**see^oh**-nays?*
pensiones?

*pohr fah-**bohr**, **ah**-gah oo-nah **lees**-tah **pah**-rah ayn-tray-**gahr**-nohs kay een-**kloo**-yay lah see-**ghee^ayn**-tay een-fohr-mah-**see^ohn pah**-rah **kah**-dah **koo^ayn**-tah day hoo-bee-lah-**see^ohn**: lah **klah**-say day **koo^ayn**-tah kay ays, ayl **sahl**-doh ays-tee-**mah**-doh, ayl **noo**-may-roh day lah **koo^ayn**-tah, ayl **nohm**-bray day lah kohm-pahn-**yee**-ah kay **tee^ay**-nay lah **koo^ayn**-tah ah-**see koh**-moh ayl **nohm**-bray, lah dee-rayk-**see^ohn** ee ayl **noo**-may-roh day tay-**lay**-foh-noh dayl rray-pray-sayn-**tahn**-tay day **koo^ayn**-tah.*

Please make a list to give us that includes the following information for each retirement account: the type of account, the estimated balance, the account number, the name of the company that holds the account, the name, address and phone number of the company and the name of the account representative.	Por favor, haga una lista para entregarnos que incluye la siguiente información para cada cuenta de jubilación: la clase de cuenta que es, el saldo estimado, el número de la cuenta, el nombre de la compañía que tiene la cuenta así como el nombre, la dirección y el número de teléfono del representante de cuenta.

---

26. Are there any ... that are the decedent's assets?

*ayk-**sees**-tahn ... kay **koo^ayn**-tahn **ayn**-tray lohs **bee^ay**-nays dayl ohk-**see**-soh/day lah ohk-**see**-sah?*
¿Existen ... que cuentan entre los bienes del occiso/de la occisa?[10]

    vehicles

*bay-**ee**-koo-lohs*
vehículos

boats	*bahr-kahs* barcas
mobile homes	*rray-**mohl**-kays* remolques
Please make a list to give us that includes the following information for each of the aforementioned assets: the type of asset, the name on the title and its physical location, the VIN number, the estimated value and the year of production of the asset.	*pohr fah-**bohr**, ah-gah oo-nah **lees**-tah **pah**-rah ayn-tray-**gahr**-nohs kay een-**kloo**-yay lah see-**ghee^ayn**-tay een-fohr-mah-**see^ohn** pah-rah **kah**-dah oo-noh day lohs **bee^ay**-nays mayn-see^oh-**nah**-dohs: lah **klah**-say day bee^ayn kay ays, ayl **nohm**-bray ayn ayl **tee**-too-loh dayl bee^ayn ee **dohn**-day say ayn-**koo^ayn**-trah ayl **tee**-too-loh, ayl **noo**-may-roh day ee-dayn-tee-fee-kah-**see^ohn** day bay-ee-koo-loh, ayl bah-**lohr** ays-tee-**mah**-doh ee ayl **ahn**-yoh day fah-bree-kah-**see^ohn** dayl bee^ayn.* Por favor, haga una lista para entregarnos que incluye la siguiente información para cada uno de los bienes mencionado: la clase de bien que es, el nombre en el título del bien y dónde se encuentra el título, el número de identificación de vehículo, el valor estimado y el año de fabricación del bien.
27. Are there any ... that are the decedent's assets?	*ayk-**sees**-tayn ... kay **koo^ayn**-tahn **ayn**-tray lohs **bee^ay**-nays dayl ohk-**see**-soh/day lah ohk-**see**-sah?* ¿Existen ... que cuentan entre los bienes del occiso/de la occisa?[10]
jewelry	***hoh^ee**-yahs* joyas
antiques	*ahn-tee-goo^ee-**dah**-days* antigüedades
collectibles	*ohb-**hah**-tohs koh-layk-see^oh-**nah**-blays* objetos coleccionables
Please make a list to give us that includes the following information for each of the aforementioned assets: the type of asset, the location and estimated value of each asset and if the asset is listed or not listed on the personal property statement.	*pohr fah-**bohr**, ah-gah oo-nah **lees**-tah **pah**-rah ayn-tray-**gahr**-nohs kay een-**kloo**-yay lah see-**ghee^ayn**-tay een-fohr-mah-**see^ohn** pah-rah **kah**-dah **oo**-noh day lohs **bee^ay**-nays mayn-see^oh-**nah**-dohs: lah **klah**-say day bee^ayn kay ays, **dohn**-day say ayn-**koo^ayn**-trah ayl bee^ayn, ayl bah-**lohr** ays-noo-may-**rah**-doh ayl bee^ayn oh noh ayn lah day-klah-rah-**see^ohn** day ay-**fayk**-tohs payr-soh-**nah**-lays.* Por favor, haga una lista para entregarnos que incluye la siguiente información para cada uno de los bienes mencionados: la clase de bien que es, dónde se encuentra el bien, el valor estimado y si se ha enumerado el bien o no en la declaración de efectos personales.
28. Was the decedent a beneficiary to any trusts?	***ay**-rah ayl ohk-**see**-soh/lah ohk-**see**-sah ayl bay-nay-fee-**see^ah**-ree^oh/lah bay-nay-fee-**see^ah**-ree^ah day ahl-**goo**-nohs fee-day^ee-koh-**mee**-sohs?* ¿Era el occiso/la occisa el beneficiario/la beneficiaria de algunos fideicomisos?[10]

*pohr fah-**bohr**, **ah**-gah **oo**-nah **lees**-tah **pah**-rah ayn-tray-**gahr**-nohs kay een-**kloo**-yay lah see-**ghee^ayn**-tay een-fohr-mah-**see^ohn** pah-rah **kah**-dah fee-day^ee-koh-**mee**-soh dayl kay ayl ohk-**see**-soh/lah ohk-**see**-sah **ay**-rah bay-nay-fee-**see^ah**-ree^oh/ah: lah **klah**-say de fee-day^ee-koh-**mee**-soh kay ays, ayl bah-**lohr** ays-tee-**mah**-doh ee lah oo-bee-kah-**see^ohn** fee-see-kah de koo^ah-lays-**kee^ayr** doh-koo-**mayn**-tohs rray-lah-see^oh-**nah**-dohs kohn ayl.*

Please make a list to give us that includes the following information for each trust of which the decedent was a beneficiary: the type of trust, the estimated value of the trust and the physical location of any documents associated with it.	Por favor, haga una lista para entregarnos que incluye la siguiente información para cada fideicomiso del que el occiso/la occisa era beneficiario/a: la clase de fideicomiso que es, el valor estimado del fideicomiso y la ubicación física de cualesquier documentos relacionados con él.[10. 3]

*pohr fah-**bohr**, **pah**-rah **kah**-dah fee-day^ee-koh-**mee**-soh kay say ah ay-noo-may-**rah**-doh, proh-pohr-**see^oh**-nay ayl **nohm**-bray, ayl **noo**-may-roh day tay-**lay**-foh-noh ee lah dee-rayk-**see^ohn** dayl fee-dee^ay-koh-mee-**sah**-ree^oh.*

Please also provide the name, telephone number and address of the trustee(s) for each trust you have listed.	Por favor, para cada fideicomiso que se ha enumerado, proporcione el nombre, el número de teléfono y la dirección del fideicomisario.

*tay-**nee**-ah ayl ohk-**see**-soh/lah ohhk-**see**-sah ahl-**goo**-nahs pahr-tee-see-pah-**see^oh**-nays soh-see^ay-**tah**-ree^ahs?*

29. Was the decedent involved in any business interests?	¿Tenía el occiso/la occisa algunas participaciones societarias?[10]

*pohr fah-**bohr**, **ah**-gah **oo**-nah **lees**-tah **pah**-rah ayn-tray-**gahr**-nohs kay een-**kloo**-yay lah see-**ghee^ayn**-tay een-fohr-mah-**see^ohn** pah-rah **kah**-dah pahr-tee-see-pah-**see^ohn** soh-see^ay-**tah**-ree^ah kay tay-**nee**-ah ayl ohk-**see**-soh/lah ohk-**see**-sah: lah **klah**-say day pahr-tee-see-pah-**see^ohn** soh-see^ay-**tah**-ree^ah (**say**-ah aym-**pray**-sah oo-nee-payr-soh-**nahl**, soh-see^ay-**dahd**, soh-see^ay-**dahd** ah-**noh**-nee-mah, soh-see^ay-**dahd** day rrays-pohn-see-bee-lee-**dahd** lee-mee-**tah**-dah), ayl bah-**lohr** ays-tee-**mah**-doh dayl fee-day^ee-koh-**mee**-soh ee lah oo-bee-kah-**see^ohn** fee-see-kah dayl nay-**goh**-see^oh ah-**see** koh-moh ayl **nohm**-bray kohm-**play**-toh ee ayl **noo**-may-roh day tay-**lay**-foh-noh day oon rray-pray-sayn-**tahn**-tay dayl nay-**goh**-see^oh.*

Please make a list to give us that includes the following information for each business interest in which the decedent was involved: the type of business (sole proprietorship, partnership, corporation, limited liability company), the estimated value of the trust and the physical location of the business interest as well as the complete name and telephone number of a business representative.	Por favor, haga una lista para entregarnos que incluye la siguiente información para cada participación societaria que tenía el occiso/la occisa: la clase de participación societaria (sea empresa unipersonal, sociedad, sociedad anónima, sociedad de responsabilidad limitada), el valor estimado del fideicomiso y la ubicación física del negocio así como el nombre completo y el número de teléfono de un representante del negocio.

*ayk-**sees**-tayn **oh**-trohs ahk-**tee**-bohs, **bee^ay**-nays **moo^ay**-blays ee/oh een-**moo^ay**-blays kay tay-**nee**-ah ayl ohk-**see**-soh/lah ohk-**see**-sah kay ah-**oon** noh say ahn mayn-see^oh-**nah**-doh?*

30. Are there any other assets the decedent possessed that have not been covered thus far?	¿Existen otros activos, bienes muebles y/o inmuebles que tenía el occiso/la occisa que aún no se han mencionado?

Could you ... what those are?	*poh-**dree**-ah ... loh kay sohn?* ¿Podría ... lo que son?
explain to someone (in Spanish)	*ayks-plee-**kahr**-lay ah **ahl**-ghee^ayn (ayn ays-pahn-**yohl**)* explicarle a alguien (en español)
describe in writing (in Spanish)	*days-kree-**beer** pohr ays-**kree**-toh (ayn ays-pahn-**yohl**)* describir por escrito (en español)
31. Have you spoken with any other attorneys about these issues?	*lay ah ah-**blah**-doh ah **oh**-troh ah-boh-**gah**-doh rray-fay-**rayn**-tay ah **ays**-tohs ah-**soon**-tohs?* ¿Le ha hablado a otro abogado referente a estos asuntos?
What is the full name of the attorney?	*koo^ahl ays ayl **nohm**-bray kohm-**play**-toh dayl ah-boh-**gah**-doh?* ¿Cuál es el nombre completo del abogado?[1,2]
32. Sign here please, if the information you have provided me is correct and complete to the best of your knowledge.	***feer**-may ah-**kee**, pohr fah-**bohr**, see lah een-fohr-mah-**see^ohn** kay may ah proh-pohr-see^oh-**nah**-doh ays bay-**ree**-dee-kah ee ah-sayr-**tah**-dah say-**goon** soo lay-**ahl** sah-**bayr** ee ayn-tayn-**dayr**.* Firme aquí, por favor, si la información que me ha proporcionado es verídica y acertada según su leal saber y entender.
33. Also, by signing this document, please understand that until you receive correspondence from us regarding this issue that details the terms of our agreement to represent you in this matter, we are not your legal representative on this or any other issue.	*ah-day-**mahs**, ahl feer-**mahr ays**-tay doh-koo-**mayn**-toh, fah-**bohr** day ayn-tayn-**dayr** kay **ahs**-tah kay say rray-**see**-bah kohn-feer-mah-**see^ohn** day noh-**soh**-trohs kohn rrays-**payk**-toh ah **ays**-tay ah-**soon**-toh ayn lah koo^ahl say day-**tah**-yahn lohs **play**-sohs day noo^ays-troh ah-**koo^ayr**-doh **pah**-rah rray-pray-sayn-**tahr**-loh/lah, noh **soh**-mohs soo rray-pray-sayn-**tahn**-tay lay-**gahl pah**-ray **ays**-tay nee neen-**goon oh**-troh ah-**soon**-toh.* Además, al firmar este documento, favor de entender que hasta que se reciba confirmación mediante correspondencia de nosotros con respecto a este asunto en la cual se detallan los plazos de nuestro acuerdo para representarlo/la, no somos su representante legal para este ni ningún otro asunto.

Notes

[1] Remember you can always ask that the caller spell the name, etc. by incorporating communication strategies from *Chapter 2—Collecting Basic Information in Person and by Phone* and referencing *Chapter 12—The Basics—I. The Alphabet.* Also, whenever possible during face-to-face encounters, allow the person with whom you are speaking to write down as much information as possible.

[2] Reference *Chapter 12—The Basics—II. Numbers.* Also, whenever possible during face-to-face encounters, allow the person with whom you are speaking to write down as much information for you as this will greatly facilitate communication and make utilizing numbers much easier since digits are represented the same in both languages.

[3] Use the *-o* ending when talking to or about a male; use the *-a* ending when talking to or about a female.

[4] In Spanish, the syntax (sentence structure) for *you (singular and formal), he/him,* and *she/her* are grammatically identical. Notice that ALL of the English questions and phrases in this chapter are written in the second person singular—*you.* Likewise, the vast majority of Spanish phrases in this book could be conveyed as *he/him* or *she/her* as well, though not noted in the English translation. If the person with whom you are speaking is the potential client, use the phrase *Referente a Ud. (In reference to you ...)* to ensure the conversation is being conducted directly with that person. If the person with whom you are speaking is inquiring on behalf of someone else, then use either *Referente a él (In reference to him ...)* or *Referente a ella (In reference to her ...)* depending upon the sex of the individual on whose behalf the person is inquiring. At anytime you wish to change the focus of the question, simply insert the expression *Referente a Ud., él* or *ella ...* before the phrase. For example, to change the focus to a female say *Referente a ella, ¿tiene trabajo actualmente? (In reference to her, is she currently employed?).* You may even insert the **proper name** of the

person accordingly to maximize comprehension—*Referente a **Carlos***. You only need to verbalize clarification when changing or clarifying the person who is the focus of the question or phrase. It is not necessary to do so before EVERY question or phrase once you establish the context of the conversation.

 [5] See *Chapter 13—Telling Time the Easy Way—Days of the Week and Month of the Year.*

 [6] Use *-lo* when talking to or about a male; use *-la* when talking to or about a female.

 [7] The symbol @ used in email addresses is called *arroba (ah-**rroh**-bah)* in Spanish.

 [8] Unlike English, Spanish makes a distinction in this case. Use *madre* if the single parent is female and use *padre* if the single parent is male.

 [9] When addressing one person use *le*; when addressing two or more use *les.*

 [10] Use *el occiso* if the decedent is male; use *la occisa* if the decedent is female.

Practical Activities

A) Oral Practice

Part I—Instructions: This activity will start out with the collection of information that would take place after obtaining general information* from the Spanish speaker. Read each numbered item below. Then, search through this chapter to the find the Spanish questions/phrases needed to obtain the requested information. Once you have done this for each situation, practice saying the necessary phrases aloud with a partner. Be aware, the phrases may not follow the order they are found in this chapter.

[* *Please reference Chapter 2—Collecting Basic Information in Person and by Phone if you would like to review this process.*]

1. Caller's nationality and race

2. Title of the discriminating party

3. Subsidized or unsubsidized rent and housing classification

4. Reasons for discrimination

5. Date of the alleged discrimination

6. Reasons for being treated unfairly

7. Address of the location where the alleged discrimination occurred

8. Manner in which the notice to vacate the premises was delivered

9. Amount of time permitted to vacate the premises

10. Type of notice that was received to vacate the premises

Part II—Instructions: Now that you and a partner have practiced the phrases and their pronunciation, work together to create the short and/or anticipated responses needed to answer each question. Remember, ALL responses will be in SPANISH. Feel free to write them out on a separate sheet of paper or notate them above. After completing the response for each question, recreate the entire interview with one of you asking the questions and the other responding. Switch roles and attempt to recreate the dialogue WITHOUT looking at the text.

B) Evictions

Part I—Instructions: In this chapter, the topic of evictions is handled from both the landlord and tenant perspective. In order to assist you in distinguishing between phrases that would be asked to one of these two parties, it is necessary to be able to identify whom is being addressed. To practice this concept, read each phrase/expression from the list below and decide if you are addressing a landlord or a tenant. Next, in the space provided after each number write **L** for landlord and **T** for tenant to indicate to whom the phrase or expression is being directed. If it could be used to address both parties, place a **B** (for both) in the space.

1. ___ ¿Cuál es la dirección completa de la propiedad sobre la cual está presentando esta queja?

2. ___ ¿Cuál es el nombre completo del inquilino cuyo nombre aparece en el contrato de arrendamiento para esta propiedad?

3. ___ ¿Cuál es el nombre completo del propietario cuyo nombre aparece en el contrato de arrendamiento para esta propiedad?

4. ___ ¿Se trata la queja de un pedido de mantenimiento?

5. __ ¿Ha infringido o actualmente está infringiendo alguna estipulación establecida por escrito en el contrato de arrendamiento?

6. __ ¿Ha recibido algunas quejas o avisos del departamento de salud pública o del departamento de aplicación de códigos municipales o del condado?

7. __ ¿Sabe si el propietario ha recibido algunas quejas o avisos del departamento de salud pública o del departamento de aplicación de códigos municipales o del condado?

8. __ ¿Cree que haya personas cuyos nombres no aparecen en el contrato de arrendamiento ocupando el local?

9. __ ¿Cuánto es el pago de arrendamiento mensual según lo estipulado por el contrato de arrendamiento?

10. __ Según el contrato de arrendamiento, ¿se requería que el inquilino entregara una notificación de la intención de desocupar la vivienda con noventa días de antelación?

11. __ Según el contrato de arrendamiento, ¿se requería que entregara Ud. una notificación de la intención de desocupar la vivienda con noventa días de antelación?

12. __ ¿Les explicaron y/o les proporcionaron expresamente los plazos y condiciones del contrato de arrendamiento a los inquilinos autorizados?

13. __ ¿Le explicaron y/o le proporcionaron expresamente los plazos y condiciones del contrato de arrendamiento a Ud.?

14. __ ¿Hizo que los inquilinos firmaran un contrato de arrendamiento enmendado en el cual se estipulaban los cambios?

15. __ ¿Hicieron que los otros inquilinos firmaran un contrato de arrendamiento enmendado en el cual se estipulaban los cambios?

Part II — Instructions: Randomly read each of the fifteen phrases above in SPANISH one at a time to partner who is NOT looking at this activity. Then, ask your partner to identify what he/she heard as a question directed to the landlord, the tenant or both. Lastly, reread the same phrase in SPANISH and ask your partner to interpret it into English. Help him/her out is necessary.

Follow-up: Now that you have correctly labeled the phrases/expressions above, can you visually identify the differences between the phrases directed to the landlord or the tenant? What are some of these differences? How does this help your remember for which person each phrase is used? How can you use this strategy to apply to other phrases and expressions in this chapter that are similar to assist you in differentiating between their uses?

C) "Just a few more questions ..."

Instructions: The answers to several questions are given below. However, you will need to provide the correct question that elicited each response. Take into consideration who is answering the question as well — the landlord or the tenant — based on context. Try to recall as much and/or as many of the questions as possible without the use of the text. When you have exhausted your knowledge of the necessary Spanish questions/expressions, refer to the chapter for assistance. You may also write the questions in the blanks provided or mark them in your text. You may wish to use an online bilingual dictionary to help you with words of which you are unsure. When you have completed this activity, compare your findings with those of a classmate. Help each other make any necessary corrections or changes.

1. Sí, se me dio directamente a mí.

_____

2. La persona a quien se le entregó el aviso se llama Humberto Esposito.

    _____

3. No, no hay ningún daño a la propiedad por el cual soy responsable.

    _____

4. Se lo mandó al inquilino por correo registrado.

    _____

5. Tengo correo devuelto posfechado que los inquilinos rechazaron aceptar.

    _____

D) Por favor, haga una lista … (Please, make a list …)

Part I—Instructions: This chapter contains requests for a client to create multiple lists to assist you in obtaining information. Once again, remember that this is an important communication strategy that will save both of you time and potential frustration. To facilitate this process, however, you may want to provide the client with fill-in-the-blank tables that will expedite this process. In this activity, you will create multiple sample tables which you will ask a client to complete. See *Practical Activities—Chapter 8—Family Law—letter B* for detailed instructions on creating tables BEFORE you begin this activity.

The following chart will indicate which phrases/expressions from this chapter—found in *Section III—Probate*—require that the Spanish-speaker create a list of information. First, review each question in ENGLISH and underline or highlight EACH piece of information being requested. For each phrase/expression, fill in column **A)** below.

Second, consider the pieces of information you will be obtaining. If you are requesting categories that will have multiple, similar answers, such as *"Please list the model of all cars you own, the VIN of each and the primary driver of each vehicle,"* you need only three columns and no rows. However, if you request *"Please list your last five employers and include how long you worked there, your starting salary and your ending salary,"* you would need a five row (five employers) and three column (three pieces of information for each employer) table. Do this for each phrase/expression and record your decisions in columns **B)** and **C)** on the chart.

Third, if you are working alone on this as a project, you will obviously want to pace yourself and not rush through the creation of the sixteen tables. Otherwise, it is suggested this task be divided among individuals, pairs or small groups. For example, a pair may be assigned to work on the completion of one or two tables whereas a small group may be assigned to work on the completion of two to three tables. If this is the case, complete column **D)** to include the names, pairs or group assignments so that everyone is aware of whom is responsible for which table(s).

phrase #	A) How many pieces of information are being requested?	B) How many columns will be needed for the table?	C) How many rows will be needed for the table?	D) Table completion assigned to:
8.				
9.				
10.				
11.				
13.				
14.				
15.				
16.				
17.				
23.				
24.				
25.				
26.				
27.				
28.				
29.				

Finally, after the completion of the multiple tables, have each assigned individual, pair or small group present the respective table(s) and ask that the rest of the class follow along to make sure they agree with the its construction or if changes or corrections need to be made.

Follow up: Have the parties responsible for the tables' creation recreate the table(s) on the computer for a more professional appearance. Either share an electronic version with classmates or prepare photocopies to distribute. This will get everyone well on their way to creating their bank of fill-in-the-blank tables.

E) Putting It All Together

Instructions: In the previous activity, you created multiple tables to be used to gather information from potential Spanish-speaking clients. Now, you will practice the lead in questions that result in your request for the individual to create a list of information. Once again, this activity is based strictly on *Section III—Probate* of this chapter. Aside from the lead in questions, it is not necessary to try and recall from memory the requests for lists creation. Feel free to read those directly from the text.

Recreate the following interview questions and requests in SPANISH. The gender of the decedent is indicated only one time in each number by either *(f.)* for *female* and *(m.)* for *male*.

1. What is your relationship with the decedent *(f.)*? / What is the decedent's full name?

2. What is the mailing address of the decedent *(m.)*? / Is the decedent a citizen of the U.S.?

3. What was the decedent's *(f.)* date of death? / Can you provide us with a copy of the death certificate?

4. Which of the following describes the decedent's *(f.)* marital status at the time of death: married, single, divorced, separated, widow or life partner?

5. Please make a list to give us that includes the following information for ALL of the decedent's *(m.)* surviving children: *[present appropriate table to potential client]**

6. Please make a list to give us that includes the following information for ALL of the representatives of the decedent's (f.) estate: *[present appropriate table to potential client]**

7. Are there any checking accounts, saving accounts or certificate of deposit accounts? / Please make a list to give us that includes the following information for each account: *[present appropriate table to potential client]**

8. Are there any retirement accounts, IRAs, KEOGHs, SEPPS or pensions? / Please make a list to give us that includes the following information for each retirement account: *[present appropriate table to potential client]**

* Notice it is not necessary to read off the list of information since it is already provided on the table! This cuts down greatly on the amount of oral communication required.

F) Cyber-Investigation

In BEFORE YOU BEGIN, you read about some of the challenges that Hispanics face with seeking housing. Continue investigating this subject by typing the following general search into your browsers search box: *Hispanics and fair housing.* You may even elect to try this search with and without quotation marks to get more or less information related to this topic. After glancing over the titles of your results, look for information regarding this topic that has been published within the last year. Find information on what is being done to safeguard Hispanics against discrimination when seeking housing. Is there evidence that these safeguards are working? Is it possible to eradicate housing discrimination based on race and ethnicity or will this always be an issue? Support your opinions by finding information that sustains your views. Summarize your discoveries below.

Chapter 10

Bankruptcy

Before You Begin

No ethnic or racial group is immune from the financial difficulties presented by today's economy. Across the board, people everywhere have lost jobs, gone into foreclosure on homes and suffered numerous other life-changing economic disparities. The Hispanic population is one group that has been tremendously affected by all of this. Hispanics generally earn less than African Americans and Caucasians. In turn, to compensate for the increased cost of living and the provision of basic necessities, many have began to supplement their income with credit cards. While this practice may sound all too common in today's cash-strapped society, many Hispanics find themselves unable to qualify for credit accounts that do not carry unusually high interest rates. This is primarily due to a low household income, no previous credit history and the refusal of the credit industry itself to offer competitive interest rates for first time card holders.

In regards to banking, many Hispanics, especially those who are recent arrivals, are reluctant to open accounts with U.S. financial institutions. This stems from a deep-seated distrust in the financial entities of their country of origin where many times such businesses did not act with the best interest of the client in mind. These so-called "unbanked" individuals therefore have to pursue other avenues when attempting to qualify for a loan, a mortgage, etc. and alternately have to depend on subprime lenders to fulfill their need for credit. Unable to qualify for a prime lender combined with a lack of education and understanding of the lending process, makes the Hispanic population an ideal target for subprime lenders.

I. General Information

*een-fohr-mah-**see^ohn** hay-nay-**rahl***
Información general

English	Pronunciation & Spanish
1. What is your full legal name?	*koo^ahl ays soo **nohm**-bray lay-**gahl** kohm-**play**-toh?* ¿Cuál es su nombre legal completo?[1]
2. Do you go by any other name?	***tee^ay**-nay ahl-**goon** oh-troh **nohm**-bray?* ¿Tiene algún otro nombre?
What is it?	*koo^ahl ays?* ¿Cuál es?[1]
3. Do you have any prior names?	*ah tay-**nee**-doh ahl-**goon** oh-troh **nohm**-bray ahn-tay-ree-^ohr-**mayn**-tay?* ¿Ha tenido algún otro nombre anteriormente?
What was it?	*koo^ahl foo^ay?* ¿Cuál fue?[1]

4. What is your ...

koo^ahl ays soo ...
¿Cuál es su ...

   date of birth?

fay-chah day nah-see-mee^ayn-toh?
fecha de nacimiento?[3]

   social security number?

noo-may-roh day say-goo-roh soh-see^ahl?
número de seguro social?[2]

5. Are you ...

ays-tah ...
¿Está ...

   married?

kah-sah-doh/dah
casado/a?[4]

   divorced?

dee-bohr-see^ah-doh/dah?
divorciado/a?[4]

   What year did you divorce?

ayn kay ahn-yoh say dee-bohr-see^oh?
¿En qué año se divorció?[3]

6. Are you widowed?

ays bee^oo-doh/dah?
¿Es viudo/a?[4]

   What year did you become widowed?

ayn kay ahn-yoh say bee^oo-doh/dah?
¿En qué año se hizo viudo/a?[3]

7. Does your spouse go by any other name?

tee^ay-nay soo kohn-yoo-hay ahl-goon oh-troh nohm-bray?
¿Tiene su cónyuge algún otro nombre?

   What is it?

koo^ahl ays?
¿Cuál es?[1]

8. Does your spouse have any prior names?

ah tay-nee-doh soo kohn-yoo-hay ahl-goon oh-troh nohm-bray ahn-tay-ree^ohr-mayn-tay?
¿Ha tenido su cónyuge algún otro nombre anteriormente?

   What was it?

koo^ahl foo^ay?
¿Cuál fue?[1]

9. What is your spouse's ...

koo^ahl ays ... day soo kohn-yoo-hay?
¿Cuál es ... de su cónyuge?

   date of birth?

lah fay-chah day nah-see-mee^ayn-toh?
la fecha de nacimiento[3]

   social security number?

ayl noo-may-roh day say-goo-roh soh-see^ahl?
el número de seguro social?[2]

10. Do you have any children?

tee^ay-nay ee-hohs?
¿Tiene hijos?

   How many?

koo^ahn-tohs?
¿Cuántos?[2]

   How old is each one?

koo^ahn-tohs ahn-yohs tee^ay-nay kah-dah oo-noh?
¿Cuántos años tiene cada uno?[2]

How many of them live in your home?	*koo^ayn-tohs day soos ee-hohs bee-bayn ayn soo kah-sah?* ¿Cuántos de sus hijos viven en su casa?[2]
11. Do you pay child support to any child not living with you?	*pah-gah mah-noo-tayn-see^ohn day ee-hohs pah-rah oon neen-yoh kay bee-bay foo^ay-rah day soo oh-gahr?* ¿Paga manutención de hijos para un niño que vive fuera de su hogar?
Do you pay the other parent, the state or some other entity?	*lay pah-gah ahl oh-troh pah-dray, ahl ays-tah-doh oh ah ahl-goo-nah oh-trah ayn-tee-dahd?* ¿Le paga al otro padre, al estado o a alguna otra entidad?
Where do they reside?	*dohn-day bee-bay ayl neen-yoh/lah neen-yah?* ¿Dónde vive el niño/la niña?[1, 5]
How much per month do you pay in support?	*koo^ayn-toh ays soo pah-goh mayn-soo^ahl day may-noo-tayn-see^ohn day ee-hohs?* ¿Cuánto es su pago mensual de manutención de hijos?[2]
12. If you have children that work and live at home, do they help with the monthy household expenses?	*see tee^ay-nay ahl-goo-nohs ee-hohs kay trah-bah-hahn ee bee-bayn ayn kah-sah, ah^ee-yoo-dahn kohn lohs gahs-tohs doh-mays-tee-kohs mayn-soo^ah-lays?* Si tiene algunos hijos que trabajan y viven en casa, ¿ayudan con los gastos domésticos mensuales?
How much do they contribute to the monthly household expenses?	*koo^ayn-toh dee-nay-roh kohn-tree-boo-yayn ah lohs gahs-tohs doh-mays-tee-kohs mayn-soo^ah-lays?* ¿Cuánto dinero contribuyen a los gastos domésticos mensuales?[2]
13. Are you a ...	*ays ...* ¿Es ...
disabled veteran?	*bay-tay-rah-noh/nah dees-kah-pah-see-tah-doh/dah?* veterano/a discapacitado/a?[4]
a Reservist?	*rray-sayr-bees-tah?* reservista?
Member of the National Guard?	*mee^aym-broh day lah goo^ahr-dee^ah nah-see^oh-nahl?* miembro de la guardia nacional?
Member of Homeland Defense?	*mee^aym-broh day lah say-goo-ree-dahd nah-see^oh-nahl?* miembro de la seguridad nacional?
14. Have you been on active duty (at any time) since Sept. 11, 2001?	*ah ays-tah-doh day sayr-bee-see^oh ahk-tee-boh (ayn koo^ahl-kee^ayr moh-mayn-toh) days-day ayl ohn-say day sayp-tee^aym-bray, dohs meel oo-noh?* ¿Ha estado de servicio activo (en cualquier momento) desde el 11 de septiembre, 2001?
How long?	*pohr koo^ahn-toh tee^aym-poh?* ¿Por cuánto tiempo?[2]
Is that more than 540 days?	*ay-soh ays mahs day kee-nee^ayn-tohs koo^ah-rayn-tah dee-ahs?* ¿Eso es más de 540 días?

15. Are you a resident of the state of ___?

*ays rray-see-**dayn**-tay dayl ays-**tah**-doh day ___?*
¿Es residente del estado de ___?[6]

---

16. Have you resided inside this state for at least …

*ah payr-mah-nay-**see**-doh **dayn**-troh day **ays**-tay ays-**tah**-doh pohr ahl **may**-nohs …*
¿Ha permanecido dentro de este estado por al menos …

the last ninety days?

*lohs **ool**-tee-mohs noh-**bayn**-tah **dee**-ahs?*
los últimos noventa días?

the last one hundred eighty days?

*lohs **ool**-tee-mohs see^**ayn**-toh oh-**chayn**-tah **dee**-ahs?*
los últimos ciento ochenta días?

the last year?

*ayl **ool**-tee-moh **ahn**-yoh?*
el último año?

the last two years?

*lohs **ool**-tee-mohs dohs **ahn**-yohs?*
los últimos dos años?

---

17. Have you resided at your permanent address during this time or some other?

*ah bee-**bee**-doh ayn soo dee-rayk-see^ohn payr-mah-**nayn**-tay doo-**rahn**-tay **ays**-tay **plah**-soh day tee^**aym**-poh oh ayn ahl-**goon oh**-troh **see**-tee^oh?*
¿Ha vivido en su dirección permanente durante este plazo de tiempo o en algún otro sitio?

---

18. Have you ever filed bankruptcy before, either individually or jointly?

*say ah day-klah-**rah**-doh ayn bahn-kah-**rroh**-tah **ayn**-tays, **say**-ah een-dee-bee-**doo^ahl** oh kohn-hoon-tah-**mayn**-tay?*
¿Se ha declarado en bancarrota antes, sea individual o conjuntamente?

What was the date of the filing?

*koo^ahl foo^ay lah **fay**-chah day lah day-klah-rah-**see^ohn**?*
¿Cuál fue la fecha de la declaración?[3]

In which county and state is that backruptcy court located?

*ayn kay kohn-**dah**-doh ee ays-**tah**-doh ays-**tah** ay-say tree-boo-**nahl** day bahn-kah-**rroh**-tah?*
¿En qué condado y estado está ese tribunal de bancarrota?[1]

Did you receive a bankruptcy discharge?

*rray-see-**bee^oh oo**-nah rray-ah-bee-lee-tah-**see^ohn** day bahn-kah-**rroh**-tah?*
¿Recibió una rehabilitación de bancarrota?

II. Debts

day^oo-dahs
Deudas

English	Pronunciation & Spanish
1. I need to ask you some questions regarding your debts:	*nay-say-**see**-toh ah-**sayr**-lay oo-nahs pray-**goon**-tahs **soh**-bray soos **day^oo**-dahs:* Necesito hacerle unas preguntas sobre sus deudas:[7]
2. I need to ask you some questions regarding your spouse's debts:	*nay-say-**see**-toh ah-**sayr**-lay oo-nahs pray-**goon**-tahs **soh**-bray lahs **day^oo**-dahs day soo **kohn**-yoo-hay:* Necesito hacerle unas preguntas sobre las deudas de su cónyuge:[7]
3. Do you own a house?	*ays proh-pee^ay-**tah**-ree^oh/ah day oo-nah **kah**-sah?* ¿Es propietario/a de una casa?[4]
Where is the house?	***dohn**-day ays-**tah** lah **kah**-sah?* ¿Dónde está la casa?[1, 2]
What is the address of the house?	*koo^ahl ays lah dee-rayk-**see^ohn** day lah **kah**-sah?* ¿Cuál es la dirección de la casa?[1, 2]
In what county and state is it located?	*ayn kay kohn-**dah**-doh ee ays-**tah**-doh ays-**tah** oo-bee-**kah**-dah?* ¿En qué condado y estado está ubicada?[1]
What is the remaining amount of the mortgage on the house?	*koo^ahl ays ayl **sahl**-doh day lah ee-poh-**tay**-kah day lah **kah**-sah?* ¿Cuál es el saldo de la hipoteca de la casa?[2]
Does that include an escrow account for insurance and taxes?	*een-**kloo**-yay **ays**-toh oo-nah koo^**ayn**-tah day day-**poh**-see-toh ayn gah-rahn-**tee**-ah **pah**-rah say-**goo**-roh ay eem-**poo^ays**-tohs?* ¿Incluye esto una cuenta de depósito en garantía para seguro e impuestos?
Are you behind on those payments?	*ays-**tah** ah-trah-**sah**-doh/dah ayn lohs **pah**-gohs?* ¿Está atrasado/a en los pagos?[4]
By how many months?	*pohr koo^**ayn**-tohs **may**-says?* ¿Por cuántos meses?[2]
Has your lender threatened foreclosure?	*loh/lah ah ah-may-nah-**sah**-doh soo prays-tah-**dohr** ee-poh-tay-**kah**-ree^oh kohn ay-hay-koo-**see^ohn** ee-poh-tay-**kah**-ree^ah?* ¿Lo/La ha amenazado su prestador hipotecario con ejecución hipotecaria?[8]
Have you received a court notice regarding a foreclosure hearing?	*ah rray-see-**bee**-doh oon ah-**bee**-soh hoo-dee-**see^ahl** pah-rah oo-nah ah^oo-**dee^ayn**-see^ah day ay-hay-koo-**see^ohn** ee-poh-tay-**kah**-ree^ah?* ¿Ha recibido un aviso judicial para una audiencia de ejecución hipotecaria?
What is the date of that hearing?	*koo^ahl ays lah **fay**-chah day lah ah^oo-**dee^ayn**-see^ah?* ¿Cuál es la fecha de la audiencia?[3]

4. Do you have a second mortgage or an equity line of credit on the house?	*tee^ay-nay oo-nah say-goon-dah ee-poh-tay-kah oh oo-nah lee-nay-ah day kray-dee-toh proh-pee^ah pah-rah lah kah-sah?* ¿Tiene una segunda hipoteca o una línea de crédito propia para la casa?
Who is the lender?	*kee^ayn ays ayl prays-tah-dohr?* ¿Quién es el prestador?[1]
How much are those payments?	*koo^ayn-tohs sohn lohs pah-gohs?* ¿Cuántos son los pagos?[2]
Are you behind on those payments?	*ays-tah ah-trah-sah-doh/dah ayn lohs pah-gohs?* ¿Está atrasado/a en los pagos?[4]
By how many months?	*pohr koo^ayn-tohs may-says?* ¿Por cuántos meses?[2]
Has your lender threatened foreclosure?	*loh/lah ah ah-may-nah-sah-doh soo prays-tah-dohr ee-poh-tay-kah-ree^oh kohn ay-hay-koo-see^ohn ee-poh-tay-kah-ree^ah?* ¿Lo/La ha amenazado su prestador hipotecario con ejecución hipotecaria?[8]
Have you received a court notice regarding a foreclosure hearing?	*ah rray-see-bee-doh oon ah-bee-soh hoo-dee-see^ahl pah-rah oo-nah ah^oo-dee^ayn-see^ah day ay-hay-koo-see^ohn ee-poh-tay-kah-ree^ah?* ¿Ha recibido un aviso judicial para una audiencia de ejecución hipotecaria?
What is the date of that hearing?	*koo^ahl ays lah fay-chah day lah ah^oo-dee^ayn-see^ah?* ¿Cuál es la fecha de la audiencia?[3]
5. Do you have any idea what your home is worth at this time?	*tee^ay-nay ahl-goo-nah ee-day-ah dayl bah-lohr day soo kah-sah ayn ays-tay moh-mayn-toh?* ¿Tiene alguna idea del valor de su casa en este momento?
Will you write it for me here, please?	*may loh ays-kree-bay ah-kee, pohr fah-bohr?* ¿Me lo escribe aquí, por favor?
6. How much do you owe on your house— inclusive of all loans?	*koo^ahn-toh day-bay pohr lah kah-sah—een-kloo^ee-dohs toh-dohs lohs prays-tah-mohs?* ¿Cuánto debe por la casa—incluidos todos los préstamos?[2]
7. Do you have a lease with anyone?	*tee^ay-nay oon kohn-trah-toh day ahl-kee-layr kohn ahl-ghee^ayn?* ¿Tiene un contrato de alquiler con alguien?
How much per month is your rental payment?	*koo^ahn-toh ays soo pah-goh day ahl-kee-layr mayn-soo^ahl?* ¿Cuánto es su pago de alquiler mensual?[2]
Are you behind on any payments?	*ays-tah ah-trah-sah-doh/dah ayn lohs pah-gohs?* ¿Está atrasado/a en los pagos?[4]
8. Has your landlord started any eviction process?	*ays kay ayl proh-pee^ay-tah-ree^oh ah ee-nee-see^ah-doh ayl proh-say-soh day days-ah-loh-hoh?* ¿Es que el propietario ha iniciado el proceso de desalojo?

9. Have you been given a court date?

*lay ahn ah-seeg-**nah**-doh **oo**-nah **fay**-chah day kohm-pah-ray-**sayn**-see^ah **ahn**-tay ayl tree-boo-**nahl**?*
¿Le han asignado una fecha de comparecencia ante el tribunal?

When is that?

*koo^**ahn**-doh ays?*
¿Cuándo es?³

10. Do you own or lease any other property?

*ays proh-pee^ay-**tah**-ree^oh/ah oh ah-rrayn-dah-**tah**-ree^oh/ah day **oh**-trah proh-pee^ay-**dahd**?*
¿Es propietario/a o arrendatario/a de otra propiedad?⁴

Is it ...

ays ...
¿Es ...

a second home?

*oo-nah say-**goon**-dah rray-see-**dayn**-see^ah?*
una segunda residencia?

Are you the owner or renter?

*ays proh-pee^ay-**tah**-ree^oh/ah oh ah-rrayn-dah-**tah**-ree^oh/ah?*
¿Es propietario/a o arrendatario/a?⁴

investment property?

*oo-nah proh-pee^ay-**dahd** day een-bayr-**see^oh**-nays?*
una propiedad de inversiones?

Are you the owner or renter?

*ays proh-pee^ay-**tah**-ree^oh/ah oh ah-rrayn-dah-**tah**-ree^oh/ah?*
¿Es propietario/a o arrendatario/a?⁴

a time share?

*oo-nah mool-tee-proh-pee^ay-**dahd**?*
una multipropiedad?

Are you the owner or renter?

*ays proh-pee^ay-**tah**-ree^oh/ah oh ah-rrayn-dah-**tah**-ree^oh/ah?*
¿Es propietario/a o arrendatario/a?⁴

commercial space?

*ays-**pah**-see^oh koh-mayr-**see^ahl**?*
espacio comercial?

Are you the owner or renter?

*ays proh-pee^ay-**tah**-ree^oh/ah oh ah-rrayn-dah-**tah**-ree^oh/ah?*
¿Es propietario/a o arrendatario/a?⁴

another type of property?

*oh-trah **klah**-say day proh-pee^ay-**dahd**?*
otra clase de propiedad?

Are you the owner or renter?

*ays proh-pee^ay-**tah**-ree^oh/ah oh ah-rrayn-dah-**tah**-ree^oh/ah?*
¿Es propietario/a o arrendatario/a?⁴

11. Now, I am going to talk to you about your vehicles:

*ah-**oh**-rah, lay boh^ee ah ah-**blahr** day soos bay-**ee**-koo-lohs:*
Ahora, le voy a hablar de sus vehículos:

12. How many cars are there in your household?

*koo^**ahn**-tohs **ah^oo**-tohs ah^ee koh-layk-tee-bah-**mayn**-tay **ayn**-tray lahs payr-**soh**-nahs kay ah-**bee**-tahn soo oh-**gahr**?*
¿Cuántos autos hay colectivamente entre las personas que habitan su hogar?²

13. For the ... car, is it in your name, your spouse's name, or the name of another person?

*pah-rah ayl ... **ah^oo**-toh, ays-**tah** ahl soo nohm-bray, ahl **nohm**-bray day soo **kohn**-yoo-hay oh ahl **nohm**-bray day oh-trah payr-**soh**-nah?*
Para el ... auto, ¿está al su nombre, al nombre de su cónyuge o al nombre de otra persona?

first	*pree-**mayr*** primer
second	*say-**goon**-doh* segundo
third	*tayr-**sayr*** tercer
fourth	***koo^ahr**-toh* cuarto
fifth	***keen**-toh* quinto
sixth	***sayks**-toh* sexto

14. How many vehicles are in your name or your spouse's name?	*koo^**ayn**-tohs bay-**ee**-koo-lohs ah^ee ayn soo **nohm**-bray oh ayl **nohm**-bray day soo **kohn**-yoo-hay?* ¿Cuántos vehículos hay en su nombre o el nombre de su cónyuge?[2, 9]
Do you own or lease the car?	*ah kohm-**proh** oh ahl-kee-**loh** ay-say ah^**oo**-toh?* ¿Compró o alquiló ese auto?
Who makes the payments each month—you, your spouse or both of you?	*kee^ayn **ah**-say lohs **pah**-gohs mayn-**soo^ah**-lays—oo-**stayd**, soo **kohn**-yoo-hay oh lohs dohs?* ¿Quién hace los pagos mensuales—Ud., su cónyuge o los dos?
To whom do you make payments?	*ah kee^ayn lay **pah**-gah?* ¿A quién le paga?[1]
How much are those payments?	*koo^**ahn**-toh ays ayl **pah**-goh mayn-**soo^ahl**?* ¿Cuánto es el pago mensual?[2]
Are you behind?	*ays-**tah** ah-trah-**sah**-doh/dah?* ¿Está atrasado/a?[4]
By how many months?	*pohr **koo^ahn**-tohs **may**-says?* ¿Por cuántos meses?[2]
When did you … the car?	***koo^ahn**-doh … ayl **ah^oo**-toh?* ¿Cuándo … el auto?[3]
purchase	*kohm-**proh*** compró
begin to rent	*aym-pay-**soh** ah ahl-kee-**lahr*** empezó a alquilar
Do you have any idea what the value of the car is at this time?	***tee^ay**-nay ahl-**goo**-nah ee-**day**-ah dayl bah-**lohr** dayl ah^**oo**-toh ayn **ays**-tay moh-**mayn**-toh?* ¿Tiene alguna idea del valor del auto en este momento?
What is it worth?	*koo^**ahl** ays ayl bah-lohr?* ¿Cuál es el valor?[2]

	*tee^ay-nay ahl-**goo**-nah ee-**day**-ah day **koo^ahn**-toh ays soo **day^oo**-dah toh-**tahl** …*
Do you have any idea how much you owe on …	¿Tiene alguna idea de cuánto es su deuda total …
	*dayl pah-gah-**ray** day **ah^oo**-toh?*
the car note?	del pagaré de auto?
	*koo^ahl ays ayl **sahl**-doh?*
What is that amount?	¿Cuál es el saldo?²
	*dayl **sahl**-doh dayl kohn-**trah**-toh day ah-rrayn-dee-**mee^ayn**-toh?*
balance of the lease?	del saldo del contrato de arrendamiento?
	*koo^ahl ays ayl **sahl**-doh?*
What is that amount?	¿Cuál es el saldo?²

---

	*koo^**ahn**-tahs **bahr**-kahs …*
15. How many boats …	¿Cuántas barcas …
	*koo^**ahn**-tahs moh-toh-see-**klay**-tahs …*
How many motorcycles …	¿Cuántas motocicletas …
	*koo^**ahn**-tohs bay-**ee**-koo-lohs **toh**-doh tay-**rray**-noh …*
How many ATVs …	¿Cuántos vehículos todo terreno …
	*koo^**ahn**-tahs **moh**-tohs ah-**koo^ah**-tee-kahs …*
How many jet skis …	¿Cuántas motos acuáticas …
	*ah^ee koh-layk-tee-bah-**mayn**-tay (**ayn**-tray lahs payr-**soh**-nahs kay ah-**bee**-tahn soo oh-**gahr**)?*
are there (in your household)?	hay colectivamente (entre las personas que habitan su hogar)?²
	*koo^ahl ays ayl bah-**lohr** ays-tee-**mah**-doh day **kah**-dah **oo**-noh?*
What is the approximate value of each one?	¿Cuál es el valor estimado de cada uno?²
	*ah^ee **oh**-trah **klah**-say day bay-**ee**-koo-loh rray-kray-ah-**tee**-boh ayn ayn soo oh-**gahr** kay noh say mayn-see^oh-**noh**?*
Are there any other types of recreational vehicles in your household?	¿Hay otra clase de vehículo recreativo en su hogar que no se mencionó?
	*may ays-**kree**-bay ah-**kee** pohr fah-**bohr**, kay **klah**-say day bay-**ee**-koo-loh rray-kray-ah-**tee**-boh ays?*
Will you write down for me here what type of recreational vehicle it is, please?	¿Me escribe aquí por favor, qué clase de vehículo recreativo es?
	*koo^ahl ays ayl bah-**lohr** ays-tee-**mah**-doh day **kah**-dah **oo**-noh?*
What is the approximate value of each one?	¿Cuál es el valor estimado de cada uno?²

---

	*tee^**ay**-nay ahl-**goo**-nahs **koo^ayn**-tahs **may**-dee-kahs?*
16. Do you have any medical bills?	¿Tiene algunas cuentas médicas?
	*ah kee^**ayn** lay **day**-bay?*
Who do you owe?	¿A quién le debe?¹

How much do you owe?	*koo^ahn-toh day-bay ayn toh-tahl?* ¿Cuánto debe en total?[2]
17. Do you have any student loans?	*tee^ay-nay prays-tah-mohs ays-too-dee^ahn-tee-lays?* ¿Tiene préstamos estudiantiles?
How much?	*koo^ahl ays ayl sahl-doh?* ¿Cuál es el saldo?[2]
Are these federal or private loans or a combination of both?	*sohn prays-tah-mohs fay-day-rah-lays oh pahr-tee-koo-lah-rays oh oo-nah kohm-bee-nah-see^ohn day lohs dohs?* ¿Son préstamos federales o particulares o una combinación de los dos?
18. Do you owe any back taxes for ...	*ays-tah ah-trah-sah-doh/dah ayn lohs pah-gohs day ...* ¿Está atrasado/a en los pagos de ...[4]
federal taxes?	*ee-poo^ays-tohs fay-day-rah-lays?* impuestos federales?
state taxes?	*ee-poo^ays-tohs ays-tah-tah-lays?* impuestos estatales?
property tax?	*ee-poo^ays-tohs day proh-pee^ay-dahd?* impuestos de propiedad?
Who do you owe?	*ah kee^ayn lay day-bay?* ¿A quién le debe?[1]
How much do you owe?	*koo^ahn-toh day-bay ayn toh-tahl?* ¿Cuánto debe en total?[2]
What years were these back taxes for?	*pah-rah kay ahn-yohs fees-kah-lays sohn lohs eem-poo^ays-tohs ah-trah-sah-dohs?* ¿Para qué años fiscales son los impuestos atrasados?[2]
Will you list each year and the respective amount of back taxes for each year here for me, please?	*may ay-noo-may-rah kah-dah ahn-yoh ee lah soo-mah rrays-payk-tee-bah day eem-poo^ays-tohs ah-trah-sah-dohs pah-rah kah-dah ahn-yoh ah-kee, pohr fah-bohr?* ¿Me enumera cada año y la suma respectiva de impuestos atrasados para cada año aquí, por favor?
Has legal action been taken against you for the back taxes that you owe?	*say ah aym-prayn-dee-doh ahk-see^ohn lay-gahl ayn soo kohn-trah pohr eem-poo^ays-tohs ah-trah-sah-dohs kay day-bay?* ¿Se ha emprendido acción legal en su contra por los impuestos atrasados que debe?
19. Do you pay ...	*pah-gah ...* ¿Paga ...
child support?	*mah-noo-tayn-see^ohn day ee-hohs?* manutención de hijos?
Who do you pay?	*ah kee^ayn lay pah-gah?* ¿A quién le paga?[1]
How much?	*koo^ahn-toh pah-gah?* ¿Cuánto paga?[2]

When will the child support payments end?	*koo^ayn-doh tayr-mee-nahn lohs pah-gohs day mah-noo-tayn-see^ohn day ee-hohs?* ¿Cuándo terminan los pagos de manutención de hijos?[3]
alimony?	*payn-see^ohn ah-lee-mayn-tee-see^ah?* pensión alimenticia?
Who do you pay?	*ah kee^ayn lay pah-gah?* ¿A quién le paga?[1]
How much?	*koo^ahn-toh pah-gah?* ¿Cuánto paga?[2]
When will the alimony payments end?	*koo^ayn-doh tayr-mee-nahn lohs pah-gohs day payn-see^ohn ah-lee-mayn-tee-see^ah?* ¿Cuándo terminan los pagos de pensión alimenticia?[3]

20. Do you have any credit card debts?	*tee^ay-nay day^oo-dahs day tahr-hay-tah day kray-dee-toh?* ¿Tiene deudas de tarjeta de crédito?
Do you have any idea what you may owe altogether?	*tee^ay-nay ahl-goo-nah ee-day-ah day koo^ahn-toh day-bay ayn toh-tahl?* ¿Tiene alguna idea de cuánto debe en total?
How much would that be approximately?	*koo^ahn-toh say-ree-ah say-goon soo may-hohr ah-prohk-see-mah-see^ohn?* ¿Cuánto sería según su mejor aproximación?[2]
If you could gather your statements and bring those with you to our meeting, that would be helpful.	*say-ree-ah moo^ee oo-teel see poh-dree-ah rray-koh-hayr toh-dohs soos ays-tah-dohs day koo^ayn-tah day tahr-hay-tah day kray-dee-toh ee trah-ayr-lohs ah noo^ays-trah prohk-see-mah hoon-tah.* Sería muy útil si podría recoger todos sus estados de cuenta de tarjeta de crédito y traerlos a nuestra próxima junta.

21. Do you have a recent copy of your credit report?	*tee^ay-nay oo-nah koh-pee^ah rray-see^ayn-tay day soo ees-toh-ree^ahl kray-dee-tee-see^oh?* ¿Tiene una copia reciente de su historial crediticio?
Could you bring that to our next meeting?	*poh-dree-ah trah-ayr-lah ah noo^ays-trah prohk-see-mah hoon-tah?* ¿Podría traerla a nuestra próxima junta?

22. Do you have any other loans for which you are responsible?	*ah^ee oh-trohs prays-tah-mohs pohr lohs koo^ah-lays ays rrays-pohn-sah-blay?* ¿Hay otros préstamos por los cuales es responsable?
Are they ...	*sohn ...* ¿Son ...
personal loans?	*prays-tah-mohs payr-soh-nah-lays?* préstamos personales?
payday loans?	*prays-tah-mohs day dee-ah day pah-goh?* préstamos de día de pago?

| other types of loans? | *oh*-trohs **tee**-pohs day **prays**-tah-mohs?
otros tipos de préstamos? |
| Can you list for me here to whom you owe each loan and the amount of each one? | *may ay-noo-**may**-rah ah-**kee** ah kee^ayn lay **day**-bay **kah**-dah **prays**-tah-moh ee ayl **mohn**-toh day **kah**-dah **oo**-noh?*
¿Me enumera aquí a quién le debe cada préstamo y el monto de cada uno? |

III. Judgments and Lawsuits

fah-yohs ee day-**mahn**-dahs
Fallos y demandas

English	Pronunciation & Spanish
1. Are there any judgments against you?	***tee^ay**-nay **fah**-yohs ayn soo **kohn**-trah?* ¿Tiene fallos en su contra?
In what county and state?	*ayn kay kohn-**dah**-doh ee ays-**tah**-doh?* ¿En qué condado y estado?[1]
Could you … what is each judgment for?	*poh-**dree**-ah … **pah**-rah kay ays **kah**-dah **fah**-yoh?* ¿Podría … para qué es cada fallo?
explain to someone (in Spanish)	*ayks-plee-**kahr**-lay ah **ahl**-ghee^ayn (ayn ays-pahn-**yohl**)* explicarle a alguien (en español)
describe in writing (in Spanish)	*days-kree-**beer** pohr ays-**kree**-toh (ayn ays-pahn-**yohl**)* describir por escrito (en español)
Other than the judgment, has anyone sought to collect on the judgment?	*ah-**pahr**-tay dayl **fah**-yoh **mees**-moh, ah een-tayn-**tah**-doh **ahl**-ghee^ayn koh-**brahr** oon **fah**-yoh?* Aparte del fallo mismo, ¿ha intentado alguien cobrar un fallo?
Who was it?	*kee^ayn foo^ay?* ¿Quién fue?[1]
2. Are there any judgments against your spouse?	***tee^ay**-nay soo **kohn**-yoo-hay **fah**-yohs ayn soo **kohn**-trah?* ¿Tiene su cónyuge fallos en su contra?
In what county and state?	*ayn kay kohn-**dah**-doh ee ays-**tah**-doh?* ¿En qué condado y estado?[1]
Could you … what is each judgment for?	*poh-**dree**-ah … **pah**-rah kay ays **kah**-dah **fah**-yoh?* ¿Podría … para qué es cada fallo?
explain to someone (in Spanish)	*ayks-plee-**kahr**-lay ah **ahl**-ghee^ayn (ayn ays-pahn-**yohl**)* explicarle a alguien (en español)
describe in writing (in Spanish)	*days-kree-**beer** pohr ays-**kree**-toh (ayn ays-pahn-**yohl**)* describir por escrito (en español)

Has anyone sought to collect on the judgment?

*ah een-tayn-**tah**-doh **ahl**-ghee^ayn koh-**brahr** oon **fah**-yoh?*
¿Ha intentado alguien cobrar un fallo?

Who was it?

kee^ayn foo^ay?
¿Quién fue?[1]

---

3. Do you have any pending lawsuits against you?

*ah^ee ahl-**goo**-nahs day-**mahn**-dahs payn-**dee^ayn**-tays ayn soo **kohn**-trah?*
¿Hay algunas demandas pendientes en su contra?

How many lawsuits do you have against you?

*koo^**ahn**-tahs day-**mahn**-dahs payn-**dee^ayn**-tays ah^ee ayn soo **kohn**-trah?*
¿Cuántas demandas pendientes hay en su contra?[2]

Will you list each one here for me, please?

*may ay-noo-**may**-rah kah-day **oo**-nah ah-**kee**, pohr fah-**bohr**?*
¿Me enumera cada una aquí, por favor?

In what county and state is each one?

*aynn kay kohn-**dah**-doh ee ays-**tah**-doh ays-**tah** kah-dah **oo**-nah?*
¿En qué condado y estado está cada una?[1]

Did you receive a summons (to appear)?

*rray-see-**bee^oh** oo-nah see-tah-**see^ohn** (day kohm-pah-ray-**sayn**-see^ah)?*
¿Recibió una citación (de comparecencia)?

When did you receive it?

*koo^**ayn**-doh lah rray-see-**bee^oh**?*
¿Cuándo la recibió?[3]

Are you represented by an attorney?

*ahk-too^ahl-**mayn**-tay, say ayn-**koo^ayn**-trah rray-pray-sayn-**tah**-doh/dah pohr oon ah-boh-**gah**-doh?*
Actualmente, ¿se encuentra representado/a por un abogado?

What is the attorney's name?

*koh-moh say **yah**-mah ayl ah-boh-**gah**-doh?*
¿Cómo se llama el abogado?[1]

---

4. Do you have any pending lawsuits you have filed against any other person?

*tee^**ay**-nay ahl-**goo**-nahs day-**mahn**-dahs payn-**dee^ayn**-tays kay yah ah pray-sayn-**tah**-doh **kohn**-trah oh-trah payr-**soh**-nah?*
¿Tiene algunas demandas pendientes que ya ha presentado contra cualquier otra persona?

Respond with "yes" to any of the reasons from the following list that explain what each lawsuit is regarding:

*rrays-**pohn**-dah kohn <see> ah koo^ah-lays-**kee^ayr** day lahs rrah-**soh**-nays day lah see-**ghee^ayn**-tay **lees**-tah kay ayks-**plee**-kahn day loh kay say **trah**-tah kah-dah day-**mahn**-dah:*
Responda con <sí> a cualesquier de las razones de la siguiente lista que explican de lo que se trata cada demanda:

Someone owes you for damages related to ...

*ahl-**ghee^ayn** lay **day**-bay een-daym-nee-sah-**see^ohn** rray-lah-see^oh-**nah**-dah ah ...*
¿Alguien le debe indemnización relacionada a ...

an accident?

*oon ahk-see-**dayn**-tay?*
un accidente?

an injury?	*oo-nah lay-**see**^ohn?* una lesión?
a debt?	*oo-nah **day**^oo-dah?* una deuda?
a loan?	*oon **prays**-tah-moh?* un préstamo?
an employment situation?	*oon ah-**soon**-toh lah-boh-**rahl**?* un asunto laboral?
another issue?	*oh-troh ah-**soon**-toh?* otro asunto?
Could you … what this issue is exactly?	*poh-**dree**-ah … day kay say **trah**-tah **ays**-tay ah-**soon**-toh?* ¿Podría … de qué se trata este asunto?
explain in writing	*ayks-plee-**kahr** pohr ays-**kree**-toh* explicar por escrito
tell someone (in Spanish/English)	*day-**seer**-lay ah **ahl**-ghee^ayn (ayn ays-pahn-**yohl**/een-**glays**)* decirle a alguien (en español/inglés)
Was the lawsuit filed …	*say pray-sayn-**toh** lah day-**mahn**-dah …* ¿Se presentó la demanda …
a few years ago?	***ah**-say oon pahr day **ahn**-yohs?* hace un par de años?
a year ago?	***ah**-say oon **ahn**-yoh?* hace un año?
some months ago?	***ah**-say **oo**-nohs **koo**^ahn-tohs **may**-says?* hace unos cuantos meses?
Was the lawsuit just filed?	*say ah-**kah**-bah day pray-sayn-**tahr** lah day-**mahn**-dah?* ¿Se acaba de presentar la demanda?
Where was the lawsuit filed?	***dohn**-day say pray-sayn-**toh** lah day-**mahn**-dah?* ¿Dónde se presentó la demanda?[1]
Is there a trial set?	*say ah proh-grah-**mah**-doh oon **hoo**^ee-see^oh?* ¿Se ha programado un juicio?
Who is your attorney?	***kee**^ayn ays soo ah-boh-**gah**-doh?* ¿Quién es su abogado?[1]
Do you have their phone number?	***tee**^ay-nay soo **noo**-may-roh day tay-**lay**-foh-noh?* ¿Tiene su número de teléfono?
Please write that phone number here for me.	*pohr fah-**bohr**, ays-**kree**-bah-may **ay**-say **noo**-may-roh day tay-**lay**-foh-noh ah-**kee**.* Por favor, escríbame ese número de teléfono aquí.
5. Are you expecting to file a case in the near future?	*ays-**tah** payn-**sahn**-doh pray-**sayn**-tahr **oo**-nah day-**mahn**-dah ayn ayl pohr-bay-**neer** sayr-**kah**-noh?* ¿Está pensando presentar una demanda en el porvenir cercano?

Could you … what the case is about?	*poh-**dree**-ah … day kay say **trah**-tah lah day-**mahn**-dah?* ¿Podría … de qué se trata la demanda?
explain in writing	*ayks-plee-**kahr** pohr ays-**kree**-toh* explicar por escrito
tell someone (in Spanish/English)	*day-**seer**-lay ah **ahl**-ghee^ayn (ayn ays-pahn-**yohl**/een-**glays**)* decirle a alguien (en español/inglés)
Do you have an attorney for this case?	*tee^**ay**-nay rray-pray-sayn-tah-**see^ohn** lay-**gahl** ayn **ays**-tay kah-soh?* ¿Tiene representación legal en este caso?
Who is that?	*kee^ayn ays?* ¿Quién es?[1]
Do you have their contact information?	*tee^**ay**-nay soo een-fohr-mah-**see^ohn** day kohn-**tahk**-toh?* ¿Tiene su información de contacto?
Will you write it for me here, please?	*may lah ays-**kree**-bay ah-**kee**, pohr fah-**bohr**?* ¿Me la escribe aquí, por favor?
6. Do you have any business debts?	*tee^**ay**-nay ahl-**goo**-nahs **day**^oo-dahs day nay-**goh**-see^oh?* ¿Tiene algunas deudas de negocio?
Can you list for me here to whom you owe each loan and the amount of each one?	*may ay-noo-**may**-rah ah-**kee** ah kee^ayn lay **day**-bay kah-dah **prays**-tah-moh ee ayl **mohn**-toh ah-prohk-see-**mah**-doh day **kah**-dah oo-noh?* ¿Me enumera aquí a quién le debe cada préstamo y el monto aproximado de cada uno?

IV. Monthly Income

*soo^**ayl**-doh mayn-**soo**^ahl*
Sueldo mensual

English	Pronunciation & Spanish
1. What is your average monthly income from all employment over the past six months?	*koo^ahl ays soo een-**gray**-soh mayn-**soo**^ahl may-dee^oh day **toh**-dohs lohs aym-**play**-ohs kay ah tay-**nee**-doh doo-**rahn**-tay lohs **ool**-tee-mohs say^ees **may**-says?* ¿Cuál es su ingreso mensual medio de todos los empleos que ha tenido durante los últimos seis meses?[2]
2. If you have pay stubs, can you gather the last six months for me?	*see ah kohn-sayr-**bah**-doh lohs tah-**loh**-nays day **chay**-kay, may **poo**^ay-day hoon-**tahr** ahl **may**-nohs lohs day lohs **ool**-tee-mohs say^ees **may**-says?* Si ha conservado los talones de cheque, ¿me puede juntar al menos los de los últimos seis meses?
If you can bring the most recent two stubs with you to our office, that would get things started.	*see **poo**^ay-day trah-**ayr** lohs dohs tah-**loh**-nays day **chay**-kay mahs rray-**see**^ayn-tays ah **noo**^ays-trah oh-fee-**see**-nah, poh-**day**-mohs ee-nee-**see^ahr** ayl proh-**say**-soh.* Si puede traer los dos talones de cheque más recientes a nuestra oficina, podemos iniciar el proceso.

3. What was the ... amount of this income?	*koo^ahl foo^ay ayl **mohn**-toh ... day **ays**-tay een-**gray**-soh?* ¿Cuál fue el monto ... de este ingreso?
gross	***broo**-toh* bruto[2]
net	***nay**-toh* neto[2]
4. How often are you paid?	***kah**-dah **koo^ahn**-toh loh/lah **pah**-gahn?* ¿Cada cuánto lo/la pagan?[3]
Each week?	***kah**-dah say-**mah**-nah?* ¿Cada semana?
The first and the fifteenth of the month?	*ayl pree-**may**-roh ee ayl **keen**-say dayl mays?* ¿El primero y el quince del mes?
The fifteenth and the last day of the month?	*ayl **keen**-say ee ayl **ool**-tee-moh **dee**-ah dayl mays?* ¿El quince y el último día del mes?
Every two weeks?	***kah**-dah dohs say-**may**-nahs?* ¿Cada dos semanas?
At the end of the month?	*ahl feen dayl mays?* ¿Al fin del mes?
5. What is your spouse's average net monthly income from all employment?	*koo^ahl ays ayl een-**gray**-soh mayn-**soo^ahl may**-dee^oh day **toh**-dohs lohs aym-**play**-ohs kay tee^ay-nay soo **kohn**-yoo-hay?* ¿Cuál es el ingreso mensual medio de todos los empleos que tiene su cónyuge?[2]
6. Do you receive ...	*rray-**see**-bay ...* ¿Recibe ...
child support?	*mah-noo-tahn-**see^ohn** day **ee**-hohs?* manutención de hijos?
alimony?	***oo**-nah payn-**see^ohn** ah-lee-mayn-**tee**-see^ah?* una pensión alimenticia?
a pension?	***oo**-nah payn-**see^ohn**?* una pensión?
social security?	*bay-nay-**fee**-see^ohs day say-**goo**-roh soh-**see^ahl**?* beneficios de seguro social?
disability benefits?	*bay-nay-**fee**-see^ohs day dees-kah-pah-see-**dahd**?* beneficios de discapacidad?
unemployment?	*bay-nay-**fee**-see^ohs day day-saym-**play**-oh?* beneficios de desempleo?
worker's compensation?	*een-daym-nee-sah-**see^ohn** lah-boh-**rahl**?* indemnización laboral?

financial assistance from family not living in your household?

*ah^ee-**yoo**-dah fee-nahn-**see**^ay-rah day fah-**mee**-lee^ah kay noh **bee**-bay ayn soo oh-**gahr**?*
ayuda financiera de familia que no vive en su hogar?

income from rental property?

*een-**gray**-sohs day proh-pee^ay-**dah**-days ah-rrayn-**dah**-dahs?*
ingresos de propiedades arrendadas?

7. Do you have any other source of income?

*tee^**ay**-nay ahl-**goo**-nah oh-trah foo^**ayn**-tay day een-**gray**-sohs?*
¿Tiene alguna otra fuente de ingresos?

Will you write for me here what that is, please?

*may ays-**kree**-bay ah-**kee** koo^ahl ays, pohr fah-**bohr**?*
¿Me escribe aquí cuál es, por favor?

8. Did you receive an Income Tax Refund from the IRS for previous tax years?

*ah rray-see-**bee**-doh oo-nah day-boh-loo-**see**^ohn dah eem-**poo**^ays-tohs day lohs sayr-**bee**-see^ohs day rray-kah^oo-dah-**see**^ohn day eem-**poo**^ays-tohs **pah**-rah lohs **ahn**-yohs fees-**kah**-lays ahn-tay-ree^**oh**-rays?*
¿Ha recibido una devolución de impuestos de los Servicios de Recaudación de Impuestos para los años fiscales anteriores?

How much would you estimate that total to be?

*koo^ahl say-**ree**-ah soo ah-prohk-see-mah-**see**^ohn dayl **mohn**-toh toh-**tahl**?*
¿Cuál sería su aproximación del monto total?[2]

9. Have you had money deducted from ... during the last six months?

*say lay ah day-doo-**see**-doh dee-**nay**-roh day ... doo-**rahn**-tay lohs **ool**-tee-mohs say^ees **may**-says?*
¿Se le ha deducido dinero de ... durante los últimos seis meses?

your income for a pension

*soos een-**gray**-sohs days-tee-**nah**-dohs a **oo**-nah payn-**see**^ohn*
sus ingresos destinados a una pensión

401K

*soo plahn day **koo**^ah-troh **say**-roh **oo**-noh kah*
su plan de 401K

any other retirementment benefits

*koo^ah-lays-**kee**^ayr **oh**-trohs bay-nay-**fee**-see^ohs day hoo-bee-lah-**see**^ohn?*
cualesquier otros beneficios de jubilación

What is the total for those deductions?

*koo^ahl ays lah **soo**-mah toh-**tahl** day ays-tahs day-dook-**see**^**oh**-nays?*
¿Cuál es la suma total de estas deducciones?[2]

10. Have you had money deducted from your income for the repayment of loans against ... during the last six months?

*say lay ah day-doo-**see**-doh dee-**nay**-roh day soos een-**gray**-sohs **pah**-rah ayl rray-**pah**-goh day **prays**-tah-mohs toh-**mah**-dohs day ... doo-**rahn**-tay lohs **ool**-tee-mohs say^ees **may**-says?*
¿Se le ha deducido dinero de sus ingresos para el repago de préstamos tomados de ... durante los últimos seis meses?

a 401K

*oon plahn day **koo**^ah-troh **say**-roh **oo**-noh kah*
un plan de 401K

any other retirment plan

*koo^ahl-**kee**^ayr oh-trah klah-say day plahn day hoo-bee-lah-**see**^ohn*
cualquier otra clase de plan de jubilación

What is the total for those deductions?

*koo^ahl ays lah **soo**-mah toh-**tahl** day ays-tahs day-dook-**see**^**oh**-nays?*
¿Cuál es la suma total de estas deducciones?[2]

V. Monthly Expenses

*gahs-tohs mayn-**soo^ah**-lays*
Gastos mensuales

English	Pronunciation & Spanish
1. When you meet with us, I will provide you with a worksheet for you to list all of your monthly expenses.	*koo^ahn-doh say rray-**oo**-nah kohn noh-**soh**-trohs, lay dah-**ray oo**-nah **oh**-hah day trah-**bah**-hoh ayn ayl koo^ahl ay-noo-may-rah-**rah toh**-dohs soos **gahs**-tohs mayn-**soo^ah**-lays.* Cuando se reúna con nosotros, le daré una hoja de trabajo en la cual enumerará todos sus gastos mensuales.
2. We need this information to provide to the bankruptcy court.	*nay-say-see-**tah**-mohs **ays**-tah een-fohr-mah-**see^ohn pah**-rah pray-sayn-**tahr**-lay ahl tree-boo-**nahl** day bahn-kah-**rroh**-tah.* Necesitamos esta información para presentarle al tribunal de bancarrota.
3. How much is your monthly ...	*koo^ahn-toh **pah**-gah ahl mays day ...* ¿Cuánto paga al mes de ...
mortgage payment?	*ee-poh-**tay**-kah?* hipoteca?[2]
rent payment?	*ahl-kee-**layr**?* alquiler?[2]
4. Do you have ...	*tee^**ay**-nay ...* ¿Tiene ...
a second (monthly) mortgage?	*oo-nah say-**goon**-dah ee-poh-**tay**-kah (mayn-**soo^ahl**)?* una segunda hipoteca (mensual)?
How much is it?	*koo^**ahn**-toh ays?* ¿Cuánto es?[2]
a third (monthly) mortgage?	*oo-nah tayr-**say**-rah ee-poh-**tay**-kah (mayn-**soo^ahl**)?* una tercera hipoteca (mensual)?
How much is it?	*koo^**ahn**-toh ays?* ¿Cuánto es?[2]
5. Are your property taxes escrowed into your mortgage?	*ays kay soo ee-poh-**tah**-kah een-**kloo**-yay soos eem-**poo^ays**-tohs day proh-pee^ay-**dahd**?* ¿Es que su hipoteca incluye sus impuestos de propiedad?
6. Is your homeowners insurance escrowed into your mortgage?	*ays kay soo ee-poh-**tay**-kah een-**kloo**-yay soo say-**goo**-roh day proh-pee^ay-**tah**-ree^oh day bee-**bee^ayn**-dah?* ¿Es que su hipoteca incluye su seguro de propietario de vivienda?
7. Is your homeowners or condominium association fee escrowed into your mortgage?	*ays kay soo ee-poh-**tah**-kah een-**kloo**-yay lohs oh-noh-**rah**-ree^ohs day ah-soh-see^ah-**see^ohn** day bee-**bee^ayn**-dah oh day kohn-doh-**mee**-nee^oh?* ¿Es que su hipoteca incluye los honorarios de asociación de vivienda o de condominio?

8. How much is your ... bill?

koo^ahn-toh ays soo koo^ayn-tah ...
¿Cuánto es su cuenta ...

electric

day ay-layk-tree-see-dahd?
de electricidad?²

water and sewer

day ah-goo^ah ee ahl-kahn-tah-ree-yah-doh?
de agua y alcantarillado?²

phone (land line)?

day tay-lay-foh-noh (day lee-nay-ah fee-hah)?
de teléfono (de línea fija)?²

cell phone

day tay-lay-foh-noh moh-beel?
de teléfono móvil?²

cable

day tay-lay-bee-see^ohn pohr kah-blay?
de televisión por cable?²

satellite tv

day tay-lay-bee-see^ohn bee-ah sah-tay-lee-tay?
de televisión vía satélite?²

9. Are there any other utilities for which you pay on a monthly basis not included here?

ah^ee oh-trohs sayr-bee-see^ohs pohr lohs koo^ah-lays pah-gah kah-dah mays kay noh say ahn mayn-see^oh-nah-doh aquí?
¿Hay otros servicios por los cuales paga cada mes que no se han mencionado aquí?

Will you list them for me here and write beside each one the amount, please?

may lohs ay-noo-may-rah ah-kee ee ays-kree-bay ahl lah-doh day kah-dah oo-noh koo^ahn-toh pah-gah ahl mays, pohr fah-bohr?
¿Me los enumera aquí y escribe al lado de cada uno cuánto paga al mes, por favor?

10. On average, how much do you spend each month on ...

day proh-may-dee^oh, koo^ahn-toh gahs-tah ahl mays ayn ...
De promedio, ¿cuánto gasta al mes en ...

home maintenance and repairs?

ayl mahn-tay-nee-mee^ahn-toh ee lah rray-pah-rah-see^ohn day kah-sah?
el mantenimiento y la reparación de casa?²

food?

lah koh-mee-dah?
la comida?²

clothing?

lah rroh-pah?
la ropa?²

laundry or dry cleaning?

ayl lah-bah-doh ee lah teen-toh-ray-ree-ah?
el lavado y la tintorería?²

transportation? (including gas, vehicle maintenance, tolls, parking fees, etc.)

ayl trahns-pohr-tay? (een-kloo^ee-dohs kohm-boos-tee-blay, mahn-tay-nee-mee^ayn-toh day bay-ee-koo-lohs, pay-ah-hays, tah-ree-fahs day ays-tah-see^oh-nah-mee^ayn-toh, ayt-say-tay-rah)
el transporte? (incluidos combustible, mantenimiento de vehículos, peajes, tarifas de estacionamiento, etcétera)²

recreation and entertainment?

lahs ahk-tee-bee-dah-days rray-kray-ah-tee-bahs ee ayl ayn-tray-tay-nee-mee^ayn-toh?
las actividades recreativas y el entretenimiento?²

	*lohs **gahs**-tohs day bohl-**see**-yoh pohr ah-tayn-**see**^ohn **may**-dee-kah ee dayn-**tahl**? (een-**kloo**^ee-dohs koh-**pah**-gohs ee day-doo-**see**-blays)*
out-of-pocket medical and dental care? (including co-pays and deductibles)	los gastos de bolsillo por atención médica y dental? (incluidos copagos y deducibles)[2]
	*ayl say-**goo**-roh day proh-pee^ay-**tah**-ree^oh day bee-**bee**^**ayn**-dah? (see noh say een-**kloo**-yay ayn lah ee-poh-**tay**-kah)*
homeowner's insurance? (if not included in the mortgage)	el seguro de propietario de vivienda? (si no se incluye en la hipoteca)[2]
	*ayl say-**goo**-roh day ah-rrayn-dah-**tah**-ree^oh?*
renter's insurance?	el seguro de arrendatario?[2]
	*ayl say-**goo**-roh day pohr **bee**-dah? (ah-**pahr**-tay dayl say-**goo**-roh day pohr **bee**-dah breen-**dah**-doh pohr oon aym-play-ah-**dohr**)*
life insurance? (other than the life insurance provided by an employer)	el seguro de por vida? (aparte del seguro de por vida brindado por un empleador)[2]
	*ayl say-**goo**-roh day sah-**lood**? (ah-**pahr**-tay dayl say-**goo**-roh day sah-**lood** breen-**dah**-doh pohr oon aym-play-ah-**dohr**)*
health insurance? (other than insurance provided by an employer)	el seguro de salud? (aparte del seguro de salud brindado por un empleador)[2]
	*ayl say-**goo**-roh day **ah**^oo-toh?*
automobile insurance?	el seguro de auto?[2]
	*lohs eem-**poo**^**ays**-tohs day proh-pee^ay-**dahd**? (see noh say een-**kloo**-yay ayn soo ee-poh-**tay**-kah)*
property taxes? (if not included in the mortgage)	los impuestos de propiedad? (si no se incluyen en su hipoteca)[2]

	*ah-say **pah**-gohs day **oo**-noh oh mahs bay-**ee**-koo-lohs?*
11. Are you making payments on one or more vehicles?	¿Hace pagos de uno o más vehículos?
	*ayn **koo**^**ahn**-tohs bay-**ee**-koo-lohs dee-fay-**rayn**-tays **ah**-say **pah**-gohs?*
On how many vehicles are you paying?	¿En cuántos vehículos diferentes hace pagos?[2]
	*koo^ahl ays ayl **pah**-goh (mayn-**soo**^ahl) dayl ... bay-**ee**-koo-loh?*
What is the (monthly) payment of the ... vehicle?	¿Cuál es el pago (mensual) del ... vehículo?[2]
	*pree-**mayr***
first	primer
	*say-**goon**-doh*
second	segundo
	*tayr-**sayr***
third	tercer
	***koo**^**ahr**-toh*
fourth	cuarto
	***keen**-toh*
fifth	quinto

12. Are you paying ...

pah-gah ...
¿Paga ...

child support? (not including child support that is deducted from your income)

*mah-noo-tayn-**see^ohn** day **ee**-hohs? (**ays**-toh noh een-**kloo**-yay mah-noo-tayn-**see^ohn** day **ee**-hohs kay day-**doo**-sayn day soos een-**gray**-sohs)*
manutención de hijos? (esto no incluye manutención de hijos que deducen de sus ingresos)

How much do you pay (each month)?

*koo^**ahn**-toh **pah**-gah (ahl mays)?*
¿Cuánto paga (al mes)?[2]

alimony? (not including alimony that is deducted from your income)

*payn-**see^ohn** ah-lee-mayn-**tee**-see^ah? (**ays**-toh noh een-**kloo**-yay pahn-**see^ohn** ah-lee-mayn-**tee**-see^ah kay day-**doo**-sayn day soo een-**gray**-sohs)*
pensión alimenticia? (esto no incluye pensión alimenticia que deducen de sus ingresos)

How much do you pay (each month)?

*koo^**ahn**-toh **pah**-gah (ahl mays)?*
¿Cuánto paga (al mes)?[2]

child care? (including day care, babysitting, before and after school care)

*koo^ee-**dah**-doh day lohs **ee**-hohs? (een-**kloo^ee**-dohs lah goo^ahr-day-**ree**-ah, lah bee-hee-**lahn**-see^ah day **neen**-yohs, ayl koo^ee-**dah**-doh day **neen**-yohs **ahn**-tays ee days-**poo^ays** day lah ays-**koo^ay**-lah)*
cuidado de los hijos? (incluidos la guardería, la vigilancia de niños, el cuidado de niños antes y después de la escuela)

How much do you pay (each month)?

*koo^**ahn**-toh **pah**-gah (ahl mays)?*
¿Cuánto paga (al mes)?[2]

13. Do you have any additional (monthly) expenses?

*tee^**ay**-nay **oh**-trohs **gahs**-tohs (mayn-**soo^ah**-lays) ah-dee-see^oh-**nah**-lays?*
¿Tiene otros gastos (mensuales) adicionales?

Approximately how much are your total additional (monthly) expenses?

*ah-prohk-see-mah-dah-**mayn**-tay, koo^**ahn**-tohs sohn soos **gahs**-tohs (mayn-**soo^ah**-lays) ah-dee-see^oh-**nah**-lays ayn toh-**tahl**?*
Aproximadamente, ¿cuántos son sus gastos (mensuales) adicionales en total?[2]

14. Is you spouse filing for bankruptcy as well?

*ays kay soo **kohn**-yoo-hay say ays-**tah** day-klah-**rahn**-doh ayn bahn-kah-**rroh**-tah tahm-**bee^ayn**?*
¿Es que su cónyuge se está declarando en bancarrota también?

How much is your spouse's monthly payments to creditors?

*koo^**ahn**-tohs sohn lohs **pah**-gohs mayn-**soo^ah**-lays day soo **kohn**-yoo-hay ah soos ah-kray-ay-**doh**-rays?*
¿Cuántos son los pagos mensuales de su cónyuge a sus acreedores?[2]

How much is your spouse's monthly income?

*koo^**ahn**-toh ays ayl een-**gray**-soh mayn-**soo^ahl** day soo **kohn**-yoo-hay?*
¿Cuánto es el ingreso mensual de su cónyuge?[2]

15. Do you support any additional dependents not living in your home?	*mahn-**tee^ay**-nay ah koo^ah-lays-**kee^ayr oh**-trahs payr-**soh**-nahs day-payn-**dee^ayn**-tays kay no **bee**-bayn ayn soo oh-**gahr**?* ¿Mantiene a cualesquier otras personas dependientes que no viven en su hogar?
16. How much are the regular (business) expenses (for one month) in order to ...	***koo^ahn**-tohs sohn lohs **gahs**-tohs (koh-mayr-**see^ah**-lays) nohr-**mah**-lays (pohr oon mays) **pah**-rah ...* ¿Cuántos son los gastos (comerciales) normales (por un mes) para ...
operate your business?	*mah-nay-**hahr** soo nay-**goh**-see^oh?* manejar su negocio?[2]
your profession?	*soo **klah**-say day trah-**bah**-hoh?* su clase de trabajo?[2]
operate your farm?	*mah-nay-**hahr** soo **feen**-kah?* manejar su finca?[2]

VI. Real Property and Mortgages

***bee^ay**-nays rah-**ee**-says ay ee-poh-**tay**-kahs*
Bienes raíces e hipotecas

English	**Pronunciation & Spanish**
1. Do you own your homestead real property?	*ays ayl/lah proh-pee^ay-**tah**-ree^oh/ah day lah proh-pee^ay-**dahd dohn**-day ays-**tah** see-**too^ah**-dah soo **kah**-sah?* ¿Es el/la propietario/a de la propiedad dónde está situada su casa?[10]
2. What is the date of purchase or the date you acquired your homestead?	*koo^ahl ays lah **fay**-chah day lah **kohm**-prah day **ays**-tah proh-pee^ay-**dahd** kohn **kah**-sah ee **tee^ay**-rrahs oh lah **fay**-chah ayn lah kay lah ahd-kee-**ree^oh**?* ¿Cuál es la fecha de la compra de esta propiedad con casa y tierras o la fecha en la cual la adquirió?[3]
What was the purchase price?	*koo^ahl foo^ay ayl **pray**-see^oh day **kohm**-prah?* ¿Cuál fue el precio de compra?[2]
What is the present value?	*koo^ahl ays ayl bah-**lohr** ahk-**too^ahl**?* ¿Cuál es el valor actual?[2]
3. How much do you owe to pay off your first mortgage?	***koo^ahn**-toh **day**-bay **pah**-rah rray-dee-**meer** soo pree-**may**-rah ee-poh-**tay**-kah?* ¿Cuánto debe para redimir su primera hipoteca?[2]
What are the monthly payments?	*koo^ah-lays sohn lohs **pah**-gohs mayn-**soo^ah**-lays?* ¿Cuáles son los pagos mensuales?[2]
4. Do you have a ... mortgage?	***tee^ay**-nay **oo**-nah ... ee-poh-**tay**-kah?* ¿Tiene una ... hipoteca?
second	*say-**goon**-dah* segunda

third	*tayr-**say**-rah* tercera
How much do you owe to pay off your … mortgage?	***koo^ahn**-toh **day**-bay **pah**-rah rray-dee-**meer** soo … ee-poh-**tay**-kah?* ¿Cuánto debe para remidir su … hipoteca?
second	*say-**goon**-dah* segunda[2]
third	*tayr-**say**-rah* tercera[2]
What are the monthly payments on your … mortgage?	***koo^ah**-lays sohn lohs **pah**-gohs mayn-**soo^ah**-lays day soo … ee-poh-**tay**-kah?* ¿Cuáles son los pagos mensuales de su … hipoteca?
second	*say-**goon**-dah* segunda[2]
third	*tayr-**say**-rah* tercera[2]

5. Are you current on your …	*ays-**tah** ahl **dee**-ah kohn lohs **pah**-gohs day soo …* ¿Está al día con los pagos de su …
mortgage?	*ee-poh-**tay**-kah?* hipoteca?
second mortgage?	*say-**goon**-dah ee-poh-**tay**-kah?* segunda hipoteca?
third mortgage?	*tayr-**say**-rah ee-poh-**tay**-kah?* tercera hipoteca?

6. How many months behind are you on your …	*pohr **koo^ahn**-tohs **may**-says ays-**tah** ah-trah-**sah**-doh/dah kohn lohs **pah**-gohs day soo …* ¿Por cuántos meses está atrasado/a con los pagos de su … [2, 4]
mortgage?	*ee-poh-**tay**-kah?* hipoteca?
second mortgage?	*say-**goon**-dah ee-poh-**tay**-kah?* segunda hipoteca?
third mortgage?	*tayr-**say**-rah ee-poh-**tay**-kah?* tercera hipoteca?

7. Do you own any other real property other than your homestead including any timeshare property?	*ays proh-pee^ay-**tah**-ree-oh/ah day **oh**-trohs **bee^ay**-nays ray-**ee**-says ah-**pahr**-tay day soo proh-pee^ay-**dahd** kohn **kah**-sah ee **tee^ay**-rrahs een-**kloo^ee**-dah koo^ahl-**kee^ayr** mool-tee-proh-pee^ay-**dahd**?* ¿Es propietario/a de otros bienes raíces aparte de su propiedad con casa y tierras incluida cualquier multipropiedad?[4]

	*may **poo^ay**-day ay-noo-may-**rahr** **ay**-sah een-fohr-mah-**see^ohn** ah-**kee**, pohr fah-**bohr**?*
Can you list that information here for me, please?	¿Me puede enumerar esa información aquí, por favor?

	*ah bayn-**dee**-doh oh trahs-fay-**ree**-doh proh-pee^ay-**dahd** payr-soh-**nahl** o rray-**ahl** doo-**rahn**-tay lohs **ool**-tee-mohs **koo^ah**-troh ahn-yohs?*
8. Have you sold or transferred any personal or real property in the past four years?	¿Ha vendido o trasferido propiedad personal o real durante los últimos cuatro años?

	*fah-**bohr** day ay-noo-may-**rahr** ah-**kee** loh kay say bayn-**dee^oh** ee lah **fay**-chah day **bayn**-tah / trahs-fay-**rayn**-see^ah ahl **lah**-doh day **kah**-dah ah-noh-tah-**see^ohn**.*
Please list here what was sold and provide the date of sale / transfer beside each line item.	Favor de enumerar aquí lo que se vendió y la fecha de venta / trasferencia al lado de cada anotación.

	*rray-see-**bee^oh** gah-**nahn**-see^ahs?*
9. Did you receive any proceeds (cash back)?	¿Recibió ganancias?

	*koo^ahl foo^ay ayl **mohn**-toh day lahs gah-**nahn**-see^ahs?*
What was the amount of the proceeds?	¿Cuál fue el monto de las ganancias?[2]

	*... lahs gah-**nahn**-see^ahs?*
Did you ... the proceeds?	... las ganancias?

	*gahs-**toh***
spend	¿Gastó

	*ah-oh-**rroh***
save	¿Ahorró

	*een-beer-**tee^oh***
invest	¿Invirtió

	*rray-gah-**loh***
give away	¿Regaló

	*doh-**noh***
donate	¿Donó

	*ah rray-fee-nahn-**see^ah**-doh oo-nah ee-poh-**tay**-kah ayn koo^ahl-**kee^ayr** moh-**mayn**-toh doo-**rahn**-tay lohs **ool**-tee-mohs dohs **ahn**-yohs?*
10. Have you refinanced a mortgage at any time during the previous two years?	¿Ha refinanciado una hipoteca en cualquier momento durante los últimos dos años?

	*koo^ahl foo^ay lah **fay**-chah day **see^ay**-rray?*
What was the closing date?	¿Cuál fue la fecha de cierre?[3]

	*rray-see-**bee^oh** gah-**nahn**-see^ahs ahl fohr-mah-lee-**sahr** ayl **see^ay**-rray?*
Did you receive any proceeds (cash back) from the closing?	¿Recibió ganancias al formalizar el cierre?

	*koo^ahl foo^ay ayl **mohn**-toh day lahs gah-**nahn**-see^ahs?*
What was the amount of the proceeds?	¿Cuál fue el monto de las ganancias?[2]

	*... lahs gah-**nahn**-see^ahs?*
Did you ... the proceeds?	... las ganancias?

spend	*gahs-**toh*** ¿Gastó
save	*ah-oh-**rroh*** ¿Ahorró
invest	*een-beer-**tee^oh*** ¿Invirtió
give away	*rray-gah-**loh*** ¿Regaló
donate	*doh-**noh*** ¿Donó

VII. Unsecured and Priority Debts

day^oo**-dahs noh ah-say-goo-**rah**-dahs ee day pree-oh-ree-**dahd
Deudas no aseguradas y de prioridad

English	Pronunciation & Spanish
1. What is your total credit card debt?	*koo^ahl ays ayl **mohn**-toh toh-**tahl** pah-rah soos **day^oo**-dahs day tahr-**hay**-tah day **kray**-dee-toh?* ¿Cuál es el monto total para sus deudas de tarjeta de crédito?[2]
2. How many credit cards total do you have?	***koo^ahn**-tahs tahr-**hay**-tahs day **kray**-dee-toh **tee^ay**-nay ayn toh-**tahl**?* ¿Cuántas tarjetas de crédito tiene en total?[2]
3. Have you used any of your credit cards within the last 90 days?	*ah oo-**sah**-doh **oo**-nah day soos tahr-**hay**-tahs day **kray**-dee-toh doo-**rahn**-tay lohs **ool**-tee-mohs noh-**bayn**-tah dee-ahs?* ¿Ha usado una de sus tarjetas de crédito durante los últimos noventa días?
Which one(s) have you used?	***koo^ah**-lay(s) ah oo-**sah**-doh?* ¿Cuál(es) ha usado?[1]
4. Do you have any medical bills?	***tee^ay**-nay **koo^ayn**-tahs **may**-dee-kahs?* ¿Tiene cuentas médicas?
Approximately how much do you owe in medical bills?	*ah-prohk-see-mah-dah-**mayn**-tay, koo^ahl ays ayl **mohn**-toh toh-**tahl** day lahs **koo^ayn**-tahs **may**-dee-kahs kay **day**-bah?* Aproximadamente, ¿cuál es el monto total de las cuentas médicas que debe?[2]
5. Do you have any other unsecured debts?	***tee^ay**-nay **oh**-trahs **day^oo**-dahs noh ah-say-goo-**rah**-dahs?* ¿Tiene otras deudas no aseguradas?
Approximately how much do you owe in unsecured debts?	*ah-prohk-see-mah-dah-**mayn**-tay, koo^ahl ays ayl **mohn**-toh toh-**tahl** day **ay**-sahs **day^oo**-dahs noh ah-say-goo-**rah**-dahs kay **day**-bay?* Aproximadamente, ¿cuál es el monto total de esas deudas no aseguradas que debe?[2]
6. Do you owe any taxes?	***day**-bay eem-**poo^ays**-tohs?* ¿Debe impuestos?

Are they state or federal taxes?	*sohn eem-**poo^ays**-tohs ays-tah-**tah**-lays oh fay-day-**rah**-lays?* ¿Son impuestos estatales o federales?
For what year(s)?	***pah**-rah kay **ahn**-yoh(s)?* ¿Para qué año(s)?[2]
For what property (properties)?	***pah**-rah kay proh-pee^ay-**dahd** (proh-pee^ay-**dah**-days)?* ¿Para qué propiedad(es)?[1]

VIII. Financial Accounts and Personal Property

*koo^ayn-tahs fee-nahn-**see^ah**-rahs ee proh-pee^ay-**dahd** payr-soh-**nahl***
Cuentas financieras y propiedad personal

English	Pronunciation & Spanish
1. How much cash do you have on hand?	*koo^ahn-toh dee-**nay**-roh ayn ay-fayk-**tee**-boh **tee^ay**-nay ayn soo payr-**soh**-nah ah-**oh**-rah?* ¿Cuánto dinero en efectivo tiene en su persona ahora?[2]
2. Do you have …	*tee^ay-nay …* ¿Tiene …
a bank account?	*oo-nah **koo^ayn**-tah bahn-**kah**-ree^ah?* una cuenta bancaria?
credit union account?	*oo-nah **koo^ayn**-tah kohn oo-nah koh-oh-pay-rah-**tee**-bah day **kray**-dee-toh?* una cuenta con una cooperativa de crédito?
3. How many (financial) accounts do you have?	*koo^ahn-tahs koo^ayn-tahs (fee-nahn-**see^ay**-rahs) **tee^ay**-nay ayn toh-**tahl**?* ¿Cuántas cuentas (financieras) tiene en total?[2]
4. Where do you have these accounts?	*kohn kay ayn-tee-**dah**-days (fee-nahn-**see^ay**-rahs) **tee^ay**-nay **ays**-tahs **koo^ayn**-tahs?* ¿Con qué entidades (financieras) tiene estas cuentas?[1]
Can you list the names of the bank(s) and credit union(s) here?	*may **poo^ay**-day ay-noo-may-**rahr** ah-**kee** ayl **nohm**-bray day **kah**-dah **bahn**-koh ee koh-oh-pay-rah-**tee**-bah day **kray**-dee-toh, pohr fah-**bohr**?* ¿Me puede enumerar aquí el nombre de cada banco y cooperativa de crédito, por favor?
What is the approximate balance for each of these accounts?	*koo^ahl ays ayl **sahl**-doh ah-prohk-see-**mah**-doh **pah**-rah **kah**-dah oo-nah day **ays**-tahs **koo^ayn**-tahs?* ¿Cuál es el saldo aproximado para cada una de estas cuentas?[2]
5. Is the name of any other person on these accounts?	*ays kay ayl **nohm**-bray day **oh**-trah payr-**soh**-nah ah-pah-**ray**-say ayn **ays**-tahs **koo^ayn**-tahs?* ¿Es que el nombre de otra persona aparece en estas cuentas?

What is the name that appears?	*kooo^ahl ays ayl **nohm**-bray kay ah-pah-**ray**-say?* ¿Cuál es el nombre que aparece?[1]
What are the names that appear?	*koo^ah-lays sohn lohs **nohm**-brays kay ah-pah-**ray**-sayn?* ¿Cuáles son los nombres que aparecen?[1]
What is your relationship with each person?	*koo^ahl ays soo pah-rayn-**tays**-koh kohn **kah**-dah payr-**soh**-nah?* ¿Cuál es su parentesco con cada persona?[1]
friend?	*ah-**mee**-goh/gah?* amigo/a?[1]
business partner?	***soh**-see^oh/ah?* socio/a?[1]
brother?	*ayr-**mah**-noh?* hermano?
sister?	*ayr-**mah**-nah?* hermana?
uncle?	***tee**-oh?* tío?
aunt?	***tee**-ah?* tía?
mother?	***mah**-dray?* madre?
father?	***pah**-dray?* padre?
boyfriend?	***noh**-bee^oh?* novio?
girlfriend?	***noh**-bee^ah?* novia?
cousin?	***pree**-moh/mah?* primo/prima?[1]
other (relative)?	***oh**-troh (pah-rayn-**tays**-koh fah-mee-**lee^ahr**)?* otro (parentesco familiar)?
6. Do you have outstanding security deposits with any person or business?	*tee^**ay**-nay ahl-**goo**-nohs day-**poh**-see-tohs day say-goo-ree-**dahd** payn-**dee^ayn**-tays kohn ahl-**goo**-nah payr-**soh**-nah oh nay-**goh**-see^oh?* ¿Tiene algunos depósitos de seguridad pendientes con alguna persona o negocio?
Can you list the names of the person or business here please?	*may **poo^ay**-day ay-noo-may-**rahr** ah-**kee** ayl **nohm**-bray day lah payr-**soh**-nah o ayl nay-**goh**-see^oh, pohr fah-**bohr**?* ¿Me puede enumerar aquí el nombre de la persona o el negocio, por favor?

7. Please make a list of your household items and furniture and write an approximate value beside each entry.

*pohr fah-**bohr**, **ah**-gah **oo**-nah **lees**-tah day soos ahr-**tee**-koo-lohs day **kah**-sah ee **moo^ay**-blays ee **loo^ay**-goh, ays-**kree**-bah ayl bah-**lohr** ah-prohk-see-**mah**-doh ahl **lah**-doh day **kah**-dah ah-noh-tah-**see^ohn**.*

Por favor, haga una lista de sus artículos de casa y muebles y luego, escriba el valor aproximado al lado de cada anotación.

8. Does any creditor have a security interest in any furniture that you own?

*tee^**ay**-nay ahl-**goon** ah-kray-ay-**dohr** oon day-**rah**-choh day gah-rahn-**tee**-ah rray-**ahl** ayn ahl-**goo**-nohs day lohs **moo^ay**-blays kay poh-**say**-ay?*

¿Tiene algún acreedor un derecho de garantía real en algunos de los muebles que posee?

Please write the name of the creditor here and the amount required to pay off the debt.

*pohr fah-**bohr**, ays-**kree**-bah ah-**kee** ayl **nohm**-bray dayl ah-kray-ay-**dohr** ee ayl **mohn**-toh nay-say-**sah**-ree^oh **pah**-rah rray-dee-**meer** lah **day**^oo-dah.*

Por favor, escriba aquí el nombre del acreedor y el monto necesario para redimir la deuda.

9. Do you have the right to sue anyone?

*tee^**ay**-nah ayl day-**ray**-choh day day-mahn-**dahr** ah ahl-**ghee^ayn**?*

¿Tiene el derecho de demandar a alguien?

Please write the reason why here.

*pohr fah-**bohr**, ays-**kree**-bah ayl pohr-**kay** ah-**kee**.*

Por favor, escriba el porqué aquí.

10. Did you receive a (monetary) settlement in the past year?

*rray-see-**bee^oh** oon ah-**koo^ayr**-doh (moh-nay-**tah**-ree^oh) doo-**rahn**-tay ayl **ool**-tee-moh **ahn**-yoh?*

¿Recibió un acuerdo (monetario) durante el último año?

How much was the settlement?

*koo^**ahn**-toh foo^ay ayl ah-**koo^ayr**-doh?*

¿Cuánto fue el acuerdo?[2]

Will you write down what you did with the proceeds here?

*may ays-**kree**-bay ah-**kee** loh kay ee-soh kohn lahs gah-**nahn**-see^ahs?*

¿Me escribe aquí lo que hizo con las ganancias?

11. Please make a list of any artwork, collectibles and books that you own and write the approximate value of each one beside each line item.

*pohr fah-**ohr**, **ah**-gah **oo**-nah **lees**-tah day koo^ah-lays-**kee^ayr** oh-brahs day **ahr**-tay, ohb-**hay**-tohs koh-layk-see^oh-**nah**-blays ee **lee**-brohs kay lay payr-tay-**nay**-sayn ee ays-**kree**-bah ayl bah-**lohr** ah-prohk-see-**mah**-doh ahl **lah**-doh day **kah**-day ah-noh-tah-**see^ohn**.*

Por favor, haga una lista de cualesquier obras de arte, objetos coleccionables y libros que le pertenecen y escriba el valor aproximado al lado de cada anotación.

12. Please write the value of all of your wearing apparel here.

*pohr fah-**bohr**, ays-**kree**-bah ah-**kee** ayl bah-**lohr** day **toh**-dah la **roh**-pah kay lay payr-tay-**nay**-say.*

Por favor, escriba aquí el valor de toda la ropa que le pertenece.

13. Please list any jewelry and furs that you own and write the approximate value beside each item.

*pohr fah-**bohr**, ay-noo-**may**-ray ah-**kee** koo^ah-lays-**kee^ayr** hoh^ee-yahs ee ah-**bree**-gohs ooh **prayn**-dahs day pee^ayl kay lay payr-tay-**nay**-sayn ee ays-**kree**-bah ahl **lah**-doh day **kah**-dah ah-noh-tah-**see^ohn** ayl bah-**lohr** ah-prohk-see-**mah**-doh.*

Por favor, enumere aquí cualesquier joyas y abrigos o prendas de piel que le pertenecen y escriba al lado de cada anotación el valor aproximado.

14. Does any creditor have a security interest in any jewelry or furs that you own or have purchased?

tee^ay-nay ahl-goon ah-kray-ay-dohr oon day-ray-choh day gah-rahn-tee-ah ayn ahl-goo-nahs day lahs hoh^ee-yahs oh ah-bree-gohs oh prayn-dahs day pee^ayl kay lay payr-tay-nay-sayn oh ah kohm-prah-doh?

¿Tiene algún acreedor un derecho de garantía real en algunas joyas o abrigos o prendas de piel que le pertenecen o que ha comprado?

Please write the amount required to payoff the debt here.

pohr fah-bohr, ays-kree-bah ah-kee ayl mohn-toh nay-say-sah-ree^oh pah-rah rray-dee-meer lah day^oo-dah.

Por favor, escriba aquí el monto necesario para redimir la deuda.

15. Please make a list here of any firearms, sports and other hobby equipment you own.

pohr fah-bohr, ay-noo-may-ray ah-kee toh-dahs lahs ahr-mahs day foo^ay-goh, ay-kee-poh day-pohr-tee-boh ee oh-troh ay-kee-poh pah-rah ahk-tee-bee-dah-days day oh-see^oh kay lay payr-tay-nay-sayn.

Por favor, enumere aquí todas las armas de fuego, equipo deportivo y otro equipo para actividades de ocio que le pertenecen.

16. Do you have any financial interest in insurance policies?

tee^ay-nay ahl-goo-nah pahr-tee-see-pah-see^ohn fee-nahn-see^ay-rah ayn poh-lee-sahs day say-goo-roh?

¿Tiene alguna participación financiera en pólizas de seguro?

Please list the name of each insurance company and the face value of each policy beside each line item here.

pohr-fah-bohr, ays-kree-bah ah-kee ayl nohm-bray day kah-dah kohm-pahn-yee-ah day say-goo-rohs ee ayl bah-lohr fah-see^ahl day kah-dah poh-lee-sah ahl lah-doh day lah ah-noh-tah-see^ohn rrays-payk-tee-bah.

Por favor, escriba aquí el nombre de cada compañía de seguros y el valor facial de cada póliza al lado de la anotación respectiva.

17. Do you have any annuities?

tee^ay-nay ah-noo^ah-lee-dah-days?

¿Tiene anualidades?

18. Do you have any interest in an IRA, ERISA and KEOGH PLANS or the like?

tee^ay-nay ahl-goo-nah pahr-tee-see-pah-see^ohn fee-nahn-see^ay-rah ayn oon ee ay-ray ah, lohs plah-nays ay-ree-sah y kee-ohg oo oh-trohs pohr ayl ays-tee-loh?

¿Tiene alguna participación financiera en un IRA, los planes ERISA y KEOGH u otros por el estilo?

19. Do you have stock interests in incorporated and/or unincorporated businesses?

tee^ay-nay ahl-goo-nah pahr-tee-see-pah-see^ohn fee-nahn-see^ay-rah oh tay-nayn-see-ah ayn nay-goh-see^ohs een-kohr-poh-rah-dohs ee/oh noh een-kohr-poh-rah-dohs?

¿Tiene alguna participación financiera o tenencia en negocios incorporados y/o no incorporados?[12]

20. Have you owned a business or partnership in the last six years?

ah see-doh proh-pee^ay-tah-ree^oh/ah day oon nay-goh-see^oh soh-see^oh/ah day oo-nah soh-see^ay-dahd doo-rahn-tay lohs ool-tee-mohs say^ees ahn-yohs?

¿Ha sido propietario/a de un negocio o socio/a de una sociedad durante los últimos seis años?[11]

21. Do you have any interest in partnerships or joint ventures?

tee^ay-nay ahl-goo-nah pahr-tee-see-pah-see^ohn ayn soh-see^ay-dah-days oh aym-pray-sahs kohn-hoon-tahs?

¿Tiene alguna participación en sociedades o empresas conjuntas?

22. Do you have any goverment, corporate, negotiable and/or non-negotiable instruments?

*tee^ay-nay ahl-**goo**-nah pahr-tee-see-pah-**see^ohn** ayn **tee**-too-lohs goo-bayr-nah-mayn-**tah**-lays, nay-goh-**see^ah**-blays ee/oh noh nay-goh-**see^ah**-blays?*
¿Tiene alguna participación en títulos gubernamentales, empresariales, negociables y/o no negociables?

23. Does anyone owe you money or payment of any type?

*ays kay ahl-**ghee^ayn**-lay **day**-bay dee-**nay**-roh oh **pah**-gohs day koo^ahl-**kee^ayr klah**-say?*
¿Es que alguien le debe dinero o pagos de cualquier clase?

24. Are you entitled to receive alimony, maintenance and/or support payments?

*tee^ay-nay day-**ray**-choh day rray-see-**beer** oo-nah payn-**see^ohn** ah-lee-mayn-**tee**-**see^ah** ee/oh **pah**-gohs day mah-noo-tayn-**see^ohn**?*
¿Tiene derecho de recibir una pensión alimenticia y/o pagos de manutención?

25. Are you owed any liquidated debts?

*say lay **day**-bay ahl-**goo**-nahs **day^oo**-dahs lee-kee-**dah**-dahs?*
¿Se le debe algunas deudas liquidadas?

26. Do you have ...

*tee^**ay**-nay ...*
¿Tiene ...

    any equitable estates?

*proh-pee^ay-**dah**-days pohr day-**ray**-choh day ay-kee-**dahd**?*
propiedades por derecho de equidad?

    any future estates?

*day-**ray**-choh ah **bee^ay**-nays een-**moo^ay**-blays ayn ayl foo-**too**-roh?*
derecho a bienes inmuebles en el futuro?

    life estates?

*proh-pee^ay-**dah**-days bee-tah-**lee**-see^ahs?*
propiedades vitalicias?

27. Are you a contingent and/or noncontingent beneficiary for the estate of a decedent?

*ays bay-nay-fee-**see^ah**-ree^oh/ah kohn-teen-**hayn**-tay oh noh kohn-teen-**hayn**-tay day lah proh-pee^ay-**dahd** day oon dee-**foon**-toh?*
¿Es beneficiario/a contingente o no contingente de la propiedad de un difunto?[4]

28. Do you have any contingent and/or unliquidated claims of any nature pending?

*tee^**ay**-nay ahl-**goo**-nahs rray-klah-mah-**see^oh**-nays kohn-teen-**hayn**-tays ee/oh noh sahl-**dah**-dahs day koo^ahl-**kee^ayr klah**-say ah-**oon** payn-**dee^ayn**-tays?*
¿Tiene algunas reclamaciones contingentes y/o no saldadas de cualquier clase aún pendientes?

29. Do you have any rights to ...

*tee^**ay**-nay day-**ray**-chohs ah ...*
¿Tiene derechos a ...

    patents?

*pah-**tayn**-tays?*
patentes?

    copyrights?

*day-**ray**-chohs rray-sayr-**bah**-dohs?*
derechos reservados?

    other intellectual property?

*oh-trahs proh-pee^ay-**dah**-days een-tay-layk-**too^ah**-lays?*
otras propiedades intelectuales?

30. Do you have any ...

*tee^**ay**-nay ...*
¿Tiene ...

oh-trahs lee-**sayn**-see^ahs?
other licenses?
otras licencias?

oh-trahs frahn-**kee**-see^ahs?
other franchises?
otras franquicias?

oh-trohs **bee^ay**-nays een-tahn-**hee**-blays?
other general intangibles?
otros bienes intangibles?

*pohr fah-**bohr**, ay-noo-**may**-ray toh-dohs lohs bay-**ee**-koo-lohs kay lay*
*payr-tay-**nay**-sayn ee proh-pohr-**see^oh**-nay lah een-fohr-mah-**see^ohn***
*pay-**dee**-dah:*
31. Please list any vehicles that you own
    and provide the requested information:
Por favor, enumere todos los vehículos que le
pertenecen y proporcione la información pedida:[11]

*bay-**ee**-koo-loh **oo**-noh:*
Vehicle 1:
vehículo 1:

***ahn**-yoh:*
year:
año:

***mahr**-kah:*
make:
marca:

*moh-**day**-loh:*
model:
modelo:

*dees-**tahn**-see^ah rray-koh-**rree**-dah ayn **mee**-yahs:*
mileage:
distancia recorrida en millas:

*ah^oo-toh-**mah**-tee-koh oh mah-**noo^ahl**:*
automatic/manual:
automático o manual:

*kohn-dee-**see^ohn**:*
condition:
condición:

*een-boh-loo-**krah**-doh ayn ahk-see-**dayn**-tays:*
involved in any accidents:
involucrado en accidentes:

*bah-**lohr** ah-prohk-see-**mah**-doh:*
approximate value:
valor aproximado:

***nohm**-bray ayn ayl **tee**-too-loh dayl bay-**ee**-koo-loh:*
name on vehicle's title:
nombre en el título del vehículo:

***pah**-goh mayn-**soo^ahl**:*
monthly payment:
pago mensual:

***noo**-may-roh day mayn-soo^ah-lee-**dah**-days payn-**dee^ayn**-tays:*
# of months left:
de mensualidades pendientes:

***mohn**-toh ahk-**too^ahl** dayl **prays**-tah-moh:*
current loan amount:
monto actual del préstamo:

*bay-**ee**-koo-loh dohs:*
Vehicle 2:
vehículo 2:

*bay-**ee**-koo-loh trays:*
Vehicle 3:
vehículo 3:

32. List any ... that you own here please.

*pohr fah-**bohr**, ay-noo-**may**-ray ah-**kee** koo^ah-lays-**kee**^ayr ... kay lay payr-tay-**nay**-sayn.*

Por favor, enumere cualesquier ... que le pertenecen aquí.

boats

__bahr__-kahs

barcas

watercrafts

__moh__-tohs ah-__koo^ah__-tee-kahs

motos acuáticas

33. Does any creditor have a security interest in ...

*tee^kray-nay ahl-**goon** ah-kray-ay-**dohr** day-**ray**-choh day gah-rahn-**tee**-ah rray-**ahl** ayn ...*

¿Tiene algún acreedor derecho de garantía real en ...

the boat(s)

lah(s) __bahr__-kah(s)

la(s) barca(s)

the watercraft(s)

lah(s) __moh__-toh(s) ah-__koo^ah__-tee-koh(s)

la(s) moto(s) acuática(s)

Please write the amount required to pay off each loan here.

*fah-**bohr** day ays-kree-**beer** ah-**kee** ayl **mohn**-toh nay-say-**sah**-ree-^oh **pah**-rah rray-dee-**meer** kah-dah **prays**-tah-moh.*

Favor de escribir aquí el monto necesario para redimir cada préstamo.

34. Please list any aircraft that you own.

*pohr fah-**bohr**, ay-noo-**may**-ray koo^ahl-**kee**^ayr ah-ay-roh-**nah**-bay kay lay payr-tay-**nay**-say.*

Por favor, enumere cualquier aeronave que le pertenece.

Does any creditor have a security interest in the aircraft?

*tee^**ay**-nay ahl-**goon** ah-kray-ay-**dohr** day-**ray**-choh day gah-rahn-**tee**-ah rray-**ahl** ayn lah ah-ay-roh-**nah**-bay?*

¿Tiene algún acreedor derecho de garantía real en la aeronave?

Please write the amount required to pay off the loan here.

*fah-**bohr** day ays-kree-**beer** ah-**kee** ayl **mohn**-toh nay-say-**sah**-ree^oh **pah**-rah rray-dee-**meer** ayl **prays**-tah-moh.*

Favor de escribir aquí el monto necesario para redimir el préstamo.

35. Please list your ... here and write the approximate value beside each line entry.

*pohr fah-**bohr**, ay-noo-**may**-ray ah-**kee** soos ... ee ays-**kree**-bah ayl bah-**lohr** ah-prohk-see-**mah**-doh ahl **lah**-doh day **kah**-dah ah-noh-tah-**see**^ohn.*

Por favor, enumere aquí sus ... y escriba el valor aproximado al lado de cada anotación.

office equipment

*__mah__-kee-nahs day oh-fee-**see**-nah*

máquinas de oficina

(office) furnishings

*moo^**ay**-blays (day oh-fee-**see**-nah)*

muebles (de oficina)

(office) supplies

*mah-tay-**ree**^ah-lays (day oh-fee-**see**-nah)*

materiales (de oficina)

36. Please list any machinery, fixtures, equipment and other business supplies here. Then write the approximate value beside each one.

*pohr fah-**bohr**, ay-noo-**may**-ray ah-**kee** koo^ah-lays-**kee^ayr** mah-kee-**nah**-ree^ah, een-stah-lah-**see^oh**-nays **fee**-hahs, een-stroo-mayn-**tah**-lays ee **oh**-trohs mah-tay-**ree^ah**-lays day oh-fee-**see**-nah ah-dee-see^oh-**nah**-lays. **loo^ay**-goh, ays-**kree**-bah ayl bah-**lohr** ah-prohk-see-**mah**-doh ahl **lah**-doh day **kah**-dah ah-noh-tah-**see^ohn**.*

Por favor, enumere aquí cualesquier maquinaria, instalaciones fijas, instrumentales y materiales de oficina adicionales. Luego, escriba el valor aproximado al lado de cada anotación.

37. Please list any ... here and write the approximate value beside each item.

*pohr fah-**bohr**, ay-noo-**may**-ray ah-**kee** koo^ah-lays-**kee^ayr** ... ee ays-**kree**-bah ayl bah-**lohr** ah-prohk-see-**mah**-doh ahl **lah**-doh day **kah**-dah ah-noh-tah-**see^ohn**.*

Por favor, enumere aquí cualesquier ... y escriba el valor aproximado al lado de cada anotación.

inventory

*ayk-sees-**tayn**-see^ahs*

existencias

(farm) animals

*ah-nee-**mah**-lays (day **grahn**-hah)*

animales (de granja)

crops—growing or harvested

*koh-**say**-chahs—kray-**see^ayn**-tays oh koh-say-**chah**-dahs*

cosechas—crecientes o cosechadas

farming equipment and implements

*ay-rrah-**mee^ayn**-tahs ee ay-kee-pah-**mee^ayn**-toh ah-**gree**-koh-lahs*

herramientas y equipamiento agrícolas

farm supplies

*mah-tay-**ree^ah**-lays ah-**gree**-koh-lahs*

materiales agrícolas

agricultural chemical products

*proh-**dook**-tohs **kee**-mee-kohs ah-**gree**-koh-lahs*

productos químicos agrícolas

(farm) animal feed

*ah-lee-**mayn**-toh **pah**-rah ah-nee-**mah**-lays (day **grahn**-hah)*

alimento para animales (de granja)

38. Please list any ... here and write the approximate value beside each item.

*pohr fah-**bohr**, ay-noo-**may**-ray ah-**kee** koo^ah-lays-**kee^ayr** ... ee ays-**kree**-bah ayl bah-**lohr** ah-prohk-see-**mah**-doh ahl **lah**-doh day **kah**-dah ah-noh-tah-**see^ohn**.*

Por favor, enumere aquí cualesquier ... y escriba el valor aproximado al lado de cada anotación.

electronics

*ay-layk-**troh**-nee-kah day kohn-**soo**-moh*

electrónica de consumo

computers

*kohm-poo-tah-**doh**-rahs*

computadoras

other belongings not listed above

***oh**-trahs payr-tay-**nayn**-see^ahs noh mayn-see^oh-**nah**-dahs ahn-tay-ree^ohr-**mayn**-tay*

otras pertenencias no mencionadas anteriormente

39. Does any creditor have a security interest in any ... that you own or have purchased?

*tee^**ay**-nay ahl-**goon** ah-kray-ay-**dohr** oon day-**ray**-choh day gah-rahn-**tee**-ah rray-**ahl** ayn koo^ah-lays-**kee^ayr** ... kay lay payr-tay-**nay**-sayn oh ah kohm-**prah**-doh?*

¿Tiene algún acreedor un derecho de garantía real en cualesquier ... que le pertenecen o ha comprado?

electronics	*ay-layk-**troh**-nee-kah day kohn-**soo**-moh* electrónica de consumo
computers	*kohm-poo-tah-**doh**-rahs* computadoras
other belongings not listed above	***oh**-trahs payr-tay-**nayn**-see^ahs noh mayn-see^oh-**nah**-dahs ahn-tay-ree^ohr-**mayn**-tay* otras pertenencias no mencionadas anteriormente

---

40. Have you spoken with any other attorneys about these issues?	*say ah koh-moo-nee-**kah**-doh kohn **oh**-troh ah-boh-**gah**-doh rray-fay-**rayn**-tay ah **ays**-tohs ah-**soon**-tohs?* ¿Se ha comunicado con otro abogado referente a estos asuntos?
What is full name of the attorney?	*koo^ahl ays ayl **nohm**-bray kohm-**play**-toh dayl ah-boh-**gah**-doh?* ¿Cuál es el nombre completo del abogado?¹

---

41. Please understand that until you receive correspondence from us regarding this issue that details the terms of our agreement to represent you in this matter, we are not you legal representative on this or any other issue.	*fah-**bohr** day ayn-tayn-**dayr** kay **ahs**-tah kay say rray-**see**-bah kohn-feer-mah-**see^ohn** may-**dee^ahn**-tay koh-rrays-pohn-**dayn**-see^ah day noh-**soh**-trohs kohn rrays-**payk**-toh ah **ays**-tay ah-**soon**-toh ayn lah koo^ahl say day-**tah**-yahn lohs **play**-sohs day **noo^ays**-troh ah-**koo^ayr**-doh **pah**-rah rray-pray-sayn-**tahr**-loh/lah, noh **soh**-mohs soo rray-pray-sayn-**tahn**-tay lay-**gahl pah**-ray **ays**-tay nee neen-**goon oh**-troh ah-**soon**-toh.* Favor de entender que hasta que se reciba confirmación mediante correspondencia de nosotros con respecto a este asunto en la cual se detallan los plazos de nuestro acuerdo para representarlo/la, no somos su representante legal para éste ni ningún otro asunto.

Notes

¹ Remember you can always ask that the caller spell the name, etc. by incorporating communication strategies from *Chapter 2—Collecting Basic Information in Person and by Phone* and referencing *Chapter 12—The Basics—I. The Alphabet*. Also, whenever possible during face-to-face encounters, allow the person with whom you are speaking to write down information for you.

² Reference *Chapter 12—The Basics—II. Numbers*. Also, whenever possible during face-to-face encounters, allow the person with whom you are speaking to write down as much information for you as this will greatly facilitate communication and make utilizing numbers much easier since digits are represented the same in both languages.

³ Reference *Chapter 13—Telling Time the Easy Way—II. Days of the Week and Months of the Year* for assistance with dates.

⁴ Use the -o ending when talking to or about a *male*; use the -a ending when talking to or about a *female*.

⁵ Use *el niño* when speaking of a *male child* and use *la niña* when speaking of a *female child*.

⁶ Though some states have Spanish names while others do not, using the English name will be understood as it is a proper noun which will be recognized. Therefore, there is no need to worry about the translation of the state's name.

⁷ Remember that in Spanish, the syntax (sentence structure) for *you (singular and formal)*, *he/him*, and *she/her* are grammatically identical. Therefore, to ask the same question set in the *you* and the *your spouse* forms, you only need to verbalize this shift if in the focus of your questioning once. For *Chapter 10—Bankruptcy—II. Debts*, complete questions 3-10 of this section on *Debts* first using phrase 1 "I need to ask you some questions regarding your debts." Then, repeat this series of questions using phrase 2 "I need to ask you some questions regarding your spouse's debts." It is not necessary to use the clarification phrases before EVERY question or expression once you establish the context of the conversation.

⁸ Use -lo when talking to or about a *male*; use -la when talking to or about a *female*.

⁹ Repeat the necessary questions from 17 for any additional cars that may be owned or leased.

¹⁰ Use *el propietario* when talking about a *male* and use *la propietaria* when talking about a *female*.

¹¹ Request the same detailed information provided for Vehicle 1 for ALL other vehicles as well.

¹² See *Chapter 14—Basic Legal Terminology* for the written out description of these retirement accounts in Spanish.

Practical Activities

A) From to Start to Finish: *Section I—General Information*

Instructions: All of the following activities will build upon one another since in a Bankruptcy filing, a potential client would most likely need to submit information that deals with all eight sections found in this chapter. For this activity, you will prepare a script, either by marking the necessary phrases/questions from *Section I—General Information* or writing them out on a separate sheet of paper. The SPANISH answers to the questions have been provided below and correspond to phrases/questions from *Section I*. Note that depending upon the response NOT ALL phrases/questions from this section will be needed in your script. This is noted by N/A next to the corresponding number. Where N/A is indicated, do read that question and discuss with a partner WHY it would be omitted and not asked. Learning to discern which questions are not applicable is important so as not to waste your time nor the time of your potential client. Next, practice with a partner in the form of an oral dialogue using your script and the responses provided.

1. *Me llamo Luisa Mendoza Torres.*	10. *Sí. / Tengo 3 hijos. / 3, 5, 7 / Los tres.*
2. *No, ningún otro nombre.*	11. *N/A*
3. *No, ningún nombre anterior.*	12. *N/A*
4. *El 12 de julio, 1987. / No tengo número de seguro social.*	13. *N/A*
5. *Divorciada. / En el 2009.*	14. *N/A*
6. *N/A*	15. *No.*
7. *N/A*	16. *Sí, los últimos dos años.*
8. *N/A*	17. *Sí.*
9. *N/A*	18. *No.*

B) From to Start to Finish: *Section II—Debts*

Instructions: For sections B–H of *Practical Activities* for this chapter, you will prepare various scripts. In composing this part of the script, you will select the appropriate phrases or questions from *Section II—Debts* and mark them or write them out on a separate sheet of paper. The SPANISH answers to the questions have been provided below and correspond to phrases/questions from *Section II*. Note that depending upon the response, NOT ALL phrases/questions from this section will be needed in your script. This is noted by N/A next to the corresponding phrase/question number. Where N/A is indicated, do read that question and discuss with a partner WHY it would be omitted and not asked. Next, practice with a partner in the form of an oral dialogue using your script and the responses provided. Do not forget that **Luisa** is still the potential client! *Remember too, that when writing numbers in Spanish the decimal and the comma are reversed.*

Example: In English—$1,250.74 but in Spanish—$1.250,74

1. *Sí, cómo no.*	12. *Sólo uno.*
2. *N/A*	13. *Está en mi nombre por supuesto.*
3. *N/A*	14. *Uno. / Lo he comprado. / Yo hago los pagos. / A mi hermano. / $150 al mes. / No. / En enero de 2010. / No, ninguna idea del valor. / Sí. / $2.000 /*

4. *N/A*   15. *Ninguna.*

5. *N/A*   16. *No.*

6. *N/A*   17. *No.*

7. *Sí. / $550 por mes. / Sí, por 4 pagos.*   18. *No.*

8. *Sí.*   19. *No.*

9. *Sí. / El 17 de agosto a las 9 de la mañana.*   20. *Sí. / Sí. / $3.500*

10. *No.*   21. *Sí.*

11. *Está bien.*   22. *No.*

C) From to Start to Finish: *Section III—Judgments and Lawsuits*

Instructions: You will prepare a script utilizing *Section III—Judgments and Lawsuits,* either by marking the necessary phrases/questions from this part of the chapter or writing them out on a separate sheet of paper. The SPANISH answers to the questions have been provided below and correspond to phrases/questions from *Section III.* Note that depending upon the response, NOT ALL phrases/questions from this section will be needed in your script. This is noted by N/A next to the corresponding number. Where N/A is indicated, do read that question and discuss with a partner WHY it would be omitted and not asked. Next, practice with a partner in the form of an oral dialogue using your script and the responses provided. Do not forget that **Luisa** is still the potential client!

1. *Sí. / Un fallo en el condado de Lexington, KY. / Sí, podría describirlo por escrito. / No.*

2. *N/A*

3. *No.*

4. *Sí. / Sí, un accidente. / Sí, podría explicarlo por escrito. / Se presentó la demanda hace seis meses. / En Buffalo, NY. / El Sr. John Fulano. / Sí, lo tengo. / Cómo no.*

5. *No.*

6. *No.*

D) From to Start to Finish: *Section IV—Monthly Income*

Instructions: Here, you will prepare a script, either by marking the necessary phrases/questions from *Section IV—Monthly Income* or writing them out on a separate sheet of paper. The SPANISH answers to the questions have been provided below and correspond to phrases/questions from *Section IV.* Note that depending upon the response, NOT ALL phrases/questions from this section will be needed in your script. This is noted by N/A next to the corresponding number. Where N/A is indicated, do read that question and discuss with a partner WHY it would be omitted and not asked. Next, practice with a partner in the form of an oral dialogue using your script and the responses provided. Do not forget that **Luisa** is still the potential client!

1. *$2.750*   6. *No, nada.*

2. *Por supuesto.*   7. *No.*

3. *El bruto es $2.750 pero el neto es $2.050.* 8. *No.*

4. *Cada dos semanas.*   9. *No.*

5. *N/A*   10. *No.*

E) From to Start to Finish: *Section V—Monthly Expenses*

Instructions: Again, you will prepare a script, either by marking the necessary phrases/questions from *Section V—Monthly Expenses* or writing them out on a separate sheet of paper. The SPANISH answers to the questions have been provided below and correspond to phrases/questions from *Section V*. Note that depending upon the response, NOT ALL phrases/questions from this section will be needed in your script. This is noted by N/A next to the corresponding number. Where N/A is indicated, do read that question and discuss with a partner WHY it would be omitted and not asked. Next, practice with a partner in the form of an oral dialogue using your script and the responses provided. Do not forget that **Luisa** is still the potential client!

1. *[Read to client phrase 1]*

2. *[Read to client phrase 2]*

3. *El alquiler es $400.*

4. *N/A*

5. *N/A*

6. *N/A*

7. *N/A*

8. *La cuenta de electricidad es $85 al mes. / La de agua y de alcatarillado es $25 al mes. / La de teléfono es $19,95 al mes. / No tengo móvil. / No tengo cable ni satélite.*

9. *No.*

10. *Nada. / En comida, $300 / En ropa, $50 / En lavado sólo, $25 / En trasportación, $150 / En entretenimiento, $45 / Nada. / En estos gastos. / No me corresponde. / No tengo seguro de arrendatario. / No lo tengo. / No lo tengo tampoco. / No tengo seguro de salud. / No tengo seguro de auto. / No me corresponden los impuestos de propiedad.*

11. *No.*

12. *No. / No. / En cuidado de hijos, $175 al mes.*

13. *Ninguno.*

14. *N/A*

15. *N/A*

16. *N/A*

F) Take a Break: *Section VI—Real Property and Mortgages*

Instructions: No answers are provided for **Luisa** in this section. Can you and your partner explain why based on the responses she has provided thus far?

G) From to Start to Finish: *Section VII—Unsecured and Priority Debts*

Instructions: You will prepare a script, either by marking the necessary phrases/questions from *Section VII—Unsecured and Priority Debts* or writing them out on a separate sheet of paper. The SPANISH answers to the questions have been provided below and correspond to phrases/questions from *Section VII*. Note that depending upon the response, NOT ALL phrases/questions from this section will be needed in your script. This is noted by N/A next to the corresponding number. Where N/A is indicated, do read that question and discuss with a partner WHY it would be omitted and not asked. Next, practice with a partner in the form of an oral dialogue using your script and the responses provided. Do not forget that **Luisa** is still the potential client!

1. *$3.500*

2. *Sólo dos.*

3. *Sí. / La tarjeta de Sears.*

4. *No.*

5. *No.*

6. *No estoy segura.*

H) The BIG Finish: *Section VIII—Financial Accounts and Personal Property*

Instructions: For the last part of this comprehensive activity, you will prepare a script, either by marking the necessary phrases/questions from *Section VIII—Financial Accounts and Personal Property* or writing them out on a separate sheet of paper. Unlike previous sections from this chapter, you are once again going to create fill-in-the-blank tables to provide to your potential client. This will be indicated on the table below. See *Practical Activities—Chapter 8—Family Law—letter B* for detailed instructions on creating tables BEFORE you begin this activity if you would like a review.

Also, some questions ask that the client simply write out the information. You may want to prepare a blank answer sheet beforehand where you have written down JUST the numbers that correspond to the phrases that request this so you may match up the requested information with the correct phrase/expression for context after you have completed the interview.

Again, the SPANISH answers to the questions have been provided below and correspond to phrases/questions from *Section VIII*. Note that depending upon the response NOT ALL phrases/questions from this section will be needed in your script. This is noted by N/A next to the corresponding number. Where N/A is indicated, do read that question and discuss with a partner WHY it would be omitted and not asked. Next, practice with a partner in the form of an oral dialogue using your script, the responses provided as well as the tables you created for the client to complete. Do not forget that **Luisa** is still the potential client!

1. *$30*

2. *No. / No.*

3. *N/A*

4. *N/A*

5. *N/A*

6. *N/A*

7. *[Read the phrase to the client and provide her with a **blank table** to complete that has already been prepared.]*

8. *No.*

9. *Sí. / [Read the remaining phrase to the client and provide her with a pen and an answer sheet to write out this information.]*

10. *No.*

11. *No me corresponde.*

22. *No.*

23. *Sí, un primo me debe $800.*

24. *No.*

25. *No.*

26. *No.*

27. *No.*

28. *No.*

29. *No.*

30. *No.*

31. *[Read the phrase to the client and provide her with a **blank table** to complete that has already been prepared.]*

32. *[Read the phrase to the client] No me corresponde.*

12. *[Read the phrase to the client and provide her with pen and answer sheet to write out this information.]*

13. *No me corresponde.*

14. *N/A*

15. *No me corresponde.*

16. *No.*

17. *No.*

18. *No.*

19. *No.*

20. *No.*

21. *No.*

33. *No.*

34. *[Read the phrase to the client] No me corresponde.*

35. *[Read the phrase to the client] No me corresponde.*

36. *[Read the phrase to the client] No me corresponde.*

37. *[Read the phrase to the client] No me corresponde.*

38. *[Read the phrase to the client and provide her with a **blank table** to complete that has already been prepared.]*

39. *No.*

40. *No.*

41. *[Read the phrase to the client]. Sí, comprendo.*

I) Cyber-Investigation

Congratulations, you just created a realistic FULL-LENGTH interview from start to finish. However, you noticed that many times, questions did not apply or the answer was a simple *NO*. When asked about financial accounts, real estate, stocks, etc., our fictitious character **Luisa** responded that she had none of these or that the request was not applicable to her. Look back at the General Information responses and find her immigration status. What is her status? Would this have any impact on whether or not a person like **Luisa** would or would not have access to the financial accounts to which she responded *NO*? Take this probability further and search for information on the internet that addresses how Hispanics, both legal and illegal, view financial entities such as banks and the services they offer. Does a person's immigration status necessarily influence the level of trust he/she may have in these institutions? Culturally, do Hispanics find such financial entities as important as the general population of the U.S.? How do they view investing, stocks, etc.? Find information that speaks directly about these topics and share your findings. Create a summary of this information below in the space provided.

Chapter 11

Questions Related to Medical Issues and Information

Before You Begin

Overall, Hispanics are less comfortable talking about their family medical history and are more likely to associate shame or embarrassment with details regarding the condition of their health or the health of a family member. Likewise, Hispanics tend to be less knowledgeable of their own family medical history and health-related issues than the average American citizen.

It is also valuable to understand the cultural difference that exists in the perception of pain among Hispanics and non-Hispanics. When polled, health care professionals frequently commented that their Hispanic patients appear to experience less pain even when suffering from severe illnesses and accidents in which non-Hispanic patients endured comparable discomfort and injuries. However, when Hispanic patients were asked to rate their pain/discomfort on a chart or scale, health care providers observed a noticeable increase in true pain felt by the patient in contrast to perceived pain that had been previously described.

I. Personal Information

*een-fohr-mah-**see^ohn** payr-soh-**nahl***
Información personal

English	Pronunciation & Spanish
1. What is your full name?	*koo^ahl ays soo **nohm**-bray kohm-**play**-toh?* ¿Cuál es su nombre completo?[1]
2. How do you spell your ...	***koh**-moh say ays-**kree**-bay soo ...* ¿Cómo se escribe su ...
first name?	*pree-**mayr nohm**-bray?* primer nombre?[1]
last name?	*ah-pay-**yee**-doh?* apellido?[1]
3. Please repeat.	*rray-**pee**-tah, pohr fah-**bohr**.* Repita, por favor.
4. Will you write it for me here?	*may loh ays-**kree**-bay ah-**kee**?* ¿Me lo escribe aquí?

5. Speak (more) slowly, please.	*ah-blay (mahs) days-**pah**-see^oh, pohr fah-**bohr**.* Hable (más) despacio, por favor.
6. I'm sorry.	*loh **see^ayn**-toh.* Lo siento.
7. I don't understand.	*noh kohm-**prayn**-doh.* No comprendo.
8. Write it here, please.	*ays-**kree**-bah-loh ah-**kee**, pohr fah-**bohr**.* Escríbalo aquí, por favor.
9. How old are you?	*koo^**ahn**-tohs **ahn**-yohs **tee^ay**-nay?* ¿Cuántos años tiene?[2]
10. When were you born?	*koo^**ahn**-doh nah-**see^oh**?* ¿Cuándo nació?[2]
11. Are you married?	*ays-**tah** kah-**sah**-doh/dah?* ¿Está casado/a?[3]
12. Are you divorced?	*ays-**tah** dee-boor-**see^ah**-doh/dah?* ¿Está divorciado/a?[3]
13. Are you single?	*ays sohl-**tay**-roh/rah?* ¿Es soltero/a?[3]
14. Are you widowed?	*ays **bee^oo**-doh/dah?* ¿Es viudo/a?[3]
15. What is your spouse's name?	*kohm-moh say **yah**-mah soo **kohn**-yoo-hay?* ¿Cómo se llama su cónyuge?[4]
16. Do you have any children?	*tee^**ay**-nay **ee**-hohs* ¿Tiene hijos?
Please write the name and age of each child for me here.	*pohr-fah-**bohr**, ays-**kree**-bah ayl **nohm**-bray ee lah ay-**dahd** day **kah**-dah ee-hoh ah-**kee**.* Por favor, escriba el nombre y la edad de cada hijo aquí.
Point to the name of each child that is your dependent.	*sayn-**yah**-lay-may ayl bnohm-**bray** day **kah**-dah **ee**-hoh kay ays soo day-payn-**dee^ayn**-tay.* Señáleme el nombre de cada hijo que es su dependiente.
17. What is your address?	*koo^ahl ays soo dee-rayk-**see^ohn**?* ¿Cuál es su dirección?[1, 2]
18. What is your phone number?	*koo^ahl ays soo **noo**-may-roh day tay-**lay**-foh-noh?* ¿Cuál es su número de teléfono?[2]
19. Do you work?	*trah-**bah**-hah?* ¿Trabaja?[4]
20. How long have you worked there?	*pohr koo^**ahn**-toh **tee^aym**-poh ah trah-bah-**hah**-doh ah-**yee**?* ¿Por cuánto tiempo ha trabajado allí?[2]

one day	*ah*-say oon **dee**-ah hace un día[5]
(#) days	*ah*-say (#) **dee**-ahs hace (#) días[5]
one week	*ah*-say **oo**-nah say-**mah**-nah hace una semana[5]
(#) weeks	*ah*-say (#) say-**mah**-nahs hace (#) semanas[5]
one month	*ah*-say oon mays hace un mes[5]
(#) months	*ah*-say (#) **may**-says hace (#) meses[5]
one year	*ah*-say oon **ahn**-yoh hace un año[5]
(#) years	*ah*-say (#) **ahn**-yohs hace (#) años[5]

21. What is your work address?	koo^ahl ays lah dee-rayk-**see^ohn** day soo trah-**bah**-hoh? ¿Cuál es la dirección de su trabajo?[1,2]
22. What is the phone number of your workplace?	koo^ahl ays ayl **noo**-may-roh day tay-**lay**-foh-noh day soo trah-**bah**-hoh? ¿Cuál es el número de teléfono de su trabajo?[2]
23. Can we call you at work?	poh-**day**-mohs yah-**mahr**-loh/lah ayn ayl trah-**bah**-hoh? ¿Podemos llamarlo/la en el trabajo?[6]
24. Who is your doctor?	kee^ayn ays soo dohk-**tohr** (dohk-**toh**-rah)? ¿Quién es su doctor(a)?[7]
25. Write your doctor's name here for me, please.	ays-**kree**-bah ayl **nohm**-bray day soo dohk-**tohr** (dohk-**toh**-rah) ah-**kee** pohr fah-**bohr**. Escriba el nombre de su doctor(a) aquí, por favor.[1,7]
26. Do you have health insurance?	tee^**ay**-nay say-**goo**-roh **may**-dee-koh? ¿Tiene seguro médico?
27. Respond "yes" or "no," please.	rrays-**pohn**-dah \<see\> oh \<noh\>, pohr fah-**bohr**. Responda \<sí\> o \<no\>, por favor.
28. Do you have a ... card?	tee^**ay**-nay lah tahr-**hay**-tah day ... ¿Tiene la tarjeta de ...
Medicare?	Medicare?
Medicaid?	Medicaid?
health insurance?	say-**goo**-roh **may**-dee-koh? seguro médico?

| | *say-**goo**-roh soh-**see^ahl**?* |
| Social Security? | seguro social? |

| 29. Do you have a driver's license? | *tee^**ay**-nay lee-**sayn**-see^ah **pah**-rah kohn-doo-**seer**?*
¿Tiene licencia para conducir? |

| 30. Do you have some form of (picture) I.D.? | *tee^**ay**-nay ahl-**goo**-nah **foor**-mah day ee-dayn-tee-fee-kah-**see^ohn** (kohn **foh**-toh)?*
¿Tiene alguna forma de identificación (con foto)? |

| 31. May I see it? | *poo^**ay**-doh **bayr**-lah?*
¿Puedo verla? |

| 32. I need to make a copy of your ... | *nay-say-**see**-toh sah-**kahr koh**-pee^ah day ...*
Necesito sacar copia de ... |

| Medicare Card. | *lah tahr-**hay**-tah day Medicare.*
la tarjeta de Medicare. |

| Medicaid Card. | *lah tahr-**hay**-tah day Medicaid.*
la tarjeta de Medicaid. |

| health insurance card. | *lah tahr-**hay**-tah day say-**goo**-roh **may**-dee-koh.*
la tarjeta de seguro médico. |

| Social Security Card. | *lah tahr-**hay**-tah day say-**goo**-roh soh-**see^ahl**.*
la tarjeta de seguro social. |

| driver's license. | *soo lee-**sayn**-see^ah **pah**-rah kohn-doo-**seer**.*
su licencia para conducir. |

| I.D. | *soo ee-dayn-tee-fee-kah-**see^ohn**.*
su identificación. |

II. Medical History

*ahn-tay-say-**dayn**-tays **may**-dee-kohs*
Antecedentes médicos

English	Pronunciation & Spanish
1. Now, I am going to ask you some personal health related questions.	*ah-**oh**-rah, lay boh^ee ah ah-**sayr oo**-nahs pray-**goon**-tahs payr-soh-**nah**-lays rrah-lah-see^oh-**nah**-dahs ah lah sah-**lood**.* Ahora, le voy a hacer unas preguntas personales relacionadas a la salud.
2. Respond with "yes" or "no," please.	*rrays-**pohn**-dah kohn <see> oh <noh>, pohr fah-**bohr**.* Responda con <sí> o <no>, por favor.
3. Do you suffer or have you suffered from ...	*soo-fray oh ah soo-**free**-doh day ...* ¿Sufre o ha sufrido de ...
anemia?	*ah-**nay**-mee^ah?* anemia?

arthritis?	*ahr-**tree**-tees?* artritis?
asthma?	***ahs**-mah?* asma?
cancer?	***kahn**-sayr?* cáncer?
anxiety?	*ahn-see^ay-**dahd**?* ansiedad?
depression?	*day-pray-**see^ohn**?* depresión?
sinusitis?	*see-noo-**see**-tees?* sinusitis?
bulimia?	*boo-**lee**-mee^ah?* bulimia?
anorexia?	*ah-noh-**rayk**-see^ah?* anorexia?
paralysis?	*pah-**rah**-lee-sees?* parálisis?
hemmorhoids?	*ay-moh-**rroy**-days?* hemorroides?
persistent cough?	*tohs payr-sees-**tayn**-tay?* tos persistente?
(Are you) lactose intolerant?	*een-toh-lay-**rahn**-see^ah **lahk**-tay^ah?* intolerancia láctea?
venereal diseases/STDs?	*ayn-fayr-may-**dah**-days bay-**nay**-ray^ahs?* enfermedades venéreas
hypertension/high blood pressure?	*ee-payr-tayn-**see^ohn**?* hipertensión?
hypotension/low blood pressure?	*ee-poh-tayn-**see^ohn**?* hipotensión?
heart problems?	*proh-**blay**-mahs kahr-**dee**-ah-cohs* problemas cardíacos?
circulatory problems?	*proh-**blay**-mahs seer-koo-lah-**toh**-ree^ohs?* problemas circulatorios?
nervous problems?	*proh-**blay**-mahs nayr-**bee^oh**-sohs?* problemas nerviosos?
other medical problems?	***oh**-trohs proh-**blay**-mahs **may**-dee-kohs?* otros problemas médicos?

4. Do you suffer from ...

soo-fray day ...
Sufre de ...

hyperglicemia or diabetes?

*ee-payr-glee-**say**-mee^ay oh dee^ah-**bay**-tays?*
hiperglicemia o diabetes?

hypoglycemia?

*ee-poh-glee-**say**-mee^ah?*
hipoglicemia?

hepatitis?

*ay-pah-**tee**-tees?*
hepatitis?

herpes?

***ayr**-pays?*
herpes?

HIV?

*bay-ee-**ah**-chay?*
VIH?

AIDS?

***see**-dah?*
SIDA?

any other illness?

***oh**-trah ayn-fayr-may-**dahd**?*
otra enfermedad?

5. Have you ever suffered a ...

*ah soo-**free**-doh oon ...*
¿Ha sufrido un ...

stroke?

*day-**rrah**-may say-ray-**brahl** o ah-poh-play-**hee**-ah?*
derrame cerebral o apoplejía?

heart attack?

*ah-**tah**-kay kahr-**dee**-ah-koh?*
ataque cardíaco?

6. Have you ever had surgery?

*ah tay-**nee**-doh see-roo-**hee**-ah?*
¿Ha tenido cirugía?

7. Was it ...

foo^ay ...
¿Fue ...

an appendectomy?

***oo**-nah ah-payn-dayk-toh-**mee**-ah?*
una apendectomía?

a hysterectomy?

***oo**-nah ees-tay-rayk-toh-**mee**-ah?*
una histerectomía?

breast surgery?

*day **say**-noh?*
de seno?

heart surgery?

*day koh-rah-**sohn**?*
de corazón?

colon surgery?

*day **koh**-lohn?*
de colon?

uterine surgery?

*day **oo**-tay-roh?*
de útero?

ovarian surgery?

*day oh-**bah**-ree^oh?*
de ovario?

kidney surgery?	*day rreen-**yohn**?* de riñon?
liver surgery?	*day **ee**-gah-doh?* de hígado?
stomach surgery?	*day ays-**toh**-mah-goh?* de estómago?
prostate surgery?	*day **prohs**-tah-tah?* de próstata?
a tonsillectomy?	*day ah-**meeg**-dah-lahs?* de amígdalas?
a thyroidectomy?	*day tee-**roh^ee**-days?* de tiroides?
for an ovarian cyst?	*day **kees**-tay oh-**bah**-ree-koh?* de quiste ovárico?
for kidney stones?	*day **kahl**-koo-lohs rray-**nah**-lays?* de cálculos renales?[8]
for hemorrhoids?	***pah**-rah ay-moh-**rroh^ee**-days?* para hemorroides?
for a hernia?	*day **ayr**-nee^ah?* de hernia?
another type of surgery?	***oh**-troh **tee**-poh day see-roo-**hee**-ah?* otro tipo de cirugía?[1]
8. Do you use drugs?	***oo**-sah **droh**-gahs?* ¿Usa drogas?
9. Have you ever used drugs?	*ah oo-**sah**-doh **droh**-gahs?* ¿Ha usado drogas?
10. Have you ever been treated for a drug problem?	*ah **see**-doh trah-**tah**-doh/dah pohr oon proh-**blay**-mah day **droh**-gahs?* ¿Ha sido tratado/a por un problema de drogas?[3]
11. Do you drink (alcohol)?	***toh**-mah ahl-koh-**ohl**?* ¿Toma alcohol?
12. How many drinks do you have in a week?	***koo^ahn**-tahs bay-**bee**-dahs ahl-koh-**oh**-lee-kahs **toh**-mah pohr say-**mah**-nah?* ¿Cuántas bebidas alcohólicas toma por semana?[1]
13. Do you have a history of ...	***tee^ay**-nay ees-**toh**-ree^ah day ...* ¿Tiene historia de ...
drug use?	***oo**-soh day **droh**-gahs?* uso de drogas?
arthritis?	*ahr-**tree**-tees?* artritis?

birth defects?	*day-**fayk**-tohs day nah-see-**mee^ayn**-toh?* defectos de nacimiento?
excessive bleeding?	*sahn-**grah**-doh ayk-say-**see**-boh?* sangrado excesivo?
cancer?	***kahn**-sayr?* cáncer?
colon cancer?	***kayn**-sayr dayl **koh**-lohn?* cáncer del colon?
stomach cancer?	***kahn**-sayr **gahs**-tree-koh?* cáncer gástrico?
(Age at diagnosis?)	*(ay-**dahd** ahl dee^ahg-**nohs**-tee-koh?)* (¿Edad al diagnóstico?)[2]
colitis?	*koh-**lee**-tees?* colitis?
colon polyps?	***poh**-lee-pohs dayl **koh**-lohn?* pólipos del colon?
Crohn's disease?	*ayn-fayr-may-**dahd** day krohn?* enfermedad de Crohn?
diabetes?	*dee^ah-**bay**-tays?* diabetes?
heart problems?	*proh-**blay**-mahs kahr-**dee**-ah-kohs?* problemas cardíacos?
high blood pressure?	*ee-payr-tayn-**see^ohn**?* hipertensión?
liver disease?	*ayn-fayr-may-**dahd** dayl **ee**-gah-doh?* enfermedad del hígado?
lung diseases?	*ayn-fayr-may-**dah**-days pool-moh-**nah**-rays?* enfermedades pulmonares?
thrombosis or stroke/cerebral embolism?	*trohm-**boh**-sees oh aym-boh-**lees**-moh say-ray-**brahl**?* trombosis o embolismo cerebral?
blood clots?	*koh-**ah**-goo-lohs sahn-**ghee**-nay-ohs?* coágulos sanguíneos?
tuberculosis?	*too-bayr-koo-**loh**-sees?* tuberculosis?
thyroid disease?	*ayn-fayr-may-**dahd** tee-roh^ee-**day**-ah?* enfermedad tiroidea?
ulcer?	***ool**-say-rah?* úlcera?

other health problems?	*oh-trohs proh-**blay**-mahs day sah-**lood**?* otros problemas de salud?[1]
14. Do you use tobacco products?	*oo-sah tah-**bah**-koh?* ¿Usa tabaco?
15. Have you ever used tobacco products?	*ah oo-**sah**-doh tah-**bah**-koh ayn ayl pah-**sah**-doh?* ¿Ha usado tabaco en el pasado?
16. Do you smoke?	*foo-mah?* ¿Fuma?
17. Have you ever smoked?	*ah foo-**mah**-doh?* ¿Ha fumado?

III. Medications and Pain Management

*may-day-**see**-nahs ee mah-**nay**-hoh day doh-**lohr***
Medicinas y manejo de dolor

English	Pronunciation & Spanish
1. Are you currently taking ...	*ahk-too^ahl-**mayn**-tay, ays-**tah** toh-**mahn**-doh ...* Actualmente, está tomando ...
any medication(s)?	*ahl-**goo**-nah(s) may-dee-**see**-nah(s)?* alguna(s) medicina(s)?[9]
What is it?	*koh-moh say **yah**-mah?* ¿Cómo se llama?[9]
What are they?	*koh-moh say **yah**-mahn?* ¿Cómo se llaman?[9]
vitamins?	*vee-tah-**mee**-nahs?* vitaminas?
What are they?	*koo^**ah**-lays sohn?* ¿Cuáles son?[9]
herbal supplements?	*proh-**dook**-tohs ayr-**bah**-lays?* productos herbales?
What are they?	*koo^**ah**-lays sohn?* ¿Cuáles son?[9]
2. Will you write the name here for me?	*may ays-**kree**-bay ayl **nohm**-bray ah-**kee**?* ¿Me escribe el nombre aquí?[2]
Please write the dosage your are taking beside each ... you have listed.	*pohr fah-**bohr**, ays-**kree**-bah lah **doh**-sees kay ays-**tah** toh-**mahn**-doh ahl **lah**-doh day **kah**-dah ... kay ah ay-noo-may-**rah**-doh.* Por favor, escriba la dosis que está tomando al lado de cada ... que ha enumerado.
medication	*may-dee-**see**-nah* medicina

vitamin	*vee-tah-**mee**-nah* vitamina
herbal supplement	*proh-**dook**-tohs ayr-**bahl*** producto herbal

3. Do you feel pain (now)?
*see^ayn-tay doh-**lohr** (ah-**oh**-rah)?*
¿Siente dolor (ahora)?

How long have you had this pain?
koo^ayn-toh tee^aym-poh ah-say kay tee^ay-nay ays-tay doh-lohr?
¿Cuánto tiempo hace que tiene este dolor?[2]

4. Have you had any pain (before)?
*ah sayn-**tee**-doh doh-**lohr** (**ahn**-tays)?*
¿Ha sentido dolor (antes)?

5. Do you feel worse in …
*say **see^ayn**-tay pay^ohr pohr …*
¿Se siente peor por …

the morning?
*lah mahn-**yah**-nah?*
la mañana?

the afternoon?
*lah **tahr**-day?*
la tarde?

the evening/at night?
*lah **noh**-chay?*
la noche?

6. Show me with your finger where you feel the pain.
*sayn-**yah**-lay kohn ayl **day**-doh **dohn**-day see^ayn-tay ayl doh-**lohr**.*
Señale con el dedo dónde siente el dolor.[10]

7. Is the pain …
*ays ayl doh-**lohr** …*
¿Es el dolor …

strong/severe?
*foo^**ayr**-tay?*
fuerte?

sharp?
*ah-**goo**-doh?*
agudo?

mild?
***lay**-bay?*
leve?

dull?
***sohr**-doh?*
sordo?

persistent?
*payr-see-**stayn**-tay?*
persistente?

burning?
*ahr-**dee^ayn**-tay?*
ardiente?

throbbing?
*pahl-pee-**tahn**-tay?*
palpitante?

localized?
*loh-kahl-lee-**sah**-doh?*
localizado?

8. Will you show me on this scale of one to ten the severity of the pain?

*may sayn-**yah**-lah ayn **ays**-tah ays-**kah**-lah day **oo**-noh ah dee^ays lah grah-bay-**dahd** dayl doh-**lohr**?*
¿Me señala en esta escala de uno a diez la gravedad del dolor?[11]

9. Does the pain radiate?

*say **koh**-rray ayl doh-**lohr**?*
¿Se corre el dolor?

10. Show me from where to where.

***moo^ays**-tray-may day **dohn**-day ah **dohn**-day.*
Muéstreme de dónde a dónde.

11. Are you taking any medication specifically for the pain?

*ays-**tah** toh-**mahn**-doh may-dee-**see**-nah ays-pay-see-fee-kah-**mayn**-tay **pah**-rah ayl doh-**lohr**?*
¿Está tomando medicina específicamente para el dolor?

12. Have you taken any medicine recently for the pain?

*ah toh-**mah**-doh may-dee-**see**-nah rray-see^ayn-tay-**mayn**-tay **pah**-rah ayl doh-**lohr**?*
¿Ha tomado medicina recientemente para el dolor?

13. Can you show me the prescriptions you have been given?

*may **poo^ay**-day mohs-**trahr** lahs rray-**say**-tahs kay lay ahn rray-say-**tah**-doh?*
¿Me puede mostrar las recetas que le han dado?

14. Are you currently under the care of a physician for this problem?

*ahk-too^ahl-**mayn**-tay, ays-**tah bah**-hoh lah ah-tayn-**see^ohn** may-dee-kah day oon dohk-**tohr pah**-rah **ays**-tay proh-**blay**-mah?*
Actualmente, ¿está bajo la atención médica de un doctor para este problema?

Please provide the following information for this physician: full name, office address and telephone number.

*poh fah-**bohr**, proh-pohr-**see^oh**-nay lah see-**ghee^ayn**-tay een-fohr-mah-**see^ohn pah**-rah **ays**-tay dohk-**tohr**: **nohm**-bray kohm-**play**-toh, dee-rayk-**see^ohn** dayl kohn-sool-**toh**-ree^oh ee **noo**-may-roh day tay-**lay**-foh-noh.*
Por favor, proporcione la siguiente información para este doctor: nombre completo, dirección del consultorio y número de teléfono.

15. Are you currently receiving physical therapy for this problem?

*ahk-too^ahl-**mayn**-tay, ays-**tah** ah-**see^ayn**-doh tay-**rah**-pee^ah **fee**-see-kah **pah**-rah **ays**-tay proh-**blay**-mah?*
Actualmente, ¿está haciendo terapia física para este problema?

Please provide the following information for your physical therapist: full name, office address and telephone number.

*poh fah-**bohr**, proh-pohr-**see^oh**-nay lah see-**ghee^ayn**-tay een-fohr-mah-**see^ohn pah**-rah soo tay-rah-**pees**-tah **fees**-see-koh: **nohm**-bray kohm-**play**-toh, dee-rayk-**see^ohn** dayl kohn-sool-**toh**-ree^oh ee **noo**-may-roh day tay-**lay**-foh-noh.*
Por favor, proporcione la siguiente información para su terapista físico: nombre completo, dirección del consultorio y número de teléfono.

Notes

¹ Reference *Chapter 12—The Basics—I. The Spanish Alphabet* to assist you with spelling and listening comprehension.

² Reference *Chapter 12—The Basics—II. Numbers* to assist you with numbers and listening comprehension.

³ When speaking with a *male* use the *-o* ending; when speaking with a *female* use the *-a* ending. When asking about a *male* use the *-o* ending; when asking about a *female* use the *-a* ending.

⁴ In Spanish, the syntax (sentence structure) for *you (singular and formal)*, *he/him*, and *she/her* are grammatically identical. Notice that ALL of the English questions and phrases in this chapter are written in the second person singular—*you*. Likewise, the vast majority of Spanish phrases in this book could be conveyed as *he/him* or *she/her* as well, though not noted in the English translation. If the person with whom you are speaking is the potential client, use the phrase *Referente a Ud. (In reference to you ...)* to ensure the conversation is being conducted directly with that person. If the person with whom you are speaking is inquiring on behalf of someone else, then use either *Referente a él (In reference to him ...)* or *Referente a ella (In reference to her ...)* depending upon the sex of the individual on whose behalf the person is inquiring. At anytime you wish to change the focus of the question, simply insert the expression *Referente a Ud., él or ella ...* before the phrase. For example, to change the focus to a female say *Referente a ella, ¿tiene trabajo actualmente? (In reference to her, is she currently employed?).* You may even insert the **proper name** of the person accordingly to maximize comprehension—*Referente a **Carlos**.* You only need to verbalize clarification when changing or clarifying the person who is the focus of the question or phrase. It is not necessary to do so before EVERY question or phrase once you establish the context of the conversation.

⁵ These are anticipated responses to assist you in understanding the answer you will hear. You may also wish to repeat what you hear to make sure you have correctly understood the information.

⁶ When speaking to or about a *male* use *-lo*; when speaking to or about a *female* use *-la*.

⁷ If the gender of the doctor is *male* use *-doctor*; if the gender of the doctor is *female* use *-doctora*. If the gender is not known, default to the male form. Once the client indicates whether the doctor is *male* or *female*, incorporate the correct form into the remainder of your questions where necessary.

⁸ To indicate "gallstones," say *cálculos biliares* (**kahl**-koo-lohs bee-**lee**^ah-rays).

⁹ These follow-up questions are provided for when 1) you are speaking with the person over the phone and he/she is not present to write the information out for you, or 2) the interviewee is unable to write for some reason. Also, remember to incorporate phrases from communication strategies that will assist you in spelling and/or requesting that the speaker speak slower if necessary. You may elect to reference *Chapter 2—Collecting Basic Information in Persona and by Phone* as well.

¹⁰ Feel free to use the *Human Body* diagrams as provided in the APPENDIX as visual aids. They are labeled in both Spanish and English for ease of comprehension.

¹¹ Use the *Pain Scale* provided in the APPENDIX as a visual aid to assist you with obtaining this information.

IV. Medical Information Consent Release Form¹

*forh-moo-**lah**-ree^oh day kohn-sayn-tee-**mee^ayn**-toh **pah**-rah lah dee-bool-gah-**see^ohn** day een-fohr-mah-**see^ohn may**-dee-kah*
Formulario de consentimiento para la divulgación de información médica

English	Pronunciation & Spanish
1. This is the consent to release of medical information form. Please complete it. Then, sign and date it.	***ays**-tay ays ayl fohr-moh-**lah**-ree^oh day kohn-sayn-tee-**mee^ayn**-toh **pah**-rah lah dee-bool-gah-**see^ohn** day een-fohr-mah-**see^ohn may**-dee-kah. fah-**bohr** day lay-**ayr**-loh. **loo^ay**-goh, **feer**-may-loh ee **fay**-chay-loh.* Este es el formulario de consentimiento para la divulgación de información médica. Favor de llenarlo. Luego, fírmelo y féchelo.
2. Bring it to me when you have finished.	*trah^ee-gah-may-loh **koo^ahn**-doh **ah^ee**-yah tayr-mee-**nah**-doh.* Tráigamelo cuando haya terminado.
3. I am going to mail you a consent to release of medical information form. Please complete it. Then, sign and date it and mail it back to me as soon as possible.	*lay boh^ee ah mahn-**dahr** pohr koh-**rray**-oh oon fohr-moo-**lah**-ree^oh day kohn-sayn-tee-**mee^ayn**-toh **pah**-rah lah dee-bool-gah-**see^ohn** day een-fohr-mah-**see^ohn may**-dee-kay. fah-**bohr** day lay-**ayr**-loh. **loo^ay**-goh, **feer**-may-loh, **fay**-chay-loh ee day-**boo^ayl**-bah-may-loh pohr koh-**rray**-oh tahn **prohn**-toh **koh**-moh poh-**see**-blay.* Le voy a mandar por correo un formulario de consentimiento para la divulgación de información médica. Favor de llenarlo. Luego, fírmelo, féchelo y devuélvamelo por correo tan pronto como posible.
4. Please sign here, indicating your consent to the release of medical information.	*fah-**bohr** day feer-**mahr** ah-**kee**, een-dee-**kahn**-doh soo kohn-sayn-tee-**mee^ayn**-toh **pah**-rah lah dee-bool-gah-**see^ohn** day een-fohr-mah-**see^ohn may**-dee-kah.* Favor de firmar aquí, indicando su consentimiento para la divulgación de información médica.
5. Do you understand that by signing this you give us permission to request and review your medical information according to the terms of the form?	*kohm-**prayn**-day kay ahl feer-**mahr ays**-tay fohr-moo-**lah**-ree^oh, nohs dah payr-**mee**-soh **pah**-rah pay-**deer** ee rray-bee-**sahr** soo een-fohr-mah-**see^ohn may**-dee-kah say-**goon** lohs plah-**sohs** een-dee-**kah**-dohs ayn ayl fohr-moo-**lah**-ree^oh?* ¿Comprende que al firmar este formulario, nos da permiso para pedir y revisar su información médica según los plazos indicados en el formulario?

Note

¹ A sample Medical Information Consent Release Form has been included. The English version mirrors the placement of information on the Spanish version to facilitate association of terminology found in form item number 3. *Information to be released (check all that apply).*

HIPAA* COMPLIANT *AUTHORIZATION* FOR RELEASE OF INFORMATION

Patient Name: _____

Date of Birth: _____ Social Security Number: _____

Provider/Facility Name: _____

Address: _____

    Date of Treatment: _____

1. I, _____, authorize the above-named provider/facility to release the following information to _____ and its agents for examination, copying or otherwise reproducing in any manner.

2. I further authorize representatives of _____ to meet or consult, whether in person or by telephone, with the above-mentioned provider/facility to discuss my medical condition, treatment, records, and associated tests and documentation.

3. Information to be released (check all that apply)

__ Complete medical records   __ Social History
__ Ultrasounds   __ Admission Notes
__ EKG's, Fetal Monitor Strips   __ Psychiatric Records
__ History & Physical   __ Echocardiogram Tapes
__ Substance Abuse Records   __ Consultation Notes
__ X-ray Reports   __ Videos
__ Progress Notes   __ X-ray Films
__ Tissue Blocks or Slides   __ Operative Notes
__ Radiation Records   __ Pathology Specimens
__ Evaluations & Summaries   __ Catheterization Films
__ Discharge Summary   __ CT Scans
__ Education Reports   __ Lab Reports
__ MRI Scans   __ Referral Documents
__ Notes, correspondence or records of any nature made by physicians, nurses, or other persons or facilities.
__ Any and all employment records, including time cards, payroll, vacation and sick leave reports.
__ Testimony
__ Other (specify): _____

4. I understand that if my record contains information relating to HIV infection, AIDS or AIDS-related conditions, alcohol abuse, drug abuse, psychological or psychiatric conditions or genetic testing, this disclosure will include that information. I also understand that I may refuse to sign this authorization and that my refusal to sign will not affect my ability to obtain treatment, payment for services, or my eligibility for benefits.

5. The purpose of this authorization is for full disclosure of all records for use in the investigation and possible resolution of a legal claim requiring disclosure of these records.

6. I understand that this consent may be revoked by me in writing at any time except to the extent that disclosure of information has already occurred prior to the receipt of revocation by the above-named provider. If written revocation is not received, authorization will be considered valid for the duration of my representation by the _____. To initiate revocation of this authorization, notification may be mailed to _____. If not revoked, this authorization will automatically become void when the undersigned's representation by _____ is concluded.

7. A photocopy of this authorization is to be considered as valid as the original.

8. The information used or disclosed pursuant to this authorization may be subject to re-disclosure by the recipient and may no longer be protected by Federal Law/HIPAA Privacy Rules.

This _____ day of _____, 20_____.

_____   _____
Signature   Witness

THIS AUTHORIZATION REVOKES ALL PRIOR AUTHORIZATIONS

* The Health Insurance Portability and Accountability Act

FORMULARIO DE *CONSENTIMIENTO* PARA LA DIVULAGACIÓN
DE INFORMACIÓN EN CUMPLIMIENTO CON HIPAA*

Nombre del paciente: _____

Fecha de nacimiento: _____ No. de seguro social: _____

Nombre del proveedor/del centro de servicios de salud: _____

_____

Dirección: _____

    Fechas de tratamiento: _____

1. Yo, _____, autorizo al proveedor/al centro de servicios de salud antes mencionado a entregarles la siguiente información a _____
y a sus representantes para los propósitos de examinar, fotocopiar o reproducir de cualquier manera.

2. Además, autorizo a los representantes de _____ a reunirse con o consultar con, sea en persona o por teléfono, el proveedor/el centro de servicios de salud antes mencionado para conferenciar sobre mi condición médica, tratamiento, expedientes médicos así como pruebas y documentación relacionadas.

3. Información que se entregará (marque todo lo que corresponda)

__ expedientes médicos completos   __ historia social
__ ultrasonidos   __ constancias de internamiento
__ cinta de monitoreo fetal/electro cardiograma   __ expedientes psiquiátricos
__ antecedentes médicos y examen físico   __ imágenes de ecocardiograma
__ antecedentes de abuso de sustancias   __ constancias de consultas
__ informes de radiografías   __ vidéos
__ notas de evolución médica   __ películas de radiografía
__ diapositivas o muestras de tejido   __ notas quirúrgicas
__ antecedentes de radiación   __ muestras de patología
__ evaluaciones y resúmenes   __ imágenes de cateterismo
__ resumen del alta   __ tomografías computarizadas
__ informes educativos   __ informes de laboratorio
__ imágenes de resonancia magnética   __ documentos de derivación

__ notas, correspondencia o expedientes de cualquier índole creados por médicos, enfermeros o cualesquier otras personas o centros.

__ todo expediente laboral, incluyendo tarjetas marcadoras de hora así como registros de nómina de pagos, baja por enfermedad y tiempo libre vacacional.

__ testimonio

__ otros (especifique): _____

4. Tengo entendido que este consentimiento autorizará la divulgación de información relacionada a la infección VIH, SIDA o cualquier condición relacionada al SIDA, el abuso de alcohol o drogas, trastornos psicológicos o psiquiátricos o pruebas genéticas si constituyen parte de mi expediente.

5. Esta autorización sirve para permitir la divulgación completa de todos los expedientes que se usarán en la investigación y la posible resolución de una demanda legal que requiere la divulgación de estos expedientes.

6. Tengo entendido que es mi derecho revocar este consentimiento por escrito en cualquier momento salvo hasta el momento en que ya se haya sucedido la divulgación de la información anterior al recibo de la revocación por

el proveedor antes mencionado. Si no se recibe revocación por escrito, se considerará válido la autorización por la duración de mi representación por _____. Para iniciar la revocación de esta autorización, hay que mandar por correo notificación a _____.
Si no se revoca autorización, esta se verá automáticamente vencida al concluir la representación legal del infra-scrito por _____.

7. Se considerará tan válida como la original una fotocopia de esta autorización.

8. La información utilizada o divulgada conforme a esta autorización puede verse sujeta a la redivulgación, la cual significa que ya no será protegida por la ley federal/las leyes de privacidad HIPAA.

Este el _____ día de _____, 20_____.

_____   _____
firma   testigo

ESTA AUTORIZACIÓN REVOCA TODA AUTORIZACIÓN ANTERIOR

* Ley de responsabilidad y transferibilidad de los seguros médicos

Practical Activities

A) Oral Practice

Instructions: Working in pairs and using ONLY SPANISH, recreate each encounter below according to the prompts provided. When necessary, answers to the information you are requesting have been provided in brackets to keep the conversation flowing. If no answer is provided, create your own response. After you have finished, switch roles and recreate it again, providing different phrases and expressions than those used the first time through whenever possible. Take advantage of this activity as an opportunity to practice a variety of vocabulary from *Sections I, II and III* from this chapter. You will need to implement communication strategies from *Chapter 2—Collecting Basic Information in Person and by Phone—#7* when asking someone ABOUT a client rather than speaking DIRECTLY to the client.

1. *You are asking a female client DIRECTLY a series of yes/no questions: ask if she has a doctor [no] and health insurance [no]; carries any kind of government medical assistance [yes], find out which kind; find out if she suffers or has suffered from—(choose 4 ailments from Section II—Medical History—#3); if the client suffers from—(choose 3 ailments from Section II—Medical History—#4); if she has ever had a heart attack [yes] or stroke [no].*

2. *You are asking a male client DIRECTLY for the following information: age [63]; if he is diabetic [no] or hypoglycemic [no]; uses drugs [no] or has ever used drugs [yes]; if he drinks [yes] and how many drinks he consumes per week [provide #]; has a history of (choose 4 ailments from Section II—Medical History—#13); if he smokes or has ever smoked or used tobacco products.*

3. *You are asking a Spanish-speaker ABOUT a female client who has given you permission to speak with this person regarding personal matters: any current medication [no], vitamins [yes—name 3 different types of vitamins], or supplements [no]; any surgeries [yes] and find out which ones [as you go through the list, your partner will respond yes to two different surgeries].*

B) Cognate Refresher

Part I—Instructions: Review the explanation of a *cognate* then complete the exercise:

> *"In Spanish, a cognate is a word that looks and sounds similar to the English word and has the same meaning. This makes them much easier to learn for the English speaker studying Spanish since there is instant word association."*

Below is a list of cognates from this chapter, try to write the ENGLISH word for each one without having to look back in the chapter. Check your answer by locating it in this chapter when you are done.

Spanish	English	Spanish	English
1. hipertensión		6. próstata	
2. depresión		7. ataque	
3. persistente		8. sufre	
4. aspirina		9. drogas	
5. apendectomía		10. alcohólicas	

Part II—Instructions: In Part I, you reviewed TRUE cognates. However, in Spanish, there do exists FALSE cognates* as well. Rather than explain this to you, you are going to find this information on the internet and write a *clear* and *concise* explanation of what a FALSE cognate is.

A false cognate is . . .

_____

_____

_____

_____

Next, search for COMMON FALSE COGNATES IN ENGLISH AND SPANISH on the internet and provide five examples according to the table below. An example has been given to get you started.

SPANISH	ENGLISH	
ej. bizarro	*brave*	*not bizarre.*
1.		*not*
2.		*not*
3.		*not*
4.		*not*
5.		*not*

* *While not to be confusing or deter you from speaking Spanish, it is important to understand that both true and false cognates exist. This should not be a problem for you since you are following the phrases and expressions set forth in the text. However, should you decide to expand your knowledge of the Spanish language and venture outside of this text, such knowledge will be valuable so as to avoid embarrassing situations and/or miscommunication.*

C) Requesting Medical Documents

Instructions: For each situation, request that a client complete a *Medical Information Consent Release* form using the necessary expressions to convey this message.

1. You request that a caller complete this form. You will mail it out. He is to complete it and return it to you. Ask the caller to confirm the purpose of this authorization.

2. You request that a potential client that is present in your office, complete this form. She is to fill it out completely and give it back to you. Ask her to confirm the purpose of this authorization.

D) Matching

Instructions: On the *Medical Information Consent Release* form, you will find a section which details what information is to be released. Match the Spanish information from this form with the English meaning so you can readily identify each language pair when necessary. Due to the number of possible pairs, this matching activity has been divided up into two parts.

List I

1. _____ antecedentes de radiación   a.   ultrasounds

2. _____ informes educativos   b.   MRI scans

3. _____ cinta de monitoreo/electro cardiograma   c.   education reports

4. _____ notas de evolución médica   d.   complete medical records

5. _____ informes de radiografía   e.   discharge summary

6. _____ evaluaciones y resúmenes   f.   tissue blocks or slides

7. _____ imágenes de resonancia magnética   g.   X-ray reports

8. _____ resumen de alta   h.   radiation records

9. _____ ultrasonidos   i.   history and phyical

10. _____ antecedentes médicos y examen físico   j.   substance abuse records

11. _____ diapostivas o muestras de tejido   k.   EKGs, fetal monitor strips

12. _____ expedientes médicos completos   l.   progress notes

13. _____ antecedentes de abuso de sustancias   m.   evaluations and summaries

List II

1. _____ vidéos   a.   operative notes

2. _____ documentos de derivación   b.   echocardiogram tapes

3. _____ notas quirúrgicas   c.   social history

4. _____ constancias de consulta   d.   X-ray films

5. _____ muestras de patología   e.   catherization films

6. _____ tomografías computerizadas   f.   lab reports

7. _____ constancias de internamiento   g.   consultation notes

8. _____ imágenes de cateterismo   h.   videos

9. _____ expedientes psiquiátricos   i.   pathology speciments

10. _____ informes de laboratorio   j.   CT scans

11. _____ imágenes de ecocardiograma   k.   referral documents

12. _____ películas de radiografía   l.   admission notes

13. _____ historia social   m.   psychiatric records

E) Cyber-Investigation

You read in BEFORE YOUR BEGIN that Hispanics are unlikely to be familiar with or willing to talk about their personal and family medical histories. However, knowledge of this information for healthcare providers is crucial when treating patients, regardless of race or ethnicity. Aside from the information you read at the beginning of this chapter, search for more in-depth explanations as to why Hispanics tend to be less knowledgeable about family medical history? What are some of the reasons this may be the case? Next, find the top three life-threatening diseases that afflict the Hispanic population. What are they? Would knowledge of family medical history be useful in the diagnosis of these diseases for early detection and/or treatment? Are these diseases due to life-style choices, genetics or both? Support your answers with information you find on the internet and summarize your findings below.

Chapter 12

The Basics

I. The Spanish Alphabet[1]

*ayl ahl-fah-**bay**-toh ays-pahn-**yohl***
El alfabeto español

Letter	Pronunciation	Letter	Pronunciation
A	*ah*	O	*oh*
B	*bay*	P	*pay*
C	*say*	Q	*koo*
D	*day*	R	***ay**-ray*
E	*ay*	S	***ay**-say*
F	***ay**-fay*	T	*tay*
G	*hay*	U	*oo*
H	***ah**-chay*	V	*bay,* **oo**-bay OR bay **chee**-kah
I	*ee*	W	***doh**-blay bay OR **doh**-blay **oo**-bay*
J	***hoh**-tah*	X	***ay**-kees*
K	*kah*	Y	*ee **gree^ay**-gah*
L	***ay**-lay*	Z	***say**-tah*
M	***ay**-may*	CH[2]	*chay*
N	***ay**-nay*	LL[2]	***ay**-yay*
Ñ	***ayn**-yay*	RR[2]	***ay**-rray OR **doh**-blay **ay**-ray*

Notes

[1] After practicing the alphabet, go to *Chapter 14* and practice spelling random legal terms aloud in Spanish. Learning to spell in Spanish can be very useful, especially when helping a Spanish-speaker with names, addresses, etc. in English.

[2] These three sounds, once considered letters, no longer form part of the Spanish alphabet. They have been included since they are commonly used in spelling and obviously have their own distinctive sounds.

II. Numbers[1]

*lohs **noo**-may-rohs*
Los números

Number	Pronunciation	Number	Pronunciation
0	**say**-roh	31	**tray^een**-tah ee **oo**-noh
1	**oo**-noh	40	koo^ah-**rayn**-tah
2	dohs	42	koo^ah-**rayn**-tah ee dohs
3	trays	50	seen-**koo^ayn**-tah
4	**koo^ah**-troh	60	say-**sayn**-tah
5	**seen**-koh	70	say-**tayn**-tah
6	say^ees	80	oh-**chayn**-tah
7	**see^ay**-tay	90	noh-**bayn**-tah
8	**oh**-choh	100	see^ayn
9	**noo^ay**-bay	101	**see^ayn**-toh **oo**-noh
10	dee^ays	150	**see^ayn**-toh seen-**koo^ayn**-tah
11	**ohn**-say	200	doh-**see^ayn**-tohs
12	**doh**-say	300	tray-**see^ayn**-tohs
13	**tray**-say	400	koo^ah-troh-**see^ayn**-tohs
14	kah-**tohr**-say	500	kee-**nee^ayn**-tohs
15	**keen**-say	600	say-**see^ayn**-tohs
16	dee^ay-see-**say^ees**	700	say-tay-**see^ayn**-tohs
17	dee^ay-see-**see^ay**-tay	800	oh-choh-**see^ayn**-tohs
18	dee^ay-see-**oh**-choh	900	noh-bay-**see^ayn**-tohs
19	dee^ay-see-**noo^ay**-bay	1.000	meel[2]
20	**bay^een**-tay	2.000	dohs meel
21	**bay^een**-tay ee **oo**-noh	10.000	dee^ays meel
22	**bay^een**-tay ee dohs	100.000	see^ayn meel
23	**bay^een**-tay ee trays	200.000	dohs-**see^ayn**-tohs meel
24	**bay^een**-tay ee **koo^ah**-troh	1.000.000	oon mee-**yohn**
25	**bay^een**-tay ee **seen**-koh	10.000.000	dee^ays mee-**yoh**-nays
26	**bay^een**-tay ee say^ees	20.000.000	**bay^een**-tay mee-**yoh**-nays
27	**bay^een**-tay ee **see^ay**-tay	100.000.000	see^ayn mee-**yoh**-nays
28	**bay^een**-tay ee **oh**-choh	200.000.000	dohs-**see^ayn**-tohs mee-**yoh**-nays
29	**bay^een**-tay ee **noo^ay**-bay	1.000.000.000	meel mee-**yoh**-nays[3]
30	**tray^een**-tah	2.000.000.000	dohs meel mee-**yoh**-nays[3]

Notes

[1] The Spanish spellings have not been included since they are irrelevant for your purposes.

[2] Numbers in Spanish can become quite complicated. Therefore, when working with large sums, it is best to write them out and show the person. Also, remember, that when writing numbers in Spanish, commas become decimals and decimals become commas; this is the opposite of the English style of writing numbers.

[3] In American English, *1,000,000,000* would be expressed as *one billion* which is 10^{9}. However, in Spanish, this number would be written as *1.000.000.000* and would be expressed as *mil millones*, which literally means *one thousand millions*. The same is true of *2,000,000,000* and so on. The number for *one billion* in Spanish would actually be *1.000.000.000.000* which is 10^{12} and would be expressed as *un billón* which is *one trillion* in American English.

Chapter 13

Telling Time the Easy Way

Before You Begin

The traditional way to tell time in Spanish can prove itself to be tricky for many beginning Spanish students. Rather than torture you with lengthy explanations that you will probably not remember, a simpler, however, less formal style for telling time is presented in this chapter. Although it is representative of a more vernacular register, it serves the purpose of creating a much more manageable way to tell time.

Important to note as well is that the shortened form of the date in Spanish varies from the shortened form in English. In Spanish, you always begin with the day rather than with the month. When collecting such information, always clarify or ask for clarification of dates using a calendar. You may choose to use a calendar as a visual reference to make sure there is no miscommunication. Here are a few examples:

Spanish: El 25 de marzo, 2015 = 25/3/2015 / English: March 25th, 2015 = 3/25/2015

Spanish: El 1º de abril, 2020 = 1/4/2020 / English: April 1st, 2020 = 4/1/2020

I. Time

*lah **oh**-rah*
La hora

English	Pronunciation & Spanish
1. It is (+ number) …	*ays lah (+ number) …* Es la (+ number) …[1]
	sohn lahs (+ number) … Son las (+ number) …[2]
2. … in the morning.	*… day lah mahn-**yah**-nah.* … de la mañana.[3]
3. … in the afternoon.	*… day lah **tahr**-day.* … de la tarde.[3]
4. … in the evening/at night.	*… day lah **noh**-chay.* … de la noche.[3]
5. At (+ number) …	*ah lah (+ number) …* a la (+ number) …[4]
	ah lahs (+ number) … a las (+ number) …[5]

6. What time is it?

*kay **oh**-rah ays?*
¿Qué hora es?[6]

7. At what time is it (the appointment)?

*ah kay **oh**-rah ays (lah **see**-tah)?*
¿A qué hora es (la cita)?[7]

8. It is midnight.

*ays lah may-dee^ah-**noh**-chay.*
Es la medianoche.

9. It is noon.

*ays ayl may-dee^oh-**dee**-ah.*
Es el mediodía.

10. At midnight.

*ah lah may-dee^ah-**noh**-chay.*
A la medianoche.

11. At noon.

*ahl may-dee^oh-**dee**-ah.*
Al mediodía.

12. Your appointment is …

*soo **see**-tah ays …*
Su cita es …

at one

*ah lah **oo**-nah*
a la una

at two

ah lahs dohs
a las dos

at three

ah lahs trays
a las tres

at four

*ah lahs **koo^ah**-troh*
a las cuatro

at five

*ah lahs **seen**-koh*
a las cinco

at six

ah lahs say^ees
a las seis

at seven

*ah lahs **see^ay**-tay*
a las siete

at eight

*ah lahs **oh**-choh*
a las ocho

at nine

*ah lahs **noo^ay**-bay*
a las nueve

at ten

ah lahs dee^ays
a las diez

at eleven

*ah lahs **ohn**-say*
a las once

at twelve

*ah lahs **doh**-say*
a las doce

fifteen	*ee koo^ahr-toh* y cuarto	
thirty	*ee may-dee^ah* y media	
forty-five	*koo^ah-rayn-tah ee seen-koh* cuarenta y cinco	
in the morning.	*day lah mahn-yay-nah.* de la mañana.	
in the afternoon.	*day lah tahr-day.* de la tarde.	
in the evening.	*day lah noh-chay.* de la noche.	

II. Days of the Week and Months of the Year[8]

lohs dee-ahs day lah say-mah-nah ee lohs may-says dayl ahn-yoh
Los días de la semana y los meses del año

English	Pronunciation & Spanish
1. Monday	*loo-nays* lunes
2. Tuesday	*mahr-tays* martes
3. Wednesday	*mee-ayr-koh-lays* miércoles
4. Thursday	*hoo^ay-bays* jueves
5. Friday	*bee^ayr-nays* viernes
6. Saturday	*sah-bah-doh* sábado
7. Sunday	*doh-meen-goh* domingo
8. January	*ay-nay-roh* enero
9. February	*fay-bray-roh* febrero
10. March	*mahr-soh* marzo

11. April	*ah-**breel*** abril	
12. May	***mah**-yoh* mayo	
13. June	***hoo**-nee^oh* junio	
14. July	***hoo**-lee^oh* julio	
15. August	*ah-**goh**-stoh* agosto	
16. September	*sayp-**tee^aym**-bray* · septiembre	
17. October	*ohk-**too**-bray* octubre	
18. November	*noh-**bee^aym**-bray* noviembre	
19. December	*dee-**see^aym**-bray* diciembre	
20. The appointment is scheduled for …	*say ah proh-grah-**mah**-doh lah **see**-tah **pah**-rah …* Se ha programado la cita para …[9]	
21. The (#) of (month) of (year).	*ayl (#) day ___ day ___.* El (#) de ___ de ___.[10]	
22. The first of (month).	*ayl pree-**may**-roh day ___.* El primero de ___.	

Notes

[1] This phrase is used to answer the question *¿Qué hora es?* when the answer begins with *1* (pronounced ***oo**-nah*).

[2] This phrase is used to answer the question *¿Qué hora es?* when the answer begins with *2 or more*.

[3] For simplicity's sake, use "*de la mañana*" from early morning (generally sun-up) to noon, "*de la tarde*" from noon to sun-down and "*de la noche*" from sun-down to early morning.

[4] This phrase is used to answer the question *¿A qué hora es?* when the answer begins with *1* (pronounced ***oo**-nah*).

[5] This phrase is used to answer the question *¿A qué hora es?* when the answer begins with *2 or more*.

[6] Use this question for asking the time in general.

[7] Use this question for asking at what time an event is or starts.

[8] Unlike English, days of the week and months of the year should never be capitalized. However, capitalization of these words in Spanish is often seen in journalistic style writing.

[9] Use this phrase when confirming an appointment. Complete the phrase with the appropriate follow-up (either phrase 20 or 21).

[10] Reference *Chapter 13 — The Basics — II. Numbers* to assist you with dates.

Chapter 14

Basic Legal Terminology

A

accessory	cómplice (**kohm**-plee-say)
accessory after the fact	encubridor (ayn-koo-bree-**dohr**)
accessory before the fact	cómplice instigador (**kohm**-plee-say een-stee-kah-**dohr**)
accomplice	cómplice (**kohm**-plee-say)
accused [in a criminal case]	acusado (ah-koo-**sah**-doh), inculpado (een-kool-**pah**-doh)
acquittal	absolución (ahb-soh-loo-**see^ohn**)
(to) adjourn	suspender la sesión (soos-payn-**dayr** lah say-**see^ohn**)
(to) admonish	amonestar (ah-moh-nays-**tahr**)
affidavit	declaración jurada (day-klah-rah-**see^ohn** hoo-**rah**-dah)
aforethought	premeditado (pray-may-dee-**tah**-doh), deliberado (day-lee-bay-**rah**-doh)
aggravated assault	agresión agravada (ah-ray-**see^ohn** ah-grah-**bah**-dah)
(to) aid and abet	ayudar e incitar (ah^ee-yoo-**dahr** ay een-see-**tahr**)
alibi	coartada (koh-ahr-**tah**-dah), defensa (day-**fayn**-sah)
(to) amend	enmendar (ayn-mayn-**dahr**)
appeal	apelación (ah-pay-lah-**see^ohn**)
appeal for reversal	recurso de reposición (rray-**koor**-soh day rray-poh-see-**see^ohn**)
arbitration	arbitraje (ahr-bee-**trah**-hay)
arraignment	lectura de cargos (layk-**too**-rah day **kahr**-gohs)
arrest warrant	orden de arresto (**ohr**-dayn day ah-**rrays**-toh)
arson	incendio premeditado (een-**sayn**-dee^oh pray-may-dee-**tah**-doh)
(simple) assault	agresión (ilegítima) (ah-ray-**see^ohn** ee-lay-**hee**-tee-mah)
assault and battery	agresión con lesiones (ah-gray-**see^ohn** kohn lay-**see^oh**-nays)
attorney	abogado (ah-boh-**gah**-doh)
attorney general	procurador general (proh-koo-rah-**dohr** hay-nay-**rahl**)
auto theft	robo de vehículo (**rroh**-boh day bay-**ee**-koo-loh)

B

bad check	cheque sin fondos (**chay**-kay seen **fohn**-dohs)
bail	fianza (**fee^ahn**-sah)
bail bond	bono de fianza (**boh**-noh day **fee^ahn**-sah)
bailiff	alguacil (ahl-goo^ah-**seel**)
(factual) basis	fundamento (foon-dah-**mayn**-toh)
battery	lesiones (lay-**see^oh**-nays)
bench conference	consulta en el estrado (kohn-**sool**-tah ayn ayl ays-**trah**-doh)
bench trial	jucio ante el juez (**hoo^ee**-see^oh **ahn**-tay ayl hoo^ays)
blood alcohol level	nivel de alcohol en la sangre (nee-**bayl** day ahl-koh-**ohl** ayn lah **sahn**-gray)
blood alcohol test	análisis de alcohol en la sangre (ah-**nah**-lee-sees day ahl-koh-**ohl** ayn lah **sahn**-gray)
boisterous conduct	conducta escandalosa (kohn-**dook**-tah ays-kahn-dah-**loh**-sah)
breaking and entering	allanamiento de morada (ah-yah-nah-**mee^ayn**-toh day moh-**rah**-dah)
breathalyzer	alcoholímetro (ahl-koh-oh-**lee**-may-troh)
(to) bring legal action against	entablar un juicio (ayn-tah-**blahr** oon **hoo^ee**-see^oh)
(to) bring to trial	someter a juicio (soh-may-**tayr** ah **hoo^ee**-see^ooh)
burglary	robo con escalamiento (**rroh**-boh kohn ays-kah-lah-**mee^ayn**-toh)

C

capital crime	delito con pena de muerte (day-**lee**-toh kohn **pay**-nah day **moo^ayr**-tay)
capital punishment	pena de muerte (**pay**-nah day **moo^ayr**-tay)
car theft	robo de auto (**rroh**-boh day **ah^oo**-toh)
carjacking	robo de auto con violencia (**rroh**-boh day **ah^oo**-toh kohn bee^oh-**layn**-see^ah)
case	caso (**kah**-soh), causa (**kah^oo**-sah)
(to) cease and desist	cesar y desistir (say-**sahr** ee day-sees-**teer**)
(to) charge	acusar de (ah-koo-**sahr** day)
charges	cargos (**kahr**-gohs)
child abuse	abuso de menores (ah-**boo**-soh day may-**noh**-rays)
child molestation	abuso deshonesto de un menor (ah-**boo**-soh days-oh-**nays**-toh de oon may-**nohr**)
child support	manutención de niños (mah-noo-tayn-**see^ohn** day **neen**-yohs)
collection agency	agencia de cobranza (ah-**hayn**-see^ah de koh-**brahn**-sah)
community service	servicio comunitario (sayr-**bee**-see^oh koh-moo-nee-**tah**-ree^oh)

complainant	demandante (day-mahn-**dahn**-tay)
concurrent sentences	condenas simultáneas (kohn-**day**-nahs see-mool-**tah**-nay-ahs)
consecutive sentences	condenas consecutivas (kohn-**day**-nahs kohn-say-koo-**tee**-bahs)
consent	permiso (payr-**mee**-soh)
contempt of court	contumacia (kohn-too-**mah**-see^ah)
controlled substance	sustancia regulada (soos-**tahn**-see^ah rray-goo-**lah**-dah)
corpus delicti	cuerpo del delito (**koo^ayr**-poh dayl day-**lee**-toh)
counsel	*see *attorney*
counterclaim	contrademanda (kohn-trah-day-**mahn**-dah)
court	tribunal (tree-boo-**nahl**), juzgado (hoos-**gah**-doh)
court order	orden judicial (**ohr**-dayn hoo-dee-**see^ahl**)
creditor	acreedor (ah-kray-ay-**dohr**)
crime [in general]	delincuencia (day-leen-**koo^ayn**-see^ah)
crime [capital crime]	crimen (**kree**-mayn)
crime [non-capital crime]	delito (day-**lee**-toh)
criminal history	antecedentes penales (ahn-tay-say-**dayn**-tays pay-**nah**-lays)
custodial parent	padre de custodia (**pah**-dray day koos-**toh**-dee^ah)
custody [of a child]	patria potestad, custodia (**pah**-tree^ah poh-tays-**tahd**, koos-**toh**-dee^ah)

D

damages	daños y perjuicios (**dahn**-yohs ee payr-**hoo^ee**-see^ohs)
deadline	fecha límite (**fay**-chah **lee**-mee-tay)
defendant [in a civil case]	demandado (day-mahn-**dah**-doh)
defendant [in a criminal case]	*see *accused*
defense attorney	abogado defensor (ah-boh-**gah**-doh day-fayn-**sohr**)
deferred sentence	condena aplazada (kohn-**day**-nah ah-plah-**sah**-dah)
deposition	deposición (day-poh-see-**see^ohn**)
direct evidence	prueba directa (**proo^ay**-bah dee-**rayk**-tah)
direct examination	interrogatorio directo (een-tay-rroh-gah-**toh**-ree^oh dee-**rayk**-toh)
disabled	discapacitado (dees-kah-pah-see-**tah**-doh), incapacitado (een-kah-pah-see-**tah**-doh)
discovery	divulgación de pruebas (dee-bool-gah-**see^ohn** day **proo^ay**-bahs)
(to) dismiss a charge	desestimar un cargo (days-ays-tee-**mahr** oon **kahr**-goh)
disturbing the peace	alterar el orden público (ahl-tay-**rahr** ayl **ohr**-dayn **poo**-blee-koh)
diversion program	programa de desviación (proh-**grah**-mah day days-bee^ah-**see^ohn**)
DNA sample	muestra de ADN (**moo^ays**-trah day ah day **ay**-nay)

(to) drop the charge	retirar el cargo (rray-tee-**rahr** ayl **kahr**-goh)
due diligence	diligencia debida (dee-lee-**hayn**-see^ah day-**bee**-dah)
DUI / DWI	manejar en estado de embriaguez (mah-nay-**hahr** ayn ays-**tah**-doh day aym-bree^ah-**gays**)

E

egregious	flagrante (flah-**grahn**-tay)
electronic home monitoring device	arresto domiciliario electrónico (ah-**rrays**-toh doh-mee-see-**lee^ah**-ree^oh ay-layk-**troh**-nee-koh)
embezzlement	desfalco (days-**fahl**-koh), malversación (mahl-bayr-sah-**see^ohn**)
endangerment	imprudencia temeraria (eem-proo-**dayn**-see^ah tay-may-**rah**-ree^ah)
(to) enter a plea	declararse (day-klah-**rahr**-say)
entrapment	incitación a la comisión de un delito (een-see-tah-**see^ohn** ah lah koh-mee-**see^ohn** day oon day-**lee**-toh)
ERISA	ley de seguridad de los ingresos de jubilación para los empleados (lay day say-goo-ree-**dahd** dah een-**gray**-sohs day hoo-bee-lah-**see^ohn pah**-rah lohs aym-play-**ah**-dohs)
evidence	pruebas (**proo^ay**-bahs)
evidentiary hearing	audiencia probatoria (ah^oo-**dee^ayn**-see^ah proh-bah-**toh**-ree^ah)
exemption	exención (ayk-sayn-**see^ohn**)
expenses	gastos (**gahs**-tohs)
expert witness	perito (pay-**ree**-toh), testigo pericial (tays-**tee**-goh pay-ree-**see^ahl**)
extension	prórroga (**proh**-rroh-gah)
extenuating circumstances	circunstancias atenuantes (seer-koons-**tahn**-see^ahs ah-tayn-**yoo^ahn**-tays)
extortion	extorsión (ayks-tohr-**see^ohn**)
eyewitness	testigo ocular (tays-**tee**-goh oh-koo-**lahr**)

F

factual basis	base fáctica (**bah**-say **fahk**-tee-kah)
failure to appear	falta de comparecencia (**fahl**-tah day kohm-pah-ray-**sayn**-see^ah)
fees *(attorney)*	honorarios (oh-noh-**rah**-ree^ohs)
felony	delito mayor (day-**lee**-toh mah-**yohr**)
field sobriety test	prueba de sobriedad en el campo (**proo^ay**-bah day soh-bree^ay-**dahd** ayn ayl **kahm**-poh)
(to) file a complaint	presentar una denuncia (pray-sayn-**tahr** oo-nah day-**noon**-see^ah)
(to) file a lawsuit	presentar una demanda (pray-sayn-**tahr** oo-nah day-**mahn**-dah)
filing fee	cuota de presentación (**koo^oh**-tah day pray-sayn-tah-**see^ohn**)
fine	multa (**mool**-tah)

fingerprint	huella digital (oo^ay-yah dee-hee-tahl)
first degree	en primer grado (ayn pree-mayr grah-doh)
for the record	para que conste en acta (pah-rah kay kohns-tay ayn ahk-tah)
(to) forfeit bail	perder la fianza (payr-dayr lah fee^ahn-sah)
forgery	falsificación (fahl-see-fee-kah-see^ohn)
foster care	colocación con una familia de crianza (koh-loh-kah-see^ohn kohn oo-nah fah-mee-lee^ah day kree^ahn-sah)
foster family	familia de crianza (fah-mee-lee^ah day kree^ahn-sah)
foster home	casa de crianza (kah-sah day kree^ahn-sah)
fraud	fraude (frah^oo-day)

G

garnishment (wage)	embargo de sueldos y salarios (aym-bahr-goh day soo^ahl-dohs ee sah-lah-ree^ohs)
(to) go to trial	ir a juicio (eer ah hoo^ee-see^oh)
good faith	de buena fe (day boo^ay-nah fay)
grand jury	jurado acusatorio (hoo-rah-doh ah-koo-sah-toh-ree^oh)
gross misdemeanor	delito menor grave (day-lee-toh may-nohr grah-bay)
guardian	tutor (too-tohr)
guardian ad litem	tutor ad litem (too-tohr ahd lee-taym)
(sentencing) guidelines	normas de condena (nohr-mahs day kohn-day-nah)
guilty plea	declaración de culpabilidad (day-klah-rah-see^ohn day kool-pah-bee-lee-dahd)

H

handicapped	*see disabled
harassment	acoso (ah-koh-soh)
hardened criminal	criminal empedernido (kree-mee-nahl aym-pay-dayr-nee-doh)
health insurance	seguro médico (say-goo-roh may-dee-koh)
(to) hear a case	ver un caso (bayr oon kah-soh), ver una causa (bayr oo-nah kah^oo-sah)
hearing	audiencia (ah^oo-dee^ayn-see^ah)
hearsay evidence	testimonio de terceros (tays-tee-moh-nee^oh day tayr-say-rohs)
holdup	asalto (ah-sahl-toh), atraco (ah-trah-koh)
homicide	homicidio (oh-mee-see-dee^oh)
house arrest	arresto domiciliario (ah-rrays-toh doh-mee-see-lee^ah-ree^oh)
hung jury	jurado sin veredicto (hoo-rah-doh seen bay-ray-deek-toh)

I

ignition interlock device	dispositivo de control del arranque (dees-poh-see-**tee**-boh day kohn-**trohl** dayl ah-**rrahn**-kay)
(to) impound	incautar (een-**kah**^oo-tahr)
imprisoned	en prisión (ayn pree-**see**^ohn)
in session	en sesión (ayn say-**see**^ohn)
inadmissible	inadmisible (een-ahd-mee-**see**-blay)
indecent exposure	exhibicionismo (ayk-see-bee-see^oh-**nees**-moh)
(to) indict	acusar formalmente (ah-koo-**sahr** fohr-mahl-**mayn**-tay)
indictment	acusación formal (ah-koo-sah-**see**^ohn fohr-**mahl**)
(to) initiate legal proceedings	entablar un proceso legal (ayn-tah-**blahr** oon proh-**say**-soh lay-**gahl**)
injury	lesión (lay-**see**^ohn)
IRA	cuenta personal de ahorro jubilatorio (**koo**^ayn-tah payr-soh-**nahl** day ah-**oh**-rroh hoo-bee-lah-**toh**-ree^oh)
irrelevant	no pertinente (noh payr-tee-**nayn**-tay)

J

judgment	fallo (**fah**-yoh)
(to) jump bail	fugarse estando bajo fianza (foo-**gahr**-say ays-**tahn**-doh **bah**-hoh **fee**^ahn-sah)
juror	miembro del jurado (**mee**^aym-broh dayl hoo-**rah**-doh)
jury	jurado (hoo-**rah**-doh)

K

KEOGH	plan de pensiones para profesionales autónomos (plahn day payn-**see**^oh-nays **pah**-rah proh-fay-see^oh-**nah**-lays ah^oo-**toh**-noh-mohs)
knowingly	a sabiendas (ah-sah-**bee**^ayn-dahs)

L

larceny	latrocinio (lah-troh-**see**-nee^oh)
law enforcement officer	agente del orden público (ah-**hayn**-tay dayl **ohr**-dayn **poo**-blee-koh)
law-abiding	que respeta la ley (kay rrays-**pay**-tah lah lay)
lawsuit	demanda (day-**mahn**-dah)
legal procedures	trámites legales (**trah**-mee-tays lay-**gah**-lays)
legal proceedings	actuaciones (ahk-too^ah-**see**^oh-nays)
leniency	indulgencia (een-dool-**hayn**-see^ah)
lenient	indulgente (een-dool-**hayn**-tay)

liability	responsabilidad civil (rrays-pohn-sah-bee-lee-**dahd** see-**beel**)
liable	responsable (rrays-pohn-**sah**-blay)
lie detector	polígrafo (poh-**lee**-grah-foh)
life in prison	pena de condena perpetua (**pay**-nah day kohn-**day**-nah payr-**pay**-too^ah)
life sentence	condena perpetua (kohn-**day**-nah payr-**pay**-too^ah)

M

malice	dolo penal (**doh**-loh pay-**nahl**)
mandatory minimum sentence	pena mínima obligatoria (**pay**-nah **mee**-nee-mah oh-blee-gah-**toh**-ree^ah)
manslaughter	homicidio culposo (oh-mo-**see**-dee^oh kool-**poh**-soh)
material evidence	prueba esencial (**proo^ay**-bah ay-sayn-**see^ahl**)
material witness	testigo esencial (tays-**tee**-goh ay-sayn-**see^ahl**)
mediation	mediación (may-dee^ah-**see^ohn**)
mediator	mediador (may-dee^ah-**dohr**)
medical malpractice	negligencia médica (nay-glee-**hayn**-see^ah **may**-dee-kah)
methamphetamine	metanfetamina (may-tahn-fay-tah-**mee**-nah)
Miranda rights	derechos constitucionales (day-**ray**-chohs kohns-tee-too-see^oh-**nah**-lays)
misdemeanor	delito menor (day-**lee**-toh may-**nohr**)
mistrial	juicio nulo (**hoo^ee**-see^oh **noo**-loh)
mitigating circumstances	*see extenuating circumstances
money laundering	lavado de dinero (lah-**bah**-doh day dee-**nay**-roh)
(to) monitor	monitorear (moh-nee-toh-ray-**ahr**)
motion	petición (pay-tee-**see^ohn**)
motion to dismiss	petición para desestimar una causa (pay-tee-**see^ohn pah**-rah days-ays-tee-**mahr oo**-nah **kay^oo**-sah)
murder attempt	intento de asesinato / homicidio (een-**tayn**-toh day ah-say-see-**nah**-toh / oh-mee-**see**-dee^oh)

N

(to) neglect	descuidar (days-koo^ee-**dahr**)
neglect	descuido (days-**koo^ee**-doh)
negligence	negligencia (hay-glee-**hayn**-see^ah)
no-contact order	orden que prohibe el contacto (**ohr**-dayn kay proh-**ee**-bay ayl kohn-**tahk**-toh)
no contest	no me opongo (noh may oh-**pohn**-goh)
nolo contendere	*see no contest

noncompliance	incumplimiento (een-koom-plee-**mee^ayn**-toh)
notice	notificación (noh-tee-fee-kah-**see^ohn**)
nuisance	molestia (moh-**lays**-tee^ah)

O

(to take an) oath	juramentar (hoo-rah-mayn-**tahr**)
(under) oath	bajo juramento (**bah**-hoh hoo-rah-**mayn**-toh)
(to) object	oponerse a (oh-poh-**nayr**-say ah), objetar a (ohb-hay-**tahr** ah), protestar (proh-tays-**tahr**)
off the record *[as in a description]*	extraoficial (ayks-trah-oh-fee-**see^ahl**)
off the record *[as in how something is told, etc.]*	extraoficialmente (ayks-trah-oh-fee-see^ahl-**mayn**-tay)
offender	delincuente (day-leen-**koo^ayn**-tay)
offense (civil)	*[if civil]* infracción (een-frahk-**see^oh**)
offense (criminal)	*[if criminal]* delito (day-**lee**-toh)
omnibus hearing	audiencia general (ah^oo-**dee^ayn**-see^ah hay-nay-**rahl**)
on the records	en las actas (ayn lahs **ahk**-tahs)
out-of-court settlement	acuerdo extrajudicial (ah-**koo^ayr**-doh ayks-trah-hoo-dee-**see^ahl**)
(to) overrule	denegar (day-nay-**gahr**)
overruled *[as a description]*	denegado (day-nay-**gah**-doh)
overruled *[as an interjection]*	no ha lugar (noh ah loo-**gahr**)
own recognizance	bajo palabra (**bah**-hoh pah-**lah**-brah)

P

pain and suffering	daños físicos y morales (**dahn**-yohs **fee**-see-kohs ee moh-**rah**-lays)
paraphernalia	adminículos (ahd-mee-**nee**-koo-lohs)
parole	libertad condicional (lee-bayr-**tahd** kohn-dee-see^oh-**nahl**)
pedophile	pedófilo (pay-**doh**-fee-loh)
penalty of perjury	pena de perjurio (**pay**-nah day payr-**hoo**-ree^oh)
perjury	perjurio (payr-**hoo**-ree^oh)
(to) perpetrate	perpetrar (payr-pay-**trahr**)
perpetrator	autor (ah^oo-**tohr**)
personal belongings	efectos personales (ay-**fayk**-tohs payr-soh-**nah**-lays)
personal property *[as in land, real estate, etc.]*	bienes muebles (**bee^ay**-nays **moo^ay**-blays)

personal property *[as in belongings, etc; synonym for personal belongings]*	propiedad personal (proh-pee^ay-**dahd** payr-soh-**nahl**)
petition	petición (pay-tee-**see^ohn**)
petty theft	hurto menor (**oor**-toh may-**nohr**)
plea	declaración (day-klah-rah-**see^ohn**)
plea agreement	acuerdo declaratorio (ah-**koo^ayr**-doh day-klah-rah-**toh**-ree^oh)
plea bargain	acuerdo de reducción de pena (ah-**koo^ayr**-doh day rray-dook-**see^ohn** day **pay**-nah)
(to) plead	declararse (day-klah-**rahr**-say)
(to) plead guilty / not guilty	declararse culpable / no culpable (day-klah-**rahr**-say kool-**pah**-blay / noh kool-**pah**-blay)
pleadings	alegatos (ah-lay-**gah**-tohs)
police	policía (poh-lee-**see**-ah)
police car	patrulla (pah-**troo**-yah)
police officer	agente de policía (ah-**hayn**-tay day poh-lee-**see**-ah)
possession of firearm	posesión de armas de fuego (poh-say-**see^ohn** day **ahr**-mahs day **foo^ay**-goh)
power of attorney	poder legal (poh-**dayr** lay-**gahl**)
preliminary hearing	audiencia preliminar (ah^oo-dee^ayn-see^ah pray-lee-mee-**nahr**)
pre-sentence report	informe precondenatorio (een-**fohr**-may pray-kohn-day-nah-**toh**-ree^oh)
pre-trial motion	petición previa al juicio (pay-tee-**see^ohn** **pray**-bee^ah ahl **hoo^ee**-see^oh)
prisoner	preso/a, prisionero/a (**pray**-soh/sah, pree-see^oh-**nay**-roh/rah)
probable cause	motivo fundado (moh-**tee**-boh foon-**dah**-doh)
probation	libertad vigilada (lee-bayr-**tahd** bee-hee-**lah**-dah)
probation officer	agente de libertad vigilada (ah-**hayn**-tay day lee-bayr-**tahd** bee-hee-**lah**-dah)
(to) prosecute	procesar (proh-say-**sahr**)
prosecution	fiscalía (fees-kah-**lee**-ah)
prosecutor	fiscal (fees-**kahl**)
public nuisance	alteración del orden público (ahl-tay-rah-**see^ohn** dayl **ohr**-dayn **poo**-blee-koh)

Q

| qualified | capacitado/a (kah-pah-see-**tah**-doh/dah) |

R

reasonable doubt	duda razonable (**doo**-dah rrah-soh-**nah**-blay)
(to) recess	levantar la sesión (lay-bahn-**tahr** lah say-**see^ohn**)
reckless	imprudente (eem-proo-**dayn**-tay)
reckless endangerment	imprudencia temeraria (eem-proo-**dayn**-see^ah tay-may-**rahr**-ree^ah)
(to) release	liberar (lee-bay-**rahr**)
relevant	pertinente (payr-tee-**nayn**-tay)
(to) remain silent	guardar silencio (goo^ahr-**dahr** see-**layn**-see^oh)
(to) render a verdict	emitir un veredicto (ay-mee-**teer** oon bay-ree-**deek**-toh)
repeat offender	infractor reincidente (een-frahk-**tohr** rray-een-see-**dayn**-tay)
repeat violation	reincidencia (rray^een-see-**dayn**-see^ah)
(to) report a crime	denunciar (day-noon-**see^ayr**)
(to) resist arrest	resistirse al arresto (rray-sees-**teer**-say ahl ah-**rrays**-toh)
restitution	restitución (rrays-tee-too-**see^ohn**)
restraining order	orden de restricción (**ohr**-dayn day rrays-treek-**see^ohn**)
review hearing	audiencia de revisión (ah^oo-**dee^ayn**-see^ah day rray-bee-**see^ohn**)
ruling	fallo (**fah**-yoh)

S

sanction	sanción (sahn-**see^ohn**)
scene of the crime	el lugar de los hechos (ayl loo-**gahr** day lohs **ay**-chohs)
search warrant	orden de registro (**ohr**-dayn day rray-**hees**-troh)
second degree	en segundo grado (ayn say-**goon**-doh **grah**-doh)
self-defense	autodefensa (ah^oo-toh-day-**fayn**-sah)
sentence	condena (kohn-**day**-nah)
(to) sentence	condenar (kohn-day-**nahr**)
sentencing hearing	audiencia para dictar la condena (ah^oo-**dee^ayn**-see^ah **pah**-rah deek-**tahr** lah kohn-**day**-nah)
(to) serve a sentence	cumplir una condena (koom-**pleer oo**-nah kohn-**day**-nah)
(to) serve (documents)	entregar oficialmente (ayn-tray-**gahr** oh-fee-see^ahl-**mayn**-tay)
session	sesión (say-**see^ohn**)
(to) settle	llegar a un acuerdo (yay-**gahr** ah oon ah-**koo^ayr**-doh)
settlement	acuerdo (ah-**koo^ayr**-doh)
sexual abuse	abuso sexual (ah-**boo**-soh sayk-**soo^ahl**)
sexual assault	agresión sexual (ah-gray-**see^ohn** sayk-**soo^ahl**)
sexual offender treatment	tratamiento para delincuentes sexuales (trah-tah-**mee^ayn**-toh **pah**-rah day-leen-**koo^ayn**-tays sayk-**soo^ah**-lays)

sexual offender	delincuente sexual (day-leen-**koo^ayn**-tay sayk-**soo^ahl**)
sexual offense	delito sexual (day-**lee**-toh sayk-**soo^ahl**)
shoplifting	hurto de tiendas (**oor**-toh day **tee^ayn**-dahs)
small claims court	tribunal de reclamos menores (tree-boo-**nahl** day rray-**klah**-mohs may-**noh**-rays)
sober	sobrio (**soh**-bree^oh)
speed limit	límite de velocidad (**lee**-mee-tay day bay-loh-see-**dahd**)
speedy trial	juicio sin demora (**hoo^ee**-see^oh seen day-**moh**-rah)
stalking	acecho (ah-**say**-choh)
standard sentencing range	escala normal de condena (ays-**kah**-lah nohr-**mahl** day kohn-**day**-nah)
statute of limitations	ley de prescripción (lay day prays-**kreep**-see^ohn)
(to) subpoena *(a person)*	citar (see-**tahr**)
(to) sue	demandar (day-**mayn**-dahr)
summary judgement	fallo sumario (**fah**-yoh soo-**mah**-ree^oh)
(to) summon	*see to subpoena*
summons	orden de comparecencia (**ohr**-dayn day kohm-pah-ray-**sayn**-see^ah)
(to) suppress evidence	excluir prueba (ahks-**kloo^eer proo^ay**-bah)
surveillance	vigilancia (bee-hee-**lahn**-see^ah)
suspect	sospechoso (sohs-pay-**choh**-soh)
suspended sentence	condena suspendida (kohn-**day**-nah soos-payn-**dee**-dah)
(to) swear in	juramentar (hoo-rah-mayn-**tahr**)

T

(to) take an oath	prestar juramento (prays-**tahr** hoo-rah-**mayn**-toh)
temporary restraining order	orden de protección temporal (**ohr**-dayn day proh-tayk-**see^ohn** taym-poh-**rahl**)
(to) testify	testificar (tays-tee-fee-**kahr**)
testimony	testimonio (tays-tee-**moh**-nee^oh)
theft	hurto (**ohr**-toh)
threat	amenaza (ah-may-**nah**-sah)
(to) threaten	amenazar (ah-may-nah-**sahr**)
traffic	tráfico (**trah**-fee-koh)
trespassing	entrada ilícita delictiva (ayn-**trah**-dah ee-**lee**-see-tah day-leek-**tee**-bah)
truancy	ausentismo injustificado (ah^oo-sayn-**tees**-moh een-hoos-tee-fee-**kah**-doh)

U

under oath	bajo juramento (**bah**-hoh hoo-rah-**mayn**-toh)
under penalty of	bajo pena de (**bah**-hoh **pay**-nah day)
undercover agent	agente encubierto (ah-**hayn**-tay ayn-koo-**bee^ayr**-toh)
(the) undersigned	el abajo firmante (ayl ah-**bah**-hoh feer-**mahn**-tay)

V

(to) vacate *(a ruling)*	invalidar (een-bah-lee-**dahr**)
vehicular assault	agresión vehicular (ah-gray-**see^ohn** bay-ee-koo-**lahr**)
verdict	veredicto (bay-ray-**deek**-toh)
(to) violate *(a law)*	quebrantar (kay-brahn-**tahr**), contravenir (kohn-trah-bay-**neer**)
violation *(of a law)*	contravención (kohn-trah-bayn-**see^ohn**)

W

(to) waive *(rights)*	renunciar (rray-noon-**see^ahr**)
wanton	sin sentido (seen sayn-**tee**-doh)
warning	advertencia (ahd-bahr-**tayn**-see^ah)
warrant	orden judicial (**ohr**-dayn hoo-dee-**see^ahl**)
whereabouts	paradero (pah-rah-**day**-roh)
will	testamento (tays-tah-**mayn**-toh)
willful	intencionado (een-tayn-see^oh-**nah**-doh)
willful act	acto intencionado (**ahk**-toh een-tayn-see^oh-**nah**-doh)
witness	testigo (tays-**tee**-goh)
work release	libertad para trabajar (lee-bayr-**tahd pah**-rah trah-bah-**hahr**)
writ	mandamiento judicial (mahn-dah-**mee^ayn**-toh hoo-dee-**see^ahl**)
writ of execution	mandamiento de ejecución (mahn-dah-**mee^ayn**-toh day ay-hay-koo-**see^ohn**)

Appendix

Countries/Nationalities[1]

Country *pah-**ees*** País	Nationality *nah-see^oh-nah-lee-**dahd*** Nacionalidad
Argentina *ahr-hayn-**tee**-nah* Argentina	Argentine *ahr-hayn-**tee**-noh/nah* argentino/a
Bolivia *boh-**lee**-bee^ah* Bolivia	Bolivian *boh-lee-**bee^ah**-noh/nah* boliviano/a
Chile ***chee**-lay* Chile	Chilean *chee-**lay**-noh/nah* chileno/a
Colombia *koh-**lohm**-bee^ah* Colombia	Colombian *koh-lohm-**bee^ah**-noh/nah* colombiano/a
Costa Rica ***kohs**-tah **rree**-kah* Costa Rica	Costa Rican *kohs-tah-rree-**sayn**-say* costarricense
Cuba ***koo**-bah* Cuba	Cuban *koo-**bah**-noh/nah* cubano/a
Dominican Republic *lah rray-**poo**-blee-kah doh-mee-nee-**kah**-nah* La República Dominicana	Dominican *doh-mee-nee-**kah**-noh/nah* dominicano/a
Ecuador *ay-koo^ah-**dohr** Ecuador	Ecuadorean *ay-koo^ah-toh-**ree^ah**-noh/nah* ecuatoriano/a
El Salvador *ayl sahl-bah-**dohr*** El Salvador	Salvadoran *sahl-bah-doh-**rayn**-yoh/yah* salvadoreño/a

Guatemala	Guatemalan
goo^ah-tay-**mah**-lah	goo^ah-tay-mahl-**tay**-koh/kah
Guatemala	guatemalteco/a

Honduras	Honduran
ohn-**doo**-rahs	ohn-doo-**rayn**-yoh/yah
Honduras	hondureño/a

Nicaragua	Nicaraguan
nee-kah-**rah**-goo^ah	nee-kah-rah-**goo^ayn**-say
Nicaragua	nicaragüense

Panama	Panamanian
pah-nah-**mah**	pah-nah-**mayn**-yoh/yah
Panamá	panameño/a

Paraguay	Paraguayan
pah-rah-**gwah^ee**	pah-rah-**gwah^ee**-yoh/yah
Paraguay	paraguayo/a

Peru	Peruvean
pay-**roo**	pay-**roo^ah**-noh/nah
Perú	peruano/a

Puerto Rico	Puerto Rican
poo^ayr-toh **rree**-koh	poo^ayr-toh-rree-**kayn**-yoh/yah
Puerto Rico	puertorriqueño/a

Spain	Spanish
ays-**pahn**-yah	ays-pahn-**yohl**(-lah)
España	español/a[2]

United States	American
ays-**tah**-dohs oo-**nee**-dohs	ays-tah-doh-oo-nee-**dayn**-say
Estados Unidos	estadounidense

Uruguay	Uruguayan
oo-roo-**gwah^ee**	oo-roo-**gwah^ee**-yoh/yah
Uruguay	uruguayo/a

Venezuela	Venezuelan
bay-nay-**soo^ay**-lah	bayn-nay-soh-**lah**-noh/nah
Venezuela	venezolano/a

Notes

[1] You will hear a *male* use the *-o ending* and a *female* use the *-a ending* where indicated. Otherwise, when no option is given, this indicates that the same word may be used to refer to a *male* or a *female*. For example, *costarricense* allows for no gender distinction.

[2] Notice with this word, the form referring to a *male* ends in *-l*; the *-a ending* is added to this to create the form referring to a *female*.

Major Religious Affiliations[1]

*ah-fee-lee^ah-**see^oh**-nays rray-lee-**hee^oh**-sahs preen-see-**pah**-lays*
Afiliaciones religiosas principales

Catholic	*kah-**toh**-lee-koh/kah* católico/a
Protestant	*proh-tays-**tahn**-tay* protestante
Baptist	*bah^oo-**tees**-tah* bautista
Jehovah's Witness	*tays-**tee**-goh/gah day hay-oh-**bah*** testigo/a de Jehová
Methodist	*may-toh-**dees**-tah* metodista
Lutheran	*loo-tay-**rahn**-noh/nah* luterano/a
Presbyterian	*prays-bee-tay-**ree^ah**-noh/nah* presbiteriano
Mormon	*mohr-**mohn**(-ah)* mormón/a[2]
Seventh Day Adventist	*ahd-bahn-**tees**-tah* adventista
Jewish	*hoo-**dee**-oh/ah* judío/a
Buddhist	*boo-**dee**-stah* budista
Muslim	*moo-sool-**mahn**(-ah)* musulmán/a[2]
Atheist	*ah-**tey**-oh/ah* ateo/a
Agnostic	*ahg-**nohs**-tee-koh/kah* agnóstico/a
Christian Science	*krees-**tee^ah**-noh/nah see^ayn-**tee**-fee-koh/kah* cristiano/a científico/a[1]

Notes

[1] You will hear a *male* use the *-o ending* and a *female* use the *-a ending* where indicated. Otherwise, when no option is given, this indicates that the same word may be used to refer to a *male* or a *female*. For example, *budista* allows for no gender distinction.

[2] Notice with this word, the form referring to a *male* ends in *-m*; the *-a ending* is added to this to create the form which refers to a *female*. In the case of these two words, the written accent is removed in the feminine form.

Races[1]

rah-sahs
Razas

American Indian	*een*-dee^oh nohr-tay-ah-may-ree-*kah*-noh indio norteamericano
Native Alaskan	een-*dee*-hay-nah day ah-*lahs*-kah indígena de Alaska
White or Caucasian	*blahn*-koh, kah^oo-*kah*-see-koh blanco, caucásico
Black or African American	*nay*-groh, ah-froh-ah-may-ree-*kah*-noh negro, afroamericano
Asian	ah-*see^ah*-tee-koh asiático
Native Hawaiian	ah-wah^ee-*yah*-noh hawaiano
Hawaiian Pacific Islander	een-*dee*-hay-nah day lah poh-lee-*nay*-see^ah indígena de la Polinesia
Hispanic	ees-*pah*-noh hispano

Note

[1] Only common races with which you will most likely come into contact have been listed. This is obviously not an extensive list of world races.

Parts of the Body

pahr-tays dayl **koo^ayr**-poh oo-**mah**-noh
Partes del cuerpo humano

abdomen	*ayl ahb-**doh**-mayn* el abdomen
ankle	*ayl toh-**bee**-yoh* el tobillo
arm	*ayl **brah**-soh* el brazo
armpit	*lah ahk-**see**-lah* la axila[1]
back	*lah ays-**pahl**-dah* la espalda
breast	*ayl **say**-noh* el seno
buttock	*lah **nahl**-gah* la nalga[2]
calf	*lah pahn-toh-**ree**-yah* la pantorilla
cheek	*lah may-**hee**-yah* la mejilla
chest	*ayl **pay**-choh* el pecho
chin	*lah bahr-**bee**-yah* la barbilla[3]
coccyx	*ayl **kohk**-seeks* el cóccix[4]
elbow	*ayl **koh**-doh* el codo
eye	*ayl **oh**-hoh* el ojo
eye lid	*ayl **pahr**-pah-doh* el párpado
eyebrow	*lah **say**-hah* la ceja
face	*lah **kah**-rah* la cara
finger	*ayl **day**-doh* el dedo

foot	*ayl pee^ay* **el pie**
forearm	*ayl ahn-tay-**brah**-soh* **el antebrazo**
forehead	*lah **frayn**-tay* **la frente**
groin	*lah **een**-glay* **la ingle**
hamstring	*ayl pohs-tay-**ree^ohr** dayl **moo**-sloh* **el posterior del muslo**
hand	*lah **mah**-noh* **la mano**
head	*lah kah-**bay**-sah* **la cabeza**
heel	*ayl tah-**lohn*** **el talón**
hip	*lah kah-**day**-rah* **la cadera**
inner ear	*ayl oh-**ee**-doh* **el oído**
knee	*lah rroh-**dee**-yah* **la rodilla**
leg	*lah **pee^ayr**-nah* **la pierna**
lip	*ayl **lah**-bee^oh* **el labio**
mouth	*lah **boh**-kah* **la boca**
nail	*lah **oo**-nyah* **la uña**
nape	*lah **noo**-kah* **la nuca**
navel	*ayl ohm-**blee**-goh* **el ombligo**
neck	*ayl **koo^ay**-yoh* **el cuello**
nipple *[for women]*	*ayl pay-**sohn*** **el pezón**

nipple *[for men]*	*lah tay-**tee**-yah* la tetilla
nose	*lah nah-**rees*** la nariz
outer ear	*lah oh-**ray**-hah* la oreja
palm	*lah **pahl**-mah* la palma
rib	*lah kohs-**tee**-yah* la costilla
shin	*lah ays-pee-**nee**-yah* la espinilla
shoulder	*ayl **ohm**-broh* el hombro
stomach	*ayl ays-**toh**-mah-goh* el estómago
temple	*lah see^ayn* la sien
thigh	*ayl **moos**-loh* el muslo
thorax	*ayl **toh**-rahks* el tórax
toe	*ayl **day**-doh (dayl pee^ay)* el dedo (del pie)
waist	*lah seen-**too**-rah* la cintura
wrist	*lah moon-**yay**-kah* la muñeca

Notes

¹ Another term for *axila* is *el sobaco (ayl soh-**bah**-koh).*

² The plural form of *la nalga,* which is *las nalgas,* may be considered rude by some Hispanics. Likewise, *las asentaderas (lahs ah-sayn-tah-**day**-rahs)* is a non-offensive, lower-register term that is used.

³ Another term for *barbilla* is *el mentón (ayl mayn-**tohn**).*

⁴ Another term for *cóccix* is *la rabadilla (lah rrah-bah-**dee**-yah).*

Internal Organs, Digestive System and Reproductive Organs

*lohs **ohr**-gah-nohs een-**tayr**-nohs, ayl sees-**tay**-mah dee-hays-**tee**-boh ee lohs **ohr**-gah-nohs rray-proh-dook-**tee**-bohs*
Los órganos internos, el sistema digestivo y los órganos reproductivos

anus	*ayl **ah**-noh* el ano
appendix	*ayl ah-**payn**-dee-say* el apéndice
bladder	*lah bay-**hee**-gah* la vejiga
brain	*ayl say-**ray**-broh* el cerebro
cervix	*ayl **koo^ay**-yoh dayl **oo**-tay-roh* el cuello del útero
diaphragm	*ayl dee^ah-**frahg**-mah* el diafragma
esophagus	*ayl ay-**soh**-fah-goh* el esófago
fallopian tubes	*lahs **trohm**-pahs* las trompas
gallbladder	*lah bay-**see**-koo-lah bee-**lee^ahr*** la vesícula biliar
heart	*ayl koh-rah-**sohn*** el corazón
kidneys	*lohs rreen-**yoh**-nays* los riñones
large intestine	*ayl een-tays-**tee**-noh **groo^ay**-soh* el intestino grueso
liver	*ayl **ee**-gah-doh* el hígado
lungs	*lohs pool-**moh**-nays* los pulmones
ovaries	*lohs oh-**bah**-ree^ohs* los ovarios
pancreas	*ayl **pahn**-kray-ahs* el páncreas
penis	*ayl **pay**-nay* el pene
prepuce, foreskin	*ayl pray-**poo**-see^oh* el prepucio

prostate gland	*lah **prohs**-tah-tah* la próstata
rectum	*ayl **rrayk**-toh* el recto
scrotum	*ayl ays-**kroh**-toh* el escroto
seminal vesicle	*ayl bay-**see**-koo-loh say-mee-**nahl*** el vesículo seminal
small intestine	*ayl een-tays-**tee**-noh dayl-**gah**-doh* el intestino delgado
spinal cord	*lah **may**-doo-lah ays-pee-**nahl*** la médula espinal
spleen	*ayl **bah**-soh* el bazo
stomach	*ayl ays-**toh**-mah-goh* el estómago
testicles	*lohs tays-**tee**-koo-lohs* los testículos
tongue	*lah **layn**-goo^ah* la lengua
urethra	*lah oo-**ray**-trah* la uretra
uterus	*ayl **oo**-tay-roh* el útero[1]
vagina	*lah bah-**hee**-nah* la vagina
vas deferens	*lohs kohn-**dook**-tohs day-fay-**rayn**-tays* los conductos deferentes

Note

[1] Another term for *el útero* is *la matriz (lah mah-**trees**)*.

Pain Assessment—Visual Aid

PAIN SCALE / ESCALA DE DOLOR

| (0) | 1 | 2 | 3 | 4 | (5) | 6 | 7 | 8 | 9 | (10) |

ningún
dolor
—
no pain

dolor
considerable
—
distressing
pain

dolor
intolerable
—
unbearable
pain

Parts of the Body—Visual Aid

The Human Body - Front View / El cuerpo humano - vista anterior

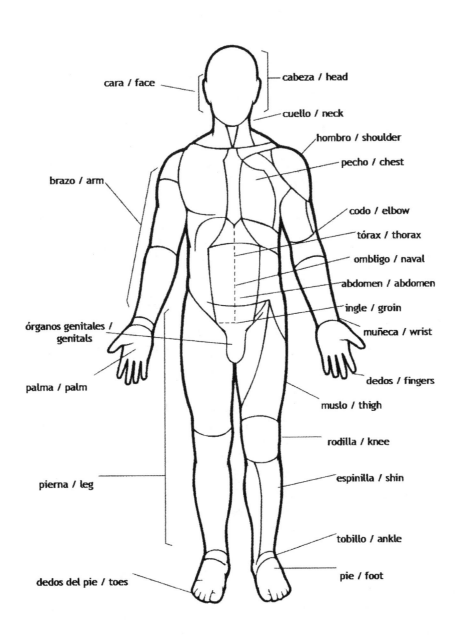

cara / face

cabeza / head

cuello / neck

hombro / shoulder

pecho / chest

brazo / arm

codo / elbow

tórax / thorax

ombligo / naval

abdomen / abdomen

ingle / groin

órganos genitales / genitals

muñeca / wrist

palma / palm

dedos / fingers

muslo / thigh

rodilla / knee

espinilla / shin

pierna / leg

tobillo / ankle

pie / foot

dedos del pie / toes

The Human Body - Rear View / El cuerpo humano - vista posterior

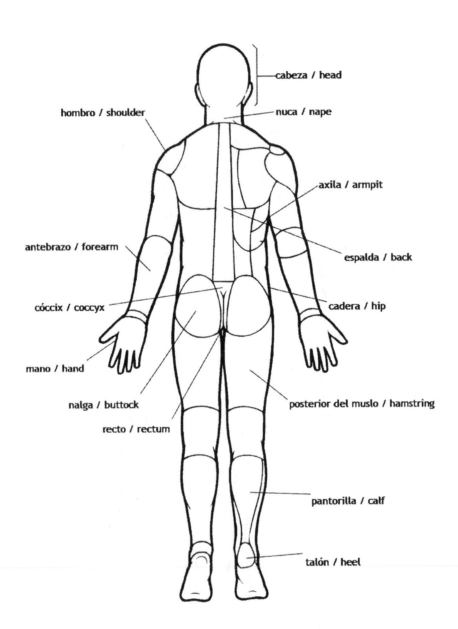

cabeza / head

hombro / shoulder

nuca / nape

axila / armpit

antebrazo / forearm

espalda / back

cóccix / coccyx

cadera / hip

mano / hand

nalga / buttock

posterior del muslo / hamstring

recto / rectum

pantorilla / calf

talón / heel

Bibliography

Bender's Forms of Discovery Interrogatories (Volumes 1 to 10A). Copyright 2010, Matthew Bender & Company, Inc., a member of the LexisNexis Group. 1 INTERROGATORIES: ACCOUNTANTS TO ATHLETICS—CHAPTER 11 ASSAULT AND BATTERY. 1 *Bender's Forms of Discovery Interrogatories* § 11 (2010).

Bender's Forms of Discovery Interrogatories (Volumes 1 to 10A). Copyright 2010, Matthew Bender & Company, Inc., a member of the LexisNexis Group. 2 INTERROGATORIES: ATTORNEYS TO AUTOMOBILES—CHAPTER 13A AUTHORIZATIONS. 2 *Bender's Forms of Discovery Interrogatories* § 13A (2010).

Bender's Forms of Discovery Interrogatories (Volumes 1 to 10A). Copyright 2010, Matthew Bender & Company, Inc., a member of the LexisNexis Group. 2 INTERROGATORIES: ATTORNEYS TO AUTOMOBILES—CHAPTER 14 AUTOMOBILES-COLLISIONS. 2 *Bender's Forms of Discovery Interrogatories* § 14 (2010).

Bender's Forms of Discovery Interrogatories (Volumes 1 to 10A). Copyright 2010, Matthew Bender & Company, Inc., a member of the LexisNexis Group. 6 INTERROGATORIES: CANCELLATION OF INSTRUMENTS TO COLLISIONS, SALVAGE AND TOWAGE—CHAPTER 40 CIVIL RIGHTS. 6 *Bender's Forms of Discovery Interrogatories* § 40 (2010).

Bender's Forms of Discovery Interrogatories (Volumes 1 to 10A). Copyright 2010, Matthew Bender & Company, Inc., a member of the LexisNexis Group. 6 INTERROGATORIES: CANCELLATION OF INSTRUMENTS TO COLLISIONS, SALVAGE AND TOWAGE. CHAPTER 42 CLAIM AND DELIVERY (REPLEVIN). 6 *Bender's Forms of Discovery Interrogatories* § 42 (2010).

Bender's Forms of Discovery Interrogatories (Volumes 1 to 10A). Copyright 2010, Matthew Bender & Company, Inc., a member of the LexisNexis Group. 9 INTERROGATORIES: DEFINITIONS TO DRUGS AND DRUGGISTS—CHAPTER 66 DIVORCE AND SEPARATION. 9 *Bender's Forms of Discovery Interrogatories* § 66 (2010).

Bender's Forms of Discovery Interrogatories (Volumes 1 to 10A). Copyright 2010, Matthew Bender & Company, Inc., a member of the LexisNexis Group. 11 INTERROGATORIES: EMPLOYMENT DISCRIMINATION TO EMPLOYMENT SUITS—CHAPTER 74 EMPLOYMENT DISCRIMINATION. 11 *Bender's Forms of Discovery Interrogatories* § 74 (2010).

Bender's Forms of Discovery Interrogatories (Volumes 1 to 10A). Copyright 2010, Matthew Bender & Company, Inc., a member of the LexisNexis Group. 15 INTERROGATORIES: JURISDICTION TO METAL FAILURE—CHAPTER 128 MEDICAL HISTORY, EXAMINATIONS, AND REPORTS. 15 *Bender's Forms of Discovery Interrogatories* § 128 (2010).

Bender's Forms of Discovery Interrogatories (Volumes 1 to 10A). Copyright 2010, Matthew Bender & Company, Inc., a member of the LexisNexis Group. 15 INTERROGATORIES: JURISDICTION TO METAL FAILURE—CHAPTER 118 LANDLORD AND TENANT. 15 *Bender's Forms of Discovery Interrogatories* § 118 (2010).

Bender's Forms of Discovery Interrogatories (Volumes 1 to 10A). Copyright 2010, Matthew Bender & Company, Inc., a member of the LexisNexis Group. 17 INTERROGATORIES: PAVEMENT AND PAVING TO PRISONS AND PRISONERS—CHAPTER 146 PERSONAL INJURIES. 17 *Bender's Forms of Discovery Interrogatories* § 146 (2010).

Bender's Forms of Discovery Interrogatories (Volumes 1 to 10A). Copyright 2010, Matthew Bender & Company, Inc., a member of the LexisNexis Group. 23 INTERROGATORIES: SLIP AND FALL TO TAXICABS—CHAPTER 177 SLIP AND FALL. 23 *Bender's Forms of Discovery Interrogatories* § 177 (2010).

Bender's Forms of Discovery Interrogatories (Volumes 1 to 10A). Copyright 2010, Matthew Bender & Company, Inc., a member of the LexisNexis Group. 26 INTERROGATORIES: UNSAFE WORKING CONDITIONS TO WITNESSES, NAMES OF—CHAPTER 209 UNSAFE WORKING CONDITIONS. 26 *Bender's Forms of Discovery Interrogatories* § 209 (2010).

Bender's Forms of Discovery Interrogatories (Volumes 1 to 10A). Copyright 2010, Matthew Bender & Company, Inc., a member of the LexisNexis Group. 27 INTERROGATORIES: WORKER'S COMPENSATION TO ZONING; INDEX TO FORMS—CHAPTER 218 WORKER'S COMPENSATION. 27 *Bender's Forms of Discovery Interrogatories* § 218 (2010).

Bender's Forms of Discovery Interrogatories (Volumes 1 to 10A). Copyright 2010, Matthew Bender & Company, Inc., a member of the LexisNexis Group. 27 INTERROGATORIES: WORKER'S COMPENSATION TO ZONING; INDEX TO FORMS—CHAPTER 219 WRONGFUL DEATH. 27 *Bender's Forms of Discovery Interrogatories* § 219 (2010).

Casablanca, Maria Isabel, and Gloria Roa Bodin. *Immigration law for paralegals.* Durham, N.C.: Carolina Academic Press, 2005.

Collin, P. H..*Spanish Law Dictionary: Diccionario de términos jurídicos.* Teddington, Middx., UK: P. Collin Pub., 1999.

"Comisión para la Igualdad de Oportunidades en el Empleo de los Estados Unidos (EEOC)." *US EEOC Home Page.* N.p., n.d.

"Discrimination Against Hispanics: Stereotypes, Hate Crimes, and Racism | CivilRightsLawFirms.com." *Civil Rights Lawyers | Attorneys for Discrimination and Harassment | CivilRightsLawFirms.com.* N.p., n.d.

"Discrimination in Metropolitan Housing Markets: National Results from Phase 1, Phase 2, and Phase 3 of the Housing Discrimination Study (HDS) | HUD USER." *HUDUSER Home Page | HUD USER.* N.p., n.d.

Garner, Bryan A., and Henry Campbell Black. *Black's law dictionary.* 7th ed. St. Paul, Minn.: West Group, 1999.

Gibson, R. Sebastian. "Discrimination Against Hispanics, Latinos and Mexican Americans, and the Need For More Civil Rights Lawyers in California." *Lawyers, Attorneys, Law Firms—Find Legal Information.* N.p., n.d.

Heines, Vivienne. "The Company You Save May Be Your Own—HispanicBusiness.com." *Hispanic News, Financial News, and Business Magazine—HispanicBusiness.com.* N.p., n.d.

"Hispanics: A Statistical Portrait." *American Renaissance.* N.p., n.d.

"Immigration Intake Questionnaire—Immigration." *Immigration Lawyer, Attorney, Law—FindLaw.* N.p., n.d.

"Impacts of Illegal Immigration: Traffic Accidents." *The Dark Side Of Illegal Immigration: Facts, Figures and Data Show A Disturbing Truth.* N.p., n.d.

Jones, Brian K. *Speak Spanish now for medical professionals: a customized learning approach for doctors, nurses, nursing and medical assistants.* Durham, N.C.: Carolina Academic Press, 2007.

Kaplan, Steven M., and Fernando Pombo. *Aspen's English-Spanish, Spanish-English Legal Dictionary. Aspen.* 2nd ed. New York: Aspen Law & Business, 2001.

Mesriani, Rodney. "Fatal Industrial Accidents: Statistics, Lawsuits, Damages and Prevention | AccidentAttorneys.com." *Accident Lawyers: Find Injury Lawyers, File a Claim, Get a Free Case Review | AccidentAttorneys.com.* N.p., n.d.

Mikkelson, Holly. *The interpreter's companion.* 4th ed. Spreckels, Calif.: ACEBO, 2000.

"Nearly Three-in-Ten Hispanic Workers Have Experienced Discrimination or Unfair Treatment at Work, CareerBuilder.com and Kelly Services Survey Shows—CareerBuilder." *Jobs—The Largest Job Search, Employment & Careers Site.* N.p., n.d.

Peña, Angel. *Guía y formularios de inmigración.* 2nd ed. Silver Spring, MD: InterMedia, 2005.

Ramey, Esq., Martin. Personal interview. 15 Nov. 2010.

Rauda, Jaime Castro. Translation Proofreader. 2013.

Reinberg, Steven. "Hispanic Workers Dying at Higher Rates Than Others—US News and World Report." *Health News Articles—US News Health.* N.p., n.d.

Schell, Debbie M., Richard E. Schell, and Kurt A. Wagner. *Inmigración y ciudadanía en los EE. UU.: preguntas y respuestas.* 1. ed. Naperville, Ill.: Sphinx Pub., 2004.

"The Hispanic Family — Hispanic Culture." *BellaOnline — The Voice of Women.* N.p., n.d.

"Translation term search | ProZ.com." *Translators & translator resources — ProZ.com.* N.p., n.d.

"U.S Hispanics having difficulty with credit card debt | Reach Hispanic." *Reach Hispanic.* N.p., n.d.

"US Immigration Forms and Fees — USCIS Forms." *Immigration Lawyer, Attorney, Law — FindLaw.* N.p., n.d.

"Word Magic | Spanish to English Translation, Dictionary & Translator / Diccionario y traductor inglés español."
Word Magic Software — English to Spanish and Spanish to English Translation Software, Online Translation and Dictionaries. N.p., n.d.

"Yahoo!." *English to French, Italian, German & Spanish Dictionary — WordReference.com.* N.p., n.d.